CREDO SERIES

The Promised One: Servant and Savior

*Based on the Curriculum Framework
Course III: The Mission of Jesus Christ
(The Paschal Mystery)*

Imprimatur Edition

GENERAL EDITOR
Thomas H. Groome, Ed. D.
*Professor Theology and Religious Education
Boston College*

VERITAS

USA Office: Frisco, Texas

www.veritasreligion.com

IMPRIMATUR EDITION

This copyrighted imprimatur edition of The Promised One: Servant and Savior *has been submitted to the USCCB Subcommittee on the Catechism for Conformity Review. Final edits, as required or recommended by the Committee, will be made to the content upon receipt of the Conformity Review Report.*

Veritas would like to thank all those who contributed to the development of this text:

CREDO SERIES CONSULTANT: Maura Hyland
PUBLISHER, USA: Ed DeStefano
WRITERS:
John Falcone (chs. 1–6) and Daniella Zsupan-Jerome (chs. 7–13)
TEXT CONSULTANTS:
Annette Honan
Ailís Travers
TEXT EDITOR: Elaine Campion
DESIGN: Lir Mac Cárthaigh

INTERNET RESOURCES
There are internet resources available to support this text. Log on to *www.credoseries.com*

NIHIL OBSTAT
Rev. Msgr. Robert M. Coerver, S.T.L.
Censor Librorum

IMPRIMATUR
† Most Reverend Kevin J. Farrell, D.D.
Bishop of Dallas
December 16, 2011

The *Nihil Obstat* and *Imprimatur* are official declarations that the work contains nothing contrary to Faith and Morals. It is not implied thereby that those granting the *Nihil Obstat* or *Imprimatur* agree with the contents, statements or opinions expressed.

Copyright © 2012 by Veritas Publications.

All rights reserved. No part of the material may be reproduced or transmitted in any form or by any means, electronic or mechanical, including photocopying or by any information or retrieval system, adapted, rented or lent without written permission from the copyright owner. Applications for permissions should be addressed to the publisher: **Veritas, 11801 Amber Valley Road, Frisco, Texas 75035-6308; info@veritasreligion.com**

See page 318 for copyright acknowledgments.

SEND ALL INQUIRIES TO:
Veritas, Customer Service
P.O. Box 789
Westerville, OH 43086
Tel. 866-844-0582
info@veritasreligion.com
www.veritasreligion.com

ISBN 978 1 84730 281 6 (Student Edition)
ISBN 978 1 84730 375 2 (Teacher Resource Edition)
ISBN 978 1 84730 376 9 (E-book: Student Edition)

Printed in the United States of America
3 4 5 6 7 8 9 / 19 18 17 16 15 14 13

CONTENTS

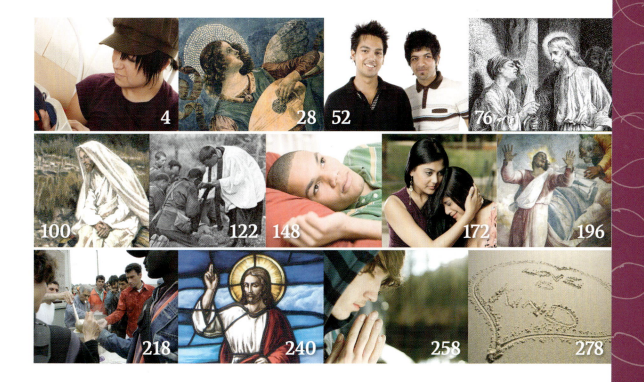

CHAPTER 1	A Good World and a Generous God	4
CHAPTER 2	The Reality of Sin and the Promise of Salvation	28
CHAPTER 3	God's Commitment, Our Hope	52
CHAPTER 4	The Word Became Flesh	76
CHAPTER 5	Thy Kingdom Come	100
CHAPTER 6	Jesus: More than Meets the Eye	122
CHAPTER 7	Victory from the Jaws of Death	148
CHAPTER 8	Christ Is Risen! He Is Risen Indeed!	172
CHAPTER 9	Bound for Glry: The Ascension, Pentecost and the Assumption	196
CHAPTER 10	Following the Way of Jesus Christ	218
CHAPTER 11	Jesus: the Way to Holiness	240
CHAPTER 12	Lord, Teach Us to Pray	258
CHAPTER 13	Jesus Christ, the Lord of Eternal Life	278
CATHOLIC PRAYERS, DEVOTIONS AND PRACTICES		302
FAITH GLOSSARY		311
ACKNOWLEDGMENTS		318
INDEX		322

CHAPTER 1

A Good World and a Generous God

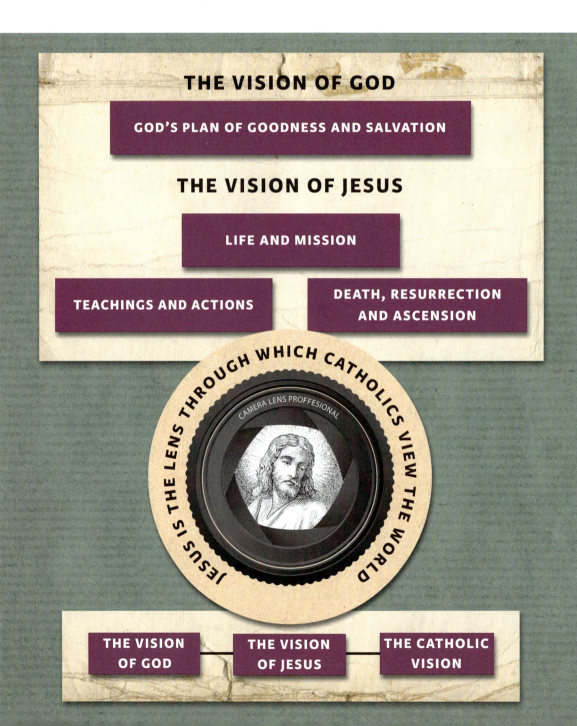

IN THIS TEXT, THE PROMISED ONE: SERVANT AND SAVIOR, we explore the mission of Jesus Christ, the incarnate Son of God and our Lord and Savior. In chapter 1 we review our faith and trust in God, whose generosity toward us knows no end or limit. We remember that God created every person in the divine image and likeness, giving each of us equal dignity. We explore that God the Blessed Trinity, one God in three Divine Persons, exists in loving relationship, and invites us to live in loving relationship with the Trinity and with one another.

LEARNING OUTCOMES

As a result of studying this chapter and exploring the issues raised, you should be able to:

- compare and contrast your vision of life with the vision of Jesus;
- understand the challenge of placing your trust in God;
- understand how the Jewish people came to place their trust in God;
- understand that Jesus is the fulfillment of the Scriptures;
- explore the meaning of fairness and generosity in the context of God's unconditional love;
- discover and understand Creation as an invitation to respond to God's unconditional love;
- articulate what it means to be created in the image and likeness of the Triune God;
- identify the symbolic significance of 'disobedience' in the story of Adam and Eve and its implications for us today;
- understand the meaning of *theosis*;
- contrast the Christian meaning of trust, fairness, generosity and respect with a purely secular or 'worldly' interpretation of these values.

FAITH-FORMATION OUTCOMES

As a result of studying this chapter and exploring the issues raised, you should also:

- recognize that the vision of Jesus is the most important 'lens' through which you view the world;
- appreciate how you can build a personal relationship of trust with God by drawing on the wisdom of the Bible and the Church;
- apply your new understanding of fairness to your life;
- appreciate and respond to the wonder and generosity of God's gift of Creation;
- identify the areas in your life where you need to undergo a conversion to values lived and taught by Christ;
- identify ways in which you can reflect God's image and likeness to others;
- identify a personal belief or rule you would like to hold on to and one you would like to change;
- be inspired by the life of Peter Maurin.

FAITH WORD: *Theosis*

LEARN BY HEART: Matthew 6:33

LEARN BY EXAMPLE: Peter Maurin

ATTEND AND REFLECT

How do you view the world?

OPENING CONVERSATION

Whether we are aware of it or not, each of us has an attitude toward life, a perspective, or point of view, through which we look at the world. This 'point of view' contributes significantly to the way we see and value people and things, and it helps shape our expectations and responses. So, how do you view the world?

- Do you see people as mostly good or mostly bad?
- Does the future (yours and the world's) seem hopeful, or are you filled with doubt?

Your answers will help you get in touch with the way you look at life, yourself, other people, things—and God. In this chapter we will explore some of the wonderful spiritual wisdom and life-giving answers our Catholic **faith** offers to these and other key questions about life. We begin by exploring three important elements of life: trust, fairness and generosity.

REFLECT AND DISCUSS

- Can we trust God? Is it better to trust people, or to keep up our guard? Think of a time when you trusted someone. Share your thoughts.
- Think of a time when you were treated fairly, and a time when you were treated unfairly. How important is it to be fair? Do you think God treats people fairly? Explain your views.
- What does it mean to be generous? Think of a time when you witnessed generosity in action. Do you think most people are generous? Do you think God is generous? Why or why not?

UNDERSTANDING YOUR VIEW OF THE WORLD

Do you prefer chocolate or vanilla ice-cream? What would you like to eat for dinner tonight? Some of our preferences are very superficial and we express them without much thought or reflection.

But our basic 'view of the world', our 'view of life', goes deeper, because we go deeper. Every person has a history, a network of relationships and a faith that shape their view of the world and influence the choices they make, which in turn give shape to their lives. Our personal history, or 'story', is shaped, in part, by the movies we have watched, the video games we have played, the books we have read, the schools we have attended, the people we love or have loved, the joys we have known and the hurts we have suffered (or inflicted), our ethnic and national identity, our family, our faith and our **Church**.

LET'S PROBE DEEPER

- List any people or experiences that are connected in your mind with how you view the world. These might include:
  - friends or relatives who have influenced you;
  - a movie, TV show or story that has influenced your outlook on life;
  - experiences that seem to back up your attitude to life;
  - a Christian belief or value that inspires you.
- What influences from Christian faith do you recognize in your view of life?
- What views or aspects of your life would you like to make more truly Christian, more Christ-like?

'POINTS OF VIEW' IN CONVERSATION

This course will challenge you to take your Catholic faith more seriously. Your faith gives expression to the Church's vision of life, the vision of Jesus Christ. The life and mission of Jesus, his teachings and actions, his Death, **Resurrection** and **Ascension**, shape every Christian's view of life and the world. Jesus is the 'lens' through which we see reality; it is his vision that shapes our viewpoint. The Church invites and helps us to discover and make the vision of Jesus, the incarnate Word of God, our vision. Understanding and taking on the mind of Christ is both challenging and a lifelong task.

Reading the Word of God, Sacred Scripture, is vital for us if we are to come to a greater understanding of Jesus' vision. Throughout this text we will provide you with many opportunities to do just that. In our exploration of Scripture we will use a technique, or process, called 'active

Four Steps for 'Active Reading' of Biblical Texts

1. Read the text carefully to get a general idea of what it is saying and how it might speak to your life.
2. Read it again. This time, when you come upon a line or word that strikes you, mark it by placing one or more of the following symbols in the left margin:
   - ¡ Candle symbol: denotes a word, phrase or sentence that gives you an insight for your life, for your relationships or for your Christian faith.
   - ▲ 'Vertical-tick' symbol: denotes 'good news'—a word, phrase or sentence that tells you something hopeful or reassuring about God's love and action in the world.
   - ▶ 'Horizontal-tick' symbol: denotes a 'challenge'—a word or phrase or sentence that challenges you to make a difficult decision or to take a risky stand.
3. Pick one or more of the Scripture passages you chose and write an explanation of your marks.
4. Reflect, either alone or with a partner, on what you are taking away from the Scripture passage for your life.

reading' to help you delve more deeply into the meaning of biblical texts. The four steps used in the 'active reading' process are described in the box above.

This course invites and challenges you to clarify your vision of life. That will involve connecting with your current viewpoint, or outlook on life, and comparing your viewpoint with the vision of Jesus. As you dig into your vision of life more deeply, you can discover what lies behind the way you see things, what you really think and why you think as you do. You will also connect with the faith-vision of the Catholic Church. This faith-vision represents the spiritual wisdom gained from two thousand years of reflection on God's Word, the Wisdom of God, revealed most fully and clearly through the life, Death, Resurrection and Ascension of Jesus Christ. As you engage in this reflection, you may be challenged to clarify your vision or views on life and on the world, and to reassess the way you live your life each day. That is what Jesus would want you to do! Remember, 'You are the salt of the earth. . . . You are the light of the world' (Matthew 5:13, 14).

THE VISION OF JESUS

The vision of Jesus may at times seem at odds with logic and common sense; it may even seem unrealistic or foolish. On the other hand, the vision of Jesus is the vision of God. The vision of Jesus blesses us with a Wisdom that goes beyond what we usually consider to be human wisdom and 'common sense'. St. Paul put it this way:

God's foolishness is wiser than human wisdom, and God's weakness is stronger than human strength.

—1 Corinthians 1:25

The four accounts of the **Gospel** challenge us to evaluate whether or not we see the world as Jesus did. Paul tells us, 'Let the same mind be in you that was in Jesus Christ' (Philippians 2:5). Here is one example of many Gospel passages that give us insight into the vision of Jesus. As you read it, apply the 'active reading' technique and compare Jesus' vision with the way you see things. Jesus said:

I tell you, do not worry about your life, what you will eat or what you will drink, or about your body, what you will wear. Is not life more than food, and the body more than clothing? . . . But strive first for the kingdom of God and his righteousness, and all these things will be given to you as well.

—Matthew 6:25, 33

OVER TO YOU
- What spiritual wisdom have you discovered in your reading of Matthew 6:25, 33?
- Now read Matthew 6:25–33, the whole passage from which the two verses were taken. How does this wisdom agree or contrast with your own view of the world?
- Working with a partner or in a small group, list and discuss all the 'challenges' that you and your classmates found in Matthew 6:25–33. Write the challenges into your journal.

ACT IT OUT
- The parable of the Good Samaritan (Luke 10:25–37) is a story of differing points of view. When Jesus told this story he was speaking to people whose point of view was that there could be no such thing as a good Samaritan. Read the story now with this in mind.
- Now pair up with a partner. Imagine that you were both among the crowd who heard Jesus tell this story. Have the conversation that you think might have happened between two people in the crowd.

REFLECT
- Has your point of view shifted as a result of today's lesson? If so, how, and what has influenced this change?

THE GOOD SAMARITAN | ENGRAVING AFTER WILLIAM HOGARTH

HEAR THE STORY

The Wisdom of Jesus

THE LAST SUPPER | 15TH-CENTURY ILLUMINATED BIBLE

OPENING JOURNAL ACTIVITY
- Write the name of a person whom you trust deeply.
- Now list all the reasons why you trust this person.
- Create a list titled 'What makes someone worthy of my trust?' List as many character traits as you can.

JESUS PLACED HIS TRUST IN HIS FATHER

Placing one's trust in someone is a decision that is not easily made. The ways we have experienced 'trust', or have seen trust in action, influence the ease or difficulty with which we trust. We may find it difficult to trust after we have experienced our trust betrayed; for example, a promise that has been made to us is broken or a friend betrays us. Our positive experiences of trust, in turn, may contribute to our ability to trust; for example, we may find it easier to trust someone whom we know has a good 'trust' track record.

How do we come to trust God? Is placing trust in God like or unlike placing our trust in ourselves or in another person? We certainly can learn much about trust from Jesus, from his actions and from his teachings, especially from the trust he placed in his Father. Jesus trusted his Father deeply and he desired that his **disciples** (that includes us) would do the same. Jesus' trust was rooted in his knowledge and love of the Father. At the Last Supper Jesus would reveal that this knowledge and love was so intimate that the Father and he were 'one'; and he prayed to the Father that the disciples would share in this oneness and intimacy:

> The glory that you have given me I have given them, so that they may be one, as we are one . . . so that the world may know that you have sent me and have loved them even as you have loved me.
> —John 17:22, 23

Jesus, the incarnate Son of God, knew God and freely willed to place his trust in the Father in a way that no one else ever did. He invites us to do the same.

OVER TO YOU
- What is Jesus saying about his relationship with you in his **prayer**? How do you respond?
- What does that mean for your life each day?

THE FULFILLMENT OF THE SCRIPTURES

'Jesus increased in wisdom and in years, and in divine and human favor' (Luke 2:52). Jesus learned from his human experiences. He grew in knowledge of Jewish history and from his experiences of Jewish culture, which had a deep impact on his view of the world. Jesus clearly lived the life of a faithful, religious Jew. He read, interpreted and often quoted the Sacred Scriptures of ancient Israel, which are now found in the Old Testament. For example, he opened the scroll of Isaiah the Prophet in the synagogue in Nazareth and deliberately selected verses from Isaiah to announce his mission. (Read Luke 4:16–21.)

Jesus' understanding of himself and of his mission was deeply biblical and based on a rock-solid trust in his Father. Central to the faith life of the Jews was their deep trust in God, who revealed himself as the One who always kept his Word. This message permeated their Scriptures—the Torah, the Prophets and the Wisdom writings. Jesus taught, 'Do not think that I have come to abolish the law or the prophets; I have come not to abolish but to fulfill' (Matthew 5:17). Jesus expressed his knowledge of the Sacred Scriptures in the way he lived his life.

LET'S PROBE DEEPER

The Law. The Law, or Torah (a Hebrew word meaning 'teachings or instructions'), consists of the Pentateuch, or first five books in the Bible: Genesis, Exodus, Leviticus, Numbers and Deuteronomy. Through the centuries many Jews and Christians believed that Moses himself wrote these five books; hence, the Law is often called 'the Law of Moses' or the 'Books of Moses'. The Law contains both the foundational stories about the origins of Israel and the establishment of the **Covenant** and the instructions (laws) on how to live in right relationship (to live the Covenant) with God and with people.

In the Law we find the Ten Commandments. Jesus combined these laws into one Great Commandment (see Matthew 22:34–40). This Law of Laws is:

You shall love the LORD your God with all your heart, and with all your soul, and with all your might.
—Deuteronomy 6:5

You shall love your neighbor as yourself. I am the LORD.
—Leviticus 19:18

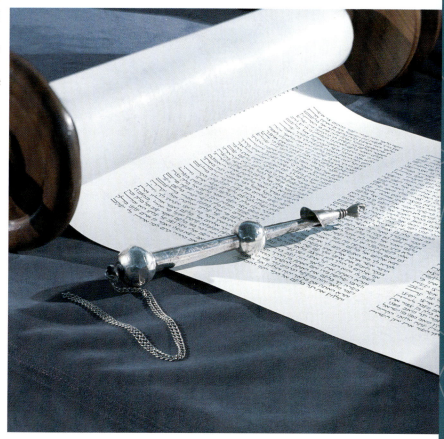

CHAPTER 1: A GOOD WORLD AND A GENEROUS GOD | HEAR THE STORY

The Prophets. The writings of the prophets record the words and actions of the 'messengers' whom God chose and sent 'to speak in his name' in the centuries before Jesus was born. The prophets helped God's people to understand the commandments of the Covenant and keep the Covenant faithfully. The message God spoke through the prophets was a two-edged sword: it promised salvation for those who trusted in God and acted with justice, but it also stated what would happen if the nation ignored God's Word.

The Bible contains the writings of eighteen prophets. These are classified as 'major' or 'minor' prophets, based on the size of their writings. First-century Jews also counted 1 Samuel and 2 Samuel, which Catholics name as historical books, among the Prophets. Here is an example from the Prophets:

The days are surely coming, says the LORD, when I will make a new covenant with the house of Israel and the house of Judah. . . . But this is the covenant that I will make . . . I will put my law within them, and I will write it on their hearts; and I will be their God and they shall be my people.

—Jeremiah 31:31, 33

The Wisdom Writings. The Bible contains seven Wisdom books, or writings. The psalms, contained within the Book of Psalms, were central to the daily life of Jews in Jesus' time, as they are to Jews and Christians today. They are religious poems set to music. Many of the psalms are attributed to the great King David (c. 900 BC), whom the Gospels tell us was an ancestor of Jesus. (Read the genealogy of Jesus in Matthew 1:1–17.) Here are a few examples of words from the Psalms that express the trust the People of God placed in God:

FOUR OLD TESTAMENT PROPHETS | ALBI CATHEDRAL, FRANCE

Liturgical Note

The Law, the Prophets and the Psalms continue to play a central role in Jewish and Christian worship today. A typical synagogue service features a reading from the Torah (a sacred 'teaching'), followed by a related reading from the Prophets that comments on the sacred 'teaching'. Numerous psalms are also recited or sung. In the **Liturgy** of the Church, the 'Liturgy of the Word', which is celebrated at every Mass, is based on this ancient synagogue practice. The first two readings at Mass on Sunday and on some feast days are readings from the Old Testament writings and, on occasions, from the New Testament letters, which build up toward the Gospel for the day. After the First Reading, a 'Responsorial Psalm' is sung or prayed aloud. The Gospel is proclaimed after the Second Reading on Sundays and after the First Reading on weekdays, announcing the Good News of Jesus and sharing his life, Death, Resurrection, Ascension and teaching.

DAVID COMPOSING THE PSALMS | 19TH-CENTURY ENGRAVING

> The Lord is my shepherd, I shall not want.
> —Psalm 23:1

> The Lord is a stronghold for the oppressed,
>   a stronghold in times of trouble. . . .
>   for you, O Lord, have not forsaken those
>   who seek you.
> —Psalm 9:9–10

The Gospels show that Jesus fulfilled the Scriptures of ancient Israel. Through studying and praying and teaching from these sacred writings, Jesus revealed God's faithful love for his people, especially for the poor and the marginalized.

SCRIPTURE ACTIVITY: COMPARE AND ANALYZE

- Work with a partner. Look up and read Matthew 19:28–30 and Psalm 22:16 and 69:22. Compare the readings.

THINK, PAIR AND SHARE

- In your journal, complete the following sentence five times by using the first five adjectives or descriptive phrases that come to mind and stating the reason you chose that descriptor: The Bible is _____ (*adjective or descriptive phrase*) because _____.
- Pair up with a partner and share your sentences. Together, discuss whether young people today see the Bible as a positive, a negative or an irrelevant factor in their lives.
- Share your best conclusions with the larger group.

THE CHALLENGE OF TRUSTING GOD

As discussed above, it is easier to trust someone who has a proven track record. The Bible is full of stories that convey the proven track record of God with his people. The truths about the relationship between God and human beings are sometimes expressed through the use of figurative and symbolic language. This language

THE ANGEL GABRIEL FROM A 15TH-CENTURY ANNUNCIATION

establish a new Covenant that would be written not in stone but in the hearts of people. (There will be more on this topic in chapter 3.)

From another perspective the inspired writers of the Old Testament pass on the faith story of the Israelites and their trust in God. This trust of the People of God is summed up in Mary's response to the angel Gabriel's announcement to her: 'Here am I, the servant of the Lord; let it be with me according to your word' (Luke 1:38). For people of faith, God's 'track record' of never-ending fidelity to his people is a 'proven' track record.

The life and worship and teachings of the Church (**Tradition**) throughout the centuries, the thinking of the Fathers and Doctors of the Church and other theologians, the life of the saints, both named and unnamed, all manifest the life-giving consequences of a life centered in God the Faithful One. Does this track record justify our own 'leap of faith'? Does its spiritual wisdom move you enough to put your trust in God?

helps to describe realities that history and science cannot grasp. (See CCC, nos. 283–289.)

The Old Testament is the story of God reaching out to the people of Israel again and again and saving his people from the consequences of their infidelity to him, from their **sin**. It is the story of God entering into Covenant with his people, freeing them from slavery and leading them to freedom, guiding them through good times and bad, and calling them to live their part of the Covenant as God's own people. Central to that story is God's promise to send the Messiah who would set his people free once and for all and

GROUP EXERCISE/DISCUSSION
⊙ Discuss and create a list of what you think are the trustworthy traits of God.

THINK, PAIR AND SHARE
⊙ Choose a partner.
⊙ Tell your partner what you would regard as their trustworthy traits.
⊙ Then reflect upon and decide which of these traits you might need to cultivate.

EMBRACE THE VISION

Our God is both fair and generous

OPENING REFLECTION

Reflecting on our experiences of fairness and generosity can help us get a glimpse of the faithful love and goodness of God, which is the foundation of our trust in him. God's dealings with human beings, however, go far beyond fairness, to generosity. 'Generosity' means giving more than what is earned or deserved or that one can even imagine. It usually has more to do with who the giver is than with what the receiver deserves.

OVER TO YOU

- Think of a time when you experienced an act of generosity.
- What was it about this act that led you to see it as an act of generosity rather than simply an act of fairness?
- When have you been generous?

SCRIPTURE ACTIVITY

Read Jesus' parable of the Laborers in the Vineyard in Matthew 20:1–16, using the four 'active reading' techniques outlined earlier in this chapter. Then discuss:

- Who, if anyone, is acting unfairly in this parable? Explain.
- Who is acting with generosity? Explain.
- What is Jesus saying about God through this parable?
- What have you learned for your life from this parable?

Think of a time when you experienced an act of generosity

GOD CREATING HEAVEN AND EARTH | VITTSKÖVLE CHURCH, SKÅNE, SWEDEN

GOD'S FAIRNESS AND GENEROSITY: EXPRESSIONS OF DIVINE LOVE

In the Bible we read, 'In the beginning . . . God created the heavens and the earth' (Genesis 1:1). This is the beginning of the truly marvelous Revelation that God is Generosity; God is the Giver of Life, the Giver of all that is good. God is always with us, bringing about his plan of goodness and creation in and through his Son, through whom all things came into being, and without whom not one thing came into being. (Read John 1:1–4).

God the Holy Spirit guides the Church, as he inspired the Sacred writers, to come to a deeper faith and trust in God, who 'not only gives [every person and thing in the universe] being and existence, but also, and at every moment, upholds and sustains them in being, enables them to act' and helps them become what they are meant to be. For those who believe in God's endless generosity, announcing our 'utter dependence' on God can be 'a source of wisdom and freedom, of joy and confidence' (CCC, no. 301). The more we reflect on God's Word, the more the Spirit leads us to discover not only God's 'generosity', but that God *is* Generosity.

God first revealed the depth of divine generosity in the story of Creation. He created 'the universe freely, directly, and without any help' (CCC, no. 317)—the light, the land and the sea; the sun and the moon; the plants, the fish and the animals—and God saw all of these as 'good'. After creating all other creatures, which he proclaimed to be good, God said,

'Let us make [man] in our image, according to our likeness; and let them have dominion over the fish of the sea, and over the birds of the air, and over the cattle, and over all the wild animals of the earth, and over every creeping thing that creeps upon the earth.'

So God created [man] in his image,
in the image of God he created them;
male and female he created them. . . .
God blessed them . . . . God saw everything that he had made, and indeed, it was very good.
—Genesis 1:26–28, 31

The depth of God's generous love is such that he creates every member of the human family in his own image and likeness. When we live as images of divine love, we give glory to God:

16 | CREDO | THE PROMISED ONE: SERVANT AND SAVIOR

> God created the world to show forth and communicate his glory. That his creatures should share in his truth, goodness, and beauty—this is the glory for which God created them.
>
> —CCC, no. 319

WHAT ABOUT YOU PERSONALLY?

- How do your words and actions give witness to your identity as an image of divine Love?

God the Creator also gave humanity 'dominion over' (the responsibility to manage and care for) God's good creation—everything. 'God created everything for man, but man in turn was created to serve and love God and to offer all creation back to him' (CCC, no. 358). The Hebrew words used in Genesis 2:15 in relation to the Earth mean 'to cultivate and develop its potential' and 'to guard it from destruction or harm'. God's own Word to us is very straightforward. The Giver of Life extends an invitation to us to join in the work of Creation. As we undertake that responsibility, that privilege, God is with us, helping and enabling us to organize our lives and our behavior in such a way that we can place ourselves in harmony with God's generous and loving plan of goodness.

REFLECT AND DISCUSS

- Reflect on and name the 'goodness' in the world, perhaps the goodness that surrounds you and that you take for granted and do not 'see' each day.
- How do these aspects of God's creation manifest God's generosity toward you? Toward the whole human family?
- How do you respond to this 'goodness'? How do your responses manifest your appreciation of God's generosity?

GIVE THANKS TO THE LORD GOD

We can easily take for granted God's amazing generosity toward us, and sometimes forget: 'Man, and through him all creation, is destined for the glory of God' (CCC, no. 353). Praying the psalms can heighten our awareness of God's goodness and generosity. In Psalm 104 the psalmist lists aspects of creation that would have been familiar to any Israelite in ancient times:

> **God created everything for man, but man in turn was created to serve and love God and to offer all creation back to him.**
>
> **CCC, NO. 358**

Bless the LORD, O my soul.
  O LORD my God, you are very great.

You make springs gush forth in the valleys;
  they flow between the hills,
giving drink to every wild animal;
  the wild [donkeys] quench their thirst.

You cause the grass to grow for the cattle,
  and plants for people to use,
to bring forth food from the earth,
  and wine to gladden the human heart,
oil to make the face shine,
  and bread to strengthen the human heart.

O LORD, how manifold are your works!
  In wisdom you have made them all;
  the earth is full of your creatures.

These all look to you
  to give them their food in due season;
when you give to them, they gather it up;
  when you open your hand, they are filled
    with good things.
        —Psalm 104:1, 10–11, 14–15, 24, 27–28

Such psalms of praise and thanksgiving reminded the Israelites of the lavish generosity of God and moved them to respond by singing his glory with worship and praise.

OVER TO YOU

- Choose the verse or phrase from Psalm 104 that you think is the best expression of gratitude to God for his generosity.
- Consider making a bookmark or a poster for your room using this phrase, so that you may be constantly reminded of the wonders of God's creation.

GOD IS ALWAYS TRYING TO 'CONVERT' US!

God created humanity with an intellect and a free will. We have the ability to know and the freedom to respond to his abundant love and generosity. From the opening chapters of Genesis and from our own experience, we know that we are also capable of choosing unwisely, making the wrong choices, setting aside God's plan and putting ourselves at odds with God and creation. Such unwise choices are out of sync with God's ways of generosity and trust.

God is always trying to 'convert' us, to 'turn us around' to living a more generous, trusting way of life

Salvation history clearly shows that we are capable of choosing to live a self-centered and not a God-centered life. But, even in the face of such choices, God does not cease to fill our lives with his generosity. Even our most selfish, self-centered and self-serving decisions cannot stop God's generosity and steadfast loyalty to us—his unconditional love for us. St. Paul explains, 'If we are faithless, [God] remains faithful—for he cannot deny himself' (2 Timothy 2:13).

'God is love' (1 John 4:8), and he always lavishes us with his generosity in the desire that we would turn toward that love. God is always inviting us to change the way we 'look at him', at ourselves, at other people and at the world, and to turn back toward him. Put another way, he is always trying to 'convert' us, to 'turn us around' to living a more generous, trusting way of life.

The depth of God's love and generosity was fully revealed in 'his freely sending of his Son for the **expiation** of our sins' (see CCC, nos. 620–621). Throughout this text we will continue to deepen our knowledge of Jesus and his mission, grow in our friendship with him, and make his wisdom the foundation of the way we look at God, at ourselves, at others and at all creation.

JOURNAL EXERCISE

Describe one aspect of your life that would benefit from a '**conversion**'.
- Write about how a Christian faith perspective could inspire and sustain your efforts.
- Now see if you can 'live' what you have described.

THINK IT THROUGH

Created in God's image and likeness

OPENING CONVERSATION
According to the Bible's first account of Creation (Genesis 1:1—2:4), every human person is created in the image and likeness of God (see Genesis 1:26).
- What do you think this Revelation means?
- How do you think you are created in the image and likeness of God?

GLIMPSE OF THE CREATOR-TRINITY
In Genesis we read, 'Let us make [man] in our image, according to our likeness' (Genesis 1:16). The Church, in light of the Revelation of Jesus Christ, has come to understand that God the Creator is the Trinity, one God in three Persons who are ever in a right and loving relationship, both within the Godhead and toward all creation. This unity, or oneness, is such that all three divine Persons always act as one.

> Though the work of creation is attributed to the Father in particular, it is equally a truth of faith that the Father, Son, and Holy Spirit together are the one, indivisible principle of creation.
> —CCC, no. 316

The names of the divine Persons—Father, Son and Holy Spirit—are not just different ways of talking about God. Father, Son and Holy Spirit are three unique 'Persons' in *perfect relationship* within the Godhead. This is a Mystery that we could never have come to know about God unless he revealed it to us and that we can never fully understand. For example, God is Father in a way that goes far beyond any human father. If you can imagine what a 'perfect' mother and father would be like, a perfect spouse or friend, then you can faintly begin to imagine what God is like: infinitely and unconditionally generous and faithful, caring and life-giving. God is far beyond the limits of any 'human' characteristic we use to describe him:

> In no way is God in man's image. He is neither man nor woman. God is pure spirit in which there is no place for the difference between the sexes. But the respective 'perfections' of man and woman reflect something of the infinite

20 | CREDO | THE PROMISED ONE: SERVANT AND SAVIOR

perfection of God: those of a mother and those of a father and husband [see Isaiah 49:14–15; 66:13; Psalm 131:2–3; Hosea 11:1–4; Jeremiah 3:4–19].

—CCC, no. 370

THINK, PAIR AND SHARE
- With a partner, read and think about this teaching of the Church: 'God's very being is Truth and Love' (CCC, no. 231).
- Where do you see people, who are images of God, living this truth about themselves?
- What happens when they do so?

THE HUMAN PERSON

This Revelation about the identity and nature of God is vital for our self-understanding and valuing of who every human person is. Why? 'The divine image is present in every man' (CCC, no. 1702). And, 'Being in the image of God the human individual possesses the dignity of a *person*, who is not just something, but someone' (CCC, no. 357). What does it mean to be a person?

First, the Catholic Church expresses the meaning of our personhood by teaching that God has revealed that he created the first humans in the state of **original holiness** and **original justice**, in a state of living in perfect harmony with him and with all creation.

Second, God has created us to be a unity of 'body' and 'soul'. The 'body' is the material aspect of the human person and the 'soul' is the person's spiritual aspect. Our body and soul are a unity that makes us one 'person'. Our souls make us persons (not objects), free (not machines). Above all, our souls give us **hope** for new life after death, an **eternal life** of living in harmony with God.

Third, 'There is a certain resemblance between the unity of the divine persons and the fraternity that men ought to establish among themselves' (CCC, no. 1890). This means that God creates us to live in community, to live in harmony with one another, to live for one another, and to develop and grow in healthy interpersonal relationships. The Church at the Second Vatican Council (restating Genesis 2:18, 23) put it this way: 'God did not create men and women as solitary beings. From the beginning "male and female God created them" (Genesis 1:27). This partnership of man and woman constitutes the first form of communion between people' (Vatican II, *Constitution on the Church in the Modern World*, no. 12).

The Human Heart

'The spiritual tradition of the Church also emphasizes the *heart*, in the biblical sense of the depth of one's being, where the person decides for or against God [see Jeremiah 31:33; Deuteronomy 6:5; 29:13; Ezekiel 36:26; Matthew 6:21; Luke 8:15; Romans 5:5].' (CCC, no. 368)

Reflecting on God's Word, the Church highlights the importance of healthy relationships for us as human beings: 'Each of the two sexes is an image of the power and tenderness of God, with equal dignity though in a different way' (CCC, no. 2335). God's own Word to us is clear: all humans are equal and connected, the same 'bone and flesh'—all members of God's family. All forms of sexism, the unjust discrimination between men and women based on gender, are contrary to both the plan of God and the dignity of the human person (see CCC, no. 2433). Created in the image of the Holy Trinity, human beings are called to respect and value one another's equality, celebrate one another's differences, and support one another in difficult times.

REFLECT AND SHARE

- Where do you see this truth being lived out? How is it being lived out? What are the results of it being lived out?
- Where do you see this truth *not* being lived out? How is it not being lived out? What are the results of it not being lived out?

LOSING AND GAINING THE 'LIKENESS OF GOD'

Our relationships, however, are not always healthy, respectful, loving and mature. Adam and Eve misused creation to serve their own desires to be other than the persons God created them to be. They disobeyed God, ate of the 'fruit of the tree in the middle of the garden', hid from God in shame, and then 'passed the buck', with neither taking responsibility for their actions (see Genesis 3).

THE EXPULSION FROM THE GARDEN OF EDEN | GUSTAVE DORÉ

Adam and Eve used creation to serve their own desires to be other than the persons God created them to be

FAITH WORD

Theosis

Theosis means 'divinization' or 'the process of becoming like God'. From the Greek word *theos*, meaning 'God', *theosis* is a central concept for many Eastern Rite Catholics. St. Athanasius, Father of the Church, wrote (about AD 319), 'The Son of God became man so that we might become God.'

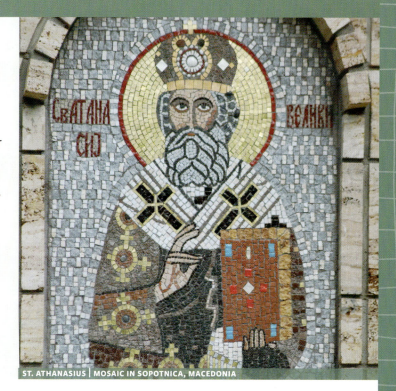

ST. ATHANASIUS | MOSAIC IN SOPOTNICA, MACEDONIA

Our first parents chose to damage their relationship with God. They lost the gifts of original holiness and original justice, of living in harmony with God, with each other and with creation. By rejecting their relationship with God, Adam and Eve and humanity 'fell' from balance, trust and justice into conflict, fear and sin. (See CCC, no. 390.) Now, irresponsibility and suffering, brokenness and loss, sickness and death are part of every human life and relationship.

Yet, humans remain essentially good; and, from the beginning, God promised Salvation. Theologians put it this way: nothing can erase the 'image of God', but sin makes us lose God's 'likeness' (see CCC, no. 705). Today, we long to 'become like God' once again; we long for *theosis*. We long to return to justice and harmony with God and one another. Catholics look for this spiritual transformation by immersing themselves in the life of Jesus and in the sacramental life of the Church.

OVER TO YOU

- Working with a partner, choose the 'best wisdom' you have learned in this chapter and discuss what difference this wisdom might make to your daily life.

JOURNAL EXERCISE

- List the five most important 'rules that you live by', your five 'personal commandments'. These may not be the rules that you are 'supposed' to follow, or even the rules that you wish you followed; rather, your list should give the rules that *actually* guide your behavior on a day-to-day basis.
- Next to each of these 'personal commandments', write two or three sentences explaining why this rule is so important to you, why you chose to adopt it, or where it came from in your life.

JUDGE AND ACT

REFLECT ON WHAT YOU HAVE LEARNED
- Reflect on what it means for the human person to be created in the image and likeness of God the Creator, the Holy Trinity.
- What **sacrifices** contribute to making trust, fairness and generosity part of our life? What sacrifices have you been challenged to make? What sacrifices are you willing to make?

COMPARE AND CONTRAST
At the end of the previous section of this chapter you listed the five most important convictions or guidelines that shape your behavior—your five 'personal commandments' as it were.
- Review your five 'personal commandments'. How do these help you put trust, fairness and generosity into action?
- How do they measure up to Jesus' standards, and how do they fall short?

LEARN BY EXAMPLE

The story of Peter Maurin

With his friend and fellow activist Dorothy Day, Peter Maurin (1877–1949) co-founded the *Catholic Worker*. The work of Peter Maurin and Dorothy Day provides us with an example of living a life based on fairness and generosity.

As a young man Peter Maurin spent time as a teacher, a religious brother and a Catholic community-organizer. At the age of thirty-two he left France, moving first to Canada and then to the United States. He worked at a variety of jobs—wandering handyman, lumberjack, miner, migrant farm-worker. For Maurin, living simply, with little money, was a gift; it gave him time to study and to think about how society could be reorganized so that 'it would be easier for people to be good'.

In 1932 Peter met Dorothy Day, with whom he discussed history—not just presidents, wars and revolutions, but the lives of holy men and women, the stories of people who had worked to make the world a better place. Maurin decided that his greatest task was to support Dorothy in creating the *Catholic Worker*, a newspaper that was launched on May 1, 1933, in the depths of the Great Depression in the United States (1929–39). Maurin wrote numerous 'Easy Essays' for the paper, in which he discussed his Catholic vision for the world. For Maurin, the practice of hospitality was key. For him, 'hospitality' meant opening our hearts and our homes to people in need. 'Modern society', he wrote, 'calls the beggar [a] bum and [a] panhandler. . . . But the Greeks used to say that people in need are ambassadors of the gods.'

Along with the newspaper, Peter and Dorothy helped create two 'Houses of Hospitality' in New York City, and a farm in Pennsylvania where the needy could live and work. Today, more than 185 Catholic Worker Houses of Hospitality and Worker Farms across the world remain committed to non-violence, voluntary poverty, prayer and hospitality for the homeless, exiled, hungry and forsaken.

THINK, PAIR AND SHARE
- With a partner, read the following 'Easy Essay' by Peter Maurin, one of many such essays published in the *Catholic Worker*.

Better or Better Off?

The world would be better off,
if people tried
to become better.

And people would
become better
if they stopped trying
to be better off.

For when everybody tries
to become better off,
nobody is better off.

But when everybody tries
to become better,
everybody is better off.

Everybody would be rich
if nobody tried
to be richer.

And nobody would be poor
if everybody tried
to be the poorest.

And everybody would be
what he ought to be
if everybody tried to be
what he wants
the other fellow to be.

- Choose one or two of the arguments expressed in this 'essay' and discuss your response to them.
- Then share some of your best conclusions with the rest of the class.

REVIEW AND JUDGE
- As you think about what you have read in this chapter, what you have written and what you have talked about, what did you find disturbing? What did you find reassuring? What did you find exciting?

- Again, if you feel comfortable, share your thoughts with a partner or small group, and then perhaps with the class.

DECIDE FOR YOURSELF
- Quietly reflect on what it means for you to be an image of the Triune God.
- Then decide on one personal belief or rule that you will definitely hold on to, and one personal belief or rule that you will definitely decide to change.

RESPOND WITH YOUR FAMILY
- As a family, choose a passage from Scripture that could be a 'family commandment', to guide the members of your family in treating one another with love that is built on trust, fairness and generosity. For example: 'In everything do to others as you would have them do to you; for this is the law and the prophets' (Matthew 7:12).
- Post your 'family commandment' in a place where it can be seen by all.

LEARN BY HEART

Strive first for the kingdom of God . . . and all these things will be given to you as well.

MATTHEW 6:33

PRAYER REFLECTION

LEADER
Sit quietly and remember that you are—as always—in the presence of the Triune God. (*Pause*)
In the name of the Father, and of the Son, and of the Holy Spirit.

ALL
Amen.

LEADER
Lord, send out your Spirit.

ALL
And renew the face of the earth.

RIGHT SIDE
Bless the Lord, O my soul.
   O Lord my God, you are very great.

LEFT SIDE
You make springs gush forth in the valleys;
   they flow between the hills,
giving drink to every wild animal;
   the wild [donkeys] quench their thirst.

ALL
Lord, send out your Spirit.
And renew the face of the earth.

RIGHT SIDE
You cause the grass to grow for the cattle,
   and plants for people to use,
to bring forth food from the earth,
   and wine to gladden the human heart,
oil to make the face shine,
   and bread to strengthen the human heart.

LEFT SIDE
O Lord, how manifold are your works!
   In wisdom you have made them all;
   the earth is full of your creatures.
These all look to you
   to give them their food in due season;
when you give to them, they gather it up;
   when you open your hand, they are filled
     with good things.

ALL
Lord, send out your Spirit.
And renew the face of the earth.

Prayers of the People

LEADER
Loving God,
your generosity surrounds us.
Send us the gift of your Spirit,
so that from day to day
we may turn our lives in your direction,
and become more and more like you.

READER
God of Generosity,
we thank you for our life, for our loved ones and for every good gift that you give.

ALL
Teach us to share your gifts with those who need them most.

READER
Sometimes we hurt one another; sometimes we hurt ourselves.

ALL
Heal our wounds and our broken relationships; teach us to open our hands and our hearts.

READER
Help us to understand the world from your point of view.

ALL
In our schools and our churches,
in our neighborhoods and society,
help us make the world a better place.

LEADER
May God bless us, protect us from all evil, and bring us to everlasting life.

ALL
Amen.

CHAPTER 2

The Reality of Sin and the Promise of Salvation

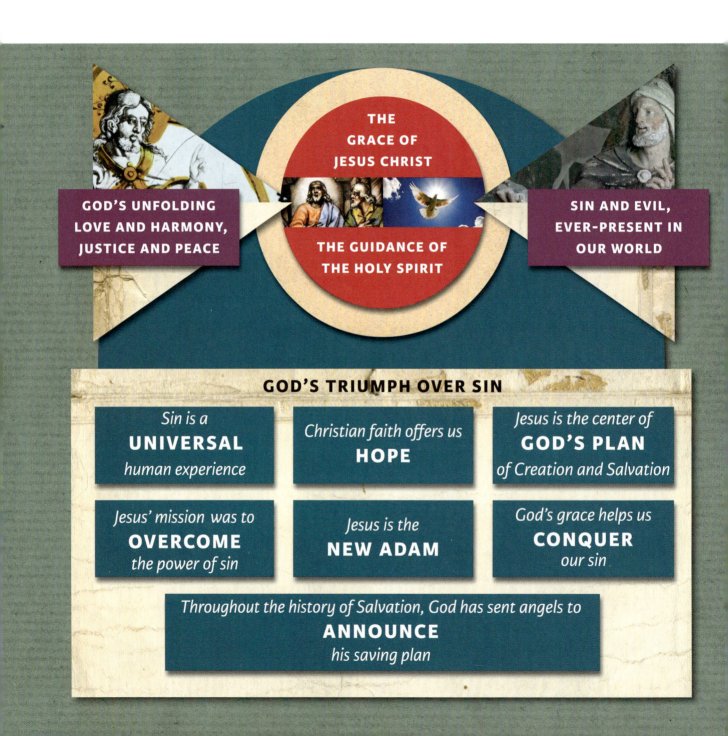

IN THIS CHAPTER WE EXPLORE THE TEACHING OF THE Catholic Church on sin—its origins and how God is at work to triumph over it. The Catholic Church teaches that the life, Death, Resurrection and Ascension of Jesus Christ are the heart of God's plan and promise to conquer sin. Jesus' mission in human history was to overcome the power and effects of sin and to restore all people to live as the free People of God. Jesus is the source of our hope that we can always say 'no' to sin and overcome its power by doing what is right and good.

LEARNING OUTCOMES

As a result of studying this chapter and exploring the issues raised, you should be able to:

- identify examples of brokenness and sinfulness in the world today;
- discover that Jesus is the beacon that lights up human history;
- understand the concepts of 'original holiness' and 'original justice';
- explore the symbolism in Genesis 2—3;
- understand why Jesus is the 'New Adam';
- understand the meaning of the term *Protoevangelium*;
- articulate the meaning of sin and how sin manifests itself in the world today;
- discover the connection between Original Sin and original justice;
- understand the teaching of the Catholic Church on angels;
- recognize God's unfolding vision of harmony, justice and peace in the face of the evil and negative forces in the world;
- understand the power each person has to challenge evil;
- understand that the Our Father calls us to turn away from evil.

FAITH-FORMATION OUTCOMES

As a result of studying this chapter and exploring the issues raised, you should also:

- identify ways in which your Christian faith can be a source of hope, meaning and inspiration for your life;
- recognize your need for God's Salvation;
- appreciate that the nature of God's love is such that no sin is unforgivable;
- grow in your awareness that we turn away from God when we sin;
- recognize that God always gives us hope through his abundant grace;
- recognize ways in which you can choose to follow God's vision;
- reaffirm your faith in the power of good to win out over evil;
- call on your guardian angel to help you recognize and overcome the power of sin in your life;
- respond to God's call to live as a disciple of Christ;
- be inspired by the story of Sr. Thea Bowman.

FAITH WORDS: Original Holiness; Original Justice; *Protoevangelium*; Sin; Original Sin

LEARN BY HEART: Romans 8:28

LEARN BY EXAMPLE: Sr. Thea Bowman, FSPA

ATTEND AND REFLECT

What is wrong with the world?

OPENING REFLECTION

We saw that God has revealed himself to be 'Truth and Love' (CCC, no. 231). When we look closely at the world in which we live, we can see that there is much truth and love, there is much goodness, love, joy and beauty; but there is also something terribly wrong.

WHERE IS THE LOVE?

In 2003, as war raged in Iraq and Afghanistan, and some marched in protest while others prepared to blow up their enemies (or themselves), the hip hop group Black Eyed Peas released the single 'Where Is the Love?', which topped the charts in over ten countries. Here are some of the lyrics:

Where Is the Love?

What's wrong with the world, mama?
People livin' like they ain't got no mamas.
I think the whole world's addicted to the
 drama,
only attracted to things that'll bring you
 trauma.
Overseas, yeah, we try to stop terrorism
but we still got terrorists here livin' in the
 USA: the big CIA,
the Bloods and the Crips and the KKK.
But if you only have love for your own race
then you only leave space to discriminate,
and to discriminate only generates hate,
and when you hate then you're bound to
 get irate. . . .

Let your soul gravitate to the love, y'all:
People killin', people dyin',
children hurt and you hear them cryin'.
Can you practice what you preach
and would you turn the other cheek?

Father, Father, Father help us.
Send some guidance from above!
'Cause people got me, got me questionin':
'Where is the love?'

EXPLORE THE LYRICS

Reread the above lyrics or listen to the song. Then, analyze the lyrics using 'active reading' markings. (You may need to review the instructions for the 'active reading' technique, which are in the opening section of chapter 1.)

- What strikes you about this song?
- What do you hear from it for your own life?
- Share your thoughts in a small group.

LET'S PROBE DEEPER

- In the song we read: 'I think the whole world's addicted to the drama.' What might be 'the drama' in your own life? Are you addicted to it? Why or why not?
- From your own experience, is 'love' enough to solve the problems in your life? In the world? Discuss.

RECOGNIZING THE BROKENNESS OF OUR WORLD

Although God has created us in the divine image and likeness, in the image and likeness of the Holy Trinity, we fall short of living up to who we were created to be. St. Paul recognized this reality. He wrote: 'I do not do the good I want, but the evil I do not want is what I do' (Romans 7:19). Similarly, Paul wrote: 'the whole creation has been groaning . . . to be set free' from brokenness and death (Romans 8:21, 22). In these two passages, St. Paul points to the brokenness within each of us personally, within the human family, and within creation as a whole.

THINK, PAIR AND SHARE

- Think about examples of brokenness and sinfulness in our world—at a personal or societal level.
- Share your examples with a partner and discuss the best Christian response to them.

REFLECT AND DISCUSS

- Reread the Black Eyed Peas' song 'Where Is the Love?'. What suggestions does it offer in answer to the question 'What's wrong with the world?'
- What do you think of this analysis?
- Call to mind some negative images you have seen in the media, in newspapers or on TV.
- What impact do such images have on the people who see them?

> St. Paul wrote: 'the whole creation has been groaning . . . to be set free' from brokenness and death

GROUP ACTIVITY
- Working in four groups, reflect on your experiences to determine which negative influences affect one of these areas:
  - Our relationships with one another
  - Our school
  - Our community
  - Our world
- Identify the *five biggest negative influences* and list them on a large sheet of paper. Save these sheets for a later project. Here are some examples from the Black Eyed Peas:
  - Drama
  - Addiction
  - Anger
  - Terrorism
  - Crime
  - Greed
  - Individual violence
  - Government violence
  - Lack of guidance
  - Discrimination
  - Negative media images
- Report your findings to the class, explaining why you believe these five influences have the most impact.

CLASS DISCUSSION
- Where do such negative influences come from? Why do they exist?
- Will violence and tragedy win out, or will healing and love have the final word?
- Who or what will be the deciding factor?

CHRISTIAN FAITH OFFERS US HOPE
In chapter 1 we explored that the story of Creation and **Salvation** began 'in the beginning' with a loving and generous God who created everything good. But the first humans rejected God's blueprint. In response to that rejection, God promised that the offspring of Eve would restore his plan of goodness, his original plan of **holiness** and justice. Genesis 3–11 goes on to describe how the descendants of Adam and Eve continued to reject God's plan of goodness and centered all things on themselves. In the stories of Cain and Abel, Noah and the flood,

and the tower of Babel, however, we read that God was faithful to his promises and called the human family and all creation back into living in harmony, trust, love and justice.

Jesus Christ, the Word of God made flesh, is the center of God's plan of Creation and Salvation. (Read John 1:1–18.) Jesus, God the Father's only Son, our brother, is the key player in the divine plan. He is the center of all Revelation and the heart of the story of Christian faith. For Christians, the life and Death-Resurrection-Ascension of Jesus (the **Paschal Mystery**) is the beacon that lights up human history. St. John's Gospel summarizes it so well:

God so loved the world that he gave his only Son, so that everyone who believes in him may not perish but may have eternal life.
—John 3:16

The coming of Jesus was a clear sign that God would not settle for what had gone wrong with the world. Jesus' mission in human history was to overcome the effects of sin. Though sin might abound, God's **grace** in Jesus Christ 'abounds all the more'; it is not sin but grace that now 'exercises dominion' over human history (Romans 5:20–21). Meanwhile, the struggle to overcome sin goes on, and the Black Eyed Peas can still sing:

Whatever happened to the values of humanity?
Whatever happened to the fairness in equality?
Instead of spreading love we're spreading animosity,
lack of understanding, leading lives away from unity.

God's work of Salvation reached its climax when God the Son became flesh in Jesus Christ. The rest of this chapter explores, first, the brokenness of our world, and second, how Jesus' victory over that brokenness can keep our faith alive and empower us with the hope to live as the People of God and disciples of Jesus, taking part in the restoration of God's loving plan of goodness.

THE ASCENSION | ANDREA MANTEGNA

[The] whole of Christ's life was a continual teaching: his silences, his **miracles**, his gestures, his prayer, his love for people, his special affection for the little and the poor, his acceptance of the total sacrifice on the Cross for the **redemption** of the world, and his Resurrection are the actualization of his word and the fulfillment of Revelation.
—*Catechism of the Catholic Church* (CCC), no. 561

JOURNAL EXERCISE

⊙ Write about how and in what situations your Christian faith offers you the most hope.

HEAR THE STORY

A story of hope

OPENING REFLECTION

Christians and Jews and Muslims have heard the story of Adam and Eve (Genesis 2:15—3:24), but those who take the time to read it for themselves might be surprised at what they find and do not find in the biblical account; for example, there is no apple, no sex, and no character called 'the Devil'! What's going on?

Recall that the biblical accounts of Creation and the Fall are neither scientific nor historical accounts as we know those literary genres today. These biblical accounts are written in a literary form that is highly symbolic. Let us revisit some of what we already know about symbols and symbolism. This is how the language of symbol was described in *God's Word Revealed in Sacred Scripture*, the first book of the *Credo* series:

> Symbols touch us on many different levels and give us ways to express ourselves in more than just words. Symbols communicate experience where words are not enough. Unlike signs (for example, a traffic light), which have just one meaning, symbols have many meanings. Symbols convey meaning when an experience is so profound that it is difficult to find the words to communicate its meaning. For example, when someone dies or when people fall in love, symbols are often used to help express and communicate the meaning of what is taking place.
>
> There are symbols that are particular to certain cultures or groups; for example, every baseball team has its own particular logo, nickname and colors, and every country has its national anthem. But there are also universal symbols that communicate across divides of time and culture; light and water are examples of universal symbols.
>
> A primary path by which we delve deeper into the meaning of things is through the creation and use of symbols. Symbols help us discern and make meaning out of life and express and share the meaning that we find.

EXPLORE THE TEXT
- Read Genesis 2:15—3:24 slowly and attentively, applying the 'active reading' technique.
- In small groups, share your most compelling active reading points.
- Discuss what you think this 'old' text means for our lives.

FAITH WORDS

Original Holiness
The grace of 'original holiness' was to share in divine life.
—CCC, no. 376

Original Justice
The inner harmony of the human person, the harmony between man and woman, and finally the harmony between the first couple and all creation, comprised the state of 'original justice'.
—CCC, no. 376

PARADISE | 12TH-CENTURY ILLUMINATED MANUSCRIPT

ORIGINAL HOLINESS AND ORIGINAL JUSTICE

Genesis 2—3 talks about the deepest realities of human experience and has played a key role in formulating the Christian outlook on life. These two biblical accounts reveal some basic truths about our first ancestors and, indeed, about ourselves. These revealed truths are:

- 'Our first parents, Adam and Eve, were constituted in an original "state of holiness and justice" ' (CCC, no. 375). They shared freely in the generous life and love of God.
- In this state of 'original holiness' and 'original justice', Adam and Eve were at harmony with God and each other, with the universe, and within their own minds and hearts.
- Adam and Eve were not slaves to selfishness, greed or bodily cravings. The work of growing, learning and living was 'not yet a burden, but rather the collaboration of man and woman with God in perfecting the visible creation' (CCC, no. 378). They did not have to suffer or die.
- This state and life of original holiness and original justice was lost for them and for all their descendants because they disobeyed God—because of **Original Sin**.
- As a result, the body has a mind of its own; injustice and tension disrupt our relationships; sickness and death are part of our lives.
- Although humans disobeyed God, God did not turn away from us. 'And when through disobedience he had lost your friendship, you did not abandon him to the domain of death. For you came in mercy to the aid of all, so that those who seek might find you. Time and time again you offered them covenants and through the prophets taught them to look forward to salvation' (*Roman Missal*, Eucharistic Prayer IV; see also CCC, no. 55).

THINK, PAIR AND SHARE

- Think of situations in your local community or in the wider world that reflect the absence of original justice.
- Share with a partner your ideas on what would need to happen for such situations to be restored to 'justice'.

RESURRECTION OF ADAM AND EVE | CHURCH OF THE HOLY SAVIOR, CHORA, TURKEY

JESUS IS THE 'NEW ADAM'

St. Paul saw a deeper sense, or meaning, in the biblical story of Adam and Eve. Paul taught that Jesus was the 'New Adam' (1 Corinthians 15:47–49), who came to correct Adam's tragic mistake:

> Therefore, just as sin came into the world through one man, and death came through sin, and so death spread to all because all have sinned. . . . Much more surely [then, has] the grace of God . . . in . . . Jesus Christ, abounded for the many.
>
> —Romans 5:12, 15

Because Jesus is the 'New Adam', Catholics see his mother, the Virgin Mary, as the 'New Eve'. Jesus and Mary lived a life free from all sin—Original Sin and personal sin. They lived a life of holiness and justice; they never lost the state of original holiness and original justice. (See CCC, no. 411.)

The biblical accounts of Creation and the Fall help us answer the question, 'What went wrong?' Through our study of Genesis 1—3 we can explore how human beings managed to turn our deep heart's desire for harmony and closeness to God into a life filled with tragedy, fear and sin.

The exploration of these accounts also helps us come to grips with the question, 'What are human beings really like?' While we long for and are capable of great goodness, the story of Adam and Eve reveals how capable we are of sin.

Finally, this ancient biblical story frames and prefigures Jesus' birth, life, Death and Resurrection. It gives final clarity to the promise made in Genesis 3:15 and answers the question 'What did Jesus save us from?' In short, it lays out the problem that Jesus came to fix.

GROUP ACTIVITY

- Working in four groups, read Genesis 2:15—3:24 once again.
- Then each group takes one of the following questions:
  – What do you learn about God and God's attitude toward human beings from this story?
  – What do you learn about human beings from this story?
  – What are the most important symbols in this story and what do they symbolize?
  – What wisdom does this story hold for your life today?
- Prepare a short presentation of your conclusions for the class.

A STORY OF HOPE

Genesis 2—3 is a story of both tragedy and hope. In Genesis 3:14–19 we read about God's response to both the serpent and Eve and Adam. Then in Genesis 3:15 we find the first promise of Salvation. God tells the serpent:

'I will put enmity between you and the woman,
 and between your offspring and hers;
he will strike your head,
 and you will strike his heel.'

—Genesis 3:15

This is the first announcement of Salvation to be found in Sacred Scripture. Symbolically speaking, the serpent represents evil, and the 'offspring' who will lead the battle and conquer evil prefigures Jesus, the Son of the New Eve, Mary. Tradition names this announcement 'the **Protoevangelium** ("first gospel"): the first announcement of the Messiah and Redeemer, of a battle between the serpent and the Woman, and of the final victory of a descendant of hers' (CCC, no. 410). Jesus is the offspring of the Woman; in him God fulfilled his promise. Jesus is the One who restores our ability to share in God's life—the life that God offered to people 'in the beginning'. The *Protoevangelium* illustrates and gives us insight into the nature of God's Truth and Love, of his generosity and fidelity to his creation.

Even as our first ancestors turned their backs on God's original plan of goodness, God's immediate response was to promise to send a Savior. Likewise, no matter what our sin might be, God is always reaching out to us, calling on us to trust in and return to the embrace of his love; God never gives up on us. (Recall the **parable** of the Prodigal Son/Forgiving Father in Luke 15:11–32.) Where our first ancestors got it wrong, Jesus gets it right—for us.

FAITH WORD

Protoevangelium

The term *protoevangelium* literally means 'first gospel' and refers to the very first Revelation we have in the Bible that God would send a Savior. In Genesis 3:15 God promises to send an 'offspring of the woman', who will crush the head of the serpent—the symbol of **temptation** and sin. (See CCC, nos. 410–411.)

OVER TO YOU

- Think of a recent incident with a family member, friend, teacher, coach or classmate where you 'got it wrong'.
- Spend a few minutes reflecting on this incident in light of the wisdom you have learned so far.
- Asking for God's guidance, prepare an apology to the person involved. You might even choose to put it in a letter.

EMBRACE THE VISION

Down but not out

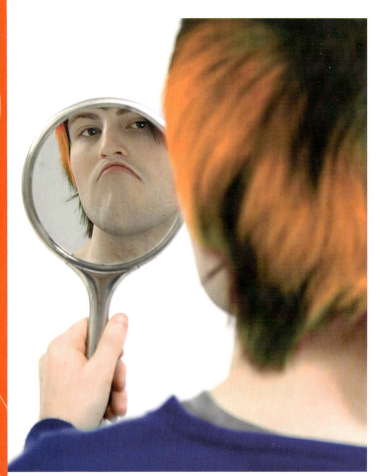

or the necessary consequence of an inadequate social structure.

In the words of St. Maximus the Confessor (580–662), sin distorts our quest for *theosis*; it turns our desire to become 'like' God into a competition 'against' God. In describing the first sin, and hence all sin, the *Catechism* teaches:

> In that sin man *preferred* himself to God and by that very act scorned him. He chose himself over and against God, against the requirements of his creaturely status and therefore against his own good. Constituted in a state of holiness, man was destined to be fully 'divinized' by God in glory. Seduced by the devil, he wanted to 'be like God', but 'without God, before God, and not in accordance with God' [St. Maximus the Confessor].
>
> —CCC, no. 398

OVER TO YOU

- Looking at the world around you, where do you see the greatest evidence of sin, of people putting themselves before God?

OPENING REFLECTION

Sin is a universal experience. You have experienced sin in many ways and, by now, you have come to realize that sin and its effects have many faces. At its root, sin is a total or partial rejection of God, of his love and of his plan of goodness for the world. Sin is 'an abuse of the freedom that God gives to created persons so that they are capable of loving him and loving one another' (CCC, no. 387). Sin is not simply a psychological weakness, a mistake,

GOD'S GRACE WILL HELP US TO CONQUER OUR SIN

God's Revelation in the biblical accounts of Creation and the Fall helps us understand the different dimensions and consequences of sin. The first sin was the moment when Adam allowed 'his trust in his Creator' to 'die in his heart'. It was the free act by which our first ancestors 'abused' their God-given freedom. They chose to overstep their human limits, to disobey God's command, and so to act as if they were God. (See CCC, nos. 396–397.)

THINK, PAIR AND SHARE

God said to Adam, 'You may freely eat of every tree of the garden; but of the tree of the knowledge of good and evil you shall not eat, for in the day that you eat of it you shall die' (Genesis 2:16–17).

- With a partner, imagine and act out the conversation Adam and Eve might have had in light of this command from God.

Adam and Eve had developed a 'distorted image' of God (CCC, no. 399). They began to fear God and to question God's goodness. We can imagine them saying, 'Maybe God enjoys bossing us around. Maybe God forbids us from doing certain things because God wants us to be ignorant. Why do we need such rules anyway?' This 'distorted image' led them to sin.

As a consequence of their sin, our first ancestors lost original holiness and original justice. They were expelled from the garden, from Paradise—a symbol of our living in a state of original holiness and original justice. The human family experienced its first Exile. The Church has always understood this Revelation to mean that the human condition as we know it and the inclination toward sin cannot be understood apart from the Original Sin.

> Following St. Paul, the Church has always taught that the overwhelming misery which oppresses men and their inclination toward evil and death cannot be understood apart from their connection with Adam's sin and the fact that he has transmitted to us a sin with which we are all born afflicted, a sin which is the 'death of the soul' [Council of Trent].
> —CCC, no. 403

Many still have the same distorted image of God that led Adam and Eve to sin. But all is not dark and lost. The promise of Salvation brings light and hope to the darkness of the Fall. Jesus Christ is that light (John 8:12), who clearly reveals to us who God truly is. Today, we are his disciples, and we are called to be lights in the world (Matthew 5:14). Christ has crushed the serpent's head; sin and evil no longer have power over us. We are free to choose the light rather than the darkness.

REFLECT AND DISCUSS

- Think of some 'dark' places in the world today—in your own neighborhood or in the wider world.
- Who brings light to this darkness?

FAITH WORD

Sin

Sin is an offense against God as well as against reason, truth, and right conscience; it is a failure in genuine love for God and neighbor caused by a perverse attachment to certain goods. It wounds the nature of man and injures human solidarity. It has been defined as 'an utterance, a deed, or a desire contrary to the eternal law' (CCC, no. 1849).

—*United States Catholic Catechism for Adults* (USCCA), 528

The Church baptizes for the remission of sins even tiny infants who have not committed personal sin.

CCC, NO. 403

WHAT ABOUT YOU PERSONALLY?

⊙ As a disciple of Jesus Christ, how and where can you bring light into the world?

ORIGINAL SIN

The *Catechism* teaches, 'By yielding to the tempter, Adam and Eve committed a *personal sin*, but this sin affected *the human nature* that they would then transmit *in a fallen state*' (CCC, no. 404). Sin is a 'universal' aspect of human existence; our hearts are 'wounded' and 'divided'; we are born into a world where something is wrong and needs to be put right. (See CCC, nos. 401, 402, 404, 1707.) We are attracted and susceptible to sin. Life is no longer free from conflict and disunity, suffering and death. We are in need of Salvation. Reflecting on the reality of evil and sin, the Church teaches:

The whole of human history has been the story of our combat with the powers of evil, stretching, as our Lord tells us, from the very dawn of history until the last day. Finding themselves in the battlefield, men and women have to struggle to do what is right, and it is at great cost to themselves, and aided by God's grace, that they succeed in achieving their own inner integrity.

—Vatican II, *Constitution on the Church in the Modern World,* no. 37

OVER TO YOU

⊙ Think of the events of the past week that have been reported on the news. Where do the reports show the effects of Original Sin in the world? What do they say about the human struggle to overcome evil?

God offers us both hope and help to deal with our struggle to overcome evil. In Baptism we receive the free gift of **sanctifying grace** and are restored to a life of holiness. The graces of Baptism cannot be earned; they flow from the love and generosity of God.

This is why Catholics baptize infants. 'Because of this certainty of faith, the Church baptizes for the remission of sins even tiny infants who have not committed personal sin' (CCC, no. 403). Baptism welcomes infants into a new way of life. It unites them with Christ. Baptism restores our relationship with God, and, in spite of the fact that human nature remains broken, it turns us back toward God and empowers us to live with the confident hope that evil and sin and death will not have the final victory over us. We receive the graces to live as children of God and to take part in Christ's work to recreate a world of justice through our participation in the Sacraments and in the life of the Church.

WHY DID GOD ALLOW SIN TO HAPPEN?

People have always asked, 'Why does God allow evil, sin and death to exist?' Why did God not stop the first humans from sinning, and so prevent their (and our) suffering and facing the pain and the reality of death?

Evil is a reality that people have always and will always seek to explain—and, perhaps, try to explain away. The struggle to understand and cope with evil, sin and death is central to human life. God has responded to our search. God inspired the human authors of the Bible to write not only Genesis 1—3 but also Job and other parts of Sacred Scripture so as to provide us with a hope-filled vision of life in our struggle with evil. God's own Word and promise to us is that he is present with us, guiding us and giving us strength and vision to weather successfully the storms of life.

> The fact that God permits physical and even moral evil is a mystery that God illuminates by his Son Jesus Christ who died and rose to vanquish evil. Faith gives us the certainty that God would not permit an evil if he did not cause a good to come from that very evil, by ways that we shall fully know only in eternal life.
> —CCC, no. 324

God has proven over and over again that we can trust in his Word. 'We know that all things work together for good for those who love God' (Romans 8:28). While 'evil never becomes a good', we know and have experienced that good can arise out of evil. In the end, God gives us the grace we need to face and overcome evil and death.

RESEARCH AND RESPOND

Death is one of the greatest consequences of Original Sin.
- Find an adult who is willing to share their feelings about death. Ask how she or he coped when someone they loved died. How did her or his faith help? How did her or his hope help?
- What have you learned from this person's sharing for your own faith?

WE HAVE REASON TO SING!

When officials of the Roman Empire first encountered the followers of Jesus, they noticed something peculiar about them. Plinius Caecilius (61–112), an imperial magistrate under the Roman Emperor Trajan, who was emperor from 98 to 117, wrote with some amazement, 'These Christians are accustomed to sing.' What was it

FAITH WORD

Original Sin

Original sin is the personal sin of disobedience by the first human beings, resulting in the deprivation of original holiness and justice and the experience of suffering and death.
—USCCA, 522

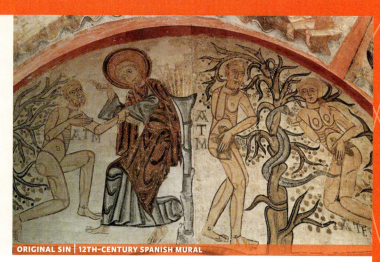

ORIGINAL SIN | 12TH-CENTURY SPANISH MURAL

that inspired the members of the early Church to sing?

The early Church followed the example of the Israelites. In times of suffering and tribulation the Israelites, as Jews do today, sang of their trust in God and their hope in his promises. (Read Psalm 140 and Psalm 146.) The early disciples of Jesus trusted in God in the midst of their suffering and persecution, and in that suffering they sang God's praise. The verses from Psalm 146 inspired the great Gospel songwriter Joseph Lowry (1826–99) to write one of our most moving spirituals, 'How Can I Keep from Singing?':

> My life flows on in endless song,
> Above earth's lamentation.
> I hear the real though far off hymn
> That hails a new creation.
>
> No storm can shake my inmost calm
> While to that Rock I'm clinging.
> Since love is Lord of Heav'n and earth,
> How can I keep from singing?

REFLECT AND DISCUSS
- What is the Rock that is referred to in the song?
- What is the Rock in your own life at this time?

In the history of our country and throughout the world today we can find many examples of Christians who continue to trust in God in the face of suffering. They may be holding on for dear life, but they remember that God is in charge, that God always gives hope, that, by God's abundant grace, good can and will triumph over evil, in our lives and our world. At the Easter Vigil each year, the Church proclaims this faith: 'O happy fault . . . which gained for us so great a Redeemer!' Things may have been good before our first ancestors sinned, but 'the glory of the new creation' established by Jesus Christ will be even greater. (See CCC, nos. 374, 412.)

OVER TO YOU
- Ask your parents and/or grandparents to talk to you about what has sustained their faith in stormy times.

THINK IT THROUGH

Rejecting evil

OPENING REFLECTION

From a human perspective, evil and sin, suffering and death are very real. Just as real, and even more powerful, is God's 'strength and gentleness', which 'guides human and cosmic history' (CCC, no. 395). Martin Luther King, Jr. spoke of this power:

> Let us remember that there is a creative force in this universe, working to pull down the gigantic mountains of evil, a power that is able to make a way out of no way and transform dark yesterdays into bright tomorrows. Let us realize the arc of the moral universe is long but it bends toward justice.

Only 'at the end' will we understand how God has bent the arc of the universe; only when God has finished his work of Salvation will we see how God brought justice and peace out of evil and sin (see CCC, no. 314). This is why the Church teaches that in the conflict with death and violence, life and love will have the last word and prevail. That is God's promise, God's own Word to us!

WHAT ABOUT YOU PERSONALLY?

How do you keep faith and hope alive?
- Pick a song, poem, video or artwork that lifts you up when you are 'feeling under'.
- Post a link to it on your blog or social networking site, or post a copy of it on the refrigerator at home.
- Add a short caption, explaining how it lifts you up.

THE EXISTENCE AND WORK OF ANGELS

Sacred Scripture and Sacred Tradition speak of angels as God's messengers and our helpers in the divine plan of Salvation. At the beginning of time God created spiritual beings—angels—and corporeal or bodily beings—human beings. Angels are servants and messengers of God, who glorify God without ceasing. They are purely spiritual creatures who have intelligence and will. Throughout the history of Salvation, God has sent angels to announce his saving plan to human beings.

For example, in the Old Testament we read that, among the many roles angels played in human life, they:
- closed the earthly paradise (Genesis 3:24);
- protected Lot (Genesis 19);
- served Hagar and her child (Genesis 21:17);
- interceded with Abraham when he was about to sacrifice his son (Genesis 22:11–12);

- led the people of God as they entered the Promised Land (Exodus 23:20–23);
- announced births and God calling people to serve him (Judges 13:6–7; Luke 1:11–17);
- assisted the prophets (Isaiah 6:6).

Perhaps the examples we remember best are those connected with the birth, Death and Resurrection of Jesus:
- The angel Gabriel announced to Mary that she would give birth to Jesus, who would be the Savior of the world. (See Luke 1:26–38.)
- An angel told Joseph in a dream to take Mary as his wife. (See Matthew 1:20.)
- Angels gave praise to God at the birth of Jesus. (See Luke 2:14.)
- Angels gave Jesus strength in the Garden of Gethsemane. (See Matthew 26:53.)
- Angels first proclaimed the good news of Jesus' Resurrection. (See Matthew 28:5–6.)

Sacred Tradition teaches that angels continue to play a role in human life. As St. Basil put it, 'Beside each believer stands an angel as protector and shepherd.' Each human life is surrounded by the watchful care of angels, from infancy to death.

RESEARCH AND SHARE
- The Bible is not the only medium filled with the stories of angels and the role they play in human life. Work in small groups.
  – Research the centrality of angels in themes of literature, in the lyrics of songs and in the visual media.
  – Share the results of your group's research with the other groups.

CLASS DISCUSSION
- Why do you think these 'angel stories' capture the attention of so many people?
- Do 'angel stories' get your interest and attention? Why or why not?
- Do you ever pray to your guardian angel? Why or why not?

ANGEL MUSICIAN | MELOZZO DA FORLI

Angels gave praise to God at the birth of Jesus, singing, 'Glory to God in the highest'

FALLEN ANGELS

Sacred Scripture also speaks of a sin of angels (2 Peter 2:4) and fallen angels, who work against God and his plan of Creation and Salvation. We call these angels 'fallen' because we believe that 'the devil and other demons were indeed created naturally good by God, but they became evil by their own doing' (Lateran Council IV [1215] in CCC, no. 391). The fallen angels made an irrevocable choice which rendered their sin unforgivable.

At the beginning of Jesus' public ministry, the Devil tempts him to abandon his mission for his own power and glory. After the third temptation, Luke writes, 'When the devil had finished every test, he departed from him until an opportune time' (Luke 4:13). Jesus rejected the Devil's temptation three times; but the Devil will continue his work until the end.

In speaking to the Jews who had denied that he was a true descendant of Abraham, Jesus has this to say of 'the Devil': 'He was a murderer from the beginning and . . . there is no truth in him. . . . For he is a liar and the father of lies' (John 8:44). Check out and look carefully at the stories of Jesus identifying and overpowering demons in the Gospel of Mark: an 'unclean' spirit (Mark 1:21–27); a 'strong man' (the tyrant or bully known as 'Satan' in Mark 3:27); a 'legion' or army of occupation (Mark 5:9); a spirit that shuts the mouths of young people and makes them hurt their own bodies (Mark 9:14–29).

The Catholic Church teaches that good and bad angels can have a real effect on our lives. The existence of evil in its many forms is a reality that tempts us to weaken our faith and trust in God. But we believe and trust that Goodness and Love and Life, God, will prevail.

THE TEMPTATION OF JESUS | 16TH-CENTURY POLYCHROME SCULPTURE, VARALLO, ITALY

REFLECT AND DECIDE
- How do you think your guardian angel might help you?
- Jesus called Satan 'the father of lies'. What are the effects of lying? Can lying ever be justified? Explain.

ACT IT OUT
- Organize a 'daytime talk show' on the theme of 'Young people who lie to their parents'. The roles might be:
  - Talk show host
  - A young person who has lied to his or her mother
  - The mother
  - The young person's teacher
  - The rest of the class as the 'studio audience'
- Use these steps in the development of your production:
  - The host asks the young person to tell his or her story. (*No more than one minute*)
  - The host invites the parent and the teacher to respond. (*No more than one minute each*)
  - The host fields questions and comments from the studio audience. (*No more than five minutes in total*)

The Devil is the master of deceit. Satan's 'workings' are subtle and modern, and his false 'promises' can look rather appealing, much as they did to Adam and Eve

- After the segment is over, discuss:
  – How does lying affect our relationships with other people?
  – How do people feel about themselves when they lie?
  – What is the best decision—for life—that we can make about lying?

EXPELLING MODERN DEMONS

Even today, there are powers in the world working against the Reign of God. On one side there is God's unfolding love and harmony, justice and peace. On the other are 'the powers of evil', which exert a 'negative influence' through the individual actions and 'communal situations' of human beings; as evil spreads, it even infects organizations and produces 'structures of sin' (see CCC, nos. 408, 1869).

When we pronounce or renew our baptismal profession of faith, we answer the following questions: 'Do you reject Satan? And all his works? And all his empty promises?' When we answer 'Yes' or 'I do', we commit ourselves to acting as Jesus did, to living as his disciples. We promise to work at casting out the demons of modern-day life from our personal life and from the structures of society that are 'sinful'. These promises might be easier to keep if the Devil, or Satan, appeared as a talking snake, or a bright red demon with horns and a tail. But the Devil, the Evil One, is the master of deceit. Satan's 'workings' are much more subtle and modern, and his false 'promises' can look rather appealing, much as they did to Adam and Eve.

Sometimes, for example, it is easier to join the crowd and treat certain people as outcasts or outsiders, instead of challenging the spirit of discrimination that labels them in this way. Joined to Christ at Baptism, we have Christ's vision and receive the grace to see through such deceit and to respond as Jesus did, 'Away with you, Satan! Worship the Lord your God, and serve only him' (see Matthew 4:10).

The truth is that in life we can be moved by good spirits or bad spirits, by angels or devils if you like. We must be constantly alert for the kinds of 'spirits' that may be driving us to decisions and choices. Christians throughout the centuries have used the biblical phrase '**discernment** of spirits' to describe this naming and testing process (see 1 Corinthians 12:10 and 1 John 4:1). The Good News is that, through our union with Christ, we have the vision and wisdom and grace of God to recognize and follow the 'good spirits' in our lives, as we take part in building and preparing for the coming of the **Kingdom of God**.

As human beings, we will always struggle to do what is right, to follow the Great Commandment and live a life of holiness and justice. This may not be so easy. However, 'aided by God's grace' we can achieve 'inner integrity' or harmony with ourselves, with God and with others (see CCC, nos. 408–409, 1707).

GROUP ACTIVITY
- Working in groups, list any forces that you believe are trying to dominate or influence young people's lives in a negative way. These are the negative 'spirits'—the demons—of our modern world.
- Still working in groups, name the opposite, positive 'spirits' that stand against each of these modern demonic forces. For example, the opposite of 'a spirit of bigotry' might be 'a spirit of respect for all people'.

JOURNAL EXERCISE
- Select one negative or positive 'spirit' discussed within the group. Reflect on ways in which that 'spirit' is helping you to live as a disciple of Christ or is an obstacle to your living as a disciple of Christ. Write your reflections in your journal.
- Pray to the Holy Spirit to guide you in living a holy and just life.

Aided by God's grace we can achieve 'inner integrity' or harmony with ourselves, with God and with others

JUDGE AND ACT

REFLECT ON WHAT YOU HAVE LEARNED

We have the freedom to turn our back on God and his love and generosity. We are capable of hurting one another and ourselves. Sin can infect such social institutions as a school or a neighborhood, and local, state and national governments. Sin can snowball into such sinful 'isms' as racism, sexism and ageism. Sinful choices can give rise to the seeking of peace through violence and unjust war. This is not the way God wants us to live. However, we can turn in trust and hope to the healing power of God's love, the grace of Jesus Christ and the guidance of the Holy Spirit. Through Jesus, we too can conquer sin and death.

REVIEW AND EVALUATE

- Define 'sin' in your own words.
- Explain how your ideas about sin have changed or remained the same as you worked through this chapter.
- In view of your definition of 'sin', do you believe Jesus has 'conquered' sin? Explain your answer.

JOURNAL EXERCISE

- Which negative spirit is exerting the most powerful force over your life right now? Write about it.
- Then engage in a conversation with Jesus about this 'spirit'. Record what you think he might say.

LEARN BY EXAMPLE

The story of Sr. Thea Bowman, FSPA

Bertha Bowman was born in Yazoo City, Mississippi in 1937. Her parents, Theon, a doctor, and Mary Esther, a teacher, sent her to a Catholic school, and she was baptized as a Catholic when she was ten years old. At the age of sixteen, Bertha joined the Franciscan Sisters of Perpetual Adoration and took the name Thea, which means 'belonging to God', in honor of her father.

Sr. Thea studied English literature and language arts in college and earned a PhD from the Catholic University of America. In her teaching Sr. Thea used storytelling and preaching, acting and singing, poetry and prayer to encourage people to discover their talents and the importance of their cultural heritage in shaping their identity. Sr. Thea often said, 'I like being black, I like being myself, and I thank God for making me my black self.' Sr. Thea would say, 'Be woman, be man, be priest, be Irish American, be Italian American, be Native American, be African American, but be one in Christ.'

Sr. Thea helped found the Institute for Black Catholic Studies at Xavier University in New

Orleans, Louisiana. The center helps educators, ministers and leaders to celebrate and serve the Black Catholic community. In explaining the purpose of the institute, she said, 'We do

48 | CREDO | THE PROMISED ONE: SERVANT AND SAVIOR

not want to change the theology of the church. We just want to express theology within the roots of our black spiritual culture.'

Reflecting on her life, Sr. Thea stated in a TV interview, 'I think the difference between me and some other people is that I'm content to do my little bit. Sometimes people think they have to do big things in order to make change. But if each one of us would light a candle, we'd have a tremendous light.'

Sr. Thea died of cancer in 1990 and was buried next to her mom and dad. Her tombstone reads: 'She tried.'

REFLECT AND DISCUSS
- What do you admire most about Sr. Thea Bowman?
- What can you learn from her example for your own life?

WHAT ABOUT YOU PERSONALLY?
- Think of one personal relationship in your life that is broken and that you would like to put right. What does your faith suggest you can do? What will you do?
- Think of one situation in your school or neighborhood that is broken and that you would like to rectify. What does your faith suggest you can do? What will you do?

RESPOND WITH FAMILY AND FRIENDS
- Talk with family members about how to figure out what are good influences on your family life and what are negative ones. Talk about how you can sharpen your discernment as a family, how you can work together to root out one of the negative influences, and how your faith can help in this work of opposing **social sin**.
- With a friend or friends, choose some social sin that is evident among young people today. Discuss the roots of the sin and what practical action you might take to counteract it.

JOURNAL REFLECTION
- Think about what you have read, what you have written and what you have talked about as you studied this chapter.
- What did you find challenging and why?
- What did you find reassuring and why?
- What did you find exciting and why?

LEARN BY HEART

We know that all things work together for good for those who love God.

ROMANS 8:28

PRAYER REFLECTION

Preparation

- Quietly reflect on the good and negative 'spirits', or influences, in life today that you identified during your study of this chapter.
- Then brainstorm as a class and select three contrasting 'spirits' that you believe reflect the most pressing needs in your class, school, local community or in the world.
- Include these in the appropriate parts of the Prayer Reflection.

LEADER
Sit quietly and remember that you are—as always—in the presence of God. (*Pause*)
In the name of the Father, and of the Son, and of the Holy Spirit.

ALL
Amen.

LEADER
We believe that Jesus came to restore within us the life that sin has taken away.
We have been buried with Christ in Baptism so that we may rise with him to new life.
Now we remember and remake the promises of our own Baptism. (*Pause.*)
Let us pray for God's wisdom and strength. (*Pause for silent prayer*)

READER
Do you reject Satan?
ALL
I do.

READER
And all his works?
ALL
I do.

READER
And all his empty promises?
ALL
I do.

READER
Do you reject the evil spirits at work in the world, such as injustice and hatred, sexism, racism, ageism?
ALL
(Name others) I do.

READER 1
Will you keep these beliefs and commitments?
ALL
I will, with the help of God.

LEADER
Let us pray that the Spirit of Jesus
will heal everything that is broken:
in our lives, in our relationships and in our world.

Do you believe that Christ will triumph over sin,
that good will triumph over evil,
that life will triumph over death?
ALL
I do.

READER
Lord, cast out the spirit of _____.
ALL
And give us a spirit of _____.

READER
Lord, cast out the spirit of _____.
ALL
And give us a spirit of _____.

READER
Lord, cast out the spirit of _____.
ALL
And give us a spirit of _____.

READER
Let us pray for the needs of other people:
for strangers, family and friends.

All pray silently, or speak prayers out loud.

READER
By awesome deeds you answer us with
 deliverance,
O God of our salvation.
ALL
Lord God, Father, Son and Holy Spirit,
you are the hope of the ends of the earth
and of all the farthest seas.

LEADER
May God bless us, protect us from all evil and bring us to everlasting life.
ALL
Amen.

CHAPTER 3

God's Commitment, Our Hope

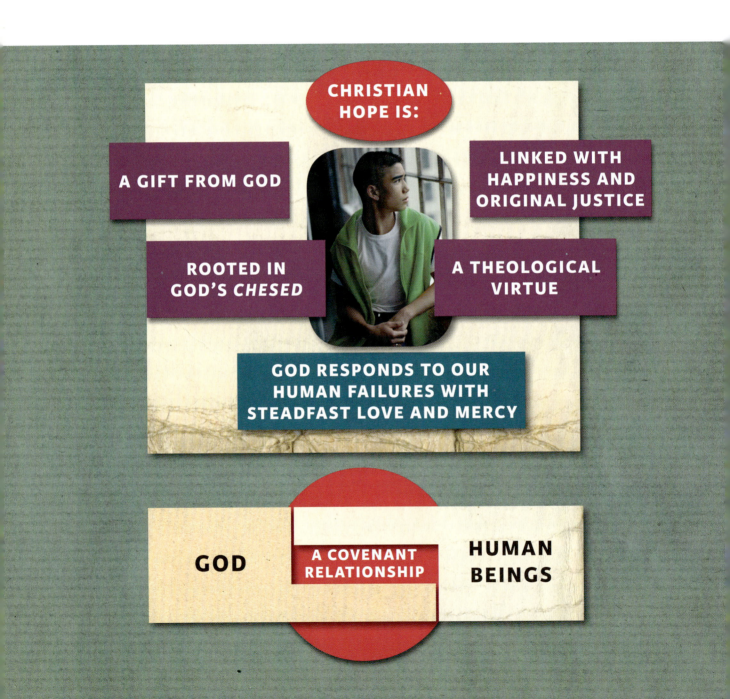

IN THIS CHAPTER WE EXPLORE THE NATURE OF Christian hope. Hope is the oxygen of the human heart! Human beings live in hope, sometimes even 'hoping against hope'. We explore both the history of the fulfillment of God's promise to send the Savior and the Covenant binding God and his people in an irrevocable partnership that is the basis of the hope of Jews and Christians. God's Word to us is that all of God's promises have been fulfilled in Jesus Christ. This is the hope that the Church announces and bears witness to in the world today.

LEARNING OUTCOMES

As a result of studying this chapter and exploring the issues raised, you should be able to:

- explore how, for Christians, hope, happiness and original justice are intrinsically linked;
- understand the Hebrew word *chesed*;
- recognize God's Covenants as our most important source of Christian hope;
- know the meaning of the story of Cain and Abel;
- recognize instances of sinfulness in the world today;
- know the meaning of the story of Ruth and Naomi;
- describe the characteristics of God's steadfast love for humanity;
- understand how God's Covenants reveal God's commitment to order, unity, justice and right relationship;
- understand that we are bound by the same Covenant;
- identify hopes that you are prepared to 'live for' and perhaps even 'die for';
- understand the meaning of 'foreshadowing' and 'typology' in the context of the Old Testament;
- understand that the 'suffering Servant of God' in the writings of Isaiah prefigures Jesus;
- understand the responsibility of disciples of Jesus to work at alleviating the suffering of others, even if that means suffering ourselves.

FAITH-FORMATION OUTCOMES

As a result of studying this chapter and exploring the issues raised, you should also:

- grow in your awareness that God created us to love and to be loved;
- articulate instances where your faith in God gives you hope;
- recognize how Cain's struggle with sin and evil reflects our own daily struggle with sin and evil;
- reflect on how Abraham's faith can inspire you to keep your faith alive;
- work at fulfilling the personal demands of your Covenant with God;
- appreciate that it is sometimes necessary to suffer in order to do what is right;
- recognize times in your life when God answered your prayers;
- be inspired by the story of St. Damien of Molokai.

FAITH WORD: *Chesed*

LEARN BY HEART: Genesis 9:14–15

LEARN BY EXAMPLE: St. Damien of Molokai

THE STORY OF GOD'S PEOPLE

- **INFIDELITY AND FIDELITY**
- **SIN AND STEADFAST LOVE**
- **SLAVERY AND LIBERATION**
- **EXILE AND FREEDOM**
- **PROMISE AND FULFILLMENT**
- **THE 'NEW COVENANT' IN JESUS**

ATTEND AND REFLECT

Where is our hope?

OPENING REFLECTION
Sometimes, hope is all we have: hope that things will turn out right; hope that a loved one will follow through on her or his promise; hope that love will overcome an obstacle; hope that God will be there to meet us when we step out into the unknown.

A QUICK CHECK
Before moving on, do the following 'quick check'—perhaps teaming up with a partner to compare and share your views.
- How would you describe hope?
- What gives you hope in your life right now?
- How can you be a source of hope for others?

EXPRESSING HOPE THROUGH ART
Artists have always used the medium of art to express different aspects of the human condition. The installation shown here is the work of a young artist called 'Know Hope'. Born in California, Know Hope lives in Tel Aviv, Israel, and travels around the world creating contemporary art. Like the name that this artist has chosen for himself, his art points toward hope. He says:

> [My art] is all about real life, and collective human struggle. It mirrors what I see around me in the heartbroken world I live in. I think all of my art is both optimistic and pessimistic. . . . The art happens in devastating circumstances, sure, but there are always moments of connection and hope.

KNOW HOPE | HOW WE GOT THERE/LIKE PIGEONS IN THE RAIN (DETAIL)

GROUP ACTIVITY
Work in small groups to examine and analyze Know Hope's installation.
- What do you notice about the figures?
- Make a list of all the symbolic elements you can find and discuss what you think each of these elements might mean.
- What parts of the artwork are pessimistic? What parts are optimistic?
- What does this artwork say to you about hope? About living as Jesus lived?
- Share your best conclusions with the rest of the class.

JOURNAL EXERCISE
- Draw an image or symbol that speaks to you of hope.

WHAT IS HOPE?
Hope brings a sense of optimism to our life journey. We often hear and perhaps use such statements as 'I hope my team wins!', 'I hope I pass this test!', 'I hope my grandma gets through

her operation well!' The sacred authors of Scripture used the word 'hope' more than 140 times. Paul, in his letter to Titus, writes: 'This Spirit he poured out on us richly through Jesus Christ our Savior, so that, having been justified by his grace, we might become heirs according to the hope of eternal life' (Titus 3:6–7). In the Letter to the Hebrews the sacred author writes, 'Let us hold fast to the confession of our hope without wavering, for he who has promised is faithful' (Hebrews 10:23).

This message of hope has been proclaimed constantly by the Church from her beginning. Today, in Evening Prayer (Vespers) of the Liturgy of the Hours for those who have died, the Church sings out:

Leader: In you, O Lord, is our hope.
People: We shall never hope in vain.
Leader: We shall dance and rejoice in your mercy.
People: We shall never hope in vain.

Hope is a gift from God. It is 'the theological virtue through which a person both desires and expects the fulfillment of God's promises of things to come' (*United States Catholic Catechism for Adults* [USCCA], 515). This virtue both reflects God's desire for the balance, the goodness and the right relationship that human beings had with him, with one another and with all creation 'in the beginning' and empowers us to strive to restore that balance in our lives.

WHAT ABOUT YOU PERSONALLY?
- How does your Christian faith give you hope?
- What difference does your faith make in tough times? For example, when school is not going well; when family relationships are strained; when friendships are undergoing difficulties and so forth.

CHESED—STEADFAST LOYALTY AND LOVE
Christian hope is rooted in our faith and trust in God's fidelity to his people. We can get a glimpse of that fidelity in the commitment of our parents who cared enough to share the gift of life with us, bring us into the world, and be with us in good times and bad, helping us grow into the person God created and blessed us to be. The Hebrew word for 'commitment' is **chesed** (pronounced 'heh-sed'). While the word *chesed* has been translated into English in a variety of ways, such as 'merciful' or 'gracious', or 'loving kindness', 'tenderness', '**compassion**' and 'steadfast love', *chesed* is a Hebrew word whose meaning no one English word can capture fully and adequately.

Christian hope is rooted in our faith and trust in God's fidelity to his people.

The sacred authors of the Old Testament often describe God as *chesed*. Through God's self-Revelation, they and God's people came to see that *chesed* is a key attribute of God as well as a quality that describes the relationship between God and the human family. God's initial commitment to us is his giving us life and sharing his own divine life with us. From that first moment of our creation, God's *chesed*, his commitment to us, has never failed. And in describing Moses' encounter with God on Mount Sinai, the *New Revised Standard Version* (NRSV) of the Bible and the *New American Bible* (NAB) both refer to God as 'merciful and gracious' and 'abounding in steadfast love and faithfulness' (Exodus 34:6). (Read Exodus 34:1–9.)

OVER TO YOU

- Give another biblical example or tell a story of God's *chesed*. What message of hope do you hear in that story?

God calls us to be *chesed* people. He commands us to be faithful to and to live up to our identity as images and likenesses of God. We are to be people who abound in *chesed*—a love that is generous beyond expectations, a love that never stops giving. (Recall Luke 10:25–37, the parable of the Good Samaritan.) Above all, *chesed* is that faithful love that binds us to God. *Chesed* is a way of being faithful in love to God, to ourselves and to our neighbor, as the Great Commandment teaches.

FAITH WORD

Chesed

Chesed is the Hebrew word for 'commitment'. The sacred authors of the Old Testament often described God's steadfast loyalty and love by using the word *chesed*. *Chesed* is committed love. *Chesed* is a key attribute of God as well as a quality that describes the relationship between God and the human family. *Chesed* is often translated as 'covenant love', a term that describes the nature and depth of the relationship that binds God with people and, in turn, people with God.

COVENANT *CHESED*

Chesed is also at the heart of the Covenant that God and his people freely enter into, which is why some biblical scholars choose to translate *chesed* as 'covenant love'. In biblical times, people did not enter a covenant lightly and with protective preconditions. A covenant was not an 'If Agreement'. The parties did not say, 'I will stick with you *if* you stick with me; I will do this *if* you do that.' Parties did not simply enter a covenant; they 'cut' a covenant. This is how the sacred writer describes the 'cutting' of the covenant between God and Abraham:

> [God] said to [Abraham]: 'Bring me a heifer three years old, a female goat three years old, a ram three years old, a turtle dove, and a young pigeon.' [Abraham] brought [God] all these and cut them in two, laying each half over against the other. . . When the sun had gone down and it was dark, a smoking fire-pot and a flaming torch passed between these pieces.
> —Genesis 15:8–10, 17

In their commentary on these verses, biblical scholars describe a ceremony in which the parties then walked between the sacrificed animals, declaring, 'Let the same happen to me if I break this covenant.' A covenant was an irrevocable 'commitment', for better or worse; it was a commitment for which those involved were willing freely to give their life, their blood, to enter and to keep.

REFLECT AND DISCUSS
- Does the commitment described by the sacred authors reflect the nature of commitments we make today? Explain.
- Do young people today enter their commitments seriously? Flippantly? Explain.

THE GOD OF THE COVENANT

In the Book of Exodus God names himself YHWH, 'I AM who I AM'. (See Exodus 3:13–15.) God's Word is who he is. God always keeps his Word. Because God had given his Word, Abraham, Moses, David and their descendants were people of hope. They were filled with the desire and the expectation that God's promises to them would come true.

Christians, too, are a people of hope. The Christian story, the heart of the human story, is a story of hope. God has given us his Word in Jesus. Jesus Christ, the Word of God made flesh and the New and Everlasting Covenant, declared, 'This is my blood of the covenant, which is poured out for many for the forgiveness of sins' (Matthew 26:28). We live in the hope that the Reign, or Kingdom, of God will come about as Jesus announced, inaugurated and continues to work to bring to fulfillment at the end of time. Our faith in Christ gives us the vision to keep on hoping, even when the odds against doing so are enormous.

WHAT ABOUT YOU PERSONALLY?
- Think of something in your life or in our world that seems 'hopeless'.
- What might keep you hoping against hope?
- How might your faith sustain your 'hope against hope'?

'CUTTING' THE COVENANT | 18TH-CENTURY ENGRAVING

HEAR THE STORY

Sin and steadfast love

OPENING ACTIVITY/DISCUSSION
- Our lives are filled with songs. Think of songs you know that speak words of hope—or of hopelessness. Share your examples with the class.
- What are the most common causes of hopelessness reflected in these songs?
- How might Christian faith offer hope in these situations?

GOD'S 'STEADFAST LOVE'
The symbolic and pre-historical stories of Genesis 3–11 (Adam and Eve, Cain and Abel, Noah and the Great Flood, and the Tower of Babel) set the stage for God's Covenant history with humankind. These foundational stories describe a relentless escalation of brokenness and sin within the world. They describe the consequences of the efforts of humans to struggle to be 'like' God without being close to God—the disruption of the balance of family, society and nature.

Chapters 5 through 11 of Genesis continue to reveal that God's Word endures in the face of evil and sin, and that sin and its destructive consequences do not always begin with dramatic choices. Reading and pondering the meaning of these stories can open our eyes to see that our sinful choices, no matter how 'small' we think those choices are, do violence to God's loving plan of goodness for creation.

OVER TO YOU
Reflect on how these seemingly simple actions might have significant consequences:
- You tell your parents you are studying, when in fact you are playing an online game with your friend.
- Your pocket money is running low. You see a five-dollar bill on your mom's bedside table. You take it.
- You spread a rumor that is untrue about someone in your class.
- Your parents are away for the weekend. You invite a gang of friends to your house for a party. You know your parents wouldn't approve.
- You join with others in excluding another student from your group.

At the same time, God's constant and consistent response is: 'I invite you into loving relationships with one another, with nature and with me.' God's *chesed* toward us, his commitment to set things right, is constant and firm, even in the worst of times.

CAIN AND ABEL: SIN AND HOPE

The story of Cain and Abel reveals that sin turns differences and disappointments into hatred and tragedy. How does God respond? God perseveres in *chesed*; God IS who God IS. Before reading this story, let's take a brief look at protagonists in it.

Eve: In Hebrew, Eve's name means 'mother of all that live'. Her son Cain is the first person ever to be *born* (instead of being created directly by God, as Adam and Eve were). Her second son is named Abel.

Cain: The name 'Cain' means 'maker' or 'producer'. Cain must have been proud to be the first farmer, the first to provide food for his family.

Abel: The name 'Abel' means 'puff of air'. Abel, the younger brother, the 'wanna-be', is always following Cain around. When Cain becomes a farmer, Abel becomes a shepherd. When Cain makes a sacrifice to God, so does Abel.

EXPLORE THE TEXT

⊙ Read Genesis 4:1–16 using the 'active reading' technique (described in the opening section of chapter 1) and discuss your markings with a partner.

In the story of Cain and Abel, even when one brother murders another, God's steadfast love and mercy is the divine response. Rather than imposing a death penalty on Cain, God puts a mark on Cain that protects him from being murdered in the future. But there are consequences. Abel is still dead; Cain can never face his family again. Cain even believes that God will turn away from him. Perhaps it is Cain who has decided to hide from God's face.

TALK IT OVER

⊙ What message of hope does the Cain and Abel story offer you as a young person today?

NOAH AND THE GREAT FLOOD

In the story of Noah and the Great Flood (Genesis 6:5—9:17), 'The LORD saw that the wickedness of [man] was great in the earth, and that every inclination of the thoughts of their hearts was only evil continually. . . . So the LORD said. . . . "I am sorry that I have made them." ' (Genesis 6:5, 7), and so he undoes all that was described in the first chapter of Genesis. Only Noah, who 'was a righteous man, blameless in his generation' (Genesis 6:9), and his family, along with enough animals to repopulate a purified world, survive.

God gives Noah and his children two guidelines to keep evil and wickedness in check. They must not murder, and they must respect the life within all living beings (Genesis 9:4–6). Then the Lord enters a Covenant with Noah, with the entire human family and all of creation, saying, 'I have set my bow in the clouds. . . . When . . . the bow is seen in the clouds, I will remember my covenant that is between me and you and every living creature' (Genesis 9:13–15).

CAIN AND ABEL | SAN JUAN DE LA PEÑA MONASTERY, HUESCA, SPAIN

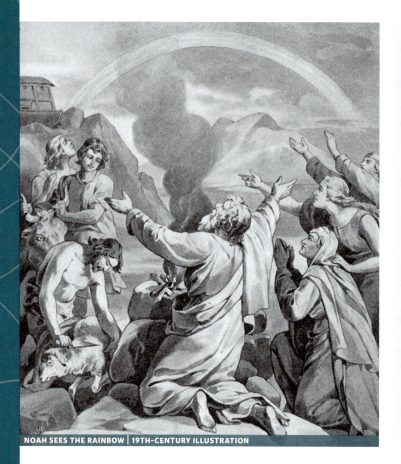

NOAH SEES THE RAINBOW | 19TH-CENTURY ILLUSTRATION

> God makes the rainbow a sign of his Covenant commitment. What else in creation might remind you of your Covenant with God?

WHAT ABOUT YOU PERSONALLY?
⊙ God makes the rainbow a sign of his Covenant commitment. What else in creation might remind you of your Covenant with God?

The Covenant with Noah is a sign of God's steadfast love and commitment to every community and person, to every race and ethnic group. God does not promise to preserve life *if* we refrain from killing. God will always preserve life; the response demanded of humans is the same—to respect life always. Our Catholic faith calls us to choose what is life-enhancing and life-preserving; in other words, to subscribe to a 'culture of life' in every aspect of our lives and society.

EXPLORE AND REFLECT
⊙ Check out these passages:
   – Genesis 4:23–24 (sin and revenge)
   – Genesis 6—8 (sin and ecological disaster)
   – Genesis 9:18–27 (sin and slavery)
   – Genesis 11:1–9 (sin and false pride in technology and the desire of a single nation to control the world)
⊙ In light of the biblical passages you have just read, where do you recognize similar sinfulness in today's world?

RUTH AND NAOMI: THE EFFECTS OF STEADFAST LOVE
The sacred authors pass on many other stories in which steadfast love, commitment and friendship prevail. One such story is that of Ruth and Naomi. The historical setting of the Book of Ruth is the period of the Judges (Ruth 1:1), which biblical scholars set to be from 1200 to 1050 BC. While biblical scholars do not agree on the date of the writing of the Book of Ruth, many do agree that the sacred author put into writing a story that had long been part of the oral tradition of the Israelites. Scholars agree that one of the main purposes of the story of Ruth and Naomi was to provide models of *chesed* for God's people.

GROUP ACTIVITY

Before we read Ruth and Naomi's story, let us take a moment to identify what true friendship looks like in your life.

- Working in small groups, brainstorm all the possible characteristics of the 'loyal friend'.
- Then agree on a definition of true friendship.
- Display the various definitions.
- Now read Ruth 1:6–22.

In the Book of Ruth we hear that Naomi and her Israelite family move to Moab in search of food, that her sons marry Moabite women, that her husband and two sons die, and that her daughter-in-law Ruth, an Israelite, refuses to leave her side. Together, Naomi and Ruth return to Israel and build a new family. At first, Naomi begs Ruth to save herself, to go back to her own parents' house. She knows that she cannot offer Ruth security or stability in ancient Israel. Recall their dialogue:

So [Naomi] said, 'See, your sister-in-law has gone back to her people and to her gods; return after your sister-in-law.'

But Ruth said,
'Do not press me to leave you
   or to turn back from following you!
Where you go, I will go;
   where you lodge, I will lodge;
your people shall be my people,
   and your God my God.
Where you die, I will die—
   there I will be buried.
May the LORD do thus and so to me,
   and more as well,
if even death parts me from you!'
—Ruth 1:15–17

TALK IT OVER

- Ruth's promise to Naomi is often read as one of the readings at Catholic weddings. Why do you think that is so?

> Where you go, I will go;
> where you lodge, I will lodge
> your people shall be my people,
> and your God my God.
>
> **RUTH 1:16**

CHAPTER 3: GOD'S COMMITMENT, OUR HOPE | HEAR THE STORY | 61

THE DESCENDANTS OF RUTH: THE CHESED LEGACY

Ruth's great-grandson, David, grew up to become a king of Israel (see Ruth 4:17, 22), with whom God also entered a Covenant. In Psalm 89 the psalmist proclaims:

I will sing of your steadfast love, O Lord, for ever; . . .

You said, 'I have made a covenant with my chosen one,
  I have sworn to my servant David:
'I will establish your descendants for ever;
  and build your throne for all generations.'
      —Psalm 89:1, 3–4

Jesus was a descendant of David, making him also a descendant of Ruth. (See Matthew 1:16; Luke 1:32; 2:4). At the same time, Ruth prefigures Mary, the mother of Jesus 'of the house of David' (see Matthew 1:16, 20; Luke 2:4; 3:31). Jesus is the ultimate model of *chesed* love. For Christians, this kind of steadfast love is the web that holds the universe together. We receive such love from God, we offer it back to God, and we share it from person to person. Such love gives hope for ever.

OVER TO YOU

- Compare your definition of true friendship to the *chesed* relationship between Ruth and Naomi.
- How do you think your idea of true friendship measures up to the model of Ruth and Naomi?

GROUP DISCUSSION

Working in small groups, recall the key truths revealed in the story of Naomi and Ruth. Then discuss:

- What does this story reveal about God's steadfast love? Explain.
- Think of situations in today's world where we find the same type of love and commitment as existed in the relationship between Naomi and Ruth.
- What is the best insight you have gained so far about keeping hope alive and about steadfast love?

How do you think your idea of true friendship measures up to the model of Ruth and Naomi?

EMBRACE THE VISION

A covenant relationship

OPENING REFLECTION

The Bible is the story of the Fall and Redemption, of man's sin and God's generosity and steadfast love, which is at the heart of the Covenant God and his People have entered. Human beings have not always kept their word and their part of the Covenant. The same is not true of God. Beginning with the *Protoevangelium* in Genesis 3:15, God has always kept his commitment to humanity to restore order, unity and harmony, the state of original holiness and original justice.

GROUP ACTIVITY

- Brainstorm examples of the disharmony you see within creation.
- Discuss ways in which young people can take part in God's work of restoring that harmony.

COVENANT WITH ABRAHAM

In the rest of the Bible, from Genesis 12 on, we read the story of the history of God, the Promise-Keeper, entering and keeping his Covenant and promises to his people.

Now the Lord said to Abram, 'Go from your country and your kindred and your father's house to the land that I will show you. I will make of you a great nation, and I will bless you, and make your name great, so that you will be a blessing. I will bless those who bless you, and the one who curses you I will curse; and in you all the families of the earth shall be blessed.'

—Genesis 12:1–3

Abram's response is described briefly in the next two verses:

So Abram went, as the Lord had told him; and Lot went with him. Abram was seventy-five years old when he departed from Haran. Abram took his wife Sarai and his brother's son Lot, and all the possessions that they had gathered, and the persons whom they acquired in Haran; and they set forth to go to the land of Canaan.

—Genesis 12:4–5

Abram, whom God would later rename Abraham, and his family were nomads who lived around 1800 BC in Haran in Mesopotamia in the ancient Middle East (modern-day Iraq). He and his family believed in many gods, as did the people of Mesopotamia. Yet Abram believed and trusted and committed himself to the One True God. This faith of Abraham in the One True God

became the foundation of the life of Abraham and his descendants, so much so that professing it daily became central to the life of the Israelites, 'Hear, O Israel, the Lord our God is one Lord'.

The next ten chapters of Genesis pass on an amazing and heartbreaking real-life faith-adventure. Abram and Sarai pack up and leave their homeland and journey to a new home. Abram rescues his relatives from danger and famine, celebrates the miraculous pregnancy of his wife and the birth of his son, and struggles with family drama; and we are told, he even dares to bargain with God, and wins. Through it all, God remains steadfastly loyal to Abram, and affirms the Covenant. Open your Bible and prayerfully read Genesis 17:1–7.

Abraham responds to God's *chesed* with his own steadfast loyalty. He dares to obey God and to give up the most precious gift he could imagine, his son Isaac. (Read about God's command to Abraham to sacrifice his son Isaac in Genesis 22:1–19.)

JOURNAL EXERCISE
- Choose an amazing or challenging moment from your own life.
- Write a conversation in which you tell God about this event and its impact on you.
- Then imagine and write down what God might say in response.

EXPLORE THE TEXT
- Here is a list of some highlights from Abraham's story. With a partner, choose one of these events. Read the passage, applying the 'active reading' technique.

EVENT	CHAPTER AND VERSES IN GENESIS
Abram and Sarai in Egypt	12:10–20
Lot's captivity and rescue	14:1–16
A son is promised to Abraham and Sarah	18:1–15
The birth of Isaac	21:1–7
Judgment pronounced on Sodom	18:16–33
God's command to sacrifice Isaac	22:1–19

THE SACRIFICE OF ISAAC | KARL REIHING

- Prepare a role-play, with one of you taking the role of Abraham and the other the role of God. 'Abraham' tells 'God' about this day in his life, explaining what happened and describing how he feels. 'God' responds.
- Afterward, discuss what this story tells you about God's relationship with Abraham.

God kept his promises to Abraham and his wife Sarah and their descendants—to their son Isaac and his wife Rebekah; to Abraham's grandson Jacob (also called 'Israel') and his wives Rachel and Leah; to their twelve sons, who became the leaders of the Twelve Tribes of Israel, and all their children for ever. Abraham said yes to God's invitation and his family grew to become the People of God, whom the Bible names the Israelites, the Hebrews and the Jews. The story of God's people in the Old Testament is a story of infidelity and fidelity, slavery and liberation, and of exile and freedom. Jesus Christ is the 'new and everlasting Covenant', the ultimate fulfillment of God's promises and Covenant to Abraham and his descendants— and to all humanity.

COVENANT WITH ISRAEL

In the Books of Exodus, Leviticus, Numbers and Deuteronomy, of the Torah, the sacred authors pass on the faith story of God re-establishing his relationship with the descendants of Abraham and entering the Covenant with the Israelites. The story is dramatic. The God of Abraham gives his Word to Moses, who had fled from Egypt to Midian. Well aware of the sins of the Hebrews who were enslaved in Egypt, God reaffirms his steadfast love to them, and promises to save the Israelites from slavery in Egypt and lead them in freedom to a new land, saying:

REBEKAH | JOHANNES TAKANEN

I have observed the misery of my people who are in Egypt; I have heard their cry on account of their taskmasters. Indeed, I know their sufferings, and I have come down to deliver them from the Egyptians.

—Exodus 3:7–8

The Lord God then protects them from Pharaoh and the 'angel of death', and saves the fleeing Hebrews from the Egyptian army by parting the waters of the Red Sea. In response to their complaining against him and Moses during their exodus in the desert, the Lord God feeds the wandering Israelites. And when they reach Mount Sinai, the Lord God calls Moses to come up the mountain for a face-to-face conversation, during which the Lord reasserts his fidelity to the Israelites, the descendants of Abraham, and invites them to enter the Covenant with him:

Moses went up to God; the LORD called to him from the mountain, saying, 'Thus, you shall say

MOSES WITH THE TEN COMMANDMENTS | BRUGES, BELGIUM

The Decalogue, the law written on the heart of every person, is the law of the Covenant, which Jesus came not to abolish but to fulfill

Decalogue, which 'express man's fundamental duties towards God and towards his neighbor' (*Catechism of the Catholic Church* [CCC], no. 2072). The Decalogue, the law written on the heart of every person, is the law of the Covenant, which Jesus came not to abolish but to fulfill.

GROUP WORK

- In small groups, discuss which of the Ten Commandments have the most influence in your life, and in what way.

THE PROPHETS

Living a Torah lifestyle, the visible sign of one's commitment to God's Covenant, was not and is not easy. The ancient Israelites turned power and wealth, comfort and popularity into false gods. Through it all, God responded with *chesed*. Judges, kings, prophets and others were inspired to admonish and remind God's people that they were unfaithful and needed to return to their Covenant commitment.

The Bible celebrates these prophets and many other leaders, who were both faithful and, sometimes, not very faithful to God. Miriam, Hannah, Esther, and other women; political leaders such as David and Solomon; military leaders (the Bible calls them 'judges') such as Deborah and Samson—all these and more helped the people of Israel to survive and to remember the Covenant

to the house of Jacob, and tell the Israelites: You have seen what I did to the Egyptians, and how I bore you on eagles' wings and brought you to myself. Now, therefore, if you obey my voice and keep my covenant, you shall be my treasured possession out of all the peoples. Indeed, the whole earth is mine, but you shall be for me a priestly kingdom and a holy nation. These are the words that you shall speak to the Israelites.'

So Moses came, summoned the elders of the people, and set before them all these words that the LORD had commanded him. The people all answered as one: 'Everything that the LORD has spoken we will do.'

—Exodus 19:3–8

Moses then returns up the mountain and receives the Ten Commandments, or the

66 | CREDO | THE PROMISED ONE: SERVANT AND SAVIOR

commitment. Yet, even some of these had serious shortcomings. For example, Moses tested God and was not permitted to enter the Promised Land; Samson was a seriously bad judge of character; King David committed murder and adultery. The struggle between sin and virtue in God's people is the same struggle that every human must face.

In the eighth century BC God chose and sent the prophet Hosea (c. 750 BC) to the Israelites. Hosea, who himself suffered from a marriage in which his spouse was unfaithful to him, describes the Covenant binding God and his people as a marriage—a committed partnership between the people of Israel and God. After addressing the people of Israel's numerous acts of infidelity, Hosea, speaking in God's name, concludes:

> I will heal their disloyalty;
> I will love them freely,
> for my anger has turned from them.
> —Hosea 14:4

Nothing can or will ever shatter God's loyalty to the Covenant. God had promised that the people of Israel and the throne of David, its greatest king, would last for ever: 'Your house and your kingdom shall be made sure for ever before me; your throne shall be established for ever' (2 Samuel 7:16). God always keeps his Word. God's love for us is for ever. This we know and have seen revealed above all in Jesus Christ.

OVER TO YOU

- Who would you recognize as a modern-day prophet, and why?
- Imagine something prophetic that you could do within the next twenty-four hours. Remember, being prophetic does not involve foretelling the future but helping people to be faithful to their Covenant with God.

THINK IT THROUGH

Promise and fulfillment

OPENING REFLECTION

Nelson Mandela (b. 1918), the great leader of South Africa's struggle against apartheid and for freedom, spent twenty-seven years in prison on Robben Island, many of those years in solitary confinement. While in solitary confinement, and when things might have seemed hopeless, he wrote:

> I have cherished the ideal of a democratic and free society in which all persons live together in harmony and with equal opportunities. It is an ideal which I hope to live for and to achieve. But if needs be it is an ideal for which I am prepared to die.

ROBBEN ISLAND PRISON BUILDING, SOUTH AFRICA

OVER TO YOU

- What might you learn from Nelson Mandela about hope?
- What are some hopes that you are prepared to 'live for'?
- Might there be hopes that you would 'die for'? Explain.
- Can you think of anyone else, from history or the present day, who displays the same hope and courage as Nelson Mandela?

THE PROMISE OF A WORLD RENEWED, A NEW CREATION

'Through the prophets, God forms his people in the hope of salvation, in the expectation of a new and everlasting Covenant intended for all, to be written on their hearts' (CCC, no. 64). Through the prophet Jeremiah, the Lord promised a 'new covenant' that

. . . will not be like the covenant that I made with their ancestors when I . . . [brought] them out of the land of Egypt—a covenant that they broke. . . . But this is the covenant that I will make with the house of Israel. . . : I will put my law within them, and I will write it on their hearts; and I will be their God, and they shall be my people.

—Jeremiah 31:32–33

This 'new covenant' came about in Jesus Christ through the saving Mystery of his life, Death, Resurrection and Ascension. Each of the Covenants God and the people of ancient Israel entered foreshadowed Christ and his Paschal Mystery. Jesus is the promised Savior, the One announced by the prophets. Jesus is the 'new and everlasting covenant' between God and humanity. While the Covenants of old were often sealed in the blood of animals, Jesus' own blood is the blood of the new and everlasting Covenant. (See Matthew 26:28.) The Catholic Church proclaims this Revelation at the celebration of the Eucharist, during the words of the Institution Narrative.

THINK, PAIR AND SHARE

- At Mass during the Consecration we hear the words, 'Do this in memory of me'. What do these words say to you? Are they simply speaking about what is happening right there at Mass? What else might they be saying about the past and about the future? Share your thoughts with a partner.

TYPOLOGY IN THE OLD TESTAMENT

The Old Testament records the history and the hopes of the ancient Israelites and points in a prophetic and 'hidden' way to the coming of Jesus and to his Paschal Mystery. In literature, 'foreshadowing' means dropping hints or clues about what will happen later in a story. To read the Bible 'typologically' means recognizing a kind of 'foreshadowing' in the Bible. (See Romans 5:14.) Let us look at the Suffering Servant in the writings of the prophet Isaiah to explore what 'foreshadowing' means to interpreting Scripture.

THE SUFFERING SERVANT

First, let us review the historical setting of the 'Suffering Servant Songs' in the writings attributed to the prophet Isaiah. In 587 BC the Babylonian armies evicted the people of Jerusalem from their homes and took them into exile. The people of Israel's Northern Kingdom of Judah had already been sent into a similar exile in 721 BC. During the Exile in Babylonia (587–539 BC), the Israelites were a small minority living in a foreign country, whose inhabitants worshiped many gods. During this Exile the Israelites struggled with tenacity to preserve their religion. Living among their captors and oppressors, the exiled Israelites were mocked for depending on the love and loyalty of a God who apparently could not save them from the power of the gods of Babylon.

How were they to hope against hope to be saved and to return to their beloved land? God chose the prophet Isaiah (a name that means 'God is salvation') to deliver a message and vision of hope to the Israelites. Central to that message are the four 'Suffering Servant Songs' in the Book of the Prophet Isaiah. (See Isaiah 42:1–7; 49:1–7; 50:4–9 and 52:13—53:12.) The sacred author of these 'Servant Songs' proposed that the Exile was a form of purification for a people who had not been faithful to their Covenant commitment. This purification would end, and they would be freed by the Servant of YHWH, who would suffer because of his fidelity to YHWH. Through these inspired Servant Songs, which Isaiah preached sometime around 550 BC, God speaks to his people:

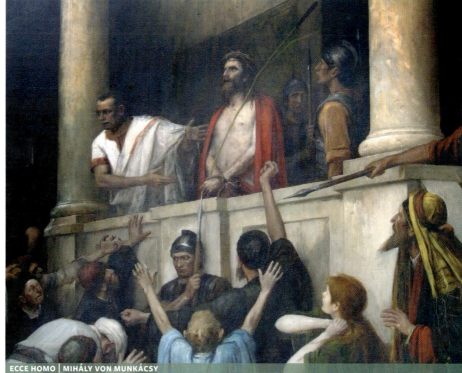

ECCE HOMO | MIHÁLY VON MUNKÁCSY

See, my servant shall prosper [says God];
 he shall be exalted and lifted up,
 and shall be very high.

I will give [him] as a light to the nations,
 that my salvation may reach to the end of the earth.

He was despised and rejected by others;
 a man of suffering and acquainted with infirmity; . . .
 —so marred was his appearance, beyond human semblance.

He was wounded for our transgressions,
 crushed for our iniquities; . . .
 and by his bruises we are healed.

He was oppressed, and he was afflicted,
 yet he did not open his mouth,
like a lamb that is led to the slaughter.

They made his grave with the wicked
 and his tomb with the rich . . .
yet he bore the sin of many.
 —Isaiah 52:13; 49:6; 53:3; 52:14; 53:5, 7, 9, 12

Through the steadfast love and obedience of this true and faithful servant, God's *chesed* would be revealed to everyone, and sinfulness would be washed away.

JOURNAL EXERCISE
- Imagine you are among the Israelites living in Exile. You hear the preaching of Isaiah. What do you hear? What is your response? Write your thoughts.
- Now return to the present. What kind of exile might young Christians live in today? Where do you find a message of hope? Write your thoughts.

WHO IS THE SUFFERING SERVANT?
First, the Suffering Servant represents the entire people of Israel; they may be mocked and temporarily defeated, but God will save them. Second, the Suffering Servant represents the 'remnant' of true believers: those exiled Jews who have maintained their commitment to God in very difficult circumstances. Third, the Suffering Servant prefigures Jesus Christ. Jesus is the ultimate revelation of the *chesed* of God.

Jesus is the Suffering Servant. He is the Savior and Redeemer, first promised in Genesis 3:15, freeing humanity from Exile in a land of suffering and death, and who brings salvation to the ends of the earth. Jesus is the Lamb of God who takes away the sin of the world (John 1:29). He is lifted high on the Cross (John 12:32–33), tortured (John 19:1–2) and brutally put to death (John 19:16–18). In becoming man, the Son of God embraced our brokenness and suffering. He suffered the consequences of being faithful to the Father and

What kind of exile might young Christians live in today?

to the mission he was sent to do. He paid the ultimate price of the sacrifice of the Cross for our sins and to reconcile and make us one again with God.

Living in a broken world, Jesus predicted his suffering (see Matthew 16:21–23; John 12:27–36) and the suffering that anyone who follows God's plan will face. (See Matthew 16:24–26.) The agony of facing that suffering was so intense that Jesus himself prayed that he might avoid being crucified. But his *chesed* was far stronger than the suffering he would face. (Read Luke 22:42.)

CROSSING OF THE RED SEA | HANS JORDAENS III

JOURNAL EXERCISE
- Reflect on how your relationship with God helps you when the right choice is also a painful one.
- Write your reflections in your journal.

EMBRACING THE OLD TESTAMENT
God is the author of all Scripture. From her beginning the Church has treasured the Old Testament as a source of Revelation, Salvation history, wisdom and prayers. 'The New Testament lies hidden in the Old [Testament] and the Old Testament is unveiled in the New' (CCC, no. 129). This is why the Church teaches that Christians need the Old Testament and the New Testament to hear the fullness of God's 'saving truth' and to guide and sustain our faith and our hope and our love.

There is an inherent unity blending the Testaments, and that unity is Jesus Christ. 'All Sacred Scripture is but one book, and this one book is Christ' (CCC, no. 134). The God who created the universe in original holiness and original justice is the same God who promised to conquer the sin and death caused by the Fall; the same God who called and entered a Covenant with Abraham and his descendants; the same God who freed the Israelites from slavery in Egypt and entered the Covenant with Moses and the Israelites at Mount Sinai; the same God who forgave his people and delivered them from Exile; the same God who revealed himself in Jesus, the Lord and the Savior, the Messiah and the Suffering Servant; the same God who delivered the human family from the power of sin and death; the same God who raised Jesus from death and gave us the hope and promise of eternal life.

At the time of Jesus, many Jews lived in hope for a different kind of savior and messiah. Some were hoping primarily for a 'political' messiah—one who would release them from the power of the Romans to live once again as a free people. This desire and expectation is reflected in the words of the two disciples on the Road to Emmaus, who tell the Stranger (the Risen Christ) of their disappointment in Jesus because they 'had hoped that he was the one to redeem Israel' (Luke 24:21). Even as Jesus explained to them that the Messiah was the 'suffering servant', they still did not recognize him. It was only when he went on with them, ate with them and broke bread with them, that their eyes were opened to see that the Scriptures were indeed fulfilled in their Lord, who suffered and died and rose from the dead.

OVER TO YOU
- Think of a time when you felt that God gave you what you really needed. Write a brief prayer of thanks to God.

JUDGE AND ACT

REVIEW WHAT YOU HAVE LEARNED
- Look back over this chapter and recognize the best lessons you have learned—about hope, faithful love, God's promises and the mission of Jesus.
- Then think about how you can put these insights and wisdom 'to work' in your life now.

THROUGH SUFFERING TO JUSTICE
The life, Death, Resurrection and Ascension of Jesus Christ is the path to eternal life and happiness. 'Christ's death is both the *Paschal sacrifice* that accomplishes the definitive redemption of men . . . and the *sacrifice of the New Covenant,* which restores men to communion with God. . . .' (CCC. no. 613). Jesus clearly revealed that doing God's will, living as faithful disciples of the Suffering Servant, is not always easy; but, by God's grace, it is possible to live the Covenant we have freely entered into with God.

Christians, as Jesus the Suffering Servant did, take on suffering, our own and that of others, face to face, to live and love as Jesus commanded us.

Jesus, the Suffering Servant Messiah, commanded his disciples to work to bring about the new creation, the Kingdom of God, that he inaugurated. We are to minister with those who are suffering and working against the forces that cause suffering. (Recall Matthew 25:35–36.) We are to live the Works of Mercy, no matter the cost.

Christians know now that living as people of the 'new and everlasting Covenant' requires us to do the works of compassion—to live the Works of Mercy. We are to join with Christ, the loyal Suffering Servant, to prepare the way for the coming of the Kingdom of God, when the desires and expectations of the human heart will finally be realized.

LEARN BY EXAMPLE

The story of St. Damien of Molokai

Jef de Veuster was born in Flanders, Belgium in 1840. His parents sent him to study business, but he decided to become a priest. He changed his name to 'Damien', in honor of an ancient saint who refused to accept payment for healing the sick. Damien soon impressed Church officials with his commitment, and they sent him to serve the poor in Hawaii, where he volunteered to be the pastor of a colony of lepers at Kalawao, on the island of Molokai.

Damien arrived at Kalawao in 1873. With his own hands he built and painted houses, constructed furniture and made coffins for the dead. He organized a farm and succeeded in getting the Government to provide him with food, medicine and supplies; he also convinced leaders from other religions to send him money, doctors and nurses.

Damien's work with the lepers did not come easy. He was notoriously hot tempered and sometimes rude. The smell of leprosy and infection often made him sick. But his love was stronger than his personal discomfort. He said, 'Every day I work with these people, touch them, clean their wounds, breathe the air they breathe. Every day I dig their graves and bury their dead.' After twelve years at Kalawao, Damien contracted leprosy, and he died five years later.

Like Abraham, Damien left his country, his family and his father's house; like Ruth, he lived, died and was buried with the people he loved. Today, Damien is honored as a patron of people with leprosy, or Hansen's disease, and HIV/AIDS. His life continues to inspire those who are looked down upon to stand up and be treated like human beings. Many Christian churches recognize him as a person of true *chesed*. On October 11, 2009, Pope Benedict XVI canonized Damien. This means that we can ask him to pray for us and, more important, he is someone we can try to imitate in our own lives.

OVER TO YOU
- What do you recognize as some social or cultural forms of 'leprosy' today?
- How does St. Damien inspire you to respond to them?

TALK IT OVER
There are always moments in history when it might seem as if hope is lost. For example, in Germany under National Socialism—Nazism—it looked as if this cruel and destructive ideology could not be defeated. Likewise, Pol Pot, the Cambodian dictator who was responsible for killing millions of his own people, appeared to be invincible. But the Hitlers and Pol Pots are always brought down, even if they first cause terrible suffering. Evil cannot ultimately triumph—this is our hope because of our faith in God.
- How might your faith in God help to keep your hope alive, even in the face of evil?

JOURNAL EXERCISE
- From your faith perspective, define how you now understand both 'hope' and '*chesed*'.
- Has working through this chapter changed your thinking about God? About what it

CHAPTER 3: GOD'S COMMITMENT, OUR HOPE | JUDGE AND ACT | 73

means to live as a child of God? Explain.
- How can you be a person of hope, a light in the world?

RESPOND WITH FAMILY AND FRIENDS
- Try to make an opportunity to share some thoughts and insights from this chapter with your family or friends. As a conversation starter, you might read this opening verse of a classic poem on hope by the great American poet Emily Dickinson (1830–86), or you might prefer to choose a more contemporary poem or song that speaks of steadfast love and hope and commitment.

> Hope is the thing with feathers
> That perches in the soul,
> And sings the tune without the words,
> And never stops at all.

WHAT WILL YOU DO NOW?
- Think about practical things you will do to be a witness of hope by living according to the criteria set out in Matthew 25:35–36. Be sure to ask God for the help you need—hope, courage, generosity, loving kindness, covenant love, or whatever—to fulfill your decision.

LEARN BY HEART

When . . . the bow is seen in the clouds, I will remember my covenant that is between me and you and every living creature.

GENESIS 9:14—15

74 | CREDO | THE PROMISED ONE: SERVANT AND SAVIOR

PRAYER REFLECTION

LEADER
Sit quietly and remember that you are—as always—in the presence of God. (*Pause*)
In the name of the Father, and of the Son, and of the Holy Spirit.

ALL
Amen.

LEADER
We remember we are in the presence of our God, whose love for us is always steadfast.
Loving Creator,
you are a maker and keeper of promises,
you are a God of loving kindness,
a God of faithful covenant love.
Teach us to love what you love,
and to want what you want,
for ourselves, for one another and for the world.
We ask this in Jesus' name.

ALL
Amen.

READER
Read 1 Peter 3:13–18 from a Bible.

Pause for a moment of silent prayer.

LEADER
In you, O Lord, is our hope.

ALL
We shall never hope in vain.

LEADER
We shall dance and rejoice in your steadfast love.

ALL
We shall never hope in vain.

LEADER
Let us pray.
The Lord promises us:
I will give you a new heart, a new spirit within you,
for I will be your strength.

ALL
Deep within, I will plant my law:
Not on stone, but in your hearts.
Follow me, I will bring you back.
You will be my own
and I will be your God.

LEADER
See my face, and see your God, for I will be your hope.

All repeat refrain.

LEADER
Return to me, with all your heart, and I will bring you back.

All repeat refrain. Pause for a moment of silent prayer.

LEADER
May God bless us and all people, protect us from all evil, and bring us to everlasting life.

ALL
Amen.

CHAPTER 4

The Word Became Flesh

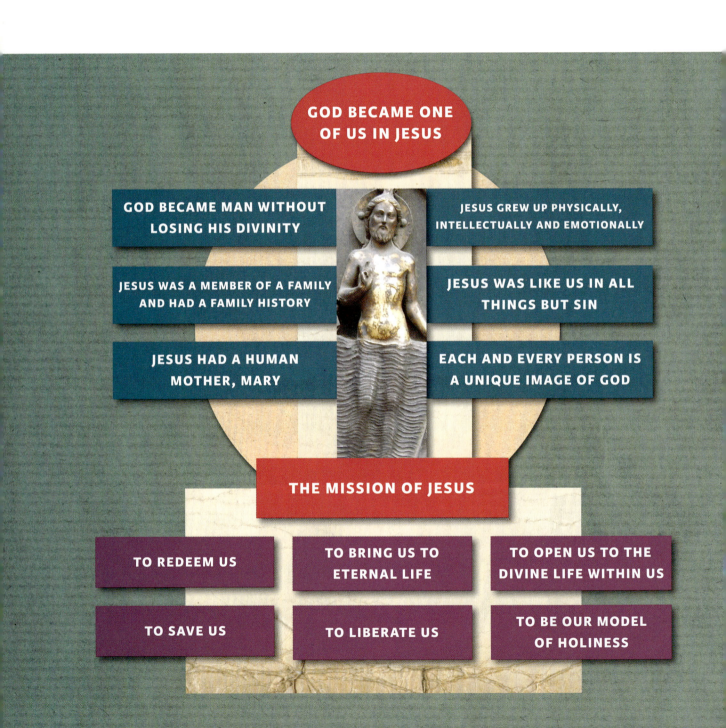

THIS CHAPTER FURTHER EXPLORES MANY OF THE implications of the Incarnation and looks at the life of Jesus. Jesus, like every young person reading this book, was a member of a family and had a family history; he lived in a neighborhood and country and shared in that culture and history. He faithfully practiced Judaism; he worshiped regularly and followed the Law of Moses. Jesus, the incarnate Son of God, had a unique mission from God; he was the Savior of the world, sent to heal what sin had broken and to show human beings how to live as faithful children of God.

MARY'S 'YES' TO GOD

MARY, MOTHER OF JESUS, MOTHER OF GOD

MODEL BELIEVER AND FAITHFUL SERVANT OF GOD

MODEL OF STEADFAST DEVOTION

MARY HAD A UNIQUE ROLE IN GOD'S PLAN OF SALVATION

LEARNING OUTCOMES

As a result of studying this chapter and exploring the issues raised, you should be able to:

- increase your understanding of the Incarnation;
- explore the faith and courage behind Mary's 'Yes' to God;
- discover that we express our faith when we pray the Hail Mary and the *Magnificat*;
- grow in your awareness and understanding of Joseph, the husband of Mary, as a person of great faith and courage;
- understand how the Incarnation was foreshadowed in the Old Testament and fulfilled in Jesus;
- recognize the significance of the fact that God chose people whom society considered powerless and weak to bring his promise of Salvation to fulfillment;
- understand the phrase 'expiate our sins';
- understand St. Anselm's theology on the Incarnation;
- become familiar with the 'Jesus Prayer';
- articulate the significance of the titles Christ, Messiah, Lord and Son of God;
- recognize opportunities where Christians can take a stand for their faith.

FAITH-FORMATION OUTCOMES

As a result of studying this chapter and exploring the issues raised, you should also:

- appreciate and value your own uniqueness;
- think about what God becoming man means for your life and your faith;
- identify Annunciation-type experiences in your life;
- recognize these experiences as opportunities to say 'Yes' to God's invitation to put your faith into action;
- see Joseph as a role model for you;
- link the teachings of the Catholic Church on the meaning of the Incarnation with your own understanding of this mystery of faith;
- be inspired by the example of Saints Perpetua and Felicity.

FAITH WORDS: Perpetual Virginity of Mary; Expiation; Atonement

LEARN BY HEART: Jesus Prayer

LEARN BY EXAMPLE: Saints Perpetua and Felicity

ATTEND AND REFLECT

How was Jesus like us?

DID YOU KNOW?

No two people in the world have:
- exactly the same DNA—except genetically identical twins.
- the same fingerprints—even identical twins!
- the same pattern in the iris of their eye.

GOD BECAME ONE OF US IN JESUS

Every human being is a *unique person*: each and every person, in our own unique way, is a unique image of God. Each one of us has a unique body, a unique way of speaking and acting, a unique outlook on life, a unique sense of humor, a unique vocation to fulfill in life . . . and the list goes on.

God has revealed that God the Son, Almighty God—YES, the Loving Creator and Sustainer of all the universe and its countless galaxies and planets—became one of us. This Mystery of Faith, the **Incarnation**, is the most unique event in human history and summarizes the very heart of Christian faith—God became man in Jesus without giving up his divinity.

Almighty God became a carpenter, learned and spoke a language, had a family history and practiced the customs of his religion and culture. He was like us, like you, in all things but sin.

Jesus of Nazareth, born a Jew of a daughter of Israel at Bethlehem at the time of King Herod the

Great and the emperor Caesar Augustus [about 4 BC], a carpenter by trade, who died crucified in Jerusalem under the procurator Pontius Pilate during the reign of the emperor Tiberius [about AD 30], is the eternal Son of God made man.
—*Catechism of the Catholic Church (CCC)*, no. 423

To someone brought up as a Christian, this claim may sound perfectly normal; to a non-believer it might sound foolish. Read what St. Paul says of 'Christ the power of God and the wisdom of God' (1 Corinthians 1:23–24). He admits that the idea of God becoming man in Jesus—who was later crucified for us—can seem foolish. Yet this is God's own Revelation to us and is the very foundation of Christian faith.

OVER TO YOU
- Pause for a moment. Think about the amazing faith claims being made: though fully divine, Jesus was also fully man in all ways except sin. Jesus, the one divine Person in whom the divine nature and a human nature were united, was born, grew up, lived and died in a particular time and place.
- Try to imagine yourself hearing these faith claims of Christians for the first time. What might be your reflections and responses?

THINK, PAIR AND SHARE
In 2004, CNN aired a special documentary called *The Mystery of Jesus,* which featured this painting based on the work of a forensic artist. The artist recreated the face of a typical working man from first-century Palestine: weathered, dark-skinned, Middle Eastern; in other words, the kind of face that a man in the time of Jesus might have had. Discuss with a partner:
- How does this image compare to the images of Jesus with which you are familiar?
- Which is more appealing, and why?
- What is your own image of Jesus?

Though fully divine, Jesus was also fully man in all ways except sin. Jesus was one divine Person in whom the divine nature and a human nature were united

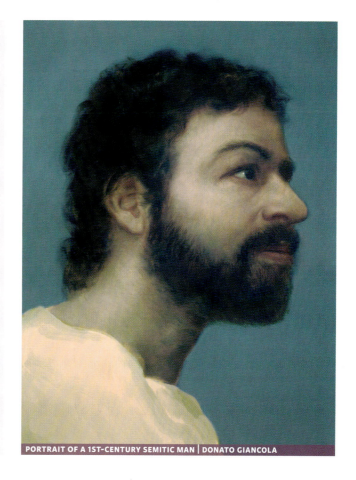

PORTRAIT OF A 1ST-CENTURY SEMITIC MAN | DONATO GIANCOLA

CORONATION OF THE VIRGIN | COREGGIO

The Son of God came down from heaven and by the Holy Spirit was incarnate of the Virgin Mary

THE WORD BECAME FLESH

The English word 'incarnation' comes from the Latin '*in + carne*', literally meaning 'into the flesh'. John's Gospel expresses the faith of the Church in the Incarnation this way:

In the beginning was the Word, and the Word was with God, and the Word was God. . . . And the Word became flesh and lived among us, and we have seen his glory . . . full of grace and truth.
—John 1:1, 14

'The Word became flesh.' The Son of God 'came down from **heaven**, and by the Holy Spirit was incarnate of the Virgin Mary, and became man' (Nicene Creed). 'Without losing his divine nature he has assumed human nature' (CCC, no. 479). As we learned in *Son of God and Son of Mary*, the second book in the *Credo* series, the Church names the mystery of the union of the divine nature and a human nature in the one divine Person, Jesus, the '**hypostatic union**'. Jesus had a human body and a human soul, a human intellect and a human will. The God-Person Jesus, in whom divine nature and human nature were united, grew up physically, intellectually and emotionally. As Luke's Gospel reveals, 'The child grew and became strong, filled with wisdom; and the favor of God was upon him' (Luke 2:40).

TALK IT OVER

- Over the centuries, Christians have developed many analogies and theologies to talk about the meaning and purpose of the Mystery of the Incarnation. For example, John the Evangelist wrote, 'For God so loved the world that he gave his only Son, so that everyone who believes in him may not perish but may have eternal life' (John 3:16).
- What do you think it means for our lives today that God became man?

80 | CREDO | THE PROMISED ONE: SERVANT AND SAVIOR

HEAR THE STORY

Mary's 'Yes'

OPENING CONVERSATION

- Have you ever had such an amazing experience or heard such an amazing story that you wondered whether you were dreaming? Share your stories of such experiences.

MARY'S 'YES'

The Incarnation came about 'at the time appointed by God', at the time God chose to complete in Mary all the preparations for Christ's coming among the People of God first made in Genesis 3:15. By the actions of the Holy Spirit in her, the Father gives the world Emmanuel, 'God-with-us'. (See CCC, no. 744.) The New Testament account of the Incarnation begins with the event that we know as the Annunciation, which is recorded in Luke 1:26–38. Luke begins, 'The angel Gabriel was sent by God to a town in Galilee called Nazareth, to a virgin engaged to a man whose name was Joseph, of the house of David. The virgin's name was Mary' (Luke 1:26–27). We can imagine how utterly amazed Mary must have been when the angel greeted her:

THE ANNUNCIATION | SIMONE MARTINI

Greetings, favored one! The Lord is with you.... You will conceive in your womb and bear a son, and you will name him Jesus.... And the Lord God will give to him the throne of his ancestor David.
—Luke 1:28, 31–32

This peasant girl, around fourteen years old, was, like so many of her contemporaries, filled with hope as she waited for the Messiah whom the Lord God had promised to send to her and her people. Like many of her Jewish peers, Mary was already betrothed; that is, engaged to be married. Scripture tells us that Mary was truly confused by the angel's words. Why would the king and messiah promised by God come through me? How can this be? To quiet her confusion and strengthen her faith, the angel responded, giving her both an explanation and a sign:

The Holy Spirit will come upon you, and the power of the Most High will overshadow you; therefore the child to be born will be holy; he

will be called Son of God. And now, your relative Elizabeth in her old age has also conceived a son. . . . For nothing will be impossible with God.
—Luke 1:35–37

OVER TO YOU
- Have you ever been confused by an unexpected announcement? What was your response?
- What does Mary's confusion say about her faith? Her trust in God?

MADONNA AND CHILD | BALLYMOTE, SLIGO, IRELAND

THE BLESSED VIRGIN MARY

The virgin birth has been and continues to be a source of confusion for many believers and non-believers. This mystery of faith that Revelation so clearly teaches, while it cannot be explained by medical science, is a truth of faith that we profess with Mary herself. Mary's virginity celebrates a paradox: Jesus' mother was a virgin all her life—before the conception of Jesus, during the conception and birth of Jesus, and after the birth of Jesus. The Church names this mystery of faith the '**perpetual virginity of Mary**'.

Some say that references in the Bible to Jesus' 'brothers and sisters' contradict the faith of the Church in Mary's perpetual virginity. The Church responds to this objection by stating that we need to interpret the use of the phrase 'brothers and sisters' in the context of how that term was used in the time in which the sacred authors wrote. Then, 'brothers and sisters' had a broader meaning than 'siblings', and was used to refer to cousins or other close relatives. (See CCC, no. 500.) So its use by the sacred authors does not contradict Mary's perpetual virginity.

Mary's virginity holds deeper meaning for those who believe; it points to the reality that Salvation is a complete gift from God and to the completeness of Mary's steadfast devotion to God. It underlines how Salvation comes as a miracle of God's love for us. The unique grace of Mary's perpetual virginity also suggests how the Holy Spirit 'gives birth' to the life of faith and devotion. Mary is the new Eve. Jesus' virginal conception points to him as the 'New Adam', since his humanity was formed directly by God. Mary is indeed the highly favored one of God; she is full of grace.

> **The unique grace of Mary's perpetual virginity suggests how the Holy Spirit 'gives birth' to the life of faith and devotion**

FAITH WORD

Perpetual Virginity of Mary

The perpetual virginity of Mary states the faith of the Church that 'Mary was a virgin in conceiving Jesus, in giving birth to him, and in remaining always a virgin ever after'.
—*United States Catholic Catechism for Adults* (USCCA), 523

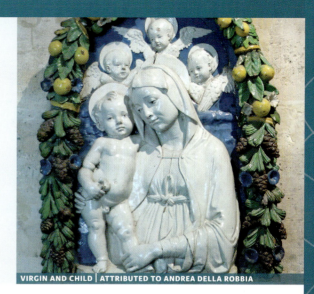

VIRGIN AND CHILD | ATTRIBUTED TO ANDREA DELLA ROBBIA

Mary, who responded to God in the simple faith-filled words 'Here am I, the servant of the Lord; let it be with me according to your word' (Luke 1:38), is the model believer and faithful servant of God prefigured by Sarah, Ruth and Hannah, the mother of the prophet Samuel (see 1 Samuel 1:1—2:11), and the other women of faith of ancient Israel. Mary said 'Yes' to God. God had kept his Word to his people; and Mary responded by giving her word in return. She embraced a message so amazing, with a love so complete, that it all must have seemed to her almost 'unbelievable'. But the testing of her love had just begun.

THINK, PAIR AND SHARE

Imagine Mary and Joseph, to whom an angel also appeared (read Matthew 1:18–25), trying to explain to their family and neighbors that Mary had conceived a baby purely by the power of the Holy Spirit. Perhaps, not everyone received Mary's good news the way Elizabeth did.
- With a partner, read Luke 1:26–38 again. Then discuss:
  – What might have gone through Mary's head and heart at the Annunciation?
  – Why do you think Mary accepted God's invitation to her to become the mother of Jesus?

WHAT ABOUT OUR OWN ANNUNCIATIONS?

We can be going about our business, and suddenly be invited to make a commitment: to go out on a limb and stand up for what is right; to strike out on an amazing and heartbreaking adventure. Each invitation is unique. The British-born American poet Denise Levertov (1923–97) describes such annunciations:

> Aren't there annunciations
> of one sort or another
> in most lives?
>   Some unwillingly
> undertake great destinies,
> enact them in sullen pride,
> uncomprehending.
>   More often
> those moments
>   when roads of light and storm
>   open from darkness in a man or woman,
> are turned away from
> in dread, in a wave of weakness, in despair
> and with relief.
> Ordinary lives continue.
>   God does not smite them.
> But the gates close, the pathway vanishes.

REFLECT AND SHARE
- Think of the most challenging invitation to which you have ever responded 'Yes'.

- What amazing and life-giving act of faith might God be inviting you to say yes to right now?
- How does the example of Mary's yes inspire your own yes?

MARY—MODEL OF STEADFAST DEVOTION

Shortly after her experience of the Annunciation, Mary set out 'with haste' to visit Elizabeth in response to the 'sign' the angel gave her. 'And now, your relative Elizabeth in her old age has also conceived a son.... For nothing will be impossible with God' (Luke 1:36–37). The journey from Mary's home in Nazareth in Galilee to Elizabeth's home in the hill country of Judea (see Luke 1:39) was a four-day journey over very difficult terrain. As Mary approached Elizabeth, Elizabeth's unborn son, John the Baptist, sensed the presence of Jesus, and stirred in Elizabeth's womb. Luke writes:

THE VISITATION | 16TH-CENTURY GERMAN ALTARPIECE

> Elizabeth was filled with the Holy Spirit and exclaimed with a loud cry, 'Blessed are you among women, and blessed is the fruit of your womb.... For as soon as I heard the sound of your greeting, the child in my womb leapt for joy.'
> —Luke 1:41–42, 44

In response, Mary praised God for the fulfillment of his promise, saying, 'My soul magnifies the Lord, / and my spirit rejoices in God my Savior, / for he has looked with favor on the lowliness of his servant' (Luke 1:46–48). We now know this canticle, or song, of praise as the *Magnificat*.

OVER TO YOU

- Read this beautiful canticle 'magnifying' God's greatness and recalling God's covenant love toward the poor in Luke 1:46–55.
- When have you experienced such great joy that you praised God?

Blessed are you among women, and blessed is the fruit of your womb.

LUKE 1:41

Then the Gospel account of Mary's visit, which the Church calls the Visitation and remembers and celebrates each year on May 31, ends abruptly, 'And Mary remained with her for about three months and then returned to her home' (Luke 1:56), presumably before the birth of John the Baptist.

The story of the Visitation manifests Mary's love for both God and Elizabeth. Though pregnant herself, Mary made a difficult journey in order to help Elizabeth. Mary praised God's greatness and, in the first months of her own pregnancy, she stayed with and cared for the elderly Elizabeth during the last three months of Elizabeth's pregnancy.

THINK, PAIR AND SHARE
- What do Mary's words and actions tell you about her?
- Have you ever responded to someone in need as Mary did? Share your story with a partner.
- How might Mary's words and actions inspire you?

HONORING THE VIRGIN MOTHER
The Church from her beginning has praised and thanked God for the Incarnation. Among those acts of praise and thanksgiving are the many ways in which the Church honors Mary, the Mother of God (*Theotokos*), the Mother of Jesus, the Mother of the Church and 'mother of all believers'. The most widely used Catholic devotion in honor of Mary is the praying of the Hail Mary.

The Hail Mary takes its name from the angel Gabriel's greeting to Mary. The prayer is divided into two parts. The first part combines Gabriel's greeting to Mary at the Annunciation (Luke 1:28) with Elizabeth's words of greeting at the Visitation (Luke 1:42). In this part of the Hail Mary, which predates the second part, we profess the Church's faith that God chose Mary to have a unique and privileged place in the fulfillment of the divine plan of Salvation. The second part of the Hail Mary is a prayer of petition, in which we acknowledge our faith in the unique role Mary continues to have in God's saving plan.

The words of the Hail Mary, as we pray them in the Church in the West today, developed over many centuries and were formulated and given their final form during the sixteenth century in the Roman Breviary of 1568. The two main versions of the Hail Mary are:

Hail Mary

WESTERN/LATIN CATHOLIC VERSION
Hail Mary, full of grace,
the Lord is with thee;
blessed art thou among women,
and blessed is the fruit of thy womb, Jesus.
Holy Mary, Mother of God,
pray for us sinners,
now and at the hour of our death. Amen.

EASTERN/GREEK CATHOLIC VERSION
Mother of God and Virgin, rejoice!
Mary full of grace,
the Lord is with thee.
Blessed art thou amongst women,
and blessed is the fruit of thy womb,
for thou hast given birth
to the Savior of our souls.

The Hail Mary clearly states that the Catholic Church's beliefs about and devotion to Mary are connected to their beliefs about Christ. Her Son, Jesus, is the incarnate Son of God, in whom the divine nature and a human nature are united. Mary is indeed 'full of grace'; she is 'blessed among all women'.

REFLECT AND DECIDE
- What is the best lesson you have learned from the faith and devotion of Mary?
- What is your favorite prayer to Mary?

EMBRACE THE VISION

Jesus, the Promised Savior and Messiah

OPENING REFLECTION

The heart of Christianity is a *Person*, not an idea. At the heart of being a Christian is being a faithful disciple of the Teacher, an apprentice of the Master. But being a disciple-apprentice of Jesus does not simply mean living in a student–teacher relationship. Jesus invites us to live in an intimate relationship; he invites us to be one with him as he and the Father are one. We must also give witness to our relationship with Jesus. All Christians are called to share their faith, first by living it. Every day we have opportunities to witness to our faith by living as disciples of Jesus.

OVER TO YOU

- What parts of Jesus' life would you like to learn more about?
- What aspects of your relationship with Jesus would you like to deepen? And what might help you to do this?

JOSEPH, HUSBAND AND FOSTER-FATHER

Many people played a significant role in Jesus' life, particularly Mary, his mother, and her husband, Joseph, whom God chose to care for Mary and Jesus. The Hebrew name for 'Joseph' means 'one who increases' or 'one who repeats' or 'one who fulfills'. It is a common name in the Bible that comes from the Hebrew verb *yasap*, meaning 'to add', 'to increase', 'to do again' or 'to repeat'. In the Infancy Narrative of Matthew's account of the Gospel, which was written between AD 80 and 90 primarily for Jews who had become Christians, we see some of the key 'salvation stories' of the ancient Israelites 'repeated'. For example, in Joseph 'of the house of David', we see Jesus' connection to the family of David and God's promise to David. In the flight of the Holy Family to Egypt and the angel's announcement that it was safe to go home, we see the story of the enslavement of the Hebrews in Egypt, God's freeing them and their journey to the land that God promised would be their new home.

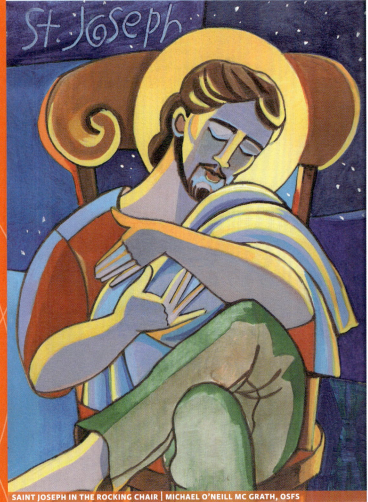

SAINT JOSEPH IN THE ROCKING CHAIR | MICHAEL O'NEILL MC GRATH, OSFS

Matthew states that Joseph was 'a righteous man' (*New Revised Standard Version* [NRSV], Matthew 1:19). Other English translations of the Bible read 'a just man' (*New American Bible* [NAB], Matthew 1:19). The use of both words, 'righteous' and 'just', to translate the Hebrew word, helps us to understand the character of Joseph. He was a man who strove to live in right relationship (a just relationship in biblical terms) with God; he was 'obedient', and sought to conform his will to God's will.

Matthew tells us that when Joseph learned that Mary was pregnant, he was 'unwilling to expose her to public disgrace' (Matthew 1:19). Matthew continues:

> But just when he had resolved to do this, an angel of the Lord appeared to him in a dream and said, 'Joseph, son of David, do not be afraid to take Mary as your wife, for the child conceived in her is from the Holy Spirit. She will bear a son, and you are to name him Jesus, for he will save his people from their sins.'
> —Matthew 1:20–21

THE DREAM OF SAINT JOSEPH | ANTON RAPHAEL MENGS

Joseph could simply have dismissed this as 'only a dream'. But clearly, he, like Mary, was a person of great faith. And he 'did as the angel of the Lord commanded him; he took her as his wife, but had no marital relations with her until she had borne a son; and he named him Jesus' (Matthew 1:24–25).

IMAGINE AND DISCUSS
- Imagine Mary and Joseph, an engaged couple, planning their marriage. What might they have wished for themselves and their family?
- Imagine how that changed when Mary said yes to the angel. Where do you think Joseph found the strength to cope with this challenge?

LITTLE—BUT *MUCH*—IS KNOWN ABOUT JOSEPH

The Gospels tell us little about Joseph; but the little they tell us tells us a great deal! Matthew describes Joseph as a man of courage who, at great risk, would fulfill his vocation and commitment to care for Mary and her Son, Jesus. This courage came to the fore soon after the birth of Jesus when the local ruler, King Herod, tried to have the newborn Jesus murdered because he had heard that a 'child has been born king of the Jews' (Matthew 2:2). Not knowing who this 'child' might be and fearing for his throne, Herod ordered that all the young children around Bethlehem be killed. In the midst of this 'terror' in the streets of Bethlehem, Joseph listened to another dream and took his family to Egypt under cover of darkness.

Joseph, the husband of Mary and the foster-father of Jesus, was not unlike the 'Joseph' who lived in Egypt, who was also a man of great faith and who responded to his dreams. Joseph, the husband of Mary, trusted that the God of Abraham, who had freed the Hebrews from

Who are the father figures in your life?

suffering and slavery in Egypt during the reign of a ruthless pharaoh, would once again save him and his family. Further dreams helped Joseph to know when to return to Israel, and directed him back to their home at Nazareth in Galilee, where they settled down. (Read Matthew 2:13–23.)

The Gospels also tell us that Joseph made his living and cared for the Holy Family as a *tekton* (Matthew 13:55); the word means 'skilled craftsman', though it is most often translated 'carpenter'. (Many New Testament scholars now interpret the word *tekton* to mean a craftsman skilled in the use of wood and stone, such as a house-builder.) The people of Nazareth referred to the adult Jesus as 'the carpenter' (Mark 6:3), which indicates that Joseph would have taught Jesus the skills of his trade, as was the custom among Jews in the time of Jesus.

The Holy Family lived faithfully according to the Law of Moses and practiced their beliefs as Jews. For example, Joseph and Mary presented the child Jesus in the Temple and dedicated him to the Lord, as was required by Jewish law. Joseph and Mary joined their relatives for the annual celebration of Passover in Jerusalem when Jesus was twelve years old. This is the last mention of Joseph in any of the Gospels. Read that great story in Luke 2:41–50.

Joseph was a person of faith and courage, kindness and compassion. He was devoted both to God and to Mary and her Son, Jesus.

OVER TO YOU

- Who are the father figures in your life? These may include your biological or foster or adoptive father and/or others who have acted in a fatherly way toward you. Choose one of these father figures and reflect:
  – What do you admire most about this person?
  – What is his most difficult trait, as far as you are concerned?
  – What is the greatest influence he has had on your life to date?

FORESHADOWINGS OF A SPECIAL TASK

God entrusted Mary and Joseph with the care of Jesus, and, through their steadfast love of him, Jesus 'grew and became strong, filled with wisdom' (Luke 2:40) and 'increased in wisdom and in years, and in divine and human favor' (Luke 2:52). Guided in his upbringing by Mary and Joseph, and through his own increasing sense of his divine identity, Jesus grew to understand the mission he had come to fulfill as Messiah and Savior of the world.

According to the four accounts of the Gospel, Jesus' mission as Messiah and Savior was foreshadowed throughout the Old Testament, for God 'makes everything converge on Christ: all the rituals and sacrifices, figures and symbols' of the Old Testament are fulfilled in Jesus (CCC, no. 522). The Incarnation itself was foreshadowed in an ancient promise from the Book of Isaiah. Matthew, echoing Isaiah 7:14, writes:

'Look, the virgin shall conceive and bear a son,
    and they shall name him Emmanuel',
which means, 'God is with us.'
—Matthew 1:23

There are many other examples of Old Testament writings that prefigure or foreshadow Christ which the Church proclaims during her celebration of the Liturgy. For example, at Mass on Christmas Day we remember that, throughout the Old Testament, the Messiah promised by God is a descendant of David. On the night of Jesus' birth, an angel appeared to a group of shepherds in fields near the place where Jesus was born, and announced, 'I am bringing you good news of great joy for all the people: to you is born this day in the city of David a Savior, who is the Messiah, the Lord. . . . You will find a child wrapped in bands of cloth and lying in a manger' (Luke 2:10–12).

On the Solemnity of Epiphany we read Matthew's account, echoing Micah 5:2, that 'wise men from the East' (or magi) traveled to Bethlehem to pay homage to the newborn king. The visit by the wise men from the East (Gentiles, perhaps from Persia, Syria or Arabia) points to the good news that Jesus is the Savior of all people.

All of the stories in the Infancy Narratives—a pregnant elderly woman, a young virgin giving birth in a stable, visits from poor shepherds and wandering foreigners, a refugee family that must flee in the middle of the night—recall the unity of the one message proclaimed through the Old Testament and fulfilled in the New Testament. They recall the universality of the love of God for all people and for all his creation. 'Against all human expectation God chooses those who were considered powerless and weak to show forth his faithfulness to his promises' (CCC, no. 489).

REFLECT AND SHARE

Family stories often become an important part of who we are.
- What is your favorite story from your own childhood?
- Which story from Jesus' infancy and early childhood do you think had the most impact on him, as his parents retold it through the years?
- How do you think Jesus would have felt about this story?
- In light of your own faith, what does this story say to you?

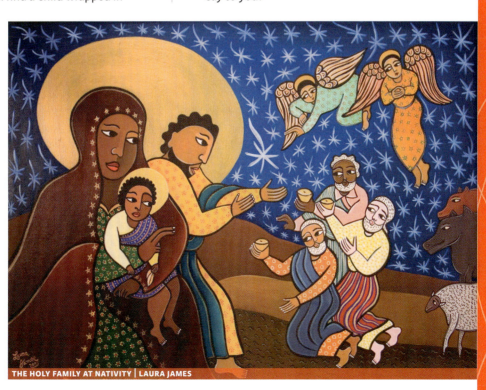
THE HOLY FAMILY AT NATIVITY | LAURA JAMES

THINK IT THROUGH

Jesus came to set things right

OPENING CONVERSATION

The Holy Spirit calls us to the lifelong task of deepening our understanding of Jesus and our relationship with him, for 'only he can lead us to the love of the Father in the Spirit and make us share in the life of the Holy Trinity' (CCC, 426).

- Which of the following dimensions of the Incarnation do you find most appealing now, and why?
    - Jesus had a body
    - Jesus was a child, as you were
    - Jesus was a teen, as you are
    - Jesus was a friend to his peers
    - Jesus belonged to a family

JESUS CAME TO EXPIATE OUR SINS

One way to talk about God's saving work through Jesus is to say that Jesus 'expiates' our sins. The verb 'to expiate' literally means 'to restore a situation of complete harmony' (Latin *pietas*), to fix a broken relationship and 'to set things right'. Around AD 1098, the great theologian and Doctor of the Church St. Anselm, Archbishop of Canterbury in Great Britain, wrote a treatise on Jesus' work of expiation, entitled *Cur Deus Homo*? (Why Did God Become Human?). When people sin, Anselm argued, we disrupt God's order within the universe, we knock things out of kilter. Good deeds cannot make up for our sins because we are supposed to do good deeds anyway. We need to have things set right in a way that goes above and beyond what our own limited human efforts can achieve.

Anselm (1033–1109) lived in the beginning of the Early Middle Ages. He used the analogy of 'allegiance to a feudal lord' in his writings, an analogy that spoke to the life experience of the people of his time. Anselm asked his readers to imagine themselves as a knight or a baron, owing allegiance to their feudal lord. He reminded them that disobedience would not only be an insult to the lord's honor; but, if uncorrected, it could unleash disorder throughout society. He then concluded: you owe it to your lord, and to society, to set things right, to re-establish harmony.

Anselm then went on to ask, 'What about disobeying God?' If one disobeys the Lord God, Anselm reasoned, only God is powerful enough to set things right. A divine debt demands divine payment. But, he continued to argue, the one paying the debt must also be able to represent us—the debtors, those in need of expiation. This is why, beyond all human expectation, God became one of us in Jesus. As man, the Son of God could represent us; and as God, he was capable of paying our debt.

The obedience of the one divine Person, Jesus, who was both Second Person of the Trinity and fully human, went above and beyond human obedience. It erased the disorder caused by our sins and set the universe right. Jesus effected, or brought about, our at-one-ment—**atonement**—with God.

FAITH WORDS

Expiation

The act of redemption and atonement for sin which Christ won for us by the pouring out of his blood on the Cross, by his obedient love even 'to the end' (John 13:1). The expiation of sins continues in the mystical body of Christ and the communion of saints by joining our human acts of atonement to the redemptive action of Christ, both in this life and in **Purgatory**.

Atonement

By his suffering and death on the Cross, Jesus freed us from our sins and brought about our reconciliation with God the Father.
—*United States Catholic Catechism for Adults*, 505

THE DESCENT FROM THE CROSS | REMBRANDT

WHAT DO YOU THINK?

- What might the fact that Jesus came to expiate our sins mean for your life now?

THE MISSION OF JESUS

The Church uses many titles and other theological descriptions of Jesus and his work, or mission. Here are several, which we will continue to explore in more detail throughout the *Credo* series:

Jesus redeemed us: The Church teaches that Jesus 'redeemed' us from our sins, and so we give him the title 'Redeemer'. *Re-demeo* means to 'pay the price'. Today we use the word 'redeem' in relation to shopping (redeeming a coupon to purchase an item). In biblical times, one redeemed slaves to purchase their freedom. So, the members of the early Church applied this terminology to describe Jesus' mission among us. In the First Letter of Peter, written between AD 60 and 65 to recently converted Christians whose faith was weak and who were ready to abandon the faith, we read, 'You were [redeemed] from the futile ways inherited from your ancestors, not with perishable things like silver or gold, but with the precious blood of Christ' (1 Peter 1:18–19). Jesus 'paid the price' for our sins and 'bought us back' from the bondage of sin.

Jesus saved us: The name 'Jesus' means 'savior'. The incarnate Son of God lived among us to save us from our sins. The angel said to Joseph, 'Joseph, Son of David, do not be afraid to take Mary as your wife, for the child conceived in her is from the Holy Spirit. She will bear a son, and you are to name him Jesus, for he will save his people from their sins' (Matthew 1:20–22). Jesus saved us from the powers of evil, from all that can destroy us, so that we might have 'life in abundance' (see John 10:10), here and hereafter.

ST. PAUL | 19TH-CENTURY ENGRAVING

St. Paul wrote, 'For freedom Christ has set us free. Stand firm, therefore, and do not submit again to a yoke of slavery'

Jesus came to bring us to eternal life: The Gospel of John teaches that the Incarnation reveals the depth of God's love. 'For God so loved the world that he gave his only Son, so that everyone who believes in him may not perish but may have eternal life' (John 3:16). Notice that there is no mention of sin in this explanation of the Incarnation, only of God's love, with the ultimate intention being to bring us to eternal life.

Jesus liberated us: We can also say that Jesus came to liberate us and set us free, especially from sin and the power of evil. St. Paul wrote, 'For freedom Christ has set us free. Stand firm, therefore, and do not submit again to a yoke of slavery' (Galatians 5:1). So the Church teaches that Christ has 'set us free from sin', and she rightfully describes Christ as the 'Liberator'.

By freeing some individuals from the earthly evils of hunger, injustice, illness and death [see John 6:5–15; Luke 19:8; Matthew 11:5], Jesus performed messianic signs. Nevertheless he did not come to abolish all evils here below [see Luke 12:13–14; John 18:36], but to free men from the gravest slavery, sin, which thwarts them in their vocation as God's sons and causes all forms of human bondage [see John 8:34–36].
—CCC, no. 549

Jesus came to open us to the divine life within us: The Greek word *theosis* summarizes the response of the Churches in the East to St. Anselm's question, '*Cur Deus Homo?*' (Why did God become a man?). The word *theosis*, as we have already seen, means 'to divinize'; in other words, to enable us to realize and live up to the divine life that is within us—to live the life of holiness as we have been created to do. St. Athanasius (c. 296–373), who is acknowledged to be one of the greatest teachers of the Church on the Incarnation, summarized this belief of the Church in his statement, 'The Son of God became man so that we might become God.'

Jesus came to be our model of holiness: The Son of God came among us to show us how to live a life of holiness. Summarizing the Scriptures, Jesus taught that we are to love God and our neighbor as ourselves as he himself did. Jesus commanded, 'Take my yoke upon you, and learn from me' (Matthew 11:29) and 'Love one another as I have loved you' (John 15:12); and he proclaimed, 'I am the way, and the truth, and the life' (John 14:6). To live as a disciple of Jesus will bring us to eternal life. (Read John 10:27–28.)

THINK, PAIR AND SHARE
- With a partner, discuss each of the Church teachings above and note which of them makes most sense to you. Explain the reasons for your choice. You don't have to agree with your partner.

WHAT'S IN A NAME?
In the Bible and biblical times, the name of a person often captured the essence of that person's role in the saving plan of God. Recall that God changed Abram's name to Abraham, and the angel commanded that Joseph name his wife's Son Jesus, 'for he will save his people from their sins'. The name 'Jesus' is a translation of the Hebrew *Yehoshuah*, or *Joshua*, which means 'God saves'. Like the Old Testament leader Joshua, Jesus saves his people—not from Canaanite enemies, but from oppression, sin and death.

In the Bible, the connection between a person's name and who they were was inseparable. This is at the foundation of the Second Commandment, 'You shall not take the name of the Lord your God in vain' and the Church's tradition of showing respect for the holy name of Jesus. Let us review some of the other key names/titles for Jesus:

Christ/Messiah

The Hebrew word for 'anointed one' is *messiah*, which is translated *christos* in Greek and *christ* in English. The ancient Israelites held an anointing ritual to install those who had been chosen for a special work of service, or mission. They would pour sacred oil over these 'chosen ones', or anoint them, to signify that they had been chosen, filled with the Spirit of God and set aside for this special work. Among those anointed were priests and kings and sometimes prophets. The works of people who were anointed included defeating an enemy, offering animals for the Temple sacrifice, or leading the nation in God's name. For example, see Exodus 29:7; Leviticus 8:12; 1 Samuel 9:16; 1 Samuel 10:1; 1 Samuel 16:1, 12–13; 1 Kings 1:39; 1 Kings 19:16.

Within this context, God promised to send 'The Anointed One', the Christ. Hence the title 'Christ' names and identifies Jesus to be the Anointed One whom God sent to fulfill his promises. Luke proclaims, 'God anointed Jesus of Nazareth with the Holy Spirit and with power' (Acts of the Apostles 10:38). Jesus' mandate and mission came directly from God: he was sent to restore the holiness and justice that was central to the original, divine plan of Creation.

THE BAPTISM OF JESUS | ANDREA PISANO

CHAPTER 4: THE WORD BECAME FLESH | THINK IT THROUGH | 93

CHRIST IN MAJESTY | SALISBURY CATHEDRAL, ENGLAND

> Jesus is the 'Lord of history', and we, his disciples, wait 'in joyful hope' for the day when his Lordship will be complete and God's Reign is fully realized

Lord

The people of ancient Israel considered the divine name YHWH that God revealed to Moses to be so sacred it was ineffable, unspeakable, not to be uttered by any person. In its place they used the name 'Lord'. Within this context we can see the significance of the early Church addressing and naming Jesus 'Lord', and Jesus using the divine name to identify himself. (See Matthew 7:21; 22:41–46.) The *Catechism* sums up the apostolic faith of the Church:

> By attributing to Jesus the divine title 'Lord', the ... Church ... affirms from the beginning that the power, honor and glory due God the Father are due also to Jesus.
>
> —CCC, no. 449

Jesus is the 'Lord of history', and we, his disciples, wait 'in joyful hope' for the day when his Lordship will be complete and God's Reign is fully realized. Meanwhile we pray, 'Lord God, Lamb of God, you take away the sin of the world; have mercy on us.'

Son of God

The term 'son of God' was used in a variety of ways by the sacred writers of the Scriptures; sometimes, to describe a person known and revered as holy, who obeyed God's will and God's law. In short, a 'son of God' was a person steadfastly loyal and faithful in his love for God and all that God required. Such a 'son of God' prefigured the 'Son of God', who would come and live among us.

Jesus revealed himself to be uniquely the Son of God; 'he is the only Son of the Father (see John 1:14, 18; 3:16, 18); he is God himself (see John 1:1)' (CCC, no. 454), and he and the Father are one (see John 14:11; 17:11). Jesus was fully divine and fully human, true God and true man. Jesus was not a human person with God dwelling inside of him; he was a divine Person in whom the divine nature and a human nature were united. So Jesus could say to his disciples, 'No one knows the Father except the Son and anyone to whom the Son chooses to reveal him' (Matthew 11:27).

TALK IT OVER

- Which of these titles of Jesus do you prefer, and why?

94 | CREDO | THE PROMISED ONE: SERVANT AND SAVIOR

WHAT ABOUT YOU PERSONALLY?
- 'Jesus is in charge.' Do you really think so? What could this mean for you at this moment in your life?

THE JESUS PRAYER
The 'Jesus Prayer' is one of the oldest of Christian prayers, dating in its original form to the words the two blind men cried out to Jesus in Matthew 20:31. It was formalized by the Orthodox Church in the fifth century.

Lord Jesus Christ, Son of God,
Señor Jesucristo, Hijo de Dios,
have mercy on me, a sinner.
ten piedad de mi un peccador.

The Jesus Prayer is a uniquely clear statement of the Church's faith in Christ, the Savior of the world.

The Jesus Prayer:
- addresses Jesus the man by name and declares him to be the Christ, the Anointed One of God, as well as the Lord of our lives;
- declares Jesus to be the Son of God, and therefore divine;
- declares Jesus to be in the position of judgment and mercy;
- confesses that we are sinners requiring God's saving grace.

Praying the Jesus Prayer regularly both confesses our faith in Jesus to be our Lord and Savior and Redeemer, and petitions the Lord to fill our life with his saving grace. Memorizing the Jesus prayer and invoking the name Jesus in prayer regularly is one way we can pray 'without ceasing', as Paul encouraged us to do. (See 1 Thessalonians 5:17.)

JESUS HEALS A BLIND MAN | ENGRAVING AFTER ALEXANDRE BIDA

JUDGE AND ACT

REVIEW WHAT YOU HAVE LEARNED

For believers, the Incarnation represents a series of 'marvelous exchanges'. Human beings have been made 'sharers in the divinity of Christ who humbled himself to share our humanity' (CCC, no. 526). The King of Heaven became the Son of Mary, born in a stable, his crib a humble manger, without ever ceasing to be God.

- What stands out as the most important things you have learned in this chapter?
- What was unexpected? Disturbing? Reassuring?
- Decide how you will put these insights or wisdom 'to work' in your life.

LEARN BY EXAMPLE

The story of St. Perpetua and St. Felicity

The lives of Saints Perpetua and Felicity are the faith stories of two women who knew how to put this same wisdom into action. In the year AD 203, Christianity was continuing to spread through northern Africa, and the Roman authorities were becoming alarmed. Christians were considered atheists and troublemakers, who openly and adamantly refused to worship the traditional gods of the Romans. During this time, the Roman Emperor Septimus Severus (who reigned from 193 to 211) made it a crime against the State for anyone to convert to Christianity. As a result, Christians, especially in North Africa, were routinely arrested, enslaved and often executed. Perpetua and Felicity were among those martyred for their faith during the persecution of Septimus Serverus.

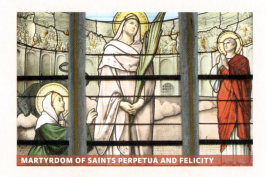

MARTYRDOM OF SAINTS PERPETUA AND FELICITY

Perpetua was the daughter of a prominent Roman citizen and mother of a newborn boy; Felicity, Perpetua's servant, was eight months pregnant at the time of her arrest. Expecting to be executed for giving bold witness to her faith in Christ, Perpetua asked her mother to raise her son. To her father, who begged her to renounce her faith, she wrote, 'I cannot call myself by any other name than what I am, Christian.' Another Christian family adopted Felicity's newborn daughter. Perpetua and Felicity were sentenced to be set upon by wild animals in the city stadium and then executed. Before their deaths, Perpetua explained their decision, 'We have come this far of our own free will, and for this reason: so that our freedom might not be denied.' The two women stood hand in hand with dignity and grace in the face of a jeering crowd. Perpetua, brave until the end, even guided the trembling hand of her executioner, so that his sword would strike her throat.

Perpetua and Felicity willingly joined their sufferings to those of Christ. They chose to obey God and to worship the Son of God, and not to obey the Government and the false gods of Rome. These two **martyrs** represent steadfast loyalty to Christ, freedom of **conscience** and courageous resistance to public pressure. The fearless witness of these African women inspired many others to become Christians. They put their bodies on the line to proclaim that Jesus alone is 'Lord'.

MEMBERS OF PAX CHRISTI PROTESTING AGAINST THE IRAQ WAR IN LONDON, ENGLAND, 2005

WHAT ABOUT YOU PERSONALLY?

- What situations at home, in school and with friends invite you to put yourself on the line in order to stand up for what is right and to live as a disciple of Jesus?
- Reflect for a moment on some of the 'false gods' of our day. Do you ever feel pressured by peers into worshiping a 'false god'? Explain.
- What may be the negative consequences for you if you give witness to your faith in Christ and refuse to go along with the crowd?
- How can the example of Perpetua and Felicity inspire you?

RESPOND WITH FAMILY AND FRIENDS

Pax Christi is an example of an organization that puts the same wisdom into action.

- Research this organization and find out what it says about a particular armed conflict that is currently taking place.
- Based on what you have learned in this chapter and from Pax Christi, write a letter about this conflict to one of your political representatives. Be sure to include in the letter your thoughts on how the Gospel goals of Pax Christi can contribute to long-lasting peace.

JOURNAL EXERCISE

- Read and reflect on these words of Jesus: 'See, I am sending you out like sheep into the midst of wolves; so be wise as serpents and innocent as doves. Beware of them, for they will hand you over to councils and flog you in their synagogues; and you will be dragged before governors and kings because of me, as a testimony to them and the Gentiles' (Matthew 10:16–18).
- Write about what these words tell you about the potential cost of giving witness to Jesus, your Lord and Savior.

WHAT WILL YOU DO NOW?

- What choice or choices can you make to give witness to your faith in Christ, right here and right now?

LEARN BY HEART

Lord Jesus Christ, Son of God, have mercy on me, a sinner.

JESUS PRAYER

PRAYER REFLECTION

LEADER
Sit quietly and remember that you are—as always—in the presence of God. (*Pause*)
In the name of the Father, and of the Son, and of the Holy Spirit.
ALL
Amen.

LEADER
God our Loving Creator,
the Incarnation of your Son
is more wonderful than words can describe.
You sent your only Son, Jesus:

READER 1
To show us how to be holy.
READER 2
To make us more like you.
READER 3
To show us the depth of your love.
ALL
Lord Jesus, Son of God, have mercy.

READER 1
To free us from oppression.
READER 2
To conquer sin and death.
READER 3
To give us courage and confidence.
ALL
Lord Jesus, Son of God, have mercy.

LEADER
Lord, God,
To set the universe right and to lead us to eternal life,
fill us with your Holy Spirit
and help us to join in the prayer of Mary,
who said 'Yes' to everything in your divine plan of Salvation.
RIGHT SIDE
I acclaim the greatness of the Lord,
I delight in God, my Savior,
who regarded my humble state.
LEFT SIDE
Truly from this day on
all ages will call me blest.

ALL
My soul magnifies the Lord!

RIGHT SIDE
For God, wonderful in power,
has used that strength for me.
LEFT SIDE
Holy is the name of the Lord!
Whose mercy embraces the faithful,
one generation to the next.
ALL
My soul magnifies the Lord!

RIGHT SIDE
The mighty arm of God
scatters the proud in their conceit,
pulls tyrants from their thrones,
and raises up the humble.
LEFT SIDE
The Lord fills the starving
and lets the rich go hungry.
ALL
My soul magnifies the Lord!

RIGHT SIDE
God rescues lowly Israel,
recalling the promise of mercy:
LEFT SIDE
the promise made to our ancestors,
to Abraham's heirs for ever.
ALL
My soul magnifies the Lord!

LEADER
Strengthen us, God,
to love and support one another,
and to confess that you alone are Lord.
We ask this in Jesus' name.
ALL
Amen.

LEADER
May God bless us and all people,
protect us from evil,
and bring us to everlasting life.
ALL
Amen.

CHAPTER 5

Thy Kingdom Come

JESUS, EXEMPLAR AND ROLE MODEL *PAR EXCELLENCE*

- JESUS IS **THE WAY,** AND THE TRUTH, AND THE LIFE
- JESUS IS THE **MASTER,** WE ARE HIS APPRENTICES
- WE ARE TO MODEL OUR LIVES AND OUR FAITH **ON JESUS**
- JESUS **RESISTED** TEMPTATION
- JESUS' LIFE, DEATH AND RESURRECTION MODELED GOD'S UNCONDITIONAL LOVE FOR US

IN THIS CHAPTER WE EXPLORE JESUS, OUR EXEMPLAR and role model. Jesus is the Master and we are his apprentices. Everything about Jesus' life—his words, his example, his miraculous actions and the puzzling (yet compelling) stories that he told—reveals God's reign of love and compassion, peace and justice. We look to the Scriptures to see how Jesus grew in his understanding of and commitment to his mission, so that we too can grow strong, be filled with wisdom and live as his loyal disciples.

LEARNING OUTCOMES
As a result of studying this chapter and exploring the issues raised, you should be able to:

- identify people whom you consider to be good role models;
- consider how we sometimes choose bad role models;
- explore how Jesus can be the ultimate role model for you;
- learn about how Jesus responded to temptation;
- find contemporary images to describe the Kingdom of God;
- understand the impact Jesus' proclamation about the Kingdom of God would have had on the Jewish people of his time;
- understand the reversal of power and powerlessness that God's Kingdom represents;
- explore the miracles of Jesus as indicators of God's Reign;
- focus on the significance of the actions of Jesus in the story of the feeding of the five thousand;
- explore the literary genre of 'parable', with reference to the parables of the Mustard Seed and the Wedding Feast;
- understand the meaning of the words *metanoia*, *kairos* and *basileia*;
- reflect on the Kingdom of God as a Kingdom of restored justice.

FAITH-FORMATION OUTCOMES
As a result of studying this chapter and exploring the issues raised, you should also:

- understand how biblical role models can inspire you;
- consider yourself as a role model;
- renew your commitment to your baptismal promise to live as a disciple of Jesus;
- appreciate how Jesus' example can help you when you face temptations;
- integrate the wisdom and insight from the miracle of the feeding of the multitude into your own life;
- appreciate how the teachings of Jesus can inspire your own commitment to the values of the Kingdom;
- articulate the changes you will make in your life so as to sow the seeds of the Kingdom of God;
- be inspired by the words and actions of Pope Benedict XVI and Severn Cullis-Suzuki.

FAITH WORD: Parables

LEARN BY HEART: Luke 4:4

LEARN BY EXAMPLE: Pope Leo XIII

JESUS' PUBLIC LIFE BEGAN WITH HIS BAPTISM

JESUS PROCLAIMED THE KINGDOM OF GOD

JESUS REVEALED THE KINGDOM THROUGH MIRACLES AND PARABLES

THE KINGDOM INVITATION IS TO ALL

ATTEND AND REFLECT

How do we choose our role models?

OPENING ACTIVITY

It is hard to imagine a world without role models: people whose style or skills, values or personal qualities we admire—and consciously, and sometimes unconsciously, imitate.
- List three people (living or dead, real or fictional) that you consider to be role models. For each person, name one character trait, value or accomplishment that you admire.
- Now contribute one or two of the 'admirable traits' you have named to a larger 'class list'. Display this list where it is visible for all to see.

TALK IT OVER
- What do you notice about the qualities listed by the group? What values do they mostly represent?
- How did people's faith in God influence their choice of 'admirable traits'?

CHOOSING ROLE MODELS

The following 'types of people' are widely admired by young people today.

The Artist—model of creativity and success

Many artists, especially singers and musicians, become role models for young people.
- What artists do you look up to, and why?

The Leader—model of power and service

Leaders, in any field or profession, naturally serve as role models; for example, religious leaders, political leaders, business leaders, teachers and so on.
- What leaders do you admire, and why?

The Activist—model of courage and hope

The activist is usually an idealist, someone who is driven by a vision of how they would like the world to be, and so their actions are often aimed at bringing about such a world.
- What activists do you admire, and why?

DR. MARTIN LUTHER KING, JR. WAS INSPIRED BY ABRAHAM LINCOLN

GROUP WORK

Work in small groups, each group brainstorming examples of people from each of the above categories, from fiction or real life, whom contemporary young people idolize. Then discuss:
- Why are some young people attracted to these types of characters?
- What problems can be associated with the way of life of each of these types of people?
- Talk about how you can recognize the faults and failings of your role models while still admiring their good qualities.
- How can your Christian faith help you to discern the type of people that deserve our admiration and those that do not?

JOURNAL EXERCISE
- Recall some of the 'learn by example' characters you have studied so far in the *Credo* series.
- Choose one that you particularly admire and write a few paragraphs explaining what it is you admire about that person. Mention how he or she has influenced your thinking or lifestyle.

JESUS AS EXEMPLAR, OR ROLE MODEL *PAR EXCELLENCE*

For Christians, Jesus is the role model *par excellence*; he is the Master that we, his apprentices, follow and desire to be like. Jesus is 'the way, and the truth, and the life' (John 14:6). Just imagine if you were truly to follow 'the way' who is Jesus—how loving, faithful, kind, compassionate and full of hope you would be.

Think how clearly your life would reflect that of a faithful and loyal child of God; reflect the image of the God who created you. Jesus' coming among us; his life, his words and his actions; his suffering and Death; his Resurrection and return to his Father—all these reveal and model God's unconditional love for us. To live as disciples, we are to give witness to and return God's love by loving our neighbors and ourselves.

REFLECT AND DISCUSS

In considering the question of how Jesus is your role model and the role model for all Christians, discuss:
- How did Jesus use his creativity, and how do you use yours?
- How did Jesus deal with violence and frustration? What about yourself?
- How did Jesus define success? How do you define it?

JOURNAL EXERCISE
- Choose one of the questions listed above and write a personal response to it.

WHAT ABOUT YOU PERSONALLY?
- Where do you stand now in relation to choosing your role models? What guidelines will you follow from here on?

HEAR THE STORY

Jesus proclaimed a new message

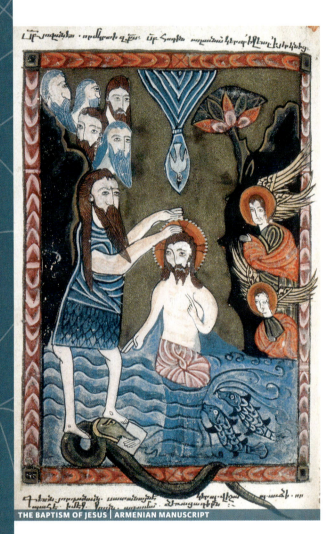

THE BAPTISM OF JESUS | ARMENIAN MANUSCRIPT

OPENING CONVERSATION
Christians have been joined to Christ the Way in Baptism.

For those of you who were baptized:
- What does your Baptism mean to you?
- What significance do you think it holds for how you live your life and the choices you make from day to day?

If you have not been baptized:
- What difference do you think being baptized into a community of faith could make to your life?
- Do you see any difference in the lives of baptized people and non-baptized people? Explain.

JESUS' PUBLIC LIFE BEGAN WITH HIS BAPTISM

All four accounts of the Gospel agree that 'Jesus' public life begins with his baptism by John in the Jordan' (*Catechism of the Catholic Church* [CCC], no. 535; see Matthew 3:13–17; Mark 1:9; Luke 3:21–22). When the Church speaks of and celebrates the Solemnity of the Baptism of the Lord on the Sunday after the Epiphany, she uses the word 'baptism' in a different way than she uses the word 'baptism' to identify the sacramental Baptism of people. In a general, or a generic way, the word or ritual of 'baptism' means the celebration of one's decision to die to an old lifestyle and to mark the beginning of a renewed life, of a deeper commitment to God. One's 'baptism' signifies the turning of one's life toward God and a life of obedience and loyalty to God. The Sacrament of Baptism, while similar, is uniquely different. The Sacrament of Baptism is 'birth into the new life in Christ' (CCC, 1277). Sacramental Baptism is:

> a rich reality that includes forgiveness of original sin and all personal sins, birth into the new life by which man becomes an adoptive son of the Father, a member of Christ and a temple of the Holy Spirit.
> —CCC, no. 1279

At first John refused to baptize Jesus, saying that it was he himself who needed to be baptized by Jesus. But Jesus insisted and John consented. The baptism of Jesus, the incarnate Son of God, was not a baptism for the forgiveness of sins. It is the sign that 'all the Old Covenant prefigurations find their fulfillment in Christ Jesus' (CCC, no. 1223). It is the announcement of the beginning of Jesus' mission among us. 'The Spirit who had hovered over the waters of the first creation descended then on the Christ as a prelude of the new creation, and the Father revealed Jesus as his "beloved Son" [see Matthew 3:16–17]' (CCC, no. 1224).

Jesus' gesture is a manifestation of his self-emptying, or *kenosis* (see Philippians 2:7). Jesus' baptism by John in the waters of the Jordan foreshadowed his suffering, Death and Resurrection. Through consenting to his baptism by John, Jesus symbolically took on the brokenness of human sin and proclaimed his steadfast loyalty to the fulfillment of his mission as Savior. Paul, in the Letter to the Philippians, describes that mission as the model for our own life as his disciples:

Let the same mind be in you that was in Christ Jesus,
 . . . who though he was in the form of God
 did not regard equality with God
 as something to be exploited,
but emptied himself,
 taking the form of a slave,
 being born in human likeness.
And being found in human form,
 he humbled himself
 and became obedient to the point of death—
 even death on a cross.

Therefore God also highly exalted him
 and gave him the name
 that is above every name,
so that at the name of Jesus
 every knee should bend,
 in heaven and on earth and under the earth,
and every tongue should confess
 that Jesus Christ is Lord,
 to the glory of God the Father.
—Philippians 2:5–11

In the Gospel accounts of the baptism of Jesus we see that the mission of Jesus is indeed the work of the Holy Trinity. The Son of God had been sent in the name of God, who is Father, Son and Holy Spirit, to bring about the divine plan of Salvation for all of humanity. Just as you were baptized 'in the name of the Father, and of the Son, and of the Holy Spirit', so the whole Blessed Trinity was present at the baptism of Jesus.

HISTORICAL SITE OF THE BAPTISM OF CHRIST, JORDAN

WHAT ABOUT YOU PERSONALLY?
- How might the Holy Spirit be inviting you to live your Baptism and put Christian faith into practice in new situations and creative ways?

CLASS DISCUSSION
Share your opinions about adults making religious decisions for their children.

JESUS RESISTED TEMPTATION
Jesus was fully human in all ways except sin, and no sooner had he been baptized, the Evangelists tell us, than the forces of evil tore at his mind and heart and will. They bombarded him with self-serving reasons for why he should renege on keeping his commitment to his Father and to his mission. Immediately after his account of the baptism of Jesus, Mark the Evangelist writes:

> And the Spirit immediately drove him out into the wilderness. He was in the wilderness for forty days, tempted by Satan; and he was with the wild beasts; and the angels waited on him.
> —Mark 1:12–13

In other words, Jesus was tempted; he faced the temptations that all humans face as they strive to live in harmony with their Creator, with one another and with all creation.

The Old Testament reveals that the Israelites who had recently been liberated from slavery in Egypt faced similar temptations. On their way to the land that God had promised them, the people of Israel wandered in the desert for forty years; this was also a time of great temptation for them, to which they sometimes gave in. These events of the Exodus prefigure Jesus living in the 'wilderness' (a term some translate as 'desert') for forty days of prayer and fasting when he was 'tempted by the devil' (Luke 4:1–13; Matthew 4:1–11; Mark 1:12–13), whose efforts failed.

The Devil, however, was determined to continue his efforts to get Jesus to turn his back on his Father and on his mission. Luke writes, 'When the devil had finished every test, he departed from him until an opportune time' (Luke 4:13). Jesus would continue to encounter the demons during his ministry; for example, see Luke 4:41; 8:26–39.

Being fully human, Jesus experienced temptation as we do. In his steadfast loyalty he revealed, and 'role-modeled' for us, the human response to temptation. God is always ready to help us resist temptation—no matter how attractive the consequences of giving in to temptation might appear to be.

OVER TO YOU
- Think about the times you were tempted. Did you reach out to the Lord for strength? Explain.
- Surely, you will be tempted in the future. How might Jesus serve as a role model to help you in those moments?

THE TEMPTATION OF CHRIST | ENGRAVING AFTER ALEXANDRE BIDA

Temptation entices us to continue down the road of the old Adam and not to travel the path of the New Adam, Jesus Christ

CHOOSING GOD'S WAY

Temptation entices us to continue down the road of the old Adam and not to travel the path of the New Adam, Jesus Christ. As Jesus did, we need to meet temptations head on, unmask their deception, and follow the Way, who is Jesus. We need to cooperate with the Holy Spirit to use our reason (intellect), our knowledge of the Truth and our free will to choose what is true and good.

Each of the three dimensions of the Temptation of Jesus represents the opposite of God's vision for holiness and justice, which is at the heart of the divine plan of Creation. First, the Devil tempted the famished Jesus, who had fasted for forty days, to turn stones into bread (see Matthew 4:3 and Luke 4:3). By so doing, the Devil was tempting Jesus to use his power and gifts not only to nourish his hunger but also to seek security through material possessions, 'bread'. Jesus, echoing Deuteronomy 8:3, responded, 'It is written, "One does not live by bread alone"' (Luke 4:4).

Next, the Devil tempted the physically weakened Jesus and 'showed [Jesus] . . . all the kingdoms of the world' (Luke 4:5). By so doing, the Devil tempted Jesus, the All-powerful One, into believing that he, the Devil, was the source of all power and would share that power with Jesus—for the price of worshiping him and not the Father. Jesus, echoing Deuteronomy 6:13, responded, 'It is written, "Worship the Lord your God, / and serve only him"' (Luke 4:8).

Finally, the Devil tempted the tired Jesus to doubt his Father and the love that unites them and to jump off the pinnacle of the Temple to test his Father's love for him. Jesus, echoing Deuteronomy 6:16, responded, 'It is said, "Do not put the Lord your God to the test"' (Luke 4:12).

Reading and reflecting on the Gospel accounts of the Temptation of Jesus is a source of wisdom that can help us explore and discover the strength and vision to choose God's way. 'The temptation in the desert shows Jesus, the humble Messiah, who triumphs over Satan by his total adherence to the plan of salvation willed by the Father' (CCC, no. 566).

EXPLORE THE TEXT

- Working in pairs, read Luke 4:1–13.
- Discuss each of the temptations listed.
- Think of examples of similar temptations faced by young people today.
- Choose *one* of these examples and agree on what would be the best response to such a temptation, influenced by Jesus as your role model.
- Share your thoughts with the rest of the class.

JOHN THE BAPTIST IN THE WILDERNESS | BERNER NELKENMEISTER

John the baptizer appeared in the wilderness, proclaiming a baptism of repentance for the forgiveness of sins

MARK 1:4

PROCLAMATION OF THE MISSION

The Gospel of Mark tells us that, soon after Jesus' baptism and temptation, Herod Antipas, Rome's puppet-king in Galilee, placed John the Baptist under arrest, and Jesus began his public ministry. Mark writes, 'Now after John was arrested, Jesus came to Galilee, proclaiming the good news of God, and saying, "The time is fulfilled, and the kingdom of God has come near; repent, and believe in the good news"' (Mark 1:14–15). Each phrase in Mark 1:14–15 reveals something important about Jesus' message and what he would teach throughout his public ministry:

- **The time is fulfilled:** The time of foreshadowing and prophecies is over; God's promises are now coming true in Jesus. The Greek word used here for 'time' is *kairos*, meaning 'the right time', 'the proper season', 'the time of ripeness', 'the time to act'.
- **The Kingdom of God:** The Kingdom of God is the actualization of God's will for human beings proclaimed by Jesus Christ to be the reign, or rule, of justice, peace, mercy, and love, the seed of which is the Church on earth, and the fulfillment of which is in eternity. (*United States Catholic Catechism for Adults*, 517)
- **Repent:** The Old Testament term for 'repentance' is *shûv*, meaning 'to turn around'; the Greek term used in the New Testament is *metanoia*, meaning 'change your mind' or 'turn your life around'.
- **Believe:** This means both to believe with your mind and also to 'trust' with your heart.
- **Good News:** This is the term often used for 'Gospel'. In medieval English, the word was 'God-spel'. Today we say 'Gospel'.

OVER TO YOU

- What meaning has the term 'Kingdom of God' had for you up to now?
- Does it have a deeper meaning as a result of your exploration of and reflection on Jesus' statement in Mark 1:14–15? Explain.

'THE KINGDOM OF GOD IS AT HAND'

The announcement and inauguration of the Kingdom would be the central theme of Jesus' whole ministry. The Kingdom was a symbol of what God desires for all people and for creation. It signified a reign of love and kindness, of peace and justice, of holiness and fullness of life for all. The Kingdom of God does not refer to a piece of territory (as some of Jesus' contemporaries erroneously believed), but rather to a time, a space, a way of life according to what God desires for all people—the best of everything and fulfillment of the deepest desires of the human heart.

The Scriptures of ancient Israel, which today are contained in the Tanakh, are replete with teachings and images of the Kingdom of God. As a background to these readings, it is important to keep in mind what lay at the heart of the faith of the Jewish people; namely, YHWH alone is our God; YHWH alone is our king. But, in their efforts to be like their neighbors—to enjoy the same security—the elders petitioned the elderly prophet Samuel. Samuel's response foreshadowed the dire consequences that this choice would bring upon God's people. (Read 1 Samuel 8:6–9, 19–20.)

TALK IT OVER
- Have you experienced people making decisions based on the wisdom of this world rather than the wisdom of God? Explain. What were the consequences?

The Salvation history of ancient Israel from that time on is one of conflict between the values of YHWH and the Kingdom of God on the one hand and the values and practices of so many of the earthly kings, the values of the kingdom of this world. Deep within this 'sad' story of infidelity to God there was a hope—a desire and expectation—that things would be set right again.

Let us get in touch with that hope as we read an oracle of the prophet Isaiah. The oracle, biblical scholars think, was written shortly after the rule of King Ahaz (735–715 BC) and during the reform of King Hezekiah (715–687 BC)—about a hundred years before the Babylonian Exile (587–539 BC). The *New Jerome Biblical Commentary* remarks that not only was the reign of Ahaz marked by his maltreatment of the poor and other unjust policies (see Isaiah 3:13–15, 5:8–13; Micah 2:1–10), but, in his efforts to appease the Assyrians, King Ahaz replaced the altar in the Temple of Jerusalem with an Assyrian-style altar (see 2 Kings 16:10–16). Within this context read Isaiah 11:1–9, which concludes:

The wolf shall live with the lamb,
    the leopard shall lie down with the kid,
the calf and the lion and the fatling together,
    and a little child shall lead them.
The cow and the bear shall graze,
    their young shall lie down together;
    and the lion shall eat straw like the ox.
The nursing child shall play over the hole of the asp,
    and the weaned child shall put its hand in the adder's den.
They will not hurt or destroy
    on all my holy mountain;
for the earth will be full of the knowledge of the LORD
    as the waters cover the sea.
—Isaiah 11:6–9

> **The reign of King Ahaz was marked by his maltreatment of the poor and other unjust policies**

KING AHAZ | 16TH-CENTURY WOODCUT

OVER TO YOU
- Where do you see in the world around you a kingdom being built similar to the kingdom built by Ahaz?
- How are you working to build, or against the building of, such a kingdom?

'The Kingdom of God *has come near*.' This phrase can be translated in two ways: 'The Kingdom of God *is near*' and 'the Kingdom of God *is here*'. This double meaning is found throughout Jesus' teaching and throughout the Christian message. Salvation is both accomplished and still awaiting to be fulfilled; Jesus has come once and he will also come again; God's Kingdom is, in effect, both 'already here and not yet'. When we pray, 'Thy kingdom come', we are not only praying about the future, but also about the here and now.

LET'S PROBE DEEPER
- Open your copy of the New Testament and page through the Gospels according to Matthew, Mark and Luke. Notice how often Jesus teaches about the 'kingdom of God' and the 'kingdom of heaven'.
- Read Matthew 13:33 and notice what Jesus teaches. In other words, even small deeds done in keeping with God's will 'on earth' are always significant. Even a small deed for God's Reign can and will bear great fruit.

BRAINSTORM AND DISCUSS
- Brainstorm, as a class, all the places outside of Scripture you can think of that speak of God's 'kingdom' or 'the kingdom of heaven'. Include prayers, such as the Our Father, hymns, movies, and what you remember from previous theology classes. Then list the common themes that arise in relation to the use of these words.
- Now discuss:
   - In what ways, however small, can young people live for the Reign, or Kingdom, of God?
   - Imagine what the world would be like if the Kingdom of God was established. Describe such a world.

Where do you see in the world around you a kingdom being built similar to the kingdom built by Ahaz?

EMBRACE THE VISION

Unexpected Good News

OPENING REFLECTION/CONVERSATION

After returning from his temptations in the desert, Jesus announced the theme of his public ministry in the synagogue in his home town of Nazareth. The leader of the synagogue handed Jesus the scroll of the prophet Isaiah, and Jesus opened the scroll and proclaimed:

'The Spirit of the Lord is upon me,
    because he has anointed me
        to bring good news to the poor.
He has sent me to proclaim release to the captives
    and recovery of sight to the blind,
        to let the oppressed go free,
to proclaim the year of the Lord's favor.'

—Luke 4:18–19

- What do the phrases 'good news to the poor', 'release to the captives', 'sight to the blind' and 'freedom for the oppressed' mean in today's world? Give concrete examples.

TRULY GOOD NEWS—WITH SOME UNEXPECTED TWISTS

Hearing this passage, the Jews in the synagogue remembered the people of Israel's return from Babylonian Exile: a time of expectation that the 'Anointed One', the Messiah, would bring freedom and healing to God's people and would finally end their oppression. Some, if not all of them, would certainly have thought, 'Is the son of the carpenter claiming to be the Messiah?' Soon the doubts and complaints began. Somebody said of Jesus, 'Is not this Joseph's son?' (Luke 4:22). Matthew in his account of this event adds that the people in the synagogue 'were astounded and said, "Where did this man get this wisdom and these deeds of power?"'(Matthew 13:54). There was also in Jesus' words a challenge that some were not quite ready to accept. When Jesus read 'to proclaim the year of the Lord's favor', he was saying that he was inaugurating the Jubilee Year described in Leviticus 23:33–44 and 25:8–55. The Jubilee Year commanded Jews that once every fifty years, all Israelite slaves be freed, all their debts erased, and every piece of land that had been bought or sold be returned to its original owners.

REFLECT AND DECIDE

The Jubilee Year represents a simple and profound challenge to build a society upon the Great Commandment, which Jesus would teach and whose elements were revealed in the Torah. Every family should have the basics they need to survive; any 'extras' must be given up after a certain time.

- Identify three 'extras' that you enjoy owning but do not really need.
- Consider giving them to someone (a family member, friend or stranger) who needs them and would get more out of them than you do right now.

In a country town like Nazareth, many of Jesus' neighbors would have been in debt to local businessmen and struggling to pay their taxes to Rome. You can imagine how amazed they must have been when Jesus declared, 'Today this scripture has been fulfilled in your hearing' (Luke 4:21). Could it be true? If so, this would really be 'good news'! Or bad news if you wanted to hold on to your wealth!

When they heard this, all in the synagogue were filled with rage. They got up, drove him out of the town, and led him to the brow of the hill on which their town was built, so that they might hurl him off the cliff. But he passed through the midst of them and went on his way.

—Luke 4:28–30

Jesus responded to his listeners' objections and reminded them that in ancient times there was famine, drought and disease in Israel, but God sent the prophets to save and heal foreigners; prophets are never accepted at home. Jesus' proclamation was too much for his audience to handle—it obviously demanded too much of them. Jesus just about escaped with his life. Preaching and living for the Reign of God can be a dangerous business.

OVER TO YOU
- Think of examples of people who suffered or were killed because they preached and lived according to Kingdom values. What did they do?
- Have you ever found yourself in a threatening situation because of your witnessing to your faith? If so, how did you respond?

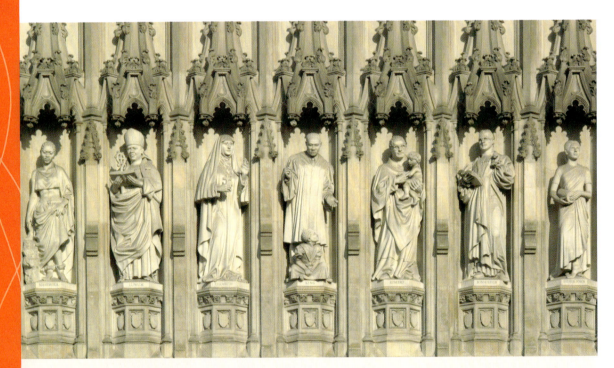

In 1998 a frieze depicting ten 20th-century martyrs from various Christian traditions was unveiled at Westminster Abbey in London, England. The ten statues are intended 'to represent all those who have died in circumstances of oppression and persecution'. Pictured above are (L–R): Manche Masemola; Anglican Archbishop Janani Luwum; Grand Duchess Elizabeth of Russia; Dr. Martin Luther King, Jr.; Archbishop Oscar Romero; Dietrich Bonhoeffer and Esther John. Also included in the frieze, but not pictured, are St. Maximilian Kolbe, Lucian Tapiede and Wang Zhiming.

THE KINGDOM INVITATION IS TO ALL

Jesus' invitation to work for the coming of the Kingdom is extended to all people. The Kingdom proclaimed and inaugurated by Jesus is not just for the 'cool' crowd, the beautiful people, or the people in leadership. The Church teaches:

> *Everyone* is called to enter the kingdom. . . . The kingdom belongs *to the poor and lowly,* which means those who have accepted it with humble hearts. [God will reveal] to the 'little ones' . . . what remains hidden from the wise and the learned.
> —CCC, nos. 543, 544

God's Kingdom is a strange Kingdom. Outsiders can become insiders, and insiders have to wait their turn. The kid next door can become God's own messenger. The hungry are filled with good things—but if you make riches your goal or 'god' in life, you will end up with nothing.

READ, REFLECT AND DISCUSS
- Read and reflect on Matthew 21:28–32, the parable of the Two Sons.
- Where do you see yourself in the story, and why?
- Keeping in mind the concluding words of Jesus (Matthew 21:31–32), who in our world today would be the first to enter the Kingdom of God?

MIRACLES AS SIGNS OF GOD'S REIGN

According to the Gospel accounts, Jesus performed many 'signs' or 'deeds of power' (Luke 19:37). These miracles, such as casting out demons, calming the storm, feeding the hungry, healing the sick and bringing the dead back to life, reveal that 'the Kingdom is present' in Jesus and that 'he was the promised Messiah' (CCC, no. 547) and manifest the nature of the Kingdom that God had begun to establish. The message: Jesus (not Satan or Caesar) is Lord!

Yet you might ask, 'Why then is there still sin and evil, illness, hunger and injustice in the world?' Jesus revealed that the saving and compassionate presence of God is at work among us and within us and within the world, partnering with us as we face these realities. 'By freeing some individuals from the earthly evils of hunger, injustice, illness and death [see John 6:5–15; Luke 19:8; Matthew 11:5], Jesus performed messianic signs. Nevertheless he did not come to abolish all evils here below [see Luke 12:13–14; John 18:36], but to free men from the gravest slavery, sin, which thwarts them in their vocation as God's sons [and daughters] and causes all forms of human bondage [see John 8:34–36]' (CCC, no. 549).

THINK, PAIR AND SHARE
- Do you think miracles happen today? Explain.
- What is the message of a miracle?

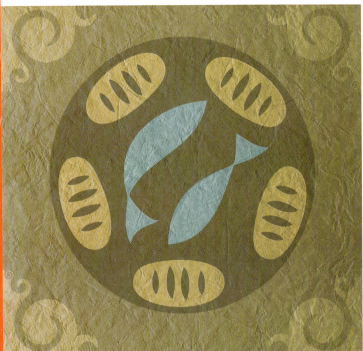

A SIGN ABOUT LIFE IN THE KINGDOM

The 'Feeding of the Multitude' is the only miracle story reported in all four accounts of the Gospel (Matthew 14:13–21, Mark 6:31–44, Luke 9:10–17 and John 6:1–14), and Mark and Matthew add a second 'Loaves and Fish' story. Feeding the hungry, and all that feeding people who are 'hungry' symbolizes, was not only a central action of the mission of Jesus; it is also central to the mission of the Church. In one account of the Feeding of the Multitude, we read that Jesus had 'compassion' on a huge crowd 'because they were like sheep without a shepherd; and he began to teach them many things' (Mark 6:34).

EXPLORE THE TEXT

- Read the account of the Feeding of the Multitude in John 6:1–14.
- Apply the 'active reading' technique (see section one of chapter 1) to John 6:5–14 and discuss your insights with a partner.
- Then discuss the following questions as a group:
  - Why do you think it was a young person who provided the five loaves and two fish?
  - Why do you think Jesus wanted the people to sit down?
  - What might the loaves of bread symbolize?
  - What might the fish symbolize?
  - In verse 12 we read: 'Gather up the fragments left over, so that nothing may be lost.' What could the fragments of food represent?
  - Does 'giving thanks' help a 'miracle' to happen? How?
  - What connections do you see between the Feeding of the Multitude and:
    ▶ the feast of Passover (John 6:4)?
    ▶ the Lord's Prayer (the Our Father)?
    ▶ the Eucharist?

In the story of the Feeding of the Multitude Jesus identified with the poor and the hungry, as God had so often done in the history of the people of ancient Israel. Jesus' response to the needs of the people revealed the saving love and compassion of the same God present and at work among them. The power of Jesus' 'thanksgiving', in Greek *eucharistia*, when lifting up the baskets of food transformed these resources in a completely unexpected way. From the generosity of a young boy, and with God's blessing, Jesus could make a little go a long way. And he can do the same for us with our 'limited' resources.

WHAT ABOUT YOU PERSONALLY?

- What are the connections between this story and your life as a young person today?
- What is the best wisdom you can take from this story for your own life?

CLASS DISCUSSION

Kingdom life includes 'release' to those in chains.
- What are the different 'chains' that entrap young people today?
- How can Jesus' message help young people to 'escape' from these chains?
- How can you help, as individuals or as a class?

THINK IT THROUGH

Puzzling through the Kingdom parables

OPENING CONVERSATION
- What are the positive aspects of puzzling through a question and figuring out the answer for yourself?
- Recall one of your favorite parables of Jesus. What wisdom does solving the puzzle of the parable reveal for you?
- Why do you think Jesus used parables so much?

FAITH WORD

Parables

A characteristic feature of the teaching of Jesus. Parables are simple images or comparisons which confront the hearer or reader with a radical choice about his invitation to enter the Kingdom of God.
—CCC, Glossary

JESUS TEACHING ON THE SEASHORE | JAMES TISSOT

THE NOT-SO-SIMPLE PARABLE

The Gospels repeat that '[Jesus] told them many things in parables' (Matthew 13:3). The English word 'parable' comes from the Greek word *parabole*, meaning 'to be similar, to be comparable'. As one dictionary describes it: 'A parable is an extended metaphor, or simile, frequently becoming a brief narrative, generally used in biblical times for didactic purposes.' One contemporary biblical scholar used this description to explain this literary form: 'Parables are tiny lumps of coal squeezed into diamonds. . . . They are not ideas at all. . . . They are the jeweled portals of another world; . . . through their surfaces are refracted lights that would otherwise blind us—or pass unseen.'

Jesus used parables—metaphors, similes and mini-stories of everyday life—to teach about the Kingdom of God. Let's read and explore the meaning of two of these parables of Jesus.

The parable of the Mustard Seed

[Jesus taught,] 'With what can we compare the kingdom of God, or what parable will we use for it? It is like a mustard seed, which, when sown upon the ground, is the smallest of all the seeds on earth; yet when it is sown it grows up and becomes the greatest of all shrubs, and puts forth large branches, so that the birds of the air can make nests in its shade.'

—Mark 4:30–32

Jesus' parables focused on topics and details familiar to his audience—nature, farming, village life, business and politics. While appearing to be simple stories, they contained complex meanings and often had an unexpected twist. They addressed many issues at once: the place of God in our lives; Jesus' role as announcer and inaugurator of the Kingdom; the Kingdom of God as it unfolds in the world; the Church is 'on earth the seed and beginning of that kingdom' (CCC, no. 541, quoting Vatican II, *Constitution on the Church*, no. 5).

TALK IT OVER
- Reread the parable of the Mustard Seed (Mark 4:30–32) and this time apply the 'active reading' technique. Share your insights with a partner.
- Then discuss as a group:
  – Why did Jesus compare the Kingdom of God to a tiny seed?
  – What do the birds represent?
  – What does the shade represent?
  – What wisdom do you hear Jesus teaching through this parable?

LET'S PROBE DEEPER
As one American writer and theologian said, 'A parable is a small story with a large point.' Let's take a closer look at the parable of the Mustard Seed and the context in which Jesus told it.
- Jesus told this story in a country setting, where people depended on their farms and their gardens for food.
- Mustard was valued as a spicy condiment.
- On the other hand, the mustard plant is a major weed. It spreads quickly and is very difficult to eliminate once it has taken root. Mustard plants hog up soil, sun and nutrients. They can easily crowd out plants used for cooking, making bread or producing a harvest for sale, and so can lead to financial losses and even starvation.
- Farmers and gardeners dislike birds because they eat the plants that humans grow.

So, continuing your discussion:
- Why does Jesus compare the Kingdom of God to a mustard plant infestation?
- For whom is this parable Good News?
- How might it be Good News for young people today?

WHAT ABOUT YOU PERSONALLY?
After his account of Jesus teaching using the parable of the Mustard Seed, Mark writes, 'With many such parables he spoke the word to them, as they were able to hear it; he did not speak to them except in parables, but he explained everything in private to his disciples' (Mark 4:33–34). Jesus' parables open our eyes to unexpected visions. Only the eyes of faith—eyes trained by following the example of Jesus—can help us make sense of the challenges that God's Kingdom presents.

- How do you view the Kingdom of God in the world today? As:
  - a tiny mustard seed?
  - a spreading mustard plant?
  - some other element in the story?
- Write your reflections in your journal.
- Then discuss the practical wisdom you can learn from this parable.

The parable of the Wedding Feast

The parable of the Wedding Feast (Matthew 22:1–14) is one of the more complex of Jesus' parables. The first half of this parable (verses 1–10) makes some familiar points. First, the Kingdom of God is like a banquet with plenty of food. Second, those who thought they would have first place, places of honor, at the banquet were badly mistaken. Instead, anyone and everyone off the street, 'both good and bad', sit at God's table. Then things begin to sound strange in the second part of the parable, verses 11–14. The King notices that one of the guests is wearing plain, off-the-street clothes. 'How did you get in here without a wedding robe?' he asks. The man is speechless. He is promptly arrested and thrown out of the Kingdom feast.

Parables open our eyes to the unexpected Good News about God's unfolding Kingdom. This was the Good News that Jesus taught and for which he gave his life.

READ, REFLECT AND DISCUSS
- Read the parable in Matthew 22:1–14 and apply the 'active reading' technique. Then share your initial insights with a partner.
- Discuss what might be the deeper meaning of 'How did you get in here without a wedding robe?'. The following might give you some ideas:
  - Some people 'dress to impress' when they go to a party. Others dress up to honor the host, or to show that they are excited about the event. Some try to present themselves in a way that is different from who they are in everyday life. How might 'dressing up' relate to life in the Kingdom of God?

OVER TO YOU
- Think of a recent incident when you *could* have stopped to celebrate the good news of a friend or family member, but you just didn't take the time. (In the words of the parable of the Wedding Feast, you did not have your 'party clothes' ready at hand.)
- Write a prayer in your journal thanking God for the gift of your friend or family member.
- Then ask God to help you recognize and celebrate future 'Kingdom moments' of shared joy as they occur.

JUDGE AND ACT

REVIEW WHAT YOU HAVE LEARNED

In describing the Kingdom of God, Jesus made bold proclamations, quoted the Scriptures of ancient Israel, performed amazing actions and told puzzling stories—all hinting at the kind of existence that the Reign of God represents.

With a partner, review the following:
- Jesus' two main announcements about the Kingdom of God (Mark 1:14–15 and Luke 4:18–19)
- Jesus' response to the Devil's temptations
- The 'sign' of the Feeding of the Multitude
- The parables of the Mustard Seed and the Wedding Feast

Then decide:
- What are the top five words or phrases that describe the Kingdom of God for you? Why did you choose these words or phrases?
- Compare your words and phrases with those of your classmates.
- Identify the five words or phrases that show up most often for the class as a whole.

WHAT ABOUT YOU PERSONALLY?
- Complete these statements:
  - The Kingdom of God is *attractive* to me because....
  - The Kingdom of God is *frightening* to me because....
- Jesus is your exemplar and primary role model. Jesus called his followers to *metanoia* or 'a change of heart', to follow 'the way, the truth and the life' that he modeled and made possible by his dying and rising. Insight and decisiveness are important steps toward embracing the Kingdom and its new ways of life. Remember the word *kairos*, which we met in section two of this chapter; it means 'the right time', 'the time of ripeness', 'the time to act'.
  - What *kairos* moments are coming up for you?
  - Reflect and then decide what practical steps you will take to make the Kingdom a reality in those moments.

A KINGDOM OF RESTORED JUSTICE

The New Testament word for 'kingdom' (the Greek word *basileia*) means 'royal rule' or 'the domain in which a king's power holds sway'. God's *Basileia* is the domain in which original justice holds sway. In Genesis 1:26 God reveals that he created human beings with the intention of giving them dominion over all of his creation. (Read Genesis 1:28–30.)

We are to care for all the elements of creation, living and non-living, as God cares for them. This responsibility extends to the respectful treatment of ourselves, others and all creation. Blessed Pope John Paul II clearly reminded us of the meaning of this biblical Revelation and teaching:

> God gave the earth to the whole human race for the sustenance of all its members, without excluding or favoring anyone. . . . The earth, by reason of its fruitfulness and its capacity to satisfy human needs, is God's first gift for the sustenance of human life.
> —John Paul II, *Centesimus Annus*, 31, quoted in *Compendium of the Social Doctrine of the Church*, no. 171

God's *Basileia* is global, not country-specific. Every person has a God-given right to these things: people living in developed countries and those living in developing countries; people who live comfortably and the well-educated; people who live in poverty, are outcast, are sick or imprisoned; the young and the elderly. The Corporal and Spiritual Works of Mercy (listed in 'Catholic Prayers, Devotions and Practices' at the back of this text) guide us in living the values of the Kingdom proclaimed by Jesus through his life and teaching.

DECIDE FOR YOURSELF
- What mustard seed can you sow now to help someone in need to experience the Reign of God in their life?
- When, where and how will you do it?

LEARN BY EXAMPLE

The story of Pope Leo XIII

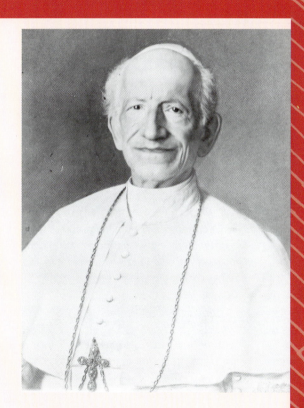

Pope Leo XIII (1810–1903) was elected Pope in 1878. Pope Leo worked tirelessly to guide and support Catholics to bring the Gospel to the modern world and live it authentically. His immense efforts and writing are the foundations of what is today known as the Social Teachings of the Catholic Church. In 1885 his encyclical *Immortale Dei* ('The Immortal God') taught the role of Catholics as citizens in the modern world. Six years later he promulgated his flagship social encyclical *Rerum Novarum* ('On new things'). This encyclical is acknowledged to be the first 'social encyclical' and the origin of the Catholic Church's social principle 'the preferential option for the poor'.

In *Rerum Novarum* Pope Leo XIII brought the teachings of the Gospel to the world in a time of immense social change. To help Catholics live the values of the Kingdom of God faithfully in the modern world, the Pope explained and applied the teachings of the Catholic Church to communism, industrialization and capitalism; to the role of labor and capital, the common good, and the rights and dignity of workers. At the beginning of the encyclical, Pope Leo XIII outlined the challenge for the Church in bringing the Gospel to the world. He taught:

> It is no easy matter to define the relative rights and mutual duties of the rich and of the poor, of capital and labor. And the

danger lies in this, that crafty agitators are intent on making use of these differences of opinion to pervert men's judgments and to stir up the people to revolt.

—*Rerum Novarum*, no. 2

In 1991 Blessed Pope John Paul II promulgated the *Centesimus Annus* ('The hundredth year') to mark the one-hundredth anniversary of *Rerum Novarum*. In describing the purpose of his encyclical, Pope John Paul II wrote that he wished 'to show the fruitfulness of the principles enunciated by Leo XIII . . . to give careful consideration to current events in order to discern the new requirements of evangelization' (*Centesimus Annus*, no. 3).

THINK, PAIR AND SHARE
- Read Matthew 13:44–53.
- Discuss with a partner how Pope Leo XIII was a wise steward of the Gospel.
- How do you see the Catholic Church today bringing the values and principles of the Gospel to current events? Be specific.

WHAT ABOUT YOU PERSONALLY?
- What current events challenge you to be a faithful disciple of Jesus and a faithful citizen?
- How do you respond to current events and issues that you know are contrary to the Gospel? Why is that?

LEARN BY HEART

One does not live by bread alone.

LUKE 4:4

PRAYER REFLECTION

Greeting

LEADER
Sit quietly and remember that you are—as always—in the presence of God. (*Pause*)
In the name of the Father, and of the Son, and of the Holy Spirit.

ALL
Amen.

Opening Prayer

LEADER
God our Creator,
    help us to see the signs of your Kingdom
    in every part of our lives.
Send your Holy Spirit
    to open our hearts to the message of Jesus
    and help us to follow in the way he has shown.
We ask this in the name of Jesus, your Son and our Messiah-Savior.

ALL
Amen.

Proclamation of and Response to the Word of God

READER
This is the Gospel of the Lord.

ALL
Praise to you, Lord Jesus Christ.

LEADER
Now reflect on and respond to the words of Jesus by prayerfully creating a doodle around one phrase of Jesus that particularly speaks to you. I will alert you when there is one minute left before the close of prayer.

The leader slowly rereads the Gospel passage several times while the students create the doodle art.

Intercessory Prayer

LEADER
I invite you to join in prayer and ask the Spirit of God for the guidance and grace to work as 'kingdom builders'. Through the power of the Holy Spirit we join with Christ in proclaiming the Kingdom of God, not only through our words but also through our deeds.

One at a time, students pray aloud their petition. After each petition, all respond, Thy kingdom come.

Concluding Prayer and Dismissal

LEADER
Thank you, God, for the food we eat
    and the beauty we create.
Fill our hearts and hands with your power,
    so that your Kingdom vision may come true
    for all your daughters and sons.
We ask this in Jesus' name.

ALL
Amen.

LEADER
May God bless us and all people,
    protect us from evil,
    and bring us to your Reign of everlasting life.

ALL
Amen.

CHAPTER 6

Jesus: More than Meets the Eye

- **JESUS WAS FULLY HUMAN AND FULLY DIVINE**
- **JESUS' MISSION WAS TO BRING ABOUT THE DIVINE PLAN**
- **JESUS INVITED HIS DISCIPLES TO JOIN HIM IN HIS MISSION**

JESUS' UNIQUE IDENTITY AND MISSION

- **JESUS REVEALED HIS MISSION THROUGH WORDS AND ACTIONS**
- **THE HOLY SPIRIT GUIDES US TO KNOW JESUS' TRUE IDENTITY**
- **THE HOLY SPIRIT ENERGIZES US TO LIVE OUR TRUE IDENTITY**

IN THIS CHAPTER WE CONSIDER THREE EPISODES IN the life of Jesus that reveal more about his identity and mission as the Promised One: Servant and Savior. We explore, in detail, the wedding feast of Cana, the Transfiguration at Mount Tabor and the institution of the Eucharist to help uncover the meaning of Jesus' saving power and his intimate love for his disciples. We then discover the significance of these Gospel passages and what they teach us about our own identity, about living as disciples of Jesus, and about our need to depend on God.

LEARNING OUTCOMES
As a result of studying this chapter and exploring the issues raised, you should be able to:

- identify how you can grow to become your true self;
- explore the Revelation of Jesus' true identity in the Gospels, the teachings of the Church and the Sacraments;
- understand how the Wedding at Cana foreshadowed the Paschal Mystery;
- appreciate the role of Mary in prompting Jesus' first miracle;
- reinterpret the Gospel account of the Transfiguration using contemporary symbols and settings;
- understand how Jesus' Apostles and disciples gradually came to be aware of his true identity;
- come to a deeper understanding of the title 'Son of Man';
- discover that Jesus' entry into Jerusalem foreshadowed both his Death and Resurrection;
- understand why the Eucharist is the 'source and summit' of the Christian life;
- understand the relationship between Passover and the Eucharist;
- understand the Eucharist as a memorial of Jesus' sacrifice on the Cross;
- understand that the Risen Jesus is really present in the Eucharist;
- explore the story of the Martyrs of the University of Central America.

FAITH-FORMATION OUTCOMES
As a result of studying this chapter and exploring the issues raised, you should also:

- recognize that there is a deeper spiritual reality behind the outward self that you present to the world;
- appreciate that Jesus' identity can help you discover your own true identity;
- assess your own experiences of the connection between suffering and glory, death and new life in light of the Transfiguration;
- understand the symbolism behind the tradition of blessing and distributing palms on Palm Sunday;
- see the connection between your celebration of the Eucharist and your life as a disciple of Jesus;
- identify how you can respond to 'acts of injustice' in your world;
- make some personal commitments in relation to the challenge that is presented in the dismissal rite at Mass.

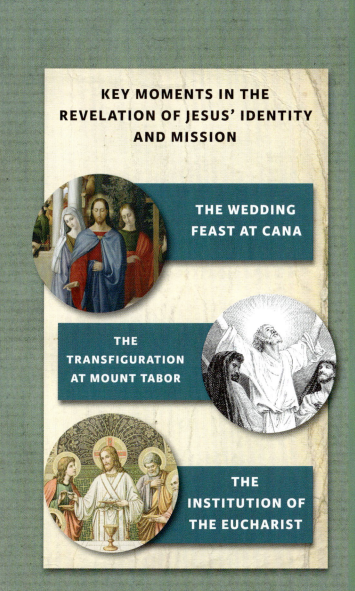

KEY MOMENTS IN THE REVELATION OF JESUS' IDENTITY AND MISSION

- THE WEDDING FEAST AT CANA
- THE TRANSFIGURATION AT MOUNT TABOR
- THE INSTITUTION OF THE EUCHARIST

FAITH WORDS: Transfiguration; Son of Man; Real Presence

LEARN BY HEART: 1 Corinthians 10:17

LEARN BY EXAMPLE: The martyrs of the University of Central America

ATTEND AND REFLECT

How do we discover our true identity?

OPENING ACTIVITY/DISCUSSION
- As a class, brainstorm as many characters as possible who have 'secret identities'— from novels and movies, from folktales, comics and real life.
- Select the three most interesting characters and assign a small group to each one.
- Each group should list the qualities of the character's two identities.
- Then decide as a class which identity would be more appealing to young people, and why.

WHAT ABOUT YOU PERSONALLY?
- What about you? Do you have a 'secret' identity? Is there more to you than meets the eye?

OUR DEEPER SIDE

As any fan can confirm, the superheroes we meet in movies often experience anxiety and inner conflict in relation to their secret identity. Should they reveal their true powers and feelings to family and friends? At the same time, of course, those family and friends already know (at least strongly suspect) what is really going on.

We too long to share what our lives are really about with our loved ones and friends. And often, those same friends and family long to learn more about our thoughts and our lives. Because God has created us in the image of God, who is a Triune Communion of Love, we are created to live in community—in communion with God and one another. We want to know others and be known.

JOURNAL EXERCISE
- Write about a part of your life that you would like to reveal to friends or family. List the reasons why you would like to share this aspect of your life with them, and the pros and cons of sharing.

CREATIVE ACTIVITY
- Draw two images, one capturing the self you show to the world, the other depicting the self you do not reveal to very many people. Keep it simple—you do not need to be good at art to do this.

EACH PERSON IS UNIQUE—AND A MYSTERY

Behind every person's physical face is a whole world of thoughts and feelings, a whole life history of experiences and relationships. Like God in whose image we are made, we are always something of a mystery, even to ourselves. Part of being human, however, is the amazing process of discovering the many different dimensions of our identity—discovering the 'mystery' of who we are.

124 | CREDO | THE PROMISED ONE: SERVANT AND SAVIOR

In our study of Scripture and the teachings of the Church we learn that figuring out who Jesus, the incarnate Son of God, is, and growing in our relationship with him, our Savior and Redeemer, is a lifelong task. But the more we discover about Jesus, the more it can help us figure out who we are, and how to live life 'abundantly' (John 10:10) as Jesus made possible for us and for all people.

We discover our identities through our relationships with other people and, ultimately, with God. When we share our experiences and our thinking with family and friends, and in prayer with God, we come to understand ourselves more clearly. Sometimes, these efforts themselves may even encourage us to try out new things and to grow.

THINK, PAIR AND SHARE
- Who has challenged you recently to try something new?
- How did you feel about their challenge?
- Discuss with a partner the challenge that Jesus offers you at this time in your life.

When we share our experiences with others we come to understand ourselves more clearly

JESUS' UNIQUE IDENTITY AND MISSION
Christians understand that there is often more to things than meets the eye. This was true of Jesus—a wandering Jewish preacher and teacher and a doer of amazing deeds—whom many often misunderstood. The Gospels tell us that even Jesus' closest disciples only came to know him and the true nature of his identity and mission over time and gradually. To some of his enemies, Jesus was a false prophet; to others he was a blasphemer and a threat to Judaism. To these enemies and other nonbelievers who radically misunderstood him and his mission, Jesus was, at the very least, a man with a dangerous and misguided vision. On the other hand, to those with the eyes of faith, Jesus was and is more than they ever could say.

JESUS SPEAKING WITH THE WOMAN OF CANAAN | FRED SHIELDS

Jesus' closest disciples only came to know him and the true nature of his identity and mission over time and gradually

Jesus was not a super hero, nor did he have 'magical' powers. Jesus was fully human and fully divine, true God and true man. Jesus is the incarnate Son of God, the Second Person of the Blessed Trinity. In other words, Jesus' power is the very power of God. This is why he could heal, teach with 'authority', bring life out of death, and create something new. As his story unfolded and his true identity emerged, people came to believe he was the Son of God; they recognized that he had the power to overcome hatred and chaos, to cast out fear and oppression. By his own dying and rising, he even had the power to overcome death. St. Paul, who first 'knew' Jesus as a threat to the teachings of Judaism and only gradually came to faith in him, proclaimed:

We have been buried with him by baptism into death, so that, just as Christ was raised from the dead by the glory of the Father, so we too might walk in newness of life.
—Romans 6:4

Like you and I have, Jesus had a calling, or a vocation—a work or mission given to him by his Father. Jesus' mission was unique—to bring about the divine, loving plan of goodness, of Creation and Salvation. It was a mission that no mere human could fulfill. It was a mission that only the God-man could fulfill, but he invited his first disciples and all the disciples who followed them to join him in fulfilling it.

The Gospels describe how Jesus' mission and his true identity unfolded over the course of his lifetime. Looking back over the story of Jesus' life, Death, Resurrection and Ascension, the first disciples and the early Church understood how events like the wedding feast at Cana and the **Transfiguration** at Mount Tabor and the institution of the Eucharist foreshadowed the most important moment of his story and mission, the Paschal Mystery of his Death–Resurrection–Ascension.

WHAT ABOUT YOU PERSONALLY?
- Which aspects of Jesus' identity do you find most inspiring, challenging or mysterious?

People express their identities by talking with and relating to others. The same was true of Jesus when he walked the roads of Galilee and the hills of Judea, and ate with his friends, with tax collectors and with scribes and Pharisees. Today, the Holy Spirit guides us to come to the knowledge of Jesus' true identity as one divine Person who was both fully divine and fully human, as is revealed in the Gospel stories and in the Church's reflection on and teachings about those stories. The same Holy Spirit energizes us to make known Jesus' identity to others and to live our true identity as his disciples.

OVER TO YOU
- Reflect on how your growing knowledge of Jesus' identity has influenced your own identity.

> **Levi gave a great banquet for [Jesus] in his house; and there was a large crowd of tax-collectors and others sitting at the table with them.**
>
> **LUKE 5:29**

JESUS EATING WITH SINNERS | ENGRAVING AFTER ALEXANDRE BIDA

HEAR THE STORY

The wedding at Cana

OPENING REFLECTION

Sometimes you meet someone and—bang!—you get a feeling. You might think, 'I know we're going to get along well' or 'I really want to come to know this person better'. Feelings are responses to our emotions, which are God's gifts to us; feelings 'are emotions or movements . . . that incline us to act or not to act in regard to something felt or imagined to be good or evil' (*Catechism of the Catholic Church* [CCC], no. 1763). Jesus himself experienced emotions and feelings; for example, he felt compassion, sadness and even anger. When we reflect on this, we can come to a deeper understanding of how Jesus was like us in all things except sin. Jesus was indeed fully human and, through his use of his feelings, he revealed to us that our own emotional responses enable us to react to good and evil.

In the Christian life, the Holy Spirit himself accomplishes his work by mobilizing the whole being, with all its sorrows, fears and sadness, as is visible in the Lord's agony and passion. In Christ human feelings are able to reach their consummation in charity and divine beatitude.
—CCC, no. 1769

FIRST IMPRESSIONS

All four accounts of the Gospel tell us that Jesus had sharp insights into the heart and character of people. For example, in the first chapter of John's Gospel the Evangelist tells us that, three days before the wedding at Cana, Jesus met and called his first disciples. In his description of the meeting and call of the first disciples, the Evangelist tells us that after two of John the Baptist's disciples heard John point Jesus out and declare, 'Here is the Lamb of God' (John 1:29, 36), they followed Jesus and spent time with him.

> **Sometimes you meet someone and you think, 'I know we're going to get along well'**

Andrew, one of the two disciples, went to his brother, Simon Peter, brought him to Jesus and announced, 'We have found the Messiah' (John 1:41). Imagine Simon Peter's excitement when Jesus spoke to him, saying, 'You are Simon son of John. You are to be called Cephas' [which is translated Peter]' (John 1:42).

REFLECT AND DISCUSS
- How do you think Andrew felt when he believed that he had found the Messiah?
- How do you think Peter felt hearing Jesus' words?
- How do you think you would have felt if you had been there?

The next day, John tells us, Jesus went on to Galilee, where he continued inviting others to follow him. First he invited Philip, who, as a result of his encounter with Jesus, went off to his friend Nathaniel and said to him, 'We have found him about whom Moses in the law and also the prophets wrote, Jesus son of Joseph from Nazareth' (John 1:45). Nathaniel, at first skeptical, accepted Philip's invitation to 'come and see' (John 1:46), and he went with him to 'see' Jesus. John describes the meeting:

> When Jesus saw Nathaniel coming towards him, he said of him, 'Here is truly an Israelite in whom there is no deceit!' Nathaniel asked him, 'Where did you come to know me?' Jesus answered, 'I saw you under the fig tree before Philip called you.' Nathaniel replied, 'Rabbi, you are the Son of God! You are the King of Israel!' Jesus answered, 'Do you believe because I told you that I saw you under the fig tree? You will see greater things than these.'
>
> —John 1:47–50

From his face-to-face life experience of meeting a 'stranger' about whom he was first very skeptical, Nathaniel came to believe and he professed his faith in Jesus to be 'Son of God' and 'King of Israel'.

WHAT ABOUT YOU PERSONALLY?
- Imagine Jesus meeting you for the first time. Remembering his divine ability to read

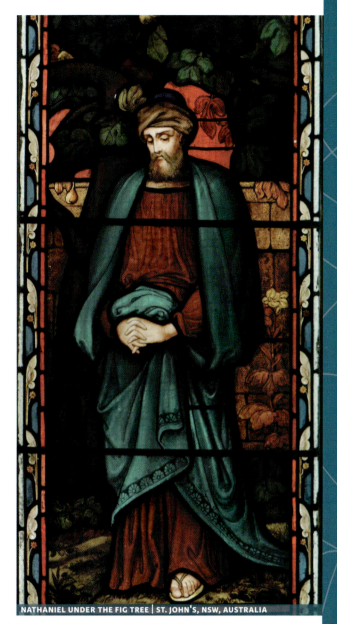

NATHANIEL UNDER THE FIG TREE | ST. JOHN'S, NSW, AUSTRALIA

your heart, what might he say about you? Summarize it in a phrase.
- Then summarize what your response to Jesus might be.

THE FIRST SIGN: A DEEPLY SYMBOLIC STORY

One of the most intriguing accounts of people coming to faith in Jesus is that of the miracle at the wedding in Cana of Galilee when Jesus changed water into wine. John tells us that three days after the calling of Philip and Nathaniel,

THE MARRIAGE AT CANA | JULIUS SCHNORR VON CAROLSFELD

Jesus and his new disciples went to a wedding to which they had been invited. It was there, John tells us, that Jesus, in response to his mother's request (John 2:3), performed the first of his 'signs . . . and revealed his glory; and his disciples believed in him' (John 2:25). This miracle, or 'sign', to use the wording of John's Gospel (John 2:11), was Jesus' first Revelation that he was someone very special—our Savior and Redeemer. The Gospel of John is the only Gospel that records this incident in Jesus' life. (You might like to review the material on the Book of Signs, the first main part of the Fourth Gospel, in *God's Word Revealed in Sacred Scripture*, the first book of the *Credo* series, where we discussed the function of the seven signs in the teaching/theology of the Fourth Gospel.)

At this point in John's narrative Jesus had been baptized (see John 1:32) but had not yet begun his public ministry. The other three Gospels, the Synoptics, record how Jesus' ministry began with the proclamation of Good News to the poor (as we saw in chapter 5). But John focuses on the wedding at Cana as the first example of Jesus' ministry and work of Salvation and the Revelation of his identity. Why is this story so important? We have already seen in the Gospel of Matthew that Jesus compared the Kingdom of Heaven to a wedding reception. (Read Matthew 22:1–14.) Telling the story of the wedding at Cana was John's way of teaching that the Kingdom had come about in Jesus.

THINK, PAIR AND SHARE

- Read John 2:1–12.
- Imagine that you were a guest at the wedding feast at Cana in Galilee and that you met Jesus there for the first time. What might have been your 'first impressions' of him?
- Share your thoughts on this with a partner.

SCRIPTURE EXERCISE

- Read John 2:1–12 again very slowly, paying close attention to every detail.
- As a group, discuss the possible symbolic meanings of the following details:
  – The third day
  – Wine

- Water
- 'My hour has not yet come.'
- 'Do whatever he tells you.'
- Saving the best for last
- Share your responses to these questions:
  - What do each of the above details foreshadow about Jesus' future actions, his saving work and destiny?
  - What teachings of the Church and Sacraments do they bring to mind?

Notice the important role of Mary, the Mother of Jesus, in prompting Jesus' first miracle. Though Jesus thought he was not ready, Mary presumed that he was and told the servants, 'Do whatever he tells you' (John 2:5). Ever since, this story has encouraged Christians to pray to Mary, asking her to intercede for them with her Son.

FORESHADOWING THE PASCHAL MYSTERY

The Cana story also points tantalizingly to the Last Supper and to Jesus' subsequent Death and Resurrection. Turning water into wine reminds us of Jesus' final meal, at which he turned the wine into his blood. As Mary, the Mother of Jesus, was present at Cana, so too was she with him at the Cross (John 19:26–27). This time Jesus made a final request of her, 'Woman, here is your son' (John 19:26). Jesus' request meant, 'Be also the Mother of the Church, my Bride.' After his death, Jesus' side would be pierced; blood and water would flow from it (John 19:34–35). The 'third day' of the wedding reception reminds us of Jesus' Resurrection, the life-changing event of his rising from the dead to new and glorified life on the third day after his execution and burial. The invitation to the great wedding feast in the Kingdom had been issued.

FIGURE OUT AND DECIDE

- What else can you learn from the account of this first sign of Jesus at the wedding celebration at Cana in Galilee for your own life?

THE CRUCIFIXION | EVGRAF SEMENOVICH SOROKIN

EMBRACE THE VISION

The Transfiguration at Tabor

THE TRANSFIGURATION | DUCCIO DI BUONINSEGNA

Jesus' teachings and actions proclaimed and established God's Kingdom. Jesus called his disciples not only to pray 'thy kingdom come' but also to do God's will 'on earth as it is in heaven' (Matthew 6:10).
⊙ How have you been working to bring about the Kingdom of God?
⊙ What role has picking up a cross played in that work?
⊙ What role has your participation in the Eucharist played in that work?

THE TRANSFIGURATION

The account of the Transfiguration, like that of the wedding feast at Cana in Galilee, is rich with symbols and meanings that the members of the early Church would have recognized as rooted in the Hebrew Scriptures. Because of this, the account of the Transfiguration deserves a very careful reading.

OPENING REFLECTION/CONVERSATION

The final week of Jesus' suffering, Death and Resurrection—his Paschal Mystery—began with his Transfiguration. The Transfiguration was a theophany, or 'appearance of God'. Central to the Transfiguration was the announcement by a voice from heaven, 'This is my Son, the Beloved; listen to him!' (Mark 9:7). It was the Revelation that Jesus is indeed the Son of God. In the Synoptic Gospels, this mission for God's Reign makes up the first half of Jesus' earthly mission. The story of his Transfiguration introduces the second half of his ministry. With the Transfiguration we begin the path toward Jerusalem and the Paschal Mystery— toward Eucharist, Cross, Resurrection and Ascension.

⊙ Quietly read Mark 9:2–10 and reflect on the story. Keep these points in mind:
  – *Six days later ... Peter and James and John (verse 2):* Readers familiar with the Hebrew Scriptures would remember that Moses took three close advisors with him to the top of Mount Sinai, and after 'six days' went up the mountain to meet with God. (Read Exodus 24:9–18.)
  – *A high mountain (verse 2):* In Salvation history, mountains bring us closer to heaven and were considered the dwelling place of God. It was on Mount Sinai that

God and the Israelites entered an eternal Covenant. (Read Exodus 19.) Elijah escaped to a tall mountain where God gave him courage to face his enemies. (Read 1 Kings 19:8–18.)

- *Dazzling white clothes (verse 3):* In the tradition of ancient Israel, brilliant light was also associated with and a sign of God's presence. Christians profess Jesus to be 'light from light'. For the early Church, white clothes were also a symbol of martyrdom; that is, of dying for one's faith. The martyrs in heaven 'have washed their robes and made them white in the blood of the Lamb' (Revelation 7:14). Jesus was the Martyr of martyrs, who, out of steadfast love and loyalty, would soon sacrifice his life on the Cross to fulfill his mission.
- *Elijah with Moses (verse 4):* Elijah and Moses received God's Revelation on a mountain. Now they were in the presence of Jesus, the fullness of God's Revelation, the Word of God himself. Coupled together, Moses and Elijah represent 'The Law and the Prophets'—an ancient Jewish expression for the Sacred Scriptures that Jesus came to fulfill. These two icons of God's people appear here to symbolize that Jesus fulfilled both the Law and the promises of the prophets.
- *Elijah (verse 4):* Elijah, the most famous of Israel's prophets, represents the struggle to overcome injustice, the invitation to return to the covenant relationship with God when we have fallen away.
- *Moses (verse 4):* Moses was the first great leader of Israel; he represents the Torah ('Law' or 'Teachings'), which governs all of Jewish life.
- *Three dwellings (verse 5):* The word for 'dwelling' in Hebrew is *shekinah*, and it is used by the sacred authors to speak of the divine glory and presence. 'Booths' or 'tabernacles' or 'tents' are other possible translations. Peter's desire to set up 'dwellings' recalls the Jewish Feast of Tabernacles. (Read Leviticus 23:39–43.)
- *The cloud (verse 7):* In the Hebrew Scriptures a cloud also symbolizes God's presence with and among his people. (Read Exodus 24:15–18.)
- *'This is my Son, the Beloved' (verse 7):* This announcement echoes God's words at the baptism of Jesus (Mark 1:11) and again establishes the true identity of Jesus.

⊙ Now re-read the text and apply the 'active reading technique' to the Transfiguration (review the instructions in chapter 1).

⊙ Discuss what the Transfiguration might mean for young people today.

FAITH WORD

Transfiguration

The word 'transfiguration' means 'change in appearance'. The Transfiguration is the mysterious event in which Jesus—in the sight of Peter, James and John—was transformed in appearance, revealing himself to be truly divine, the Son of God.

THE TRANSFIGURATION | ENGRAVING AFTER ALEXANDRE BIDA

The Transfiguration was the Revelation of Jesus' true identity. The man Jesus, whom the disciples had come to know and whom Peter, just six days before the Transfiguration, confessed to be the Messiah (see Mark 8:29), was now revealed also to be truly God. This event reflected both his public ministry and what lay ahead in Jerusalem. The disciples saw terrifying glory, but it was really 'only Jesus'. God's 'favorite' rubbed shoulders with Moses and Elijah because his life and preaching had fulfilled 'the Law and the Prophets'. Yet, his white clothes revealed that he would soon be put to death and rise to glory for faithfully and obediently bringing about God's divine plan of Salvation.

WHAT ABOUT YOU PERSONALLY?

The *Catechism* reminds us: 'Jesus went up to Jerusalem voluntarily, knowing well that there he would die a violent death' (CCC, no. 569). After the Transfiguration, Jesus could simply have relied on his power as God's own Son and avoided the suffering that he knew lay ahead of him. Yet, he wanted to move on to Jerusalem to bear witness to his Gospel and fulfill his mission by his own death.

- When have you ever had a choice between two options, and chosen the more painful path?
- How does the story of the Transfiguration help you to understand your choice in a different, Christian way?

GLORY REVEALED IN HISTORY'S DARKEST HOUR

The Transfiguration is a preview of Resurrection life and of Jesus' Second Coming again in glory, when the Reign of God will come about. 'The Transfiguration gives us a foretaste of Christ's glorious coming, when he "will change our lowly body to be like his glorious body" ' (CCC, no. 556). Jesus' path to his glory would, as he announced six days earlier, come about through his death—a path Peter had categorically refused to accept. (Read Mark 8:31—9:1). Mark writes:

CREATE 'TRANSFIGURATION NOW'

- In this activity we will retell the Transfiguration story in a format that will help you come to a deeper understanding of the Transfiguration and apply the significance of this turning-event in the life of Jesus to your own life.
- Brainstorm as a class some possible genres to use; for example:
  - Western movie
  - Sword-and-sorcery movie
  - Police drama
  - Hip-hop / Rap song
  - Country and western DVD
  - Another genre of your choice
- Break up into groups of three or four and re-write the story of Mark 9:2–10. Make sure you include the insights and questions that you identified in your close reading, but express them using symbols and settings that fit your chosen genre.
- When finished, read the story dramatically to the class.
- Discuss the messages these differing interpretations convey for young people today.

> Then he began to teach them that the Son of Man must undergo great suffering, and be rejected by the elders, the chief priests, and the scribes, and be killed, and after three days rise again.
>
> —Mark 8:31

The response of Peter, who was known as 'the Rock', showed how slow he and the other disciples were to grasp Jesus' true identity and mission: the **Son of Man**, the One who would freely offer himself for our Salvation. 'Let's stay on this mountain and build three dwellings!' Peter declared. But Jesus' business was not on *this* mountain. His business lay on the road ahead, on the road he would travel when he came down from the mountain. It lay unavoidably on another mountain, Mount Calvary, the hill of the Cross. Only after the events of Good Friday and Easter would it become clearer how suffering and glory are so often connected—for Jesus and for those who believe in him. The Crucifixion was foreshadowed in the Scriptures of ancient Israel and was now embraced by Father, Son and Spirit. In a flash, we 'confirm' Jesus' truest identity: divine and human, glory and self-sacrificing love.

Yes, Jesus would die, but he would rise again, enabling us to live beyond the power of violence and death. Christians share in the new life of Jesus, sustained by the Holy Spirit and empowered by the Sacraments of the Church.

FAITH WORD

Son of Man

Jesus used the title 'Son of Man' to identify himself and his mission in the four accounts of the Gospel (thirty times in St. Matthew, fourteen times in St. Mark, twenty-five times in St. Luke, and twelve times in St. John). Rooted in the Scriptures of ancient Israel, most especially the Books of Ezekiel and Daniel, the term 'son of man' refers to the 'ideal human', the one most faithful to YHWH.

OVER TO YOU
- Have you ever chosen the easier option, even though it was probably the wrong thing to do?
- Decide that next time you will ask Jesus to help you make the better choice.

THE FINAL JOURNEY TO JERUSALEM

'Christ's Transfiguration aims at strengthening the apostles' faith in anticipation of his Passion' (CCC, no. 568). As Jesus and his disciples made the final journey to Jerusalem, Jesus continued to heal and to teach. He focused again and again both on revealing the saving presence of God at work in and through him and on teaching clearly that his work, the work of the Messiah, included his Passion, his suffering and Death.

During these final weeks with his disciples, Jesus also prepared them for the inevitable challenges ahead and the trauma of his Crucifixion. With sad irony, the Son of Man stated, 'It is impossible for a prophet to be killed away from Jerusalem' (Luke 13:33). When he finally saw Jerusalem's skyline from afar, he wanted so much to enfold this city and its people in his arms—but he knew that fear, sin and death would have their day. He could only lament:

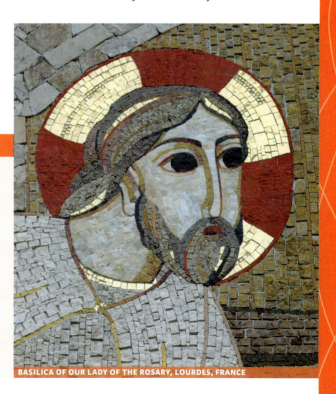

BASILICA OF OUR LADY OF THE ROSARY, LOURDES, FRANCE

Jerusalem, Jerusalem, the city that kills prophets and stones those who are sent to it! How often have I desired to gather your children together as a hen gathers her brood under her wings, and you are not willing! See, your house left to you, desolate. For I tell you, you will not see me again until you say, 'Blessed is the one who comes in the name of the Lord.'

—Matthew 23:37–39

Jerusalem 'did not recognize the time of [its] visitation from God' (see Luke 19:41–44).

REFLECT AND DISCERN

The cloud of God's presence surrounds us at all times. God is ever 'visiting' our lives, reaching out to us in the ordinary and the everyday.

- Pause and recognize a recent moment when you have experienced God's presence in your life.
- How did you respond? Might you have responded differently?

BLESSED IS THE ONE WHO COMES IN THE NAME OF THE LORD

Jesus' entry into Jerusalem foreshadowed both his suffering and his triumph and exaltation. The crowd covered the road with cloaks and palm branches (as people would for a king so that the dust of the road would not rise) to welcome Jesus as the promised Savior-King 'who comes in the name of the Lord' (Luke 19:38). Luke tells us that he was greeted with the same acclaim as people would give on the return of a king to his royal city.

> As he rode along, people kept spreading their cloaks on the road. As he was now approaching the path down from the Mount of Olives, the whole multitude of the disciples began to praise God joyfully with a loud voice for all the deeds of power that they had seen, saying,
>> 'Blessed is the king
>>> who comes in the name of the Lord!
>> Peace in heaven,
>>> and glory in the highest heaven!'
>
> Some of the Pharisees in the crowd said to him, 'Teacher, order your disciples to stop.' He answered, 'I tell you, if these were silent, the stones would shout out.'
>
> —Luke 19:36–39

This king, however, did not come with royal pomp and circumstances, returning from battle to be welcomed with glory; this king's battle and glory were yet to come.

Christians remember this event each year at the beginning of Holy Week with the celebration of the liturgy of Palm Sunday of the Lord's Passion. During this liturgy, both Jesus' kingship and his coming Passion are recalled. With palm branches in hand, we re-enact the crowd's enthusiastic welcome of the Lord with shouts of 'Hosanna!' ('Save us! Bring us salvation!'). We then enter the church to listen to the reading of the Passion from the Gospel of Matthew, or Mark, or Luke. (John's account of the Passion is always read on Good Friday.) And in the acclamation of the Preface, as we do at every celebration of the Mass, we repeat, 'Blessed is he who comes in the name of the Lord! Hosanna in the highest!', as we celebrate the Eucharist, as we re-enact and are made sharers in the one Sacrifice of Christ.

For Catholics, and for all Christians, there is no glory without daily sacrifice; there is no Resurrection victory without the Sacrifice of the Cross. Many Christians remember this connection by saving the palm branches that they receive at Church each year on Palm Sunday. Some place the palm branches around the Crucifix in their home; others fold them into crosses to wear on their clothes on Palm Sunday, or place them in their Bibles, or keep them in a special location at home.

WHAT ABOUT YOU PERSONALLY?

- Consider the connection between sacrifice and glory, between suffering and hope that these palm branches represent. Might you adopt one of the traditions around these to connect with your own life?

JOURNAL EXERCISE

Life is never a 'bed of roses' for anyone. Yet, in the story of Jesus' Transfiguration, we can see a deep connection between suffering and glory, death and new life.

- Reflect on how you can take this wisdom to heart in your own life. How might it help you with a particular issue at this time? Write your thoughts on this in your journal.

PALM SUNDAY IN GRANADA, SPAIN

THINK IT THROUGH

The First Eucharist

THE LAST SUPPER | 19TH-CENTURY GERMAN CHROMOLITHOGRAPH

is 'an efficacious sign of grace, instituted by Christ and entrusted to the Church, by which divine life is dispensed to us by the work of the Holy Spirit' (*United States Catholic Catechism for Adults* [USCCA], 526). When the Church celebrates the Sacraments, much more is happening than we see or hear or taste or touch. The saving work of Christ is taking place among us, and we are being made sharers in it. Our lives are being transformed by the grace of God.

The Eucharist, Jesus' great gift of himself, is indeed much more than words and actions, more than bread and wine. For just as God reached out to us in Jesus at a particular historical moment, so God's **real presence** continues now among us in a unique way in the Eucharist. The great outpouring of God's unconditional love for us in Jesus continues for ever through the Eucharist.

At Mass the Risen Jesus is present among us. He is present in the proclamation of the Scriptures, in the person of the priest and in the people in the pews. 'Christ . . . the eternal high priest of the New Covenant who, acting through the ministry of the priests, offers the Eucharistic sacrifice' (CCC, no. 1410). Above all, Jesus is uniquely present with us in the consecrated bread and wine. What still looks like, feels like and tastes like bread and wine is no longer bread and wine; it is the Body and Blood of Jesus Christ. When we receive Holy Communion, it is Christ himself that we receive.

Under the consecrated species of bread and wine Christ himself, living and glorious, is

REFLECT AND SHARE

- Reflect on the main feeling you associate with going to Mass. Is it positive, negative, or a mixture of both? And why do you think that you feel this way?
- Share with a partner how you might grow in your appreciation of the Eucharist.

MUCH MORE THAN MEETS THE EYE

The seven Sacraments of the Church are visible realities and signs of the invisible saving presence of the Triune God at work in our lives. Each of the seven Sacraments (Baptism, Confirmation, Eucharist, Penance and Reconciliation, Anointing of the Sick, Matrimony and Holy Orders) present in a true, real and substantial manner: his Body and his Blood, with his soul and his divinity.

—CCC, no. 1413

The Eucharist is 'the supreme expression' (CCC, no. 610) of Jesus' free and self-giving love. It is the Son of Man's continuing expression of his free choice to follow and fulfill God's plan of Salvation. The Eucharist is God's pledge of our future glory; it foreshadows the Kingdom of Heaven and is a glimpse of God's heavenly banquet. The Eucharist makes it possible for us to take part in the Paschal Mystery—the Passover of the Lord—in which the sacrificial Lamb of God leads the way from death to new life.

The Eucharist is the 'source and summit' of the Christian life (CCC, no. 1324). Jesus' gift of the Eucharist to the Church reveals who Jesus is. He is 'the living bread that came down from heaven' and 'whoever eats this bread will live for ever; and the bread that I will give for the life of the world is my flesh' (John 6:51). Eating 'the bread of life' and drinking from 'the cup of salvation' brings us into deep personal encounter with the Risen Christ and gives us the strength to live as his disciples in the world. The Eucharist is the spiritual food and drink that feeds our souls and deepens our intimacy with God. In the Eucharist, God's self-giving love continues for ever.

OVER TO YOU

Our participation in the Eucharist is our commitment to share our lives in loving sacrifice and service to the people around us, and especially to those in need.
- How would you describe your participation in the Eucharist?
- What role does the Eucharist have in your life as a disciple of Christ?

THE INSTITUTION NARRATIVE

After many journeys back and forth from Jerusalem, during which Jesus taught and healed, Jesus and his disciples arrived in Jerusalem for the last time, on the eve of the Jewish feast of Passover. Passover is the central feast in the Jewish religion. During Passover, Jews remember that God set them free from slavery in Egypt and established a Covenant of *chesed*—faithful love—with them; they remember and re-enact the events of that frightening and exhilarating night when their ancestors sacrificed and roasted a lamb, painted its blood on the front door of their home, ate the unleavened bread and drank the wine as the angel of death 'passed [them] over', allowing them to escape to freedom through the power of God; they also remember and celebrate that God and his saving love is present and at work among them now. God has been, is, and will always be faithful to the Covenant he entered into with them. (Read Exodus 12:1–13, 28–32.)

'Before he was given up to death, a death he freely accepted', Jesus, the Lamb of God, gave us the Eucharist. At the Last Supper table he changed the unleavened Passover bread and the Passover wine into his own Body and Blood; he gave the transformed bread and wine to his disciples to eat and drink, and he told them to 'do this in memory of me'. Each time the Church celebrates the Eucharist, we make our greatest prayer of thanksgiving to God. The one Sacrifice of Christ is made present again, and we are made sharers in God's greatest act of saving love for his people. St. Paul passed on the faith of the Church in Jesus' institution of the Eucharist. He wrote:

> For I received from the Lord what I also handed on to you, that the Lord Jesus on the night when he was betrayed took a loaf of bread, and when he had given thanks, he broke it and said, 'This is my body that is for you. Do this in remembrance of me.' In the same way he took the cup also, after supper, saying, 'This cup is the new covenant in my blood. Do this, as often as you drink it, in remembrance of me.' For as often as you eat this bread and drink the cup, you proclaim the Lord's death until he comes.
> —1 Corinthians 11:23–26

These words, recorded by St. Paul about thirty years after Jesus died, are the first words in the New Testament that pass on the event of the institution of the Eucharist. The Eucharist's Institution Narrative is also recorded in the later writings of the Synoptic Gospels.

The Eucharist is the celebration of the 'Passover of the Lord'; it is the new and everlasting Passover, the final Exodus. In Jesus, the Passover Lamb of God, God enters the new and everlasting Covenant, freeing us from sin and death, and offering us intimate communion in the Body and Blood of Christ. Like the Passover lamb that is sacrificed and eaten during Passover, 'our paschal lamb, Christ, [is] sacrificed' for us (1 Corinthians 5:7).

SCRIPTURE EXERCISE

- With a partner, check out and compare the accounts of the institution of the Eucharist in Matthew 26:26–30, Mark 14:22–25 and Luke 22:14–23 using 'active reading' markings. (Review the instructions in chapter 1.)
- Discuss what stands out for you in each account.

At Mass, as we conclude the Institution Narrative, the priest proclaims the 'mystery of faith'. We

THE LAST SUPPER | ENGRAVING AFTER ALEXANDRE BIDA

FAITH WORD

Real Presence

When the bread is consecrated, it is changed into Christ's Body. When the wine is consecrated, it is changed into Christ's Blood. Jesus Christ is substantially present in a way that is entirely unique. This happens through the power of the Holy Spirit and the ministry of the priest or bishop acting in the person of Christ during the Eucharistic prayer.
—USCCA, 525

respond, 'Save us, Savior of the world, for by your Cross and Resurrection you have set us free.' How true this is. Every time we celebrate Eucharist, Jesus' Death on the Cross and his Resurrection are re-enacted and made present again and again. We are made sharers in the Passover of the Lord.

OVER TO YOU
- Someone has summarized the relationship between Passover and the Eucharist this way: 'Every Eucharist is an echo of the Passover: God saving us from destruction, God setting us free from slavery.'
- What are some of the slaveries that young people can suffer today?
- Has the celebration of Eucharist ever helped you feel free or helped you to overcome something difficult? Share your story.

A MEMORIAL OF CHRIST'S SACRIFICE

St. Paul proclaimed, 'Our paschal lamb, Christ, has been sacrificed. Therefore, let us celebrate the festival' (1 Corinthians 5:7–8). 'By celebrating the Last Supper with his apostles in the course of the Passover meal, Jesus gave the Jewish Passover its definitive meaning' (CCC, no. 1340). Since the days of the early Church, Jesus' followers have celebrated the Eucharist as 'the memorial of his sacrifice' (CCC, no. 611). 'It was above all on "the first day of the week", Sunday, the day of Jesus' resurrection, that the [first] Christians met "to break bread" ' (CCC, no. 1343).

Since the early Church, Christians have celebrated the Eucharist—Jesus' New Covenant, sealed by his own blood—by remembering his words and repeating his Eucharistic actions. The Eucharist is at the center of Catholic life today, just as it was in the time of the early Church. By the power of the Holy Spirit, the Eucharist is where we encounter the Risen Jesus most intimately, an encounter through which we imagine and are sustained in living as his disciples.

The wording in the Eucharistic Prayers prayed during Mass reflects the meaning of this powerful mystery.

PASSOVER | FACSIMILE OF A 15TH-CENTURY MISSAL MINIATURE

Therefore, O Lord,
as we now celebrate the memorial of our redemption,
we remember Christ's Death
and his descent to the realm of the dead,
we proclaim his Resurrection
and his Ascension to your right hand,
and, as we await his coming in glory,
we offer you his Body and Blood,
the sacrifice acceptable to you
which brings salvation to the whole world.

Look, O Lord, upon the Sacrifice
which you yourself have provided for your Church,
and grant in your loving kindness
to all who partake of this one Bread and one Chalice
that, gathered into one body by the Holy Spirit,
they may truly become a living sacrifice in Christ
to the praise of your glory.
—From Eucharistic Prayer IV

ARMY CHAPLAIN AND NEW ZEALAND TROOPS TAKING HOLY COMMUNION DURING WORLD WAR I

WHAT ABOUT YOU PERSONALLY?
- Think for a moment about your participation in the Eucharist. How deep an experience is it for you? Do you experience it as an encounter with Christ?
- What would you change about the celebration, if you could, to deepen that experience?

Not all the members of the early Church understood fully the depth of the meaning of the Eucharist. The behavior (or mis-behavior) of some Christians at the Eucharist manifested this lack of understanding.

Paul responded to this situation in the Church in Corinth. He taught, 'The cup of blessing that we bless, is it not a sharing in the blood of Christ? The bread that we break, is it not a sharing in the body of Christ?' Then he added, 'Because there is one bread, we who are many are one body, for we all partake of the one bread' (1 Corinthians 10:16–17). Our receiving the Body of Christ bonds us together with all Christians as the Body of Christ in the world. In the Eucharist we are joined to Jesus, and together we give thanks and praise to the Father through the Holy Spirit and renew ourselves as 'one body, one spirit in Christ'.

REFLECT
Reflect on what you have learned about the Eucharist from your work on this section of the chapter.
- How has what you learned opened your eyes to see and your ears to hear what is 'really taking place' at Mass?
- What does your behavior at Mass say about your faith in Christ's presence at Mass?

THINK, PAIR AND SHARE
St. Augustine said, 'We eat the body of Christ to become the body of Christ.' St. Teresa of Ávila said, 'Christ has no body now but yours, no hands, no feet on earth but yours. Yours are the eyes through which he looks with compassion on the world. Yours are the feet with which he walks to do good. Yours are the hands with which he blesses the world.'
- Discuss what these quotations mean for you today.
- How can we connect our celebration of the Eucharist to the world today?

JUDGE AND ACT

REFLECT ON WHAT YOU HAVE LEARNED

In this chapter we have explored three important stories that reveal the true identity of Jesus. In the Wedding at Cana, the Transfiguration and the story of the First Eucharist, Jesus always presents us with much more than meets the eye: a wedding party whose symbolism connects human intimacy with miracle (John 2:1–12), a glimpse of glory and self-sacrifice that lead back down from the mountaintop into the challenges of life (Mark 9:2–10), and a Passover meal that embraces the whole mystery of Salvation (Mark 14:12, 17, 22–25).

- Look back over this chapter and reflect on the images that accompany each of these Gospel stories.
- How do you respond to these stories as a young person on a journey of faith?

LEARN BY EXAMPLE

The story of the martyrs of the University of Central America

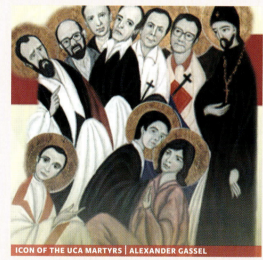

ICON OF THE UCA MARTYRS | ALEXANDER GASSEL

When Obdulio Lozano got up at six in the morning on November 16, 1989, he found eight bodies in the flower garden of the Theological Reflection Center at the University of Central America (UCA) in San Salvador, El Salvador. Two of the bodies were those of his wife, Elba, who was a cook at the university, and his teenage daughter, Celina. The other six victims were Father Ignacio Martín-Baró, the academic president of the university, and five other Jesuit priests, who were teachers and community workers, all murdered by the army during El Salvador's brutal civil war. Elba and Celina had been murdered because they had witnessed the killing of the six Jesuits.

What made these university professors so dangerous? In part, it was the message that their work represented: 'There's more going on in our society than first meets the eye.'

One of the Jesuits, Father Ignacio Martín-Baró, was born in Spain forty-seven years earlier and had worked in El Salvador for twenty-three years as a psychologist and researcher. His work included interviewing, surveying and polling people in order to hear and tell the story of the working class and the poor. His research topics included: the psychological effects of violence (war and gangs; police and army brutality), male and female imagery in media and society, the realities of inner-city life, the effect of unemployment on young people, the psychology of obedience, and—above all—how to get behind 'the hype' of politics and advertising so as to understand what is really going on.

Jesus worked to announce and bring about the Kingdom of God, the world of justice according to which God created and desires all people to live. One way Jesus did this was to reach out to the poor and those suffering from the power of injustice. Father Ignacio Martín-Baró followed the example of Jesus. He was murdered because, in his work of preaching the Gospel and serving the people of El Salvador, he uncovered the voices of ordinary people—people who wanted a better society for themselves, their families and friends. This work helped to amplify the cry for justice in his society, where injustice was often hidden or covered up. He certainly proved that there is always more going on than first meets the eye.

JUDGE AND DECIDE

Jesus' presence in the Gospel that we proclaim and hear and in the Eucharist that we share at Mass gives us strength to step up to the plate and do the same as Father Ignacio Martín-Baró.
- What are the real needs resulting from 'acts of injustice' in your school, your neighborhood and your community?
- How do you step up to the plate and address those needs?

RESPOND WITH FAMILY AND FRIENDS

- Our English word 'Mass' comes from the Latin *missa*, meaning 'to be sent'. As the closing words of the celebrant remind us, the Mass always sends us back out into the world with the commission to live our faith as disciples of Jesus, to be the Body of Christ in the world:
  – Go and announce the Gospel of the Lord.
  – Go in peace, glorifying the Lord by your life.
- Discuss with your family and friends what sources of strength and insight you can find from your faith in Jesus to live up to the challenges presented in the dismissal at the end of the Mass.

WHAT WILL YOU DO NOW?

- What personal decisions—in your head, heart or practice—will you make about the Eucharist?
- How can the Holy Spirit help you to keep these commitments?

LEARN BY HEART

We who are many are one body, for we all partake of the one bread.

1 CORINTHIANS 10:17

PRAYER REFLECTION

The Liturgy of the Hours is the official daily prayer of the Church. The sections of the prayer have been named to correspond with the 'hours' of the day when the members of the Church around the world gather to pray this prayer; hence we have Morning Prayer, Midmorning Prayer, Midday Prayer, Midafternoon Prayer, Evening Prayer and Nighttime Prayer. Our prayer reflection for this chapter is from Midday Prayer on the Solemnity of the Transfiguration.

Opening

LEADER
Sit quietly and remember that you are—as always—in the presence of God. (*Pause*)
God, come to my assistance.

ALL
Lord, make haste to help me.
Glory to the Father, and to the Son, and to Holy Spirit:
as it was in the beginning, is now, and will be for ever. Amen. Alleluia.

Hymn

ALL
Help us, O Lord, to learn
The truths thy Word imparts:
To study that thy laws may be
Inscribed on our hearts.

Help us, O Lord, to live
The faith which we proclaim,

> **God our Father,
> in the transfigured glory of
> Christ your Son,
> you strengthened our faith**

That all our thoughts and words and deeds
May glorify your name.

Help us, O Lord, to teach
The beauty of your ways,
That yearning souls may find in Christ,
And sing aloud his praise.

Psalm

LEADER
By his Gospel our Lord and Savior has lighted up for us the way to life and immortality.

GROUP 1
To you have I lifted up my eyes,
you who dwell in the heavens:
my eyes, like the eyes of slaves
on the hand of their lords.

GROUP 2
Like the eyes of a servant
on the hand of her mistress,
so our eyes are on the Lord our God
till he show us his mercy.

GROUP 1
Have mercy on us, Lord, have mercy.
We are filled with contempt.
Indeed all too full is our soul
with the scorn of the rich,
with the proud man's disdain.

ALL
Glory to the Father, and to the Son, and to Holy Spirit:
as it was in the beginning, is now, and will be for ever. Amen. Alleluia. *(Pause)*
By his Gospel our Lord and Savior has lighted up for us the way to life and immortality.

Reading

Reader reads Exodus 33:9 and 11a.

Following the reading, all reflect for a moment in silence.

Concluding Prayer

LEADER
God our Father,
in the transfigured glory of Christ your Son,
you strengthened our faith
by confirming the witness of your prophets,
and showed us the splendor of your beloved sons and daughters.
As we listen to the voice of your Son,
help us to become heirs to eternal life with him
who lives and reigns with you and the Holy Spirit,
one God, for ever and ever.

ALL
Amen.

LEADER
Look to the Lord and be enlightened.

ALL
And never let your faces be ashamed.

CHAPTER 7

Victory from the Jaws of Death

**JESUS CHRIST—
THE KEY TO UNDERSTANDING
THE MYSTERY OF SUFFERING**

- CHRISTIANS VIEW SUFFERING WITH THE EYES OF FAITH
- GOD PROMISED TO 'SAVE' US

- WE BELIEVE THAT GOD WALKS WITH US IN GOOD TIMES AND BAD
- IN JESUS WE SEE THE FULFILLMENT OF GOD'S PROMISE

- GOD IS NOT THE CAUSE OF SUFFERING
- IN JESUS' PASSION GOD SUFFERED WITH US AND FOR US

- SUFFERING IS THE RESULT OF THE REJECTION OF GOD'S PLAN
- JESUS DIED TO BRING ABOUT THE KINGDOM OF GOD'S LOVE

THE CROSS MEANS 'NEVER GIVE UP!'

JESUS IS THE SOURCE OF

- SALVATION
- JUSTIFICATION
- REDEMPTION
- SANCTIFICATION
- LIBERATION
- RECONCILIATION
- NEW CREATION
- ADOPTION AS GOD'S OWN CHILDREN

IN THIS CHAPTER WE EXAMINE MORE FULLY THE amazing dogma of Christian faith: 'Christ died for our sins in accordance with the Scriptures' (1 Corinthians 15:3). This chapter looks at only one aspect of the Paschal Mystery, the Death of Jesus, and must be coupled with the next two chapters on the Resurrection and Ascension. We explore how Jesus' death on a cross was the turning point in God's work of Salvation and that 'God's saving plan was accomplished "once for all" by the redemptive death of his Son' (*Catechism of the Catholic Church*, no. 571).

LEARNING OUTCOMES

As a result of studying this chapter and exploring the issues raised, you should be able to:

- understand the Church's teaching on human suffering;
- understand the meaning of Jesus' decision to accept suffering and death;
- understand the political, religious and historical context of first-century Palestine;
- appreciate the motivation of those who persecuted and crucified Jesus;
- recognize that the Catholic Church does not blame Jews for the crucifixion of Jesus;
- identify examples of people snatching victory from defeat;
- understand the connection between Jesus' Death and the promise God made to send a Savior who would conquer evil and sin;
- explore the Gospel accounts of Jesus' Agony in the Garden;
- identify the common evils that tempt young people;
- understand the Church's teaching that Jesus was fully human and fully divine;
- reflect on Jesus' Death as the ultimate agape love story;
- understand why the Cross means 'Never give up!';
- identify the aspects of society and of your own life that are in need of a savior or redeemer;
- be familiar with the different elements of Holy Week.

FAITH-FORMATION OUTCOMES

As a result of studying this chapter and exploring the issues raised, you should also:

- realize that human suffering can have meaning;
- understand that Jesus willingly endured crucifixion for you;
- experience the suffering and Death of Jesus as a source of courage for you;
- reflect on how you can challenge religious discrimination;
- come to a deeper understanding of what Jesus' life and Death means for you;
- recognize how faith in Jesus can help you deal with temptation;
- value the Cross as a symbol of hope and redemption;
- identify ways in which God's work of Salvation and Redemption can continue through you;
- be inspired by the story of Sr. Maura Clarke;
- consider having a crucifix in your bedroom or study area.

LEARN BY HEART: 1 Corinthians 15:3

LEARN BY EXAMPLE: Sr. Maura Clarke

ATTEND AND REFLECT

What is the meaning of suffering?

OPENING CONVERSATION

In the Hail, Holy Queen, a traditional prayer to Mary, we pray, 'To you do we send up our sighs, mourning and weeping in this valley of tears.' Suffering is a part of every human life. It is also true that great joy and happiness come our way. Yet, even in the best of times, things are never perfect; there always seems to be some kind of suffering intermingled with joy.

- Think of a time in your life when you experienced real suffering.
- What caused the suffering?
- What enabled you to endure the suffering?
- In what ways did your faith help you during your time of suffering?
- Did your experience of suffering contribute in some way to your future experiences of joy?

GROUP ACTIVITY

- Work in small groups. Search through newspapers and magazines for images that reflect suffering in the world today. Cut out the images and paste them onto a large sheet of paper to form a collage.
- Agree on a caption or title for your poster.

A CHALLENGE TO FAITH

For some people the fact of suffering is not only a roadblock to belief in God, but also a reason to deny the existence of God. If God is All-loving and Provident as Christians claim, then why, people ask, is there so much suffering. This question seems all the more reasonable at times when the world is faced with massive suffering of innocent people, as happens with such natural

THE SMOKEY MOUNTAIN RUBBISH DUMP IN MANILLA, PHILIPPINES

disasters as earthquakes and tsunamis or with such moral evils as the genocide during the Holocaust or, more recently, in Rwanda.

DISCUSS

- How might you make an argument in favor of faith in God, in spite of human suffering?

JESUS CHRIST—KEY TO UNDERSTANDING THE MYSTERY OF SUFFERING

Suffering is a 'mystery' that believers and non-believers have always struggled to understand. The use of reason and logic can never fully make sense of this mystery. Christians, however, move beyond logic and reason and view suffering with

150 | CREDO | THE PROMISED ONE: SERVANT AND SAVIOR

the eyes of faith. We deal with our experiences of suffering with God's help. We take God on his Word and trust that he is always present with us. We believe that he walks with us in good times and bad and that he shares in our laughter and in our tears.

From the opening chapters of the Book of Genesis, the Word of God is clear: God is not the cause of suffering or of physical and moral evil. Suffering in all its forms is a direct result of the rejection of God's plan of Creation; it is the consequence of humanity's attempt to go it alone and recreate the world in its own image and according to its own desires. While God did permit Adam and Eve and everyone after them to choose between good and evil, God's response to the human choice to 'go it alone' and turn away from the divine plan of goodness was and is his continuing promise to 'save' us. God promised that he would work with us to restore the world and rebuild creation according to his original plan of goodness.

In Jesus' words and actions we see both the fulfillment of this promise and the true human response to suffering. First, Jesus acknowledged, but never favored or glorified, suffering. In fact, he taught his disciples that they must work against those forces that bring about suffering. Second, in Jesus' Passion, his suffering and Death, we have the amazing testimony of the incarnate Son of God suffering in solidarity with us and for us. Through the Cross, Jesus Christ, in solidarity with all who suffer, gathered up all human suffering, helping all of us to carry our own crosses. No less is expected of us, his disciples. (Read Matthew 16:24–26; Mark 8:34–36; Luke 9:23–25.)

By his Resurrection (which is the focus of chapter 9), Jesus turned his own suffering and the

THE EXPULSION FROM EDEN | ILLUMINATED MANUSCRIPT

suffering of all humanity into new life for all people and for all of creation. In Christ and with Christ we have the power to deal with suffering and overcome it, no matter how painful that may be.

WHAT ABOUT YOU PERSONALLY?

- ◉ What does Jesus' suffering tell you about Jesus? About ourselves?
- ◉ What is your own sense of why Jesus was crucified?
- ◉ What does the symbol of the Cross mean to your own faith?

CHAPTER 7: VICTORY FROM THE JAWS OF DEATH | ATTEND AND REFLECT | 151

TALK IT OVER

Generally, people do not willingly take on suffering. However, there are times when people decide to accept suffering freely and do something that is really difficult for the sake of another person or for a cause or a belief that is dear to them—such as living as a disciple of Christ.

- Do you know any stories of people in your own family or in your neighborhood who chose to suffer for the sake of someone else or to achieve a goal in life? Share your story.
- Has anyone ever done something difficult on your behalf? What did they do and why do you think they did it?
- Did you ever act in a way that caused you to suffer on behalf of someone else, or because you believed passionately in something? If so, what was your motivation?
- What role did your Christian faith play in motivating your decision and in sustaining your actions?

JESUS FREELY ACCEPTED SUFFERING— THE CRUCIFIXION

Jesus' faithfulness to his Father and the mission he was sent to accomplish resulted in his execution by crucifixion. This was a reality that Jesus faced with great anxiety and wished might be otherwise (see Matthew 26:36–46), but that he freely accepted as the consequence of the fulfillment of his mission as the Savior of the world. In explaining the parable of the Good Shepherd, Jesus said, 'No one takes [my] life from me, but I lay it down of my own accord' (John 10:18).

The cruel practice of punishing capital crimes by crucifixion was legendary in the ancient world of Jesus' time. So, when Jesus was falsely and unjustly executed in this fashion, the members of the early Church had no need for graphic descriptions to convey the horrific nature of his death. That Jesus would willingly accept death by crucifixion to accomplish the divine plan of Salvation was beyond the comprehension of his disciples. Given the miracles that Jesus' disciples

THE CRUCIFIXION | GERHARD REMISCH

152 | CREDO | THE PROMISED ONE: SERVANT AND SAVIOR

THE CRUCIFIXION | MODOVITA MONASTERY, ROMANIA

witnessed him performing throughout his life, they would certainly have believed that he, the Son of God, could have avoided this cruel and excruciating suffering. Even Peter the Apostle rebuked Jesus for saying he must suffer and die. 'And Peter took him aside and began to rebuke him. But turning and looking at his disciples, [Jesus] rebuked Peter and said, 'Get behind me, Satan! For you are setting your mind not on divine things but on human things' (Mark 8:32–33).

OVER TO YOU
⊙ Have you ever wondered why Jesus would freely accept death by crucifixion? Explain.

In the eyes of many onlookers, Jesus' death by crucifixion was the highest form of public shame. There was nothing glorious or splendid about Calvary, also called 'The Place of the Skull' because the Romans left the bones of corpses on the hill as a warning to those who might revolt against Rome. For many of Jesus' disciples, the trauma was so dreadful and beyond their comprehension that they avoided being with him as he hung on the Cross. And, after his Death, they struggled to come to grips with the fact that their Lord and Messiah and great Teacher had died such an ignominious death. They did not understand fully what was taking place. That understanding would come later after Jesus had risen from the dead.

JOURNAL EXERCISE
Imagine yourself in Peter's position. You had left your job as a fisherman, from which you earned your livelihood and supported your family, in order to follow Jesus. You had stayed with him and traveled with him for three years. Now this man, for whom you had given up everything, has been arrested and is on trial to be shamefully executed as a criminal. Imagine you are Peter.
⊙ What are your thoughts?
⊙ What are your questions?
⊙ What might be your hopes for the future?
⊙ Write your reflections in your journal.

GROUP DISCUSSION
In the remainder of this chapter we will explore the meaning of the Passion, the suffering and Death, of Jesus. Meantime, gather in small groups and talk about what the Passion means for you now.
⊙ What parts of the Passion Narrative stand out in your mind?
⊙ What do you find most shocking or most comforting about what you remember?
⊙ What do you think you still need to learn?

CHAPTER 7: VICTORY FROM THE JAWS OF DEATH | ATTEND AND REFLECT | 153

HEAR THE STORY

The Cross: A sign of contradiction

OPENING CONVERSATION

In first-century Palestine, many Jews were hoping for a political messiah to overcome Roman rule and to restore the earthly kingdom of Israel. Some of Jesus' disciples, as the conversation on the Road to Emmaus revealed (see Luke 24:21), were among these people. Because Christ failed to meet these expectations, Paul would later write, 'We proclaim Christ crucified, a stumbling-block to Jews and foolishness to Gentiles' (1 Corinthians 1:23).

⊙ Why might Jesus' death on the Cross appear as 'a stumbling-block to Jews and foolishness to Gentiles' (non-Jews)'?

⊙ What is your response to knowing that Jesus took upon himself the horrendous suffering of crucifixion for all people—and would have done so just for you?

HISTORICAL AND POLITICAL CONTEXT OF THE CRUCIFIXION

At the time of Jesus, Judea was under the control of the Roman Republic for many years. In 4 BC, after the death of King Herod the Great, a Jew, the situation in Palestine became unstable. The Roman Emperor sent a governor to keep a lid on the situation and quell any sign of rebellion. Pontius Pilate, the fifth governor, was in power at the time of Jesus. During Pilate's governance, Jews had the freedom to run their own religious affairs, including the management of the Temple in Jerusalem. Thousands of Jewish pilgrims from all parts of the ancient world came to the Temple annually, especially at Passover time. This influx of people became, in Roman eyes, a potential cause for political uprisings.

It was during Passover that Jesus entered the city of Jerusalem to the acclaim of a crowd who chanted, 'Blessed is the king who comes in the name of the Lord!' Taking note of what was happening, some of the Pharisees, because of their fear of a negative Roman reaction, called out to Jesus, 'Teacher, order your disciples to stop.' Adding to their dismay, Jesus responded, 'I tell you, if these were silent, the stones would shout out' (Luke 19:38–40). In the eyes of the Pharisees, their worst fears—and the fears of a crackdown by Rome—were coming true. It was during this, the last, visit to Jerusalem that the tensions between Jesus and some of the key leaders of the Jews came to a head.

154 | CREDO | THE PROMISED ONE: SERVANT AND SAVIOR

The four accounts of the Gospel detail many other occasions that contributed to the conflict between Jesus and the Pharisees, scribes and other leaders. For example, John's Gospel tells the story of Jesus visiting the home of Martha and Mary and raising their brother Lazarus to life. This happened as Jesus and his disciples were *en route* to Jerusalem to celebrate their last Passover together. John the Evangelist gives his account of what happened:

The chief priests and the Pharisees called a meeting of the council, and said, 'What are we to do? This man is performing many signs. If we let him go on like this, everyone will believe in him, and the Romans will come and destroy both our holy place and our nation.' But one of them, Caiaphas, who was high priest that year, said to them, 'You know nothing at all! You do not understand that it is better for you to have one man die for the people than to have the whole nation destroyed.'

—John 11:47–50

OVER TO YOU

◉ What examples of conflict between religion and politics can you give from your study of history or your knowledge of contemporary events? How do these conflicts seem to be resolved? In favor of religion or in favor of 'politics'? Explain.

◉ Have you ever experienced a conflict in your own life between your religious beliefs and society's concerns? Explain.

JESUS AND THE JEWISH LAW

The animosity and anger that Jesus experienced from the Pharisees and some of the other Jewish leaders was not only the result of their political concerns. They often criticized Jesus for not following Jewish religious laws. Mark, in chapter 3 of his account of the Gospel, writes that Jesus, from the very beginning of his public ministry, experienced such animosity from the Pharisees. Mark tells us that, on one

occasion, Jesus and his disciples were hungry and stopped to get something to eat on the Sabbath, an action that was against Jewish law. Witnessing what Jesus was doing, the Pharisees accused Jesus of violating the command to 'keep holy the Sabbath day'. As Jesus and his disciples continued on to the synagogue, the Pharisees followed them, waiting to see if Jesus would continue to violate the Sabbath law. On entering the synagogue, Jesus invited a man 'who had a withered hand' to come to him. Jesus, knowing well that the Pharisees were out to get him, openly confronted them:

'Is it lawful to do good or do harm on the sabbath, to save life or to kill?' But they were silent. He looked around at them with anger; he was grieved at their hardness of heart and said

JESUS RAISING LAZARUS FROM THE TOMB | JAMES TISSOT

JESUS HEALING THE SICK | JAMES TISSOT

Yet others came to believe in Jesus, 'but because of the Pharisees they did not confess it, for fear that they would be put out of the synagogue: for they loved human glory more than the glory that comes from God' (John 12:42–43).

REFLECTIVE EXERCISE

John the Evangelist tells us the faith story of Nicodemus. Work with a partner and follow the three appearances of Nicodemus within John's Gospel. Begin with John 3:1–21, then read John 7:50 and 19:39. Then discuss:

- What is your interpretation of the Nicodemus story?
- Why do you think Nicodemus didn't publicly become a disciple from the beginning?
- Why do you think he came back to help bury Jesus?
- Do you imagine that he eventually became a disciple? Why or why not?
- When do you take risks because of your faith in Jesus?

JESUS PREDICTED HIS OWN CRUCIFIXION

Jesus predicted that he would suffer and die because of his works and teachings. For example, in the Gospel of Mark Jesus, after he had cured a boy 'with an unclean spirit', pulled his disciples aside from the crowds and said to them, '"The Son of Man is to be betrayed into human hands, and they will kill him, and three days after being killed, he will rise again." But they did not understand what he was saying and were afraid to ask him' (Mark 9:31–32). On another occasion, as Jesus and his disciples were traveling to Jerusalem to celebrate Passover for the last time:

to the man, 'Stretch out your hand.' He stretched it out, and his hand was restored. The Pharisees went out and immediately conspired with the Herodians against him, how to destroy him.

—Mark 3:3–6

Some of the Pharisees and other Jewish leaders truly believed that what Jesus had been teaching and doing throughout the land was contrary to Jewish law. Jesus' healing the sick and forgiving sinners were actions that they believed belonged to God alone. Other leaders and prominent Jews, such as Nicodemus and Joseph of Arimathea, did not judge Jesus so quickly and came to believe in him. These Jews followed Jesus at great risk to their position in Jewish society.

[Jesus] took the twelve disciples aside by themselves, and said to them on the way, 'See, we are going up to Jerusalem, and the Son of Man will be handed over to the chief priests and scribes, and they will condemn him to death; then they will hand him over to the Gentiles to

156 | CREDO | THE PROMISED ONE: SERVANT AND SAVIOR

be mocked and flogged and crucified; and on the third day he will be raised.

—Matthew 20:17–19

Throughout his public ministry Jesus experienced growing animosity and plotting against him and it became clearer and clearer to him that he would suffer and die because of his works and teachings. During all of this, Jesus faced his impending suffering and death with extraordinary resolve.

REFLECT

- ◉ What do you think it felt like for Jesus to be aware of the suffering and death he would inevitably face?
- ◉ What do you think helped him to 'keep on', to keep his resolve?
- ◉ When have you suspected or known the painful consequences of standing up for the truth? How did you feel as you faced what you knew you had to do?
- ◉ What helped you? Did you turn to Jesus?

THE CHARGES AGAINST JESUS

Once they resolved that Jesus had to die 'for the sake of the nation', the Jewish authorities decided to put Jesus on trial quickly. But they could not do this on their own. The Jews had no power to condemn a person to death; that was reserved by Roman law for the Governor. If the Jewish leaders wanted to execute Jesus they would need two trials, one before the High Priest and the second before Pilate. So, the Jewish leaders, especially the Temple priesthood, accused Jesus, and they drummed up support and put pressure on Pilate to try, convict and condemn Jesus to death. Pilate, afraid of threats to report him to Rome, gave in to the pressure.

Scholars point out that the authorities made two accusations against Jesus. First, Jesus committed blasphemy by claiming to be God and predicting the destruction of the Temple. Second, Jesus had committed a crime against Roman law because he claimed to be a king in opposition to Caesar and caused a riot in Galilee. (See CCC, no. 596.)

CHRIST BEFORE PILATE | MIHALY MUNKACSY

CHAPTER 7: VICTORY FROM THE JAWS OF DEATH | HEAR THE STORY | 157

LET'S PROBE DEEPER: A SCRIPTURE EXERCISE

Work in groups of four. Each member of the group reads, explores the meaning of and applies 'active reading' marks (see instructions in chapter 1) to one of these four Gospel passages: Matthew 26:57—27:24; Mark 14:53—15:15; Luke 23:1—25; John 18:12—19:16. Discuss your findings, using these questions:

- ⊙ What were the precise charges laid against Jesus by the High Priest in the Council and by the leaders before Pilate?
- ⊙ Why do you think Pilate acted as he did?
- ⊙ Give examples of times when you were aware of someone acting in this way.
- ⊙ Name one good lesson you learned from your reading of these texts.

WHO CRUCIFIED JESUS?

The Gospel presentation of the response of the Jewish leaders to Jesus and of the arrest and trial of Jesus has led many Christians to falsely accuse 'all' Jews of having Jesus killed. This false accusation of Jews has been used as an excuse to justify the oppression and persecution of Jews by Christians for many centuries. For example, during the Second World War, anti-Semitism culminated in the Holocaust, one of history's most heinous crimes. The perverse attitude that underlies this oppression and persecution is called anti-Semitism.

The Catholic Church teaches clearly that this false and dangerous charge of holding all Jews, past and present, responsible for the death of Jesus is evil and erroneous, and must end and should never be repeated again. The Church at the Second Vatican Council taught 'neither all Jews indiscriminately at that time, nor Jews today, can be charged with the crimes committed during [Jesus'] passion', and it explicitly condemned 'all hatreds, persecutions [and] displays of anti-Semitism leveled at any time or from any source against the Jews' (*Declaration on the Relation of the Church to Non-Christian Religions*, no. 4).

All we can reasonably conclude from the Gospel account is that *some* Jewish religious leaders and the Roman authorities in Jerusalem co-operated in trying and condemning and crucifying Jesus. The vast majority of the Jewish people at that time, and all of them since, are guiltless of Jesus' death. (See CCC, no. 597.) Perhaps the most touching and public moment of the Church's expression of sorrow at this 'dark' aspect of her history was Blessed Pope John Paul II's historic apology on behalf of the Church when he placed this signed note in the Wailing Wall during his visit to Jerusalem in March 2000:

God of our fathers, you chose Abraham and his descendants to bring your Name to the Nations: we are deeply saddened by the behavior of those who in the course of history have caused these your children to suffer, and asking your forgiveness we wish to commit ourselves to genuine brotherhood with the people of the Covenant.

POPE JOHN PAUL II PLACES A NOTE IN THE WAILING WALL, MARCH 2000

158 | CREDO | THE PROMISED ONE: SERVANT AND SAVIOR

In reality, all sinners, Christian and non-Christian, were the authors of Christ's Passion. 'Taking into account that our sins affect Christ himself, the Church does not hesitate to impute to Christians the gravest responsibility for the torments inflicted upon Jesus, a responsibility with which they have all too often burdened the Jews alone' (CCC, no. 598).

OVER TO YOU

The Church condemns all forms of discrimination and calls on Christians to respect people of all religious traditions.

⊙ Have you experienced instances of anti-Semitism or of prejudice toward people of other faiths?

⊙ How can Christians finally put an end to such acts of discrimination—as our faith demands?

For Pilate and the Roman authorities, the Crucifixion of Jesus involved a bit of diplomacy and legal footwork. For the Jewish leaders, it was a damage-control exercise to avoid the disaster that a full-blown Jewish revolt would have brought down on the Temple, city and nation. The Jewish Council deliberated and quickly settled on a verdict. For the Roman soldiers, the crucifixion of Jesus was part of a routine working day in a foreign posting, and they obediently and efficiently discharged their duty. For the onlookers, they were witnessing just another execution.

For the first disciples the suffering and Death of Jesus was a dreadful let-down, representing a seemingly tragic end to their hopes. But a new light, in just three days, would be shed on the tragedy of the Crucifixion, when their sorrow would be turned into overwhelming joy.

REFLECT AND DISCUSS

Christians came to name the day of Jesus' Death 'Good Friday'. We have the gift of seeing the Crucifixion in light of the Resurrection; we can see both Jesus' suffering and our own in a 'less tragic' light. Pause for a moment and listen to a reflection on these events.

The Crucifixion

This was a rough death, there was nothing tidy about it,
No sweetness, nothing noble.
Everything stuck out awkwardly and angular;
The clumsy soldier brought the wrong basket of nails. . . .
But later on, the heart edits them lovingly,
Abstracts the jeers and jags, imports a plan
Into the pain, and calls it history.
We always go back to gloss over some roughness,
To make the past happen properly as we want it to happen.
But this was a hard death. At the time,
There was no room for thought.
How often he had rehearsed and rehearsed this hour.
But when you come up against it all the good words about it
Are less than breath. It is hard to turn the other cheek
When both have been slapped.

⊙ Which lines from this poem do you find surprising or disturbing?

⊙ Which lines say most about the reality of the crucifixion of Jesus?

⊙ At this point, what is your own best understanding of the Crucifixion?

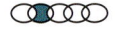 CHAPTER 7: VICTORY FROM THE JAWS OF DEATH | HEAR THE STORY | 159

EMBRACE THE VISION

Victory from defeat

OPENING CONVERSATION

- Identify examples of people who have experienced very difficult situations, perhaps in the world of sport or as a result of natural disasters, but have managed to turn such difficulties into success stories.
- Have there been times in your own life when you were in a situation that looked like disaster or when your own seeming failure was turned into success? What caused the situation to turn around? And where did you find the courage to persevere to the end?
- How can Christian faith help in such challenging situations?
- How does your own experience of suffering help you to understand how the disciples felt about the Death of Jesus?

GOD REMAINS FAITHFUL

For the disciples, the Death of Jesus was not just a setback, a twist in the road; rather, it seemed to mark the end of all their hopes and expectations. Recall the words of the disciples walking from Jerusalem to Emmaus (Luke 24:13–53). Furthermore, they were aware that Jesus had freely chosen his Passion and Death. At that time they did not understand that this was part of God's plan of Salvation.

So where did it all begin? What wisdom does God's Word in Scripture reveal to help us understand these tragic events? 'Our salvation flows from God's initiative of love for us. . .' (CCC, no. 620).

As we have studied already, it all began with our first ancestors' free and knowing choice to reject God's original plan of Creation. In the biblical account of the Fall the sacred author portrays God explaining to Adam and Eve the consequences of their choice—after they try to excuse it away. Pain, suffering and hardship would now be part of human life. While God commanded Adam and Eve to leave the Garden, God did not abandon them or the original divine plan.

While humanity would suffer, suffering would not be the final result of people's sin. God did not condemn our first ancestors and their descendants (humanity) to 'eternal' suffering, pain, punishment and separation from his love. God promised to send them a Savior who would conquer evil and sin (revisit Genesis 3:15). The woman's 'offspring' would 'strike the head' of the serpent, the symbol of evil. We now know that Jesus Christ is the woman's 'offspring'.

160 | CREDO | THE PROMISED ONE: SERVANT AND SAVIOR

JESUS—SAVIOR, MESSIAH AND SUFFERING SERVANT

Jesus was the One promised by God. He was the Savior and Messiah, who would victoriously and definitively defeat death and evil through his own suffering and Death. Jesus' whole life was both an offering to his Father and a commitment to the divine plan of Salvation. 'The desire to embrace his Father's plan of redeeming love inspired Jesus' whole life [see Luke 12:50, 22:15; Matthew 16:21–23]' (CCC, no. 607). Jesus' personal participation in the struggle and battle between good and evil, between the Kingdom of God and the kingdom of this world, was central to God's work of our Salvation and, hence, to the mission of Jesus. St. Paul sums it up thus, 'Just as one man's trespass led to condemnation for all, so one man's act of righteousness leads to justification and life for all. For just as by the one man's disobedience the many were made sinners, so by the one man's obedience the many will be made righteous' (Romans 5:18–19).

This mission of the Messiah and his unfailing commitment to the divine plan of Salvation was proclaimed in the Old Testament. In the sixth century before the coming of Christ, during the Exile of God's people, God chose the prophet Isaiah, who, to the surprise of many of his contemporaries (as it was for many of the Jews in the time of Jesus), described the Savior as One who would suffer because of his faithfulness to the LORD (YHWH). The Messiah would be a Suffering Servant.

He was despised and rejected by others;
    a man of suffering . . . and infirmity;
and as one from whom others hide their faces
    he was despised, and we held him of no account.
                                        —Isaiah 53:3

[L]ike a lamb that is led to the slaughter,
    and like a sheep that before its shearers is
        silent,
    so he did not open his mouth. . . .

ISAIAH | SAINT-GERMAIN-L'AUXERROIS, PARIS, FRANCE

They made his grave with the wicked
    and his tomb with the rich,
although he had done no violence,
    and there was no deceit in his mouth. . . .
The righteous one, my servant, shall make
        many righteous,
    and he shall bear their iniquities.
                                —Isaiah 53:7, 9, 11b

EXPLORE THE TEXT

- Read Isaiah 53:1–12. Pause and reflect as you read, and apply active reading' marks (see instructions in chapter 1).
- Which lines appeal most to you as a summary of the meaning of the Death of Jesus?
- How would you explain the Death of Jesus in your own words?

Jesus fulfilled all the characteristics of the 'suffering Servant' prophesied by Isaiah. 'By his loving obedience to the Father, "unto death, even death on a cross"' (see Philippians 2:8), Jesus fulfills the atoning mission (see Isaiah 53:10) of the suffering Servant, who will "make many righteous; and he shall bear their iniquities"' (CCC, no. 623).

OVER TO YOU

One of the most memorable acts of Jesus, the servant of God, was his washing of his disciples' feet at the Last Supper. Read that story again in John 13:1–20. Notice the sentence, 'So if I, your Lord and Teacher, have washed your feet, you also ought to wash one another's feet' (John 13:14). On another occasion Jesus said, 'The Son of Man has come not to be served but to serve, and to give his life a ransom for many' (Mark 10:45).

⊙ As a disciple of Jesus, you are an 'apprentice' to the Suffering Servant. Do you consider yourself an apprentice to Jesus, the Suffering Servant? Explain.

⊙ What are the implications of being such a 'servant'?

THE AGONY IN THE GARDEN: THE PASSION BEGINS

All three Synoptic Gospels tell of Jesus' Agony in the Garden, the night before his Crucifixion. There, we are told, he experienced the beginning of the pain he would soon suffer on Calvary. Read carefully Luke's version.

[Jesus] came out and went, as was his custom, to the Mount of Olives; and the disciples followed him. When he reached the place, he said to them, 'Pray that you may not come into the time of trial.' Then he withdrew from them about a

Events of the Passion

1. BETRAYAL BY JUDAS
MARK 14:10–11 **MATTHEW** 26:14–16
LUKE 22:3–6 **JOHN** 13:1–4

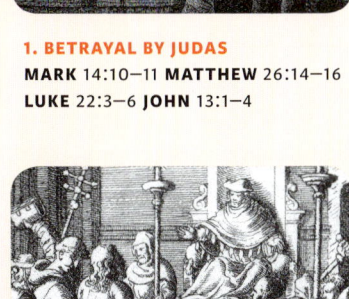

2. AGONY IN THE GARDEN OF GETHSEMANE
MARK 14:32–42 **MATTHEW** 26:36–46
LUKE 22:39–46 **JOHN** 18:1–9

3. ARREST AND IMPRISONMENT
MARK 14:43–52 **MATTHEW** 26:47–56
LUKE 22:47–53 **JOHN** 18:10–11

4. TRIAL BEFORE THE HIGH PRIEST
MARK 14:53–65 **MATTHEW** 26:57–68
LUKE 22:54A, 66–71 **JOHN** 18:12–14,
19:19–24

5. BETRAYAL BY PETER
MARK 14:66–72 **MATTHEW** 27:69–75
LUKE 22:54B–62 **JOHN** 18:15–18,
19:25–27

stone's throw, knelt down, and prayed, 'Father, if you are willing, remove this cup from me; yet, not my will but yours be done.' [Then an angel from heaven appeared to him and gave him strength. In his anguish he prayed more earnestly, and his sweat became like great drops of blood falling down on the ground.] When he got up from prayer, he came to the disciples and found them sleeping because of grief, and he said to them, 'Why are you sleeping? Get up and pray that you may not come into the time of trial.'

—Luke 22:39–46

TALK IT OVER

⊙ What does Jesus' prayer to his Father in the Garden of Gethsemane tell us about how he felt at that time?

⊙ What does it tell us about the reality of his suffering? (*Note:* Doctors tell us that the sweating of blood is a sign of extraordinary human stress.)

⊙ Twice Jesus tells the disciples to pray for the same thing. Why was this?

⊙ Imagine yourself in the position of one of the disciples of Jesus on that night. What would you have prayed for?

LET'S PROBE DEEPER

Now read about the Agony in the Garden in Matthew 26:36–46 and Mark 14:32–42. Compare Luke's account with the account in the other two Synoptics.

⊙ How does reading about Jesus' Agony in the Garden help you to understand the cost of being a faithful disciple of Jesus?

JOURNAL EXERCISE

⊙ Write the story of the Passion in one narrative, combining all the elements found in the four accounts of the Gospels.

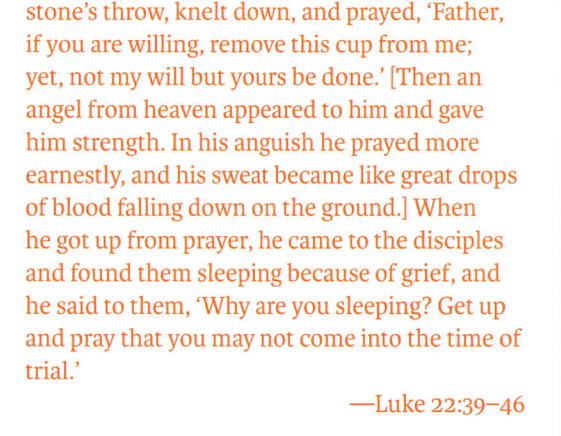

6. TRIAL BEFORE PILATE
MARK 15:1–15 **MATTHEW** 27:11–26
LUKE 23:1–5, 13–25 **JOHN** 18:28–40, 19:4–16

7. TRIAL BEFORE HEROD
LUKE 23:6–12

8. MOCKERY AND SCOURGING
MARK 15:16–20 **MATTHEW** 27:27–31
LUKE 22:63–65 **JOHN** 19:1–3

9. CARRYING THE CROSS
MARK 15:21 **MATTHEW** 27:32
LUKE 23:26–31 **JOHN** 19:17

10. CRUCIFIXION AND DEATH
MARK 15:22–40 **MATTHEW** 27:33–56
LUKE 23:32–49 **JOHN** 19:18–37

11 BURIAL
MARK 15:42–47 **MATTHEW** 27:57–61
LUKE 23:50–56 **JOHN** 19:38–42

CHAPTER 7: VICTORY FROM THE JAWS OF DEATH | EMBRACE THE VISION | 163

THINK IT THROUGH

The Passion of Jesus—its meaning for our life

JESUS PRAYING IN THE GARDEN OF GETHSEMANE | ST.-MICHAELS-KIRCHE, VERINGENDORF, GERMANY

Son of Mary, you learned that throughout the history of the Church theologians have striven to understand the Mystery of the union of the divine nature and a human nature in the one divine Person, Jesus Christ. Sometimes, in their efforts and desire to understand this great Mystery of Faith, theologians would overemphasize Jesus' divinity to the detriment or even denial of his humanity. Other times, they would overemphasize Jesus' humanity to the detriment or even denial of his divinity.

The human soul that the Son of God assumed is endowed with a true human knowledge. As such, this knowledge could not in itself be unlimited: it was exercised in the historical conditions of his existence in space and time. This is why the Son of God could, when he became man, 'increase in wisdom and in stature, and in favor with God and man' [Luke 2:52], and would even have to inquire for himself about what one in the human condition can learn only from experience.

—CCC, no. 472

Similarly . . . Christ possesses two wills and two natural operations, divine and human. They are not opposed to each other, but cooperate in such a way that the Word made flesh willed humanly in obedience to his Father all that he had decided divinely with the Father and the Holy Spirit for our salvation.

—CCC, no. 475

OPENING CONVERSATION

Imagine you are in the presence of Jesus. He encourages you, as he encouraged the disciples in the Garden of Gethsemane just before his arrest, 'Pray that you may not come into the time of trial' (Luke 22:46).

- ◉ What might be the times of trial in your life at present?
- ◉ What evil might be a threat to you at this time?
- ◉ Where do you find the vision and strength to deal with the 'trials', temptations' and 'threats' that you encounter?

JESUS—FULLY HUMAN, FULLY DIVINE

Jesus, the incarnate Son of God, was truly human and truly divine, true God and true man. In the second book of the *Credo* series, *Son of God and*

164 | CREDO | THE PROMISED ONE: SERVANT AND SAVIOR

The Nicene Creed, which we often profess at Mass on Sundays and on other feasts of the Church, was the result of the Church's efforts, under the guidance of the Holy Spirit, to state in human language this great Mystery.

Thus the Church clearly teaches that Jesus was fully divine *and* fully human in all ways except sin. Some today, as in the past, explain the Passion, the suffering and Death of Jesus, in a way that minimizes his humanity. They falsely claim that because he was truly divine he knew all about the dreadful human experiences that awaited him, which lessened the human pain and suffering he had to endure; that it was not really the same for him as it would be for a human person. Scripture clearly reveals that this position represents a false understanding of the Mystery of the Incarnation. It is clear from Jesus' Agony in the Garden that he experienced great human fear and anxiety as he came face to face with his Passion.

A DEATH FOR LOVE

The greatest act of a person, the greatest virtue, is 'love'. (See 1 Corinthians 13:13.) There are many 'love stories' of people 'dying for love of another'; some of these stories are true (for example, the love that motivated St. Maximilian Kolbe), others are fictional (such as the love of Romeo and Juliet). Recall for a moment what you learned about love in the second text of the *Credo* series, *Son of God and Son of Mary*, where you explored the difference between *eros* and *agape*. Unlike eros, agape is the love that is given totally for another. It is the love that motivates a person to give themselves so completely and unselfishly that they are willing, knowingly and freely, to sacrifice their life for another.

'The Redemption won by Christ consists in this, that . . . "he loved [his own] to the end" [see John 13:1]' (CCC, no. 621). St. Paul used the Greek word *kenosis*, which means 'an emptying', to help us understand the depth of God's love for us revealed in the Incarnation and in the suffering, Death and Resurrection of Jesus. The word *kenosis* reveals Jesus' love to be total and unconditional. It is agape. Take a moment and reread Paul's hymn in Philippians 2:5–11.

John the Evangelist also helps us understand this mystery of divine love. Sharing the faith of the Apostolic Church, he wrote: 'God so loved the world that he gave his only Son, so that everyone who believes in him may not perish but may have eternal life' (John 3:16). God the Father sent Jesus out of love for humankind, and Jesus lived and died (and rose again) because of his love for his Father and his love for us. Jesus' love for his Father and for humanity is the ultimate agape love story.

The sacrificial Death of Jesus was the consequence of the love that he had preached, in both deeds and words, throughout his life. Jesus died to bring about the Kingdom of God's

THE CRUCIFIXION | ENGRAVING AFTER ALEXANDRE BIDA

CHAPTER 7: VICTORY FROM THE JAWS OF DEATH | THINK IT THROUGH | 165

When have you been challenged to fight against sin and evil? What role did your faith play?

love. During his life he had denounced sin, evil, hypocrisy and deceit. His life lived to show the Kingdom of God alive in the world led to his persecution and death.

OVER TO YOU
- ⊙ When have you been challenged to fight against sin and evil?
- ⊙ How did you fare?
- ⊙ What role did your faith play?
- ⊙ What role might it play in the future?

WE ARE NO LONGER ENSLAVED TO SIN

In the lead up to Jesus' Passion and right through his suffering on the Cross, his love for others was foremost in his mind and heart.

Holy Father, protect them in your name that you have given me.... I am not asking you to take them out of the world, but I ask you to protect them from the evil one.... Sanctify them in the truth.... I ask not only on behalf of these, but also on behalf of those who will believe in me [because of] their word.
—John 17:11, 15, 17, 20

Love is the heartbeat of human life and the essence of the identity of a disciple of Christ. (Read John 13:34–35.) Yet, when we read the story of humanity, we might well ask 'Where is love?' From the Bible story of Cain and Abel to the war and violence that seem to be the focus of history-in-the-making today, is it any wonder there are people who think that the power of evil and sin still has control of the world and that we humans cannot say no to sin?

Many today might ask themselves, 'What was the point of the Death of Jesus if most people continue to commit sin?' God's Word to us clearly says that the struggle between love and hate, evil and goodness, virtue and sin did not end with Jesus' Death. The struggle continues, but love will be the final victor. Faith in Jesus means precisely that we are not 'condemned' to sin, not condemned to choose evil over love, but we are 'set free' to choose always what is right and good—to love as Jesus loved us, to love as God loves us. The author of the First Letter of John, writing to the early Church around AD 90, encourages us:

Beloved, let us love one another, because love is from God; everyone who loves is born of God and knows God. Whoever does not love does not know God, for God is love.
—1 John 4:7–8

166 | CREDO | THE PROMISED ONE: SERVANT AND SAVIOR

Earlier in this same letter the author admonishes his readers, 'Everyone who commits sin is guilty of lawlessness; sin is lawlessness' (1 John 3:4). Writing much earlier, St. Paul wrote, 'Christ died for our sins' (1 Corinthians 15:3) so that we might be able to resist sin and say yes to living his commandment of love, to living as children of God.

We must remember that, to God, there is no past, present or future; all moments of time are present in their immediacy. (See CCC, no. 600.) When Jesus died on the Cross he carried with him not only the sin of our first ancestors but the sins of all humanity through the ages, including our own sins. St. Paul elaborates, 'Do you not know that all of us who were baptized into Christ Jesus were baptized into his death? . . . We know that our old self was crucified with him so that the body of sin might be destroyed, and we might no longer be enslaved to sin' (Romans 6:3, 6).

JOURNAL EXERCISE

Jesus said, 'Holy Father, protect them in your name that you have given me' (John 11:7).

⊙ Imagine Jesus saying to you, 'Holy Father, protect (*your name*) whom you have given me.' Reflect on what this means for you. Write your reflections in your journal.

THE CROSS MEANS 'NEVER GIVE UP!'

Sometimes we can feel a sense of despair. We may feel helpless in seeking to thwart the seemingly endless and unstoppable cycle of war and violence, of self-serving exploitation of the poor, of death-bearing and family-destroying addiction to drugs, and so on. The Cross of Jesus is God's ultimate pledge to us that we need not and should never 'give up' in facing these and other forms of enslavement. Because of the Cross, there is always hope—in every situation.

But, we cannot work to overcome sin and evil by ourselves. Our strength and hope is rooted in God, whose unconditional and faithful love for us was revealed in Jesus and who has sent us his Spirit, our Advocate and Teacher and Guide. Because of this, we are capable of living as children of God. We have not been left alone to 'fight the good fight'. (Read 2 Timothy 4:6–7.)

CHAPTER 7: VICTORY FROM THE JAWS OF DEATH | THINK IT THROUGH

St. Peter used the word 'ransom' to describe what Jesus did for us. The verb 'ransom' means 'to buy something back'; the noun 'ransom' means 'the price paid to buy something back'. Today kidnappers and hijackers often look for ransom for their captives. In the case of Jesus, humankind was captive to sin and he gave his life as ransom. Jesus our Redeemer paid the ransom for us and restored our hope. Once again, 'Our salvation flows from God's initiative of love for us, because "he loved us and sent his Son to be the expiation for our sins" (see 1 John 4:10)' (CCC, no. 620).

The depth of God's love is so great that we can only begin to capture it in human language. Jesus is the source of salvation, justification, redemption, sanctification, liberation, reconciliation, new creation and adoption as God's own children. 'All salvation comes from Christ the Head through the Church his Body' (CCC, no. 846). No one of these teachings in and of themselves, or indeed all of them together, is sufficient to capture fully the love of God revealed in what Jesus achieved for us by his Cross and subsequent Resurrection.

GROUP ACTIVITY

- Working in small groups, list a number of things to which young people today can be captive.
- Then list what might have the power to free them from that captivity.

OVER TO YOU

- Which of the teachings of the New Testament that describe the Redemption Jesus won for us has most appeal for you at this time? Explain.
- What does the teaching you chose say to you about God's love? How can you witness that teaching and God's love?

To what things can young people be captive today? What might have the power to free them from that captivity?

JUDGE AND ACT

REFLECT ON WHAT YOU HAVE LEARNED

Think about where you now stand in relation to Jesus' suffering and Death. Focus on:

- Your understanding of this event and its enduring symbol—the Cross.
- Your decisions about the place the Cross of Christ will have in your own faith life.

REMEMBERING THE PASSION OF JESUS

Christians remember the Passion (the suffering and Death) of Jesus in a special way during Holy Week. Holy Week begins with Palm Sunday of the Lord's Passion, when we remember the triumphant entry of Jesus into Jerusalem for the celebration of the Passover with his disciples. On Holy Thursday we remember the Last Supper that Jesus shared with his disciples, during which he washed the disciples' feet. On Good Friday we remember the suffering and Death of Jesus. On both Palm Sunday and Good Friday we stand and listen to a proclamation of the Passion of Jesus. We proclaim our faith in Jesus Christ and commit ourselves to him as our Savior and Redeemer.

- What aspects of your own life now are in need of a Savior or Redeemer?
- What aspects of our society are in need of saving and redemption?

DISCUSS WITH A PARTNER

In every locality there are people and situations that need redemption.

- What people do you know who are acting to redeem and save some part of the world from the evils that are affecting it?
- How can Jesus work through you to continue God's work of salvation and redemption?

LEARN BY EXAMPLE

The story of Sr. Maura Clarke

Down through history, many people have followed Jesus' example and have suffered in solidarity with those in most need of redemption. One such person was Sr. Maura Clarke. Maura was born on January 13, 1932, and grew up in the borough of Queens in New York City. In 1950 she joined the Maryknoll Sisters. Eight years later, in 1959, she accepted the call to go to Nicaragua, where she taught and ministered in a Capuchin Franciscan parish in Siuna, a remote city in the east of the country. Friends said of Maura that she was outstanding in her generosity, and she became known to the people as 'the angel of our land'.

In response to an appeal from Archbishop Oscar Romero, Sr. Maura left Nicaragua to minister with the people of El Salvador, alongside Sr. Ita Forde, who was also a Maryknoll Sister, Sr. Dorothy Kazel, an Ursuline Sister, and Jean Donovan, a lay missionary.

Following Archbishop Romero's assassination, the threat of a violent death was ever present for these women missionaries. Maura, recognizing the dangers around her, wrote: 'My fear of death is being challenged constantly as children, lovely young girls and old people are being shot and some cut up with machetes and bodies thrown by the road and people prohibited from burying them. One cries out: Lord, how long? And then too what creeps into my mind is the little fear, or big, that when it touches me very personally, will I be faithful?'

In spite of her fears, Maura continued her work with refugees, searching out missing people, praying with the families of prisoners, burying the dead. She described her ministry as 'showing concern for the victims of injustice in today's world, for the suffering of the poor and marginalized, for the non-persons of the human family'.

On December 2, 1980, Maura Clarke was murdered along with Ita Ford, Dorothy Kazel and Jean Donovan. Dorothy and Jean had travelled to the airport to pick up Maura and Ita on their return from a meeting in Nicaragua. On the way back, they were assassinated by Salvadoran army officers, after two of them had been raped.

Because of their option to stand in solidarity with the poor of El Salvador, these women were labeled as subversives by the Salvadoran authorities. They showed themselves to be true followers of Jesus Christ, the Crucified One.

JUDGE AND DECIDE

◉ What do you find most inspirational in the story of Sr. Maura Clarke?

RESEARCH ACTIVITY

◉ Work in small groups. Review what you learned in chapters 6 and 8 of *God's Word Revealed in Sacred Scripture*, the first book of the *Credo* series, about Jean Donovan and Archbishop Oscar Romero and the political situation in El Salvador at that time. Identify other places in the world today where similar forms of oppression and injustice are happening. When you have completed your research, present your findings to the rest of the class.

JOURNAL EXERCISE

◉ Write about how you will take up the challenge to live as a disciple of Jesus.

RESPOND WITH YOUR FAMILY

Catholics have a strong tradition of having one or more crucifixes in their homes. A crucifix is a cross bearing a representation of Jesus' body.

◉ Consider introducing this practice to your family.

◉ Consider having a crucifix in your own bedroom or study area.

LEARN BY HEART

Christ died for our sins in accordance with the scriptures.

1 CORINTHIANS 15:3

PRAYER REFLECTION

Pray the Sign of the Cross together.

LEADER

Remember the words of Jesus, 'Where two or three are gathered in my name, I am there among them' (Matthew 18:20). Become aware that the Risen Jesus is present here with us. (*Pause*) Close your eyes and place yourself as an observer at Calvary on the day that Jesus was crucified. You are on a hill overlooking the scene. Imagine the sights and sounds all around. (*Pause*) Close your eyes. Open your ears. Open your hearts to hear the story again. (*Pause*)

READER

Then the soldiers led him into the courtyard of the palace; and they called together the whole cohort. And they clothed him in a purple cloak; and after twisting some thorns into a crown, they put it on him. And they began saluting him, 'Hail King of the Jews!' They struck his head with a reed, spat upon him, and knelt down in homage to him. After mocking him they stripped him of the purple cloak and put his own clothes on him. Then they led him out to crucify him.

—Mark 15:16–20

All pause for a moment of silent reflection.

LEADER

Imagine the pain Jesus experienced as the crown of thorns was placed on his head, and the humiliation as the crowd jeered and spat on him. Remember that Jesus did this for you! (*Pause*)

READER

They compelled a passer-by, who was coming in from the country, to carry his cross; it was Simon of Cyrene. . . . Then they brought Jesus to the place called Golgotha. And they offered him wine mixed with myrrh; but he did not take it. And they crucified him, and divided his clothes

among them, casting lots to decide what each should take.

—Mark 15:21–24

All pause for a moment of silent reflection.

LEADER

How do you think Simon felt? He probably didn't even know who Jesus was. (*Pause*) What do you imagine were the thoughts going through Jesus' mind as the nails pierced his hands and feet? (*Pause*) Again remember that Jesus did all of this for you! (*Pause*)

In your own heart tell the Risen Jesus how you feel about all he suffered for you. (*Pause*)

Open your eyes now and stand. (*Pause*)

Before we all pray the Sign of the Cross together, become conscious that every time we pray the Sign of the Cross we recall the Crucifixion of Jesus. This is the sign that marks us as followers of Jesus.

Pray the Sign of the Cross together.

CHAPTER 8

Christ Is Risen! He Is Risen Indeed!

THE RESURRECTION:

- REVEALS THE DIVINE PURPOSE OF THE INCARNATION
- OFFERS US THE HOPE THAT GOD HAS FULFILLED HIS PROMISES IN CHRIST
- ASSURES US OF OUR OWN RESURRECTION TO NEW LIFE AFTER DEATH

JESUS CHRIST HAS:

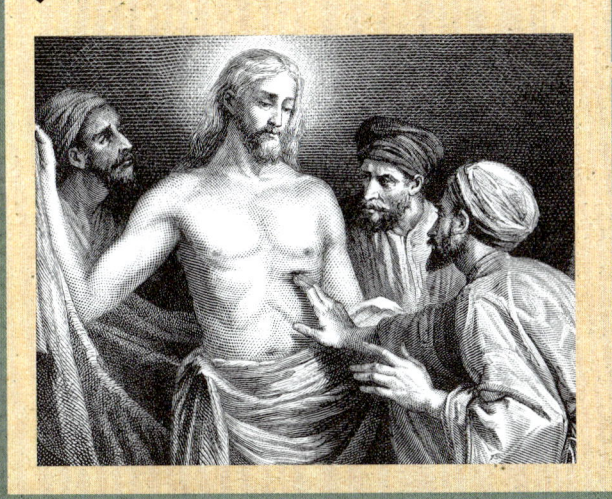

- PAVED THE WAY FOR US
- MADE US SHARERS IN THE PASCHAL MYSTERY
- GIVEN NEW MEANING TO THE REALITY OF DEATH
- DEFEATED DEATH AND ALL OF DEATH'S POWER

THIS CHAPTER WILL HELP TO DEEPEN YOUR understanding of the Resurrection of Jesus Christ, the greatest source of hope for our lives. In rising from the dead, Jesus Christ triumphed over sin and death and fulfilled his mission. The Resurrection is the ultimate seal to God's work of Salvation in Jesus Christ. The Resurrection is the foundation of the hope that both shapes our present life and paves our way home to the possibility of eternal life and happiness in the presence of God.

THE PASCHAL MYSTERY, JESUS' DEATH, RESURRECTION AND ASCENSION, IS THE HEART AND CENTER OF THE FULFILLMENT OF GOD'S SAVING PROMISE OF SALVATION AND FLOURISHING NEW LIFE

DEATH IS THE DOORWAY TO NEW LIFE

LEARNING OUTCOMES

As a result of studying this chapter and exploring the issues raised, you should be able to:

- ⊙ identify examples of good triumphing over evil;
- ⊙ understand why the Resurrection is the foundation of Christian hope;
- ⊙ recall the reactions of Jesus' disciples to the Resurrection;
- ⊙ understand the significance of the empty tomb;
- ⊙ appreciate that we remember the Resurrection when we celebrate Eucharist;
- ⊙ understand that the resurrected body of Jesus was transformed;
- ⊙ recognize the Resurrection as the definitive sign of the fulfillment of Christ's mission;
- ⊙ identify how faith in the Resurrection can enable us to restore a right relationship with God, with other people, with ourselves and with all creation;
- ⊙ understand how faith in the Resurrection should shape the lives of disciples of Jesus;
- ⊙ understand that participation in the Sacraments is at the heart of your Christian identity;
- ⊙ understand the meaning of 'symbol' in the context of the Sacraments;
- ⊙ understand the conversion of Dismas as a sign of hope for all sinners;
- ⊙ understand the importance of respecting our bodies.

FAITH-FORMATION OUTCOMES

As a result of studying this chapter and exploring the issues raised, you should also:

- ⊙ recognize how Christ's victory over death redefines the meaning of death for all people;
- ⊙ recognize times when your faith in the Resurrection gave you hope and comfort;
- ⊙ reflect on how you sustain your faith in times of doubt and fear;
- ⊙ identify ways you can share the Risen Lord's peace with others;
- ⊙ reflect on your personal image of the Risen Lord;
- ⊙ recognize signs of death and resurrection in your life;
- ⊙ assess the challenges you will face as you strive toward fullness of new life in Christ;
- ⊙ value your Baptism as the source of your discipleship of Jesus;
- ⊙ recognize the Risen Christ in the people and situations you meet every day.

LEARN BY HEART: 1 Peter 1:3

LEARN BY EXAMPLE: Dismas, the Good Thief

ATTEND AND REFLECT

Where or what is the source of our hope?

OPENING REFLECTION

The ultimate triumph of good over evil is an age-old storyline that artists and musicians, poets, novelists and playwrights have interpreted down through the ages in theater, cinema, art and literature: 'good' battles 'evil', and just when all hope seems lost, good (usually) rises to triumph over evil once and for all. Such stories point to humanity's belief in the existence and ultimate power of the good. This belief, which is embedded in the human heart, helps us find meaning in the hardships of life, and shows us how to see possibilities even in the most difficult situations.

BRAINSTORM

⊙ Think of examples of films, literature, poetry, music or art that tell the story of good triumphing over evil.

DISCUSS

⊙ Which of the examples is your favorite and why?
⊙ What makes this story especially meaningful for you?

Aslan the Great and the White Witch

One well-read story of good triumphing over evil is Aslan's victory over the White Witch in C.S. Lewis's *The Lion, the Witch and the Wardrobe*. In this story Aslan the great lion offers himself as a sacrifice to break the terrorizing spell of the White Witch over the inhabitants of Narnia. Susan and Lucy, two children who witness Aslan's sacrifice, sorrowfully look for his great and broken body the next morning. Instead, they find the table of his sacrifice broken in two, and encounter a living Aslan, greater and more glorious than before. Rejoicing in awe, the children ask Aslan to explain what has happened. Aslan tells them:

> Though the witch knew the Deep Magic, there is a deeper magic still which she did not know. Her knowledge goes back only to the dawn of time. But if she could have looked a little further back, into the stillness and the darkness before Time dawned, she would have read there a different incantation. She would have known that when a willing victim who had committed no treachery was killed in a traitor's stead, the Table would crack and Death itself would start working backwards.

174 | CREDO | THE PROMISED ONE: SERVANT AND SAVIOR

OVER TO YOU

- When have you ever been in a situation where it seemed like all hope was lost?
- What did it feel like to consider failure or defeat?
- How did hope and triumph emerge against all odds?
- Did your faith in God help to give you hope? How?

C.S. Lewis was a person of deep Christian faith, and he composed *The Lion, the Witch and the Wardrobe* as an allegory for the Paschal Mystery of Christ's suffering, Death, triumphant Resurrection and glorious Ascension. For Lewis, Aslan symbolized Jesus, who sacrificed his life and who triumphantly rose from the dead on the third day after his Crucifixion as the Risen Christ to free humanity from the bondage of sin and death. Jesus Christ made death go 'backward'— not into final death but into newness of life. Jesus' Death represented the ultimate triumph of good over evil.

REVIEW ACTIVITY

- Work with a partner. Review the passage from *The Lion, the Witch and the Wardrobe*, this time reading it with Christ's Death and Resurrection in mind. Together, list the elements of the passage that reflect the Christian story.
- Share your list with the class and discuss how *The Lion, the Witch and the Wardrobe* helps you understand the story of Christ's Death and Resurrection.

THE RESURRECTION: THE FOUNDATION OF OUR HOPE

Jesus' Passion (his suffering and Death) and Resurrection took place in Jerusalem during the Passover festivities. The first Passover prefigured the Passover of Christ, the Lamb of God. Christ's Passover opened up the possibility of deliverance from sin and death for all people of all times. The Paschal Mystery is the divine act that liberates all humanity from the bondage of sin and death once and for all and sets humanity 'right', or justifies humanity. Merited through the Passion of Christ and granted to us through Baptism, our justification 'includes remission of sins, sanctification, and the renewal of the inner man' (*Catechism of the Catholic Church* [CCC], no. 2019).

The Church since her earliest days used the term 'Mystery' to name God's work in the world,

THE RESURRECTION OF CHRIST | CONVENT OF SAN PIETRO, PERUGIA

whose meaning will become clear to us only in the eternal presence of God in heaven. The Resurrection of Jesus Christ is the foundation of Christian faith in him and in the Mystery of his life, Death, Resurrection and Ascension. St. Paul states boldly, '[I]f Christ has not been raised, then our proclamation has been in vain and your faith has been in vain. . . . If for this life only we have hoped in Christ, we are of all people most to be pitied' (1 Corinthians 15:14, 19).

Without the Resurrection, Jesus' life would simply be an epic story of a good man overcome by evil, a tragic figure meeting a violent and unjust death on a cross, after a heroic life of loving and serving people. But Jesus was not simply a good and heroic man. He was Goodness and Love itself at work among us, whose love for and service of people was not defeated by his unjust execution. Jesus rose triumphantly and defeated death itself. 'The Resurrection of the crucified one shows that he was truly 'I AM', the Son of God and God himself' (CCC, no. 653). It is this faith that gives identity and power to our discipleship. St. Paul wrote: 'For if we have been united with [Christ] in a death like his, we will certainly be united with him in a resurrection like his' (Romans 6:5).

St. Paul's teachings pass on the faith of the Church from the Apostles. Our hope in Christ is not just for this present life and its many struggles. Christ's Resurrection assures us of our own resurrection to new life after death. 'Christ's Resurrection . . . is the principle and source of our future resurrection' (CCC, no. 655). In rising from death, Christ was the first to fulfill God's promise of eternal salvation that now awaits all the faithful. Every time Christians pray the Apostles' Creed, we confess our faith 'in the resurrection of the body and life everlasting'. We are confident that Jesus Christ has paved 'the way' for us.

St. Paul does not say that the Resurrection has eradicated death from our human experience. Death in all its forms and all its traces remains part of our human experience—such is the consequence of Original Sin. But now death and its traces throughout our lives have lost their final and definitive power; death, in Paul's words, has lost its 'sting'. Because of Christ's Paschal Mystery, death is not an ending; instead, it is a passage to a new way of living, leading to new life, new opportunities and new possibilities.

REFLECT AND DISCUSS

- What are the different kinds of 'dying' that a person may experience during their life?
- Has such an experience ever happened to you? If so, what gave you hope?

What are the different kinds of 'dying' that a person may experience during their life?

DEATH—THE DOORWAY TO NEW LIFE

'The Paschal mystery has two aspects: by his death, Christ liberates us from sin; by his Resurrection, he opens for us the way to a new life' (CCC, no. 654). Living with faith in the Risen Lord and his continuing, saving and liberating presence among us, means that our day-to-day outlook can be one of hope, creativity, imagination and new life—even as we face the dead ends and closed doors of life. Because of the Risen Christ, death and all its traces lose their final power over our lives.

Through his own Death, Resurrection and Ascension, Jesus redefined and redeemed the reality of death. Death is not an ending to our life, but the doorway to a new life, which Paul describes as:

> What no eye has seen, nor ear heard,
>   nor the human heart conceived,
> what God has prepared for those who
>   love him.
>
> —1 Corinthians 2:9

By God's abundant grace given in Jesus Christ, we have the life-giving power to meet and overcome all the challenges in life—including death. 'For as all die in Adam, so all will be made alive in Christ' (1 Corinthians 15:22).

WHAT ABOUT YOU PERSONALLY?

Jesus' Resurrection does not mean that we will escape from the challenges and problems of life. What it does mean, however, is that we now have the God-given power, the grace, not to be defeated by them. On our behalf, Christ defeated death and all of death's power, which is present in many events and experiences of life on earth, such as despair, dead ends, the loss of creativity, the loss of opportunity, the loss of imagination, the consequences of sin, and feelings of alienation from self, others and God.

- In your own life, have there been times when your belief in the Resurrection of Jesus from the dead has made a significant difference? What were these times and how did your belief in the Resurrection make a difference?
- How does your belief in the Resurrection affect how you see the world?

REFLECTIVE ACTIVITY

Work with a partner or in small groups.
- Reflect together on why you think St. Paul stated that without the Resurrection of Jesus Christ our faith would be in vain.
- Then talk about how our beliefs and practices would be different if the Christian story ended at the foot of the Cross. Would it still be a story of Good News? What about our call to love and serve others?

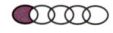 CHAPTER 8: CHRIST IS RISEN! HE IS RISEN INDEED! | ATTEND AND REFLECT | 177

HEAR THE STORY

Christ rose from the dead according to the Scriptures

OPENING REFLECTION

Take a moment to read and contemplate on this Easter poem, written by Joyce Rupp.

Easter

Sturdy, deep green tulip shoots.
How did they know it was time to push up through the
    long-wintered soil?
How did they know it was the moment to resurrect,
    while thick layers of stubborn ice still pressed the
    bleak ground flat?
But the tulips knew.
They came, rising strongly, a day after the ice died.
There's a hope-filled place in me that also knows when to
    rise,
    that waits for the last layer of ice to melt into
    obscurity.
It is urged by the strong sun warming my wintered heart.
    It is nudged by the Secret One, calling, calling, calling:
    'Arise, my love, and come.'
My heart stirs like dormant tulips and hope comes
    dancing forth.
Not unlike the Holy One kissing the morning sun,
    waving a final farewell to a tomb emptied of its
    treasure.

In New England, where Joyce Rupp lives, and in many parts of the world, spring flowers emerging from often semi-frozen ground after months of cold and darkness are an annual miracle and a joyful sign of hope and new life. Little green shoots come up from the snowy, icy, muddy ground and send a sturdy signal to the world that warmer, easier days lie ahead. Joyce Rupp compares hope within our hearts to dormant tulips, as both know to emerge against all odds and persist in signaling new life. Hope, like dormant tulips, can surprise us, especially when the world around overwhelms us with worry, stress, noise, suffering and disappointment.

WHAT ABOUT YOU PERSONALLY?

- Is there a 'hope-filled place' within you?
- What are the 'layers of ice' in your life? And where do you find 'strong sun' to melt these layers?

JOURNAL EXERCISE

- Reread and reflect on the poem 'Easter'. Then write your personal response to the poem in your journal.

178 | CREDO | THE PROMISED ONE: SERVANT AND SAVIOR

A TOMB EMPTIED OF ITS TREASURE

After the Death and burial of Jesus, Mary Magdalene went back to the tomb in which Joseph of Arimathea and Nicodemus had buried Jesus. On finding the stone that was supposed to be blocking the entrance to the tomb rolled back and the tomb empty, Mary ran to Peter and John to share her astonishing discovery. Equally astonished, perhaps even bewildered, Peter and John rushed to the tomb to see for themselves. (Read John 20:1–10.)

Peter, John and the other disciples grappled with the reality of the empty tomb—and were unsure what to make of it. The Fourth Gospel tells us that while they 'believed . . . they did not understand the scripture, that he must rise from the dead' (John 20:8–9). Jesus did foretell his Resurrection, but could it really be possible? Or did someone rob the grave and steal his body? Questions like these must have occupied their minds and hearts. The discovery of the empty tomb was 'the first step toward [their] recognizing the very fact of the Resurrection. This was the case, first with the holy women, and then with Peter' (CCC, no. 640) and the others.

THINK, PAIR AND SHARE

- Think of a time when you struggled with doubt about something you had seen or heard, or of an occasion when you had a hard time believing something or someone. Then discuss with a partner: What made it difficult to believe? What did your head tell you to do? What did your heart say to you? How did you resolve this?
- How does your experience help you to understand the disciples' difficulty in believing that Jesus had in fact risen from the dead?
- Share your best insights with the class.

The empty tomb was the first sign of Jesus' Resurrection. By itself, the empty tomb is a challenging sign. It makes us aware that something transcendent has happened. It is a sign of possibilities; its emptiness is like a holding place where we can sort out all our questions, fears, doubts, hopes and desires. Just as the experience of the empty tomb was a necessary part of Mary Magdalene's and Peter's faith journey to their belief in the Resurrection and its meaning for their lives, so too with us. Experiencing and discovering the meaning of the 'empty tombs' in our own lives is a necessary part of our spiritual growth in our life in Christ. These 'empty tomb moments' give us space to come to terms with our faith in Jesus Christ, who has risen from the dead.

MARY MAGDALENE FINDS JESUS' TOMB EMPTY | ENGRAVING AFTER ALEXANDRE BIDA

CHAPTER 8: CHRIST IS RISEN! HE IS RISEN INDEED! | HEAR THE STORY | 179

JOURNAL EXERCISE

For each of us, the empty tomb can be a symbol of unresolved questions, hopes and expectations, as it was for the first disciples.

⊙ Imagine the empty tomb in your own life right now. What questions, doubts, fears, hopes and desires would you put there? List these in your journal and explain why you chose them.

NEW LIFE, RENEWED FAITH

The disciples' experience of the Risen Lord began with the empty tomb; but it did not end there. After the Resurrection, the Risen Lord Jesus appeared many times to his disciples. As they continued to struggle with faith and doubt, they responded to their encounters with the Risen Christ in different ways: some fell down in worship (Matthew 28:9), some thought he might be a ghost (Luke 24:37), some did not recognize him right away (Luke 24:13–35, John 20:15–16), and some were outright resistant until they could touch him to make sure he was real (John 20:25). All these encounters with the Risen Lord gradually helped the disciples to cement their belief in the Resurrection. Slowly they embraced and began to share the joyful news of Christ risen from the dead. It was in this sharing of faith that the early Church was rooted.

OVER TO YOU

From their encounters with the Risen Lord, the disciples gradually came to a rock-solid faith in the Resurrection.

⊙ How have you experienced the Risen Lord in your life? What events, relationships, actions or truths have made your faith in the Resurrection real for you?

⊙ What is the best evidence you could show in your life for your belief in the Resurrection?

WITNESSES TO THE RESURRECTION

Among those disciples who encountered the Risen Lord, Mary Magdalene and Thomas the Apostle stand out as two compelling examples. Let's look at how John the Evangelist describes their encounters.

Mary Magdalene

Mary Magdalene is the first disciple to whom the Risen Lord appears. In John 20:11–18 we read that Mary Magdalene stands weeping by the empty tomb because she thinks the body of Jesus has been stolen. The Risen Lord comes to her, but she thinks he is the gardener and does not, at first, recognize him. Then he calls her by name; and hearing his voice, Mary Magdalene recognizes the Risen Christ and immediately embraces her beloved Jesus. The Risen Lord tells Mary Magdalene not to hold on to him. Instead, she must let go of him again in order to go and share the Good News of the Resurrection with others.

180 | CREDO | THE PROMISED ONE: SERVANT AND SAVIOR

Thomas the Apostle

Thomas exclaims in faith: 'My Lord and my God!'

JOHN 20:28

On that same Easter Sunday evening, 'the first day of the week', the Risen Lord's first appearance to the disciples as a group takes place. However, Thomas the Apostle is absent. When the other disciples tell him the extraordinary Good News, Thomas refuses to believe until he can touch and confirm the reality of the Risen Lord's body for himself. That same evening the Risen Lord returns to the disciples again and offers his body to Thomas to touch. Thomas exclaims in faith: 'My Lord and my God!' (John 20:28). The Risen Lord gently admonishes him, saying, 'Have you believed because you have seen me? Blessed are those who have not seen and yet have come to believe' (John 20:29). In other words, our faith, the faith of all those who believe without seeing the Risen Lord face to face, is all the more 'blessed'.

Mary Magdalene and Thomas offer us two different perspectives and insights into the gift of faith; one focuses on the power of our emotions or feelings, and the other on our intellect or reason. Perhaps Mary was initially so overwhelmed by her emotions that she, at first, failed to recognize Jesus; Thomas, on the other hand, may have so rigidly adhered to the power of his intellect, looking for empirical evidence, that he, too, at first, could not accept the fact that Jesus had risen from the dead. By sharing these two stories back to back, John the Evangelist teaches that there are many paths to faith in the Risen Lord. Faith is an invitation, calling forth a free response to relationship with the Lord that demands our whole being, mind and heart. Both in grappling with doubt and in responding to God's call in faith, we bring our whole being, mind and heart into our relationship with God.

SCRIPTURE EXERCISE

⊙ With a partner, read and compare the encounters of the Risen Lord with Mary Magdalene (John 20:11–18) and Thomas (John 20:24–29). Share your thoughts on how each of these disciples of Jesus responded to the Risen Lord. Compare Christ's message to each of them.

WHAT ABOUT YOU PERSONALLY?

⊙ Do you identify in any way with Mary Magdalene? With Thomas the Apostle? Explain.

'PEACE BE WITH YOU'

The Evangelist tells us that after Jesus' disciples had witnessed the horrors of his suffering and Crucifixion, they locked themselves in a room. They were understandably shocked, shaken and

CHAPTER 8: CHRIST IS RISEN! HE IS RISEN INDEED! | HEAR THE STORY | 181

Every time we participate in the Communion Rite we share the peace of the Risen Lord

fearful for their own lives. The Risen Lord came to them on that day of his Resurrection, and it is no surprise that the message and gift that he shared with them was one of comfort and peace. The same gift is seen in the Risen Lord's most common greeting to them, 'Peace be with you'. (See Luke 24:36; John 20:19, 21, 26.)

The peace of the Lord comforted the disciples and strengthened them in their faith. The disciples, in turn, would go forth and share the Good News of the Resurrection among themselves and with others. The Resurrection would be the foundation of their hope and make them bold witnesses for Christ, willing to sacrifice their own lives to proclaim this message. We are to share that same peace, that shalom, with others.

THINK IT OVER

Every time we participate in the Communion Rite during the celebration of Mass, we share the peace of the Risen Lord, greeting one another by using the very words of the Risen Christ, 'Peace be with you' (John 20:21).

⊙ Think about what it is like to exchange peace at Mass and to hear the words 'Peace be with you'.

⊙ Why does the Risen Lord offer us the same message of peace that he offered the first disciples?

⊙ Think about situations in your own life—in your locality, in your country and in the world—where the same gift of peace is needed right now.

182 | CREDO | THE PROMISED ONE: SERVANT AND SAVIOR

EMBRACE THE VISION

The fulfillment of God's promise

OPENING ACTIVITY

⊙ On a self-stick note, write a sign of the Resurrection that you can see in your own life or in the world around you.

⊙ Post your example with those of the other students on a large poster or notice board.

⊙ Read the various contributions and discuss your response to them.

REFLECT AND DISCUSS

Consider the image *The Risen Lord*, created by the Chinese Christian artist He Qi. The figure of the Risen Lord in the center embodies the shape of a cross. He is surrounded on four sides by smaller figures: the women and the Apostles who went to the tomb are depicted at the bottom of the image, and the other disciples, some proclaiming faith in the Resurrection and struggling with uncertainty and doubt, are shown at the top. In the forefront are bread on a paten and wine in a chalice, symbols of the Eucharist.

⊙ How does this depiction compare with your own image of the Risen Lord?

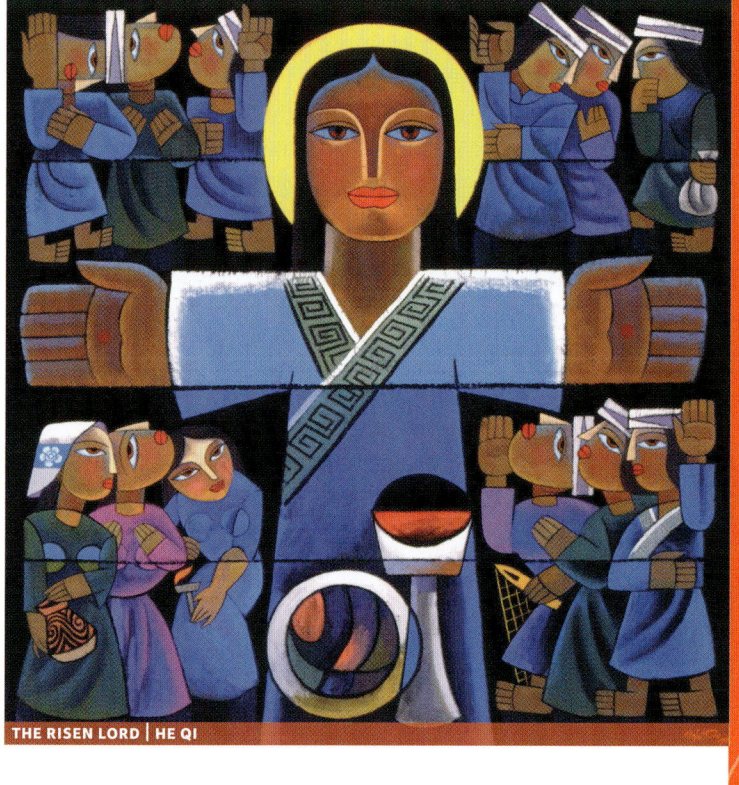

THE RISEN LORD | HE QI

JESUS IS TRANSFORMED!

'Christ's Resurrection was not a return to earthly life. . . . In his risen body he passes from the state of death to another life beyond time and space' (CCC, no. 646). The Resurrection was both a historical and a transcendent event. While the Evangelists are not specific about the nature and appearance of Jesus' risen and glorified body, we can conclude from the Resurrection Narratives that the earthly body of Jesus was totally transformed; for example, neither Mary Magdalene (read John 20:14–15) nor the two disciples on the road to Emmaus (read Luke 24:15) recognized the Risen Christ right away.

What the Evangelists do tell us is that the Risen Lord could appear and disappear at will and could enter through locked doors (read John 20:19, 26). He ate food (read Luke 24:41–43) and his body remained touchable and bore the marks of the Crucifixion (read John 20:19–20, 27). The Church, interpreting these Gospel accounts teaches:

By means of touch and the sharing of a meal, the risen Jesus establishes direct contact with his disciples. He invites them in this way to recognize that he is not a ghost and above all to verify that the risen body in which he appears

CHAPTER 8: CHRIST IS RISEN! HE IS RISEN INDEED! | EMBRACE THE VISION | 183 to them is the same body that had been tortured and crucified, for it still bears the traces of his passion. Yet at the same time this authentic, real body possesses the new properties of a glorious body: not limited by space and time but able to be present how and when he wills; for Christ's humanity can no longer be confined to earth and belongs henceforth only to the Father's divine realm.

—CCC, no. 645

WHAT ABOUT YOU PERSONALLY?

⊙ Do you ever try to imagine what the Risen Christ might have looked like? How does that help strengthen your faith in the Resurrection?

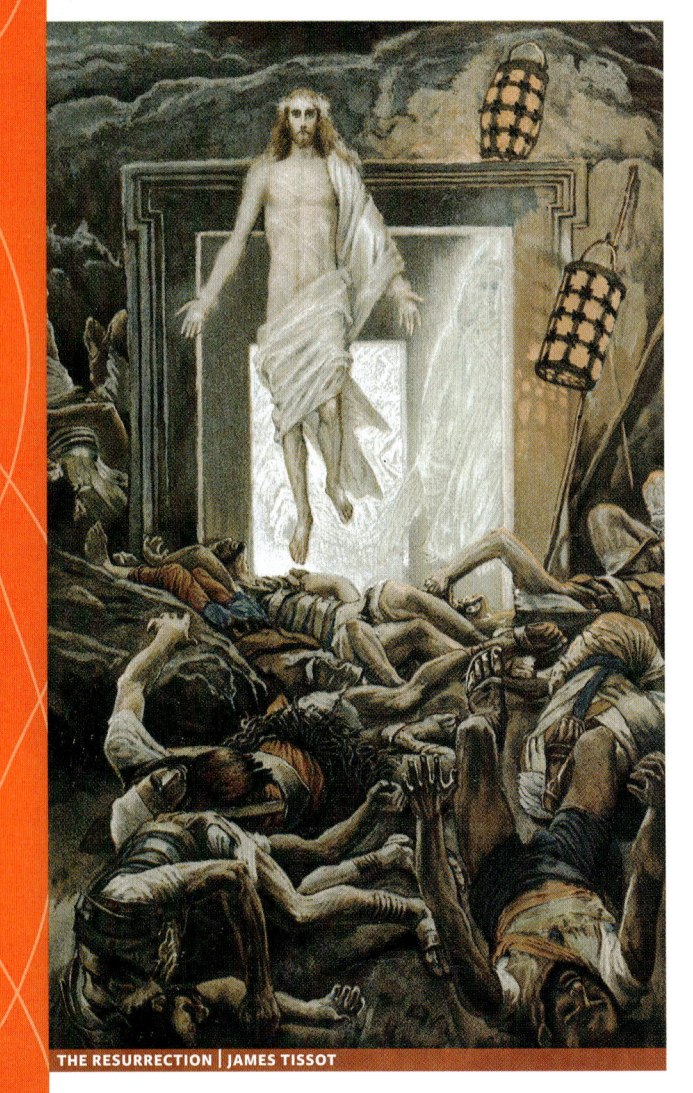

THE RESURRECTION | JAMES TISSOT

JESUS, 'A MAN OF HEAVEN'

The Church, from her earliest days, has strived, under the guidance of the Holy Spirit, to reach a deeper understanding of the meaning of the mystery of the Resurrection. In his First Letter to the Corinthians, which was written sometime between AD 52 and 57, Paul both asserts the fact and faith of the apostolic Church in the Resurrection and strives to help the Church in Corinth understand its meaning.

As part of Paul's teaching, he compares Adam, the first human created from the earth, to Christ, the 'last Adam', who is 'from heaven'. The Apostle writes, 'Thus it is written, "The first man, Adam, became a living being"; the last Adam became a life-giving spirit. . . . The first man was from the earth, a man of dust; the second man is from heaven. . . . Just as we have borne the image of the man of dust, we will also bear the image of the man of heaven' (1 Corinthians 15:45, 47, 49). While Adam of the first Creation symbolizes finitude and our Fall from God's grace, Christ as the 'last Adam' opens creation to limitless possibilities by God's grace and life-giving Spirit. The mysterious nature of Christ's risen body reflects this new order of creation and the great possibilities it offers us all.

Christ's Resurrection was not a return to earthly life, as was the case with the raisings from the dead that he had performed before Easter. . . . Christ's Resurrection is essentially different. . . . At Jesus' Resurrection his body is filled with the power of the Holy Spirit; he shares the divine life in his glorious state, so that St. Paul can say that Christ is 'the man of heaven'.

—CCC, no. 646

Whatever was the exact nature and form of the Risen Lord's body, it has become imperishable and immortal. It is no longer limited by the confines of the physical world, and it is no longer subject to suffering, finitude and limitation. Although present among his disciples in the days after the Resurrection, the Risen Christ was no longer confined to the limits of our earthly realm. Instead, the transformed body of Jesus was a sign and promise of God's eternal kingdom.

OVER TO YOU

⊙ Christ as 'the man of heaven' shatters our limits and fills our lives with possibilities. What signs have you seen in your life thus far of the possibility of resurrection?

IN FULFILLMENT OF THE SCRIPTURES

'Christ's Resurrection is the fulfillment of the promises both of the Old Testament and of Jesus himself during his earthly life' (CCC, no. 652). Jesus is the fulfillment of the Scriptures. In him all God's promises become reality. All 'Sacred Scripture is but one book, and this one book is Christ' (CCC, no. 134). The 'unity of the two Testaments proceeds from the unity of God's plan and his Revelation' (CCC, no. 140). This is why the Church has always looked to the Old Testament to come to a deeper understanding of Christ and his mission in the world.

While traveling the road to Emmaus with his dejected disciples, the Risen Jesus explained,

THE ROAD TO EMMAUS | JULIUS SCHNORR VON CAROLSFELD

'Oh, how foolish you are, and how slow of heart to believe all that the prophets have declared! Was it not necessary that the Messiah should suffer these things and then enter his glory?' Then beginning with Moses and all the prophets, he interpreted to them the things about himself in the scriptures.

—Luke 24:25–27

Many texts in the Old Testament prefigure the life and mission of Jesus, including his Resurrection. For example, Isaiah the Prophet has the image of a messiah as the Suffering Servant, the anointed one who offers his life for many, and who 'out of his anguish shall see light'. After the Risen Lord's Ascension into glory, the first disciples of Jesus and the Jews who would become believers, strived to understand Jesus, in light of the Scriptures of ancient Israel and the teachings of Jesus himself. The Church today continues this task and responsibility.

Jesus clearly and openly foretold his coming Death and Resurrection multiple times. Mark's Gospel tells us that Jesus 'began to teach them that the Son of Man must undergo great suffering, and be rejected by the elders, the chief priests, and the scribes, and be killed, and after three days rise again' (Mark 8:31; also read Mark 9:30–32, 10:32–34).

TALK IT OVER

Scripture reveals that the disciples often resisted, ignored or did not understand Jesus when he foretold his Passion and Resurrection. Mark tells us, 'For he was teaching his disciples, saying to them, "The Son of Man is to be betrayed into human hands and they will kill him, and three days after being killed, he will rise again." But they did not understand what he was saying and were afraid to ask him' (Mark 9:31–32).

⊙ Why do you think the disciples did not understand what Jesus was saying, and why were they afraid to ask?

'I AM THE RESURRECTION AND THE LIFE'

Jesus not only predicted his coming Death and Resurrection but he also revealed the deeper meaning of those events. He declared, 'I am the resurrection and the life' (John 11:25). The Paschal Mystery, Jesus' Death, Resurrection and Ascension, is the heart and center of the fulfillment of God's saving promise of Salvation and flourishing new life. Faith in Christ is the

CHAPTER 8: CHRIST IS RISEN! HE IS RISEN INDEED! | EMBRACE THE VISION | 185

THE HARROWING OF HELL | 15TH-CENTURY ENGLISH ALABASTER RELIEF

Christ's descent to the dead and his Resurrection paved the way for us to enjoy freedom from the overwhelming power of sin and death

of sin and death. By God's abundant grace, now available to us through the Paschal Mystery and our participation in the Sacraments and the life of the Church, we can live as disciples of Jesus, who is 'the resurrection and the life' (John 11:25). We can live each day with hope to dwell for ever with God in the eternal glory of heaven.

The Resurrection of the crucified one shows that he was truly 'I AM', the Son of God and God himself. So St. Paul could declare: 'What God promised to the fathers, this he has fulfilled to us their children by raising Jesus; as also it is written in the second psalm, "You are my Son, today I have begotten you" [Acts of the Apostles 13:32–33; Psalm 2:7]'.

—CCC, no. 653

REFLECT AND SHARE

- ⊙ Think of times when you experienced God's faithfulness in your life.
- ⊙ Then think of an experience that confirmed your faith in God. Why do you think this experience confirmed your faith in God?
- ⊙ Share your thoughts with a partner.

fulfillment of the divine promise and the source of that new, mysterious and glorious life. Jesus is the new and everlasting Covenant.

Through the Paschal Mystery of Christ, God fulfills the divine promise of Salvation and opens for all humanity the way into new life now and eternal life after the death of our body. For in 'his human soul united to his divine person, the dead Christ went down to the realm of the dead. He opened heaven's gates for the just that had gone before him' (CCC, no. 637). Christ's descent to the dead and his Resurrection paved the way for us to enjoy freedom from the overwhelming power

186 | CREDO | THE PROMISED ONE: SERVANT AND SAVIOR

JESUS SHOWED US WHO WE WERE CREATED TO BE

The Death and Resurrection of Jesus gives clear meaning both to his life and mission among us and to our life as his disciples. St. Irenaeus (d. 202), an influential teacher of the early Church and Bishop of Lyons, summarized the faith of the Church this way: 'Our Lord became what we are, that he might bring us to be what he is himself.' The Son of God became incarnate in Jesus that we may be made sharers in his divinity. He loved, taught, healed and served among us, revealing in his every word and action the depth of God's saving love for us and showing us who we were created to be.

In Christ, Christians 'have tasted . . . the powers of the age to come' [Hebrews 6:5] and their lives are swept up by Christ into the heart of divine life, so that they may 'live no longer for themselves but for him who for their sake died and was raised' [2 Corinthians 5:15].

—CCC, no. 655

In summary, the Resurrection reveals the divine purpose of the Incarnation and Paschal Mystery of the Son of God: all humanity is empowered to live in justice and holiness, in right relationship with our heavenly Father, and with all creation, both seen and unseen. Christ defeated death and sin, and he opened the way for all of humankind to live in shalom and eternal life with God. The deepest desire of the human heart can truly be fulfilled.

OVER TO YOU

⊙ Think of a particular relationship in your life, perhaps with a family member, a teacher or friend. Imagine the Risen Lord being present with you in your relationship. Imagine he says 'Peace be with you', as he did to his disciples after his Resurrection. What would these words challenge you to change in your relationship?

THINK IT THROUGH

Our hope of rising with Christ

OPENING REFLECTION/CONVERSATION

A typical day for them begins at 4:30 in the morning. They rise, pray and receive the Eucharist. They spend the day doing good works around the cities in which they live and serve: helping the sick, the poor, the dying. Their blue and white saris are unmistakable signs of God's hope and love for those whom society seems to have forgotten. They are the Missionaries of Charity, and their founder, now on her way to sainthood, formed this community as a sign of hope and a testament to the triumph of the Risen Lord even among the poorest of the poor. Blessed Mother Teresa of Calcutta shared the following about her experience of service:

> To those who say they admire my courage,
> I have to tell them that I would not have any
> if I were not convinced that each time
> I touch the body of a leper,

a body that reeks with a foul stench,
I touch the same Christ I receive in the
Eucharist.

⊙ From where do you draw strength when faced with the trials and struggles of life? What fuels your sense of hope and perseverance?

WE BELIEVE IN THE RESURRECTION OF THE BODY

Imagine the overwhelming joy the first disciples experienced when the reality of the Resurrection enlivened their minds and hearts. The Resurrection of Jesus Christ is joyful news: our Lord, the object of our love, returns to us triumphantly, as he predicted and promised, after the horrific suffering he endured in the final day of his life on earth. The Church has named that day 'Good Friday' in light of the Resurrection. Christ is the firstborn from the dead and the principle of our own resurrection. (See CCC, no. 658.)

> By death the soul is separated from the body, but in resurrection God will give incorruptible life to our body, transformed by reunion with our soul. Just as Christ is risen and lives for ever, so all of us will rise at the last day.
> —CCC, no. 1016

The Resurrection is joyful news because it signals the fulfillment of God's promises of the Covenant entered into with his people. It is joyful news because it is the sign and pledge of our reconciliation with God, and it enables us, gives us the grace, to live in right relationship with God, with other people

NUNS OF THE MISSIONARIES OF CHARITY AT PRAYER DURING GOOD FRIDAY

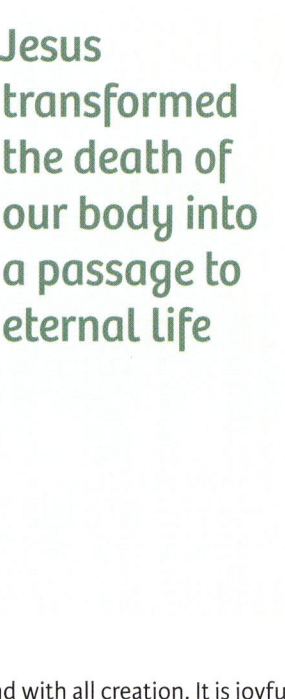

Jesus transformed the death of our body into a passage to eternal life

THE 'JAZZ FUNERAL' OF NEW ORLEANS COMBINES MOURNING WITH REJOICING

and with all creation. It is joyful news because it reveals and is the pledge of the possibility of our own resurrection at the end of time. Because Jesus rose from the dead, we believe that we, too, will rise at the end of time, and our rising, like Christ's, will include our bodies.

In the Nicene Creed we confess that we 'look forward to the resurrection of the dead'. In the Apostles' Creed we say explicitly that we 'believe in the resurrection of the body, and life everlasting'. Our belief is that God the Father will raise us up as whole persons, as he raised up Jesus.

OVER TO YOU

- Why do you think our faith in the resurrection of the body and everlasting life concludes the Creed?

'In death, the separation of the soul from the body, the human body decays and the soul goes to meet God, while awaiting its reunion with its glorified body' (CCC, no. 997). Jesus did not eradicate death, but rather emptied it of its final say over our lives, and he transformed the death of our body into a passage to eternal life instead. At the resurrection of our bodies, our souls will reunite with our risen bodies in heaven. Between our death and the resurrection of our bodies at the end of time, our souls will experience the heavenly presence of God.

GROUP ACTIVITY

Work in small groups.
- Together, read and discuss one of the following biblical passages:
  - Genesis 1:26–31: God creates the human person in God's image
  - Psalm 139:13–16: Fearfully and wonderfully made
  - John 1:14–16: The Word becomes flesh
  - John 5:1–9: Jesus heals the man by the pool of Bethzatha
  - 1 Corinthians 3:16–17: You are a temple of the Holy Spirit
  - 1 Corinthians 11:23–26: This is my body that is for you
- Use these questions to guide your discussion:
  - What does this passage reveal about the importance of our bodies?
  - What does this passage reveal about God and God's plan for us?
  - Why does our faith teach such reverence for our bodies?
  - What are some practical implications of this?
- Summarize your thoughts and share your insights with the larger group.

CHAPTER 8: CHRIST IS RISEN! HE IS RISEN INDEED! | THINK IT THROUGH | 189

The example of the historical Jesus and the reality of the Risen Christ should fill every aspect of our lives with profound hope and limitless possibilities. In Baptism we receive the call and grace of the Holy Spirit to live as disciples of Jesus. Jesus' dying and rising give direction to how we respond to that call and make it possible for us to answer the call. Our identity as disciples of Christ comes from our actual participation in the Paschal Mystery of Jesus Christ. Through regular participation in the Sacraments, especially the Eucharist, which is at the heart of who we are as members of Christ's Body, we receive God's abundant grace to live as Jesus' disciples.

OVER TO YOU

⊙ How would someone meeting you through school, through work, through your friends or family recognize you as a Christian?

LET'S PROBE DEEPER

⊙ Select one of the seven Sacraments: Baptism, Confirmation, Eucharist, Penance and Reconciliation, Anointing of the Sick, Marriage, or Holy Orders.

WE HAVE BEEN MADE SHARERS IN THE PASCHAL MYSTERY

'Christian life is already now on earth a participation in the death and Resurrection of Christ' (CCC, no. 1002). The resurrection of the body and life everlasting is not just about something we anticipate in the future. This belief shapes how we Christians live our lives each day. Joined to Christ at Baptism, we are members of the Body of Christ, the Church. We already participate in the new life made possible for us by the Risen Christ. We express our Christian identity by our efforts to live our lives as disciples of Jesus, who is 'the Way'. How we understand our world, how we make decisions, how we carry out our tasks and form relationships, reflect the reality of who we are—disciples and apprentices of the Risen Christ.

⊙ Recall some of the words, gestures, symbols, sights and sounds associated with the celebration of the Sacrament you selected. How do these communicate new life? Joy? Hope? Possibility? The triumph of the Resurrection?

⊙ Recall our opening conversation about the Missionaries of Charity and how they begin each day of service with prayer and the Eucharist. How do you think the Eucharist helps them bring joy, hope and possibility to the poorest of the poor?

WHAT ABOUT YOU PERSONALLY?

⊙ How does your sharing in the Paschal Mystery of Christ's Death and Resurrection enable you to be a messenger of hope in your family? In your school? In your parish? In your neighborhood?

190 | CREDO | THE PROMISED ONE: SERVANT AND SAVIOR

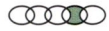

JUDGE AND ACT

REFLECT ON WHAT YOU HAVE LEARNED

⊙ What was the best insight or wisdom you gained from studying this chapter?

⊙ What real difference might it make to your daily life if you take seriously Christian faith in the Resurrection of Jesus Christ?

LEARN BY EXAMPLE

The story of Dismas, the Good Thief

The Gospel accounts of Jesus' Crucifixion tell us that two thieves were crucified along with him, 'one on his right and one on his left' (Luke 23:33), whom the tradition of the church has named Gestas and Dismas. Gestas, we are told, mocked Jesus. Dismas, on the other hand, acknowledged his sin and uttered these memorable words, 'Jesus, remember me when you come into your kingdom', to which Jesus replied, 'Truly I tell you, today you will be with me in Paradise' (Luke 23:42–43). Even in the last moments of his life, this 'good thief' was forgiven and assured of eternal life. There is always hope!

ST. DISMAS | BŘEZNICE, CZECH REPUBLIC

While suffering the excruciating pain of death by crucifixion, Dismas had hope against hope. While facing the earthly consequences of his capital crimes, he turned to Jesus in faith and hope for his own redemption. By God's grace, Dismas came to believe that Jesus' dying brings the possibility of new life in a 'new kingdom', even in the midst of the direst of circumstances. He is a lasting witness to the possibility of God's triumph over evil and death.

He is a symbol of hope and of the revelation of the mystery of God's love and mercy and a remarkable figure of faith. The Catholic Church honors the repentant Dismas as the patron of prisoners and condemned criminals, and remembers and celebrates his encounter with the crucified Lord each year on March 25.

JOURNAL EXERCISE

When it comes to the possibilities of new life offered by the Risen Christ, the limits of sin and death can sometimes seem too great a hurdle, especially if our burdens are something we think we deserve. Similarly, it can be difficult to forgive those who have hurt us, since our anger seems as just punishment for their misdeeds.

⊙ Reflect on the encounter of St. Dismas the Good Thief with the crucified Christ. By his own account, Dismas was condemned justly and deserved the sentence for his deeds (see Luke 23:41). Yet, even under the weight of his own sins and their earthly consequences, Dismas had the faith to approach Jesus with hope for his redemption.

CHAPTER 8: CHRIST IS RISEN! HE IS RISEN INDEED! | JUDGE AND ACT | 191

⊙ Now, reflect on the following questions and write your thoughts in your journal.
  – How or when have you experienced God's forgiveness in your own life? What did this feel like?
  – How does reflecting on your own forgiveness help you approach those who have hurt you? How can the new life of the Risen Christ emerge in your broken relationships?
⊙ If you feel comfortable doing so, share what you have learned from this reflection with another person.

RESPOND WITH FAMILY AND FRIENDS

When we are with our friends or family, the Risen Lord can join us in many ways. Learning something new and insightful, walking with somebody (literally or figuratively), inviting and hosting a guest, sharing in a good meal, telling our good news and joys to others are all occasions when we can encounter the presence of God with us and with those around us.

⊙ Think about how you can be more alert for God's presence in your everyday life.
⊙ Create a PowerPoint presentation showing images of where you find the Risen Lord present in your everyday life.

JUDGE AND DECIDE

All human life is sacred and we must reverence its sanctity in ourselves and others. The glorified body of Jesus Christ and the belief in the dignity of the human body and in our own bodily resurrection remind us that the wholeness of our bodies is part of God's promise of Salvation. Anything that deliberately harms the wholeness of our own bodies or the bodies of others acts against God's desire for our wholeness and the gift of eternal life offered to us through the Risen Lord.

⊙ Think about the ways you treat or maltreat and nourish your body, for example, through diet, exercise, sleep, recreation, relaxation, hygiene.
⊙ How can you honor the Risen Christ Jesus through these everyday activities?

- What are some life-giving ways to treat your body?
- What ways of treating your body are not life-giving?
- Next, think about the bodies of the people around you, the bodies of the young, elderly, healthy, weak, strong, thin, heavy, small, big, tall and short.
- How much does physical shape and size factor into how you perceive other people and form relationships?
- Do you need to reassess your criteria of evaluation?
- What can you say or do to bring the joy of the Risen Lord to those whose bodies are a target of judgment and criticism?

- How can your faith help you resist the social or cultural pressure to look a certain way?

WHAT WILL YOU DO NOW?
Responding to the concepts and challenges presented in this chapter:
- Where in our world do you think there is the greatest need for the joy and hope of the Resurrection?
- What can or will you do to 'light a candle' of hope, because you believe in the Resurrection of Jesus?
- What in this week's lesson was good news or a sign of hope for your own life? For your relationships with friends and family?

LEARN BY HEART

By his great mercy [God] has given us a new birth into a living hope through the resurrection of Jesus Christ from the dead.

1 PETER 1:3

JESUS APPEARS AFTER THE RESURRECTION | ENGRAVING AFTER ALEXANDRE BIDA

PRAYER REFLECTION

Greeting and Opening Prayer

LEADER

Sit quietly and remember that you are—as always—in the presence of God. (*Pause*)
In the name of the Father, and of the Son, and of the Holy Spirit.

ALL

Amen.

LEADER

Loving God,
through his glorious Resurrection, your Son, our
    Lord Jesus Christ, brings us new life.
Send your Holy Spirit to inspire us to live fully in
the joy and triumph of the Resurrection.
May we live as members of the Body of Christ
    who have died and risen with our Lord in the
    waters of Baptism.
We ask this in the name of Christ our Lord.

ALL

Amen.

Proclamation of the Word of God

READER

A reading from St. Paul's Letter to the Romans.
Read Romans 6:5–11.
The word of the Lord.

ALL

Thanks be to God.

Prayer of intercession

LEADER

Reflect for a few moments on the hope the Resurrection brings to the world. Think of situations and people to whom that hope can bring new life. (*Pause*)

Lord, as we rejoice in the possibilities for new life that you offer us, we pray: Bring us to new life, Lord Jesus Christ.

I now invite you to offer your needs and hopes.

Those who wish may express their petitions.

ALL

After each need or hope, respond:
Bring us to new life, Lord Jesus Christ.

LEADER

Uniting all of our needs and hopes for the triumph of the Risen Jesus Christ in our lives and in the lives of those around us, let us pray together the prayer that Jesus himself taught us.

ALL

Our Father. . . .

Exchange of Sign of Peace

LEADER

Echoing the words of the Risen Lord Jesus Christ, let us share with one another the peace of God.

ALL

Exchange a sign of peace, saying, 'Peace be with you'.

Concluding Prayer and dismissal

LEADER

Let us pray: (*Pause*)
Lord Jesus Christ, who said to your Apostles;
Peace I leave you, my peace I give you,
look not on our sins,
but on the faith of your Church,
and graciously grant her peace and unity
    in accordance with your will.
Who live and reign for ever and ever.

ALL

Amen.

LEADER

Let us share God's gift of peace with all.

ALL

Amen.

CHAPTER 9

Bound for Glory
—The Ascension, Pentecost and the Assumption

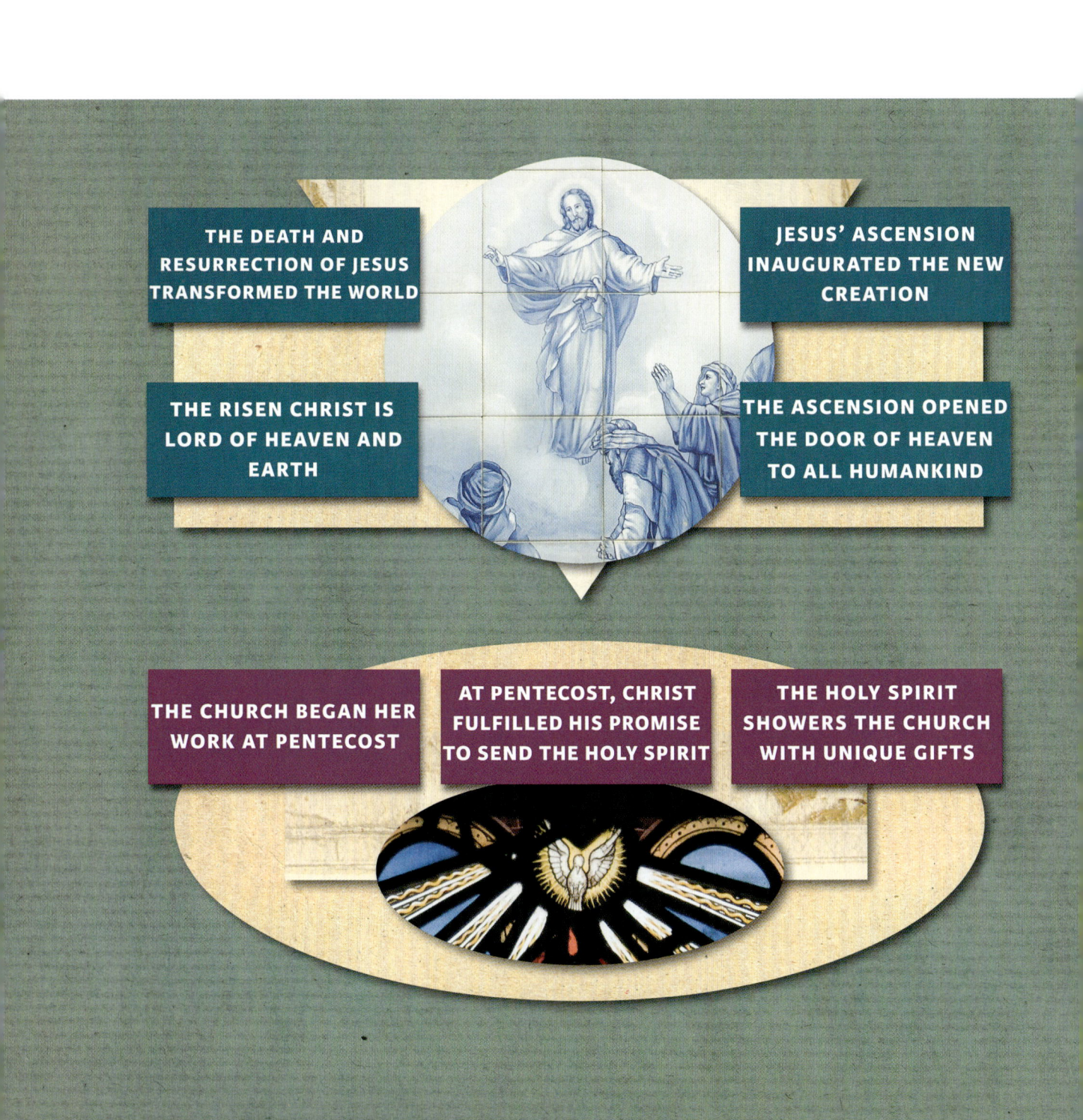

THE DEATH AND RESURRECTION OF JESUS TRANSFORMED THE WORLD

JESUS' ASCENSION INAUGURATED THE NEW CREATION

THE RISEN CHRIST IS LORD OF HEAVEN AND EARTH

THE ASCENSION OPENED THE DOOR OF HEAVEN TO ALL HUMANKIND

THE CHURCH BEGAN HER WORK AT PENTECOST

AT PENTECOST, CHRIST FULFILLED HIS PROMISE TO SEND THE HOLY SPIRIT

THE HOLY SPIRIT SHOWERS THE CHURCH WITH UNIQUE GIFTS

THIS CHAPTER WILL HELP YOU DISCOVER MORE ABOUT what the presence of the Risen Christ in heaven means for your life in faith here and now. Scripture reveals that after Jesus rose from the dead, he ascended to heaven to the right hand of God the Father. Christ then sent the Holy Spirit to continue his mission and ministry. The Spirit now empowers the Church in Jesus' work of bringing about the fullness of God's Reign on earth. The Assumption of Mary is a special sign that the Reign of God has already come and of humankind's invitation into the glory of heaven.

PENTECOST

ASCENSION

ASSUMPTION

ALL SIGNS OF THE TRIUMPH OF CHRIST

LEARNING OUTCOMES

As a result of studying this chapter and exploring the issues raised, you should be able to:

⊙ understand the meaning of the 'new creation' inaugurated by the Ascension of Jesus;

⊙ understand the meaning of the petition 'Thy Kingdom come. . . .' in the Lord's Prayer;

⊙ explore common understandings of heaven and compare them with the Church's teaching;

⊙ understand the teaching of the Catholic Church on the Ascension;

⊙ explore what Jesus' freely embracing Death on the Cross reveals about power;

⊙ explore the meaning of the story of Pentecost;

⊙ recognize the Fruits of the Holy Spirit at work in the lives of the first disciples;

⊙ understand Pentecost as the time when the Church began the work Christ gave her;

⊙ understand the meaning of the Assumption;

⊙ recognize the Assumption as a sign of hope and a promise for all people;

⊙ deepen your understanding of why Catholics pray to Mary;

⊙ explore the story of St. Lucy as a model of faith and hope.

FAITH-FORMATION OUTCOMES

As a result of studying this chapter and exploring the issues raised, you should also:

⊙ articulate ways you can work to bring about the 'new creation' that Christ inaugurated;

⊙ describe the 'power' that your faith in the Death-Resurrection-Ascension of Jesus Christ gives you to live your life;

⊙ deepen your understanding of how your life gives witness to the Fruits of the Holy Spirit;

⊙ reflect on how you experience God's promise of Salvation;

⊙ embrace Mary as your mother in faith;

⊙ ask Mary to intercede for you as you pray the Hail Mary;

⊙ express your concern for others by praying or 'interceding' for them with God;

⊙ identify one thing you will commit to do to help advance the coming of God's Kingdom.

FAITH WORDS: Ascension; Pentecost

LEARN BY HEART: Acts of the Apostles 2:3–4

LEARN BY EXAMPLE: St. Lucy

ATTEND AND REFLECT

How can we bring about the new creation?

⊙ Think about a time when you experienced a great personal accomplishment. What impact did your accomplishment have on your life? What new opportunities and new challenges did it bring? Share your story.

THE NEW CREATION HAS COME

The Death and Resurrection of Jesus reshaped and transformed the world. The Risen Christ shattered the hold of death and all of its traces over human lives. Our hopes, dreams, opportunities and challenges are changed for ever. Belief in the reality and transforming power of Christ moved St. Paul to proclaim:

If anyone is in Christ, there is a new creation: everything old has passed away; see, everything has become new!
—2 Corinthians 5:17

OPENING REFLECTION/CONVERSATION

The documentary film *Pressure Cooker* (2008) tells the true story of a class of Philadelphia high school students from poor backgrounds who are competing for scholarships in the culinary arts. For these young people, securing a scholarship is the only way they can hope to get to college and achieve success and new opportunities for themselves. The documentary focuses on three students: Erica, who comes from a broken home and cares for her blind sister; Tyree, a football enthusiast who has to support himself and his single mother, and Fatoumata, who is a recent emigrant from Africa. Helped by their tough but loving and inspirational teacher, and a lot of hard work, these three students do well in the competition. They can now look forward to lives full of opportunity and hope.

Living as a new creation in Christ does not mean being a totally different person. It means cooperating with the grace of God and discovering and using your gifts so as to become the unique person God created you to be.

TALK IT OVER

In our culture, anything that is innovative, truly new or radically improved, has instant appeal. Shiny and unblemished products, the latest fashion and technology all attract our attention.

⊙ What do you think our cultural desire for all things new has to do with the reality of the new creation offered through Christ?

⊙ Do you see these as compatible or incompatible? Explain.

⊙ Can our cultural desire for the 'new' ever be fulfilled? Explain.

198 | CREDO | THE PROMISED ONE: SERVANT AND SAVIOR

The Paschal Mystery of Christ's Death, Resurrection and Ascension set God's plan for the new creation in motion. In the Nicene Creed all Christians profess their faith in Christ, saying:

For our sake he was crucified
    under Pontius Pilate,
he suffered death and was
    buried,
and rose again on the third day
in accordance with the
    Scriptures.
He ascended into heaven
and is seated at the right hand
    of the Father.

He will come again in glory
to judge the living and the
    dead,
and his kingdom will have no end.

CHRIST IN MAJESTY | SEBASTIANO DEL PIOMBO

Jesus' Ascension inaugurated the new creation, which is also called the Kingdom, or Reign, of God, since Christ in heaven reigns over all of it. As Christ the Lord reigns in heaven, his disciples on earth work to bring about the fullness of his reign on earth until he returns in glory. We continue to follow him who is the way, the truth and the life, as we face the trials and challenges of life. To continue Jesus' work of bringing about God's Reign, Christ sends the Holy Spirit to empower us to live our Christian identity and fulfill the vocation, or mission, that God has given us.

JOURNAL EXERCISE

In the Lord's Prayer we pray, 'Thy kingdom come; thy will be done on earth as it is in heaven.' In other words, we pray for the coming of the new creation.

- ⊙ Reflect on this question: What is the will of God that Christians must do?
- ⊙ Then write a summary of your reflections in your journal.

OUR JOURNEY TO GOD

The Risen and Glorified Christ is the Lord of heaven and earth. In this chapter we will explore three dogmas of the Catholic faith that are connected to this truth. These revealed truths are: (1) Christ's own Ascension into heaven, (2) the coming of the Holy Spirit at **Pentecost**, and (3) the **Assumption** of Mary, body and soul, into heaven at the end of her life of earth. These three dimensions of our faith also point to the reality of the divine pledge of the new creation. Belief in these truths has the power to reshape how we live our lives, empowering us to do God's will 'on earth as it is in heaven' and so work to advance the fullness of the coming of God's Kingdom.

Our whole life is a journey, coming forth from and returning to God, our Creator and Life-Giver. Faith in Jesus' Ascension into heaven, and his sending the Holy Spirit to guide us toward the Reign of God, and the Assumption of Mary, assures us that we can finally rest in God and find our heart's fulfillment.

THINK, PAIR AND SHARE

- ⊙ Explore with a partner the most popular depictions of heaven that come to your mind.
- ⊙ Now draw your own image of heaven.

CHAPTER 9: BOUND FOR GLORY | ATTEND AND REFLECT | 199

It is easier for a camel to go through the eye of a needle than for someone who is rich to enter the kingdom of God

AS IT IS IN HEAVEN

We humans can only begin to imagine what heaven may be like, and our images will always fall short. St. Paul, speaking on this point, teaches:

What no eye has seen, nor ear heard,
    nor the human heart conceived,
what God has prepared for those who love him.
—1 Corinthians 2:9

This is the new order of reality that God brought about through the Death-Resurrection-Ascension of Jesus and confirmed with the Assumption of Mary. Every time we do God's will on earth, we advance the coming to completion of the Reign of God.

LET'S PROBE DEEPER

⊙ Read the following Gospel descriptions of the Kingdom of God:
  – 'Blessed are you who are poor, for yours is the kingdom of God.' (Luke 6:20)
  – 'Let the little children come to me; do not stop them; for it is to such as these that the kingdom of God belongs.' (Mark 10:14)
  – 'Cure the sick who are there, and say to them, "The kingdom of God has come near to you." ' (Luke 10:9)
  – 'Indeed, it is easier for a camel to go through the eye of a needle than for someone who is rich to enter the kingdom of God.' (Luke 18:25)

⊙ How do these references point us to what heaven may be like?

OVER TO YOU

⊙ At times, Jesus affirmed the signs of the Reign of God around him. Read Mark 12:34.
⊙ Where do you notice the signs of the Kingdom of God around you?
⊙ How does experiencing the Kingdom of God make you feel?
⊙ What can you do today that will be a sign of the Kingdom of God?

HEAR THE STORY

The Ascension

OPENING REFLECTION

In the springtime it is not uncommon to find a baby bird that has fallen out of its nest in its efforts to learn to fly. For nestlings, learning to fly is a lesson in tough love. Eventually parent birds begin to stay away from the nest for longer periods of time to coax the little ones to move out of the nest on their own. Leaving the nest on their own for the first time is the greatest leap of a nestling's short life. At times, these nestlings end up on the ground, but, with their parents' guidance and protection, it is likely that they will eventually succeed.

WHAT ABOUT YOU PERSONALLY?

- On finding a nestling on the ground, many of us would be tempted to take it home to 'rescue' it, thinking that it fell out of its nest too soon. Why might this be a bad idea?
- What is the biggest leap you have ever taken? Who helped you along?

- The Bible images God as a 'mother eagle'. For example, in Exodus we read, 'I bore you on eagles' wings and brought you to myself' (Exodus 19:4). Why might this be a fitting image for God?
- When do you experience God as both a tough and protective parent?

WHY DO YOU STAND LOOKING UP TOWARD HEAVEN?

The Ascension marks the end of the forty days the Risen Christ spent among his disciples, 'appearing to them . . . and speaking about the kingdom of God' (Acts of the Apostles 1:3). The Gospels reveal that after those forty days, Christ was taken up into heaven to sit at the right hand of God the Father. Before his ascent into glory, Christ promised the disciples that the Holy Spirit would empower them to become his witnesses to Jews and Gentiles—to all peoples. (Read Mark 16:19–20 and Luke 24:50–53.) The Acts of the Apostles describes the scene with a bit more detail.

So when they had come together, they asked him, 'Lord, is this the time when you will restore the kingdom to Israel?' He replied, 'It is not for you to know the times or periods that the Father has set by his own authority. But you will receive power when the Holy Spirit has come upon you; and you will be my witnesses in Jerusalem, in all Judea and Samaria, and to the ends of the earth.' When he had said this, as they were watching, he was lifted up, and a cloud took him out of their sight. While he was

CHAPTER 9: BOUND FOR GLORY | HEAR THE STORY | 201

going and they were gazing up towards heaven, suddenly two men in white robes stood by them. They said, 'Men of Galilee, why do you stand looking up towards heaven? This Jesus, who has been taken up from you into heaven, will come in the same way as you saw him go into heaven.'

—Acts of the Apostles 1:6–11

OVER TO YOU

⊙ Imagine yourself standing among Jesus' disciples, gazing upward as he disappears. What might be going through your mind? What fears might you have? What might be your best hopes?

The Risen Lord who had spent forty amazing days with his disciples was now leaving their sight once again. They had thought they had lost him once already with his Death on the Cross and his burial in the tomb. But three days later, his glorious Resurrection had filled them with hope and healed their sorrows with great joy. Now they watched as he left them again. Perhaps they asked themselves: Will he return? When and in what form? What are we supposed to do in the meantime?

The Ascension of the Risen Lord into divine glory seals our Christian faith in and hope for the resurrection of our body and our everlasting life. Although the Second Person of the Trinity has always existed with God, the Ascension of the incarnate Son of God takes the humanity of Jesus Christ into divine glory. The Ascension of Jesus Christ opens the door of heaven to all humankind.

JOURNAL EXERCISE

⊙ Ponder the metaphor of the life of faith being compared to a baby bird learning to fly. How are God's actions toward us like those of a parent bird caring for a nestling? How are they different?

⊙ Write your thoughts on this in your journal.

THE ASCENSION | AZULEJOS TILES IN LAMA, PORTUGAL

202 | CREDO | THE PROMISED ONE: SERVANT AND SAVIOR

THE CHALLENGE OF THE ASCENSION

With Christ's Ascension, the disciples began to understand more clearly that they were facing a great but challenging opportunity. They saw the promise of the Resurrection fulfilled, and their hope of the glory of eternal life in God's eternal presence strengthened. 'Jesus Christ, having entered the sanctuary of heaven once and for all, intercedes constantly for us as the mediator who assures us of the permanent outpouring of the Holy Spirit' (*Catechism of the Catholic Church* [CCC], no. 667).

Like any of us, the disciples had a long way to go before they learned to fly. But what did it mean to learn to fly as a disciple of the Glorified Lord, now seated at the right hand of the Father? The Letter to the Ephesians, which is one of the assigned readings for the Solemnity of the Ascension, gives us this insight:

I therefore, the prisoner in the Lord, beg you to lead a life worthy of the calling to which you have been called, with all humility and gentleness, with patience, bearing with one another in love, making every effort to maintain the unity of the Spirit in the bond of peace.
—Ephesians 4:1–3

Jesus Christ did not leave his disciples to face this great but challenging opportunity unprepared. His whole life, his words, actions and teachings, all served to help his disciples to understand his mission and to continue it after he left. The Scriptures reveal that between the Resurrection and the Ascension, Jesus mentored them in their role as disciples of the Kingdom of God. In the Acts of the Apostles, Luke writes, 'After his suffering he presented himself alive to them by many convincing proofs, appearing to them over the course of forty days and speaking about the kingdom of God' (Acts of the Apostles 1:3). In his account of the Gospel, St. Luke also tells us that, as the Risen Lord traveled the road to Emmaus with the two distraught disciples, he helped them to understand what the Scriptures taught about the Messiah, the Suffering Servant of God. (Read Luke 24:27.) The disciples relied on these teachings and the stories they recalled from the life of Jesus to grow into their role as disciples of the Lord.

FAITH WORD

Ascension

The entry of Jesus' humanity into divine glory to be at the right hand of the Father; traditionally, this occurred forty days after Jesus' Resurrection.
—*United States Catholic Catechism for Adults*, 504

THE ASCENSION | 8TH-CENTURY ANGLO-SAXON IVORY

WHAT ABOUT YOU PERSONALLY?

⊙ Have you ever faced a great but challenging opportunity? What promises and challenges did it offer?
⊙ How can faith in the Paschal Mystery help you and other people to face the challenges of life?

TALK IT OVER

⊙ Working with a partner, browse the Bible to find passages that help you meet the challenges you face in life. As you do so, discuss the following questions and share your insights:
  – Why are the passages you chose meaningful for you?
  – How do they encourage you in your faith?
  – How do they help you make difficult decisions?

CHAPTER 9: BOUND FOR GLORY | HEAR THE STORY | 203

GOD INVITING CHRIST TO SIT AT HIS RIGHT HAND | PIETER DE GREBBER

As the *Catechism* teaches, 'The lifting up of Jesus on the cross signifies and announces his lifting up by his Ascension into heaven, and indeed begins it' (CCC, no. 662). Jesus did not gain his power at the right hand of God by violence, force, aggression, bullying or intimidation, but by self-sacrifice and service to his Father and to all humanity. In other words, Jesus revealed the true nature of 'power', the power of God at work in our lives.

We often experience the exercise of 'power' as the use of force and violence; and we can easily and mistakenly associate force and violence as essential components of power. Jesus turned this understanding of power inside out. Instead of fighting violence with violence, Jesus exercised true power by submitting to death on the Cross. Jesus' Death, Resurrection and Ascension reveal that true power is exercised in acts of love and not hate, of peace and not violence, of truth and not deceit and falsehood—of serving rather than being served.

Next time you see a Crucifix, stop and take a look at it anew as one of the most profound images of 'power' we have as Christians—of the power of God at work in our lives.

REFLECT AND DECIDE
- Consider a scenario where a person is being bullied by others.
- Who appears to be the most powerful?
- In light of what you have read and heard about Jesus, where is the true power in this scenario? Explain your answer.

JOURNAL EXERCISE
- Reflect on your life and the lives of those around you. Who do you consider to be the powerful? Why do you consider them to be so? Who seems to be the powerless? Why do you consider them so? How does their power compare to the power of Christ as revealed through the Cross?
- Write your reflections in your journal.

CREATIVE EXERCISE
- Still working in pairs, choose one of the passages that you selected for the previous activity and create a poster, using the passage as the focal point.
- Display all the different passages and read the different choices from the whole group.

AT THE RIGHT HAND OF THE FATHER
In describing the Ascension in his account of the Gospel, St. Mark writes that the Risen Jesus 'sat down at the right hand of God' (Mark 16:19). The phrase 'to sit at the right hand of God' was a common expression in the culture of the peoples of the ancient world. Mark and other sacred authors of the New Testament used this phrase to signify God's glory, power and authority and to help us understand the significance of the Ascension. That the Risen Jesus now 'sits at the right hand of God' reveals that, with the Father and the Holy Spirit, Christ 'has gone into heaven and is at the right hand of God, with angels, authorities, and powers made subject to him' (1 Peter 3:22) and exercises the glory, power and authority of God over all of creation. (See CCC, no. 663.)

The Son of Man's path to greatness and 'glory' was fundamentally connected to his Death.

204 | CREDO | THE PROMISED ONE: SERVANT AND SAVIOR

EMBRACE THE VISION

The experience of Pentecost

OPENING ACTIVITY/DISCUSSION

- Read and reflect on the account of Pentecost in Acts 2:1–12.
  - What are your first thoughts about the Pentecost event?
  - What do you feel passionate about? And how do you express this strong sentiment?

- How does passion for something motivate you differently than other things in your life (duty, obligation and so on)?
- Now read this poetic interpretation of the Pentecost event:

Pentecost-Poem

In the upper room
Pentecostal wind
swirled like a tornado of grace
and fiery tongues
burned language into stutterers.

O Spirit,
stir our passion again!
Light wildfires
and spin them past
our tame intentions.

Huff and puff till you blow down
the shutters we hide in,
scarred by earlier zests,
more cowardly and cynical
than once upon a time

when we inhaled your fire
and gulped your windstorms
like tap water
and laughed at those
who counseled caution.

THINK, PAIR AND SHARE

- With a partner, analyze 'Pentecost-Poem', which was written by Sr. Patricia Schnapp, RSM. As you do so, notice all the verbs, adjectives and images she uses to describe the action of the Holy Spirit and list them in three groups.
- Notice all the verbs she uses to describe our human actions. How do the human actions change in the course of the poem?

- Ponder the image of shutters as those panels that are meant to protect our homes from the power of the wind. What do you think the poet is referring to when she points out the shutters we hide in? What are some of the shutters in your life? Why are they in place? How may they keep out God's 'tornado of grace'?

CHAPTER 9: BOUND FOR GLORY | EMBRACE THE VISION | 205

Sr. Patricia Schnapp's 'Pentecost' recalls the coming of the Holy Spirit to the disciples of Jesus gathered in the upper room ten days after the Ascension. It also describes how we may experience the life-giving power of the same Holy Spirit in our own lives. According to the poem, it is the Spirit of God that stirs our passions and fills us with a sense of true power, enabling us to overcome our fears and face the obstacles of life. We experience the Holy Spirit, the Third Person of the Trinity who is inseparable from the Father and the Son, as God's movement of grace, or life-giving breath, which animates us to live as disciples of Jesus.

EMBOLDENED WITH THE LANGUAGE OF FAITH

After Christ ascended into divine glory, he fulfilled his promise to send the Holy Spirit. Luke writes that the disciples who 'numbered about one hundred and twenty persons', including 'certain women' and 'Mary, the mother of Jesus' (Acts of the Apostles 1:14–15), were gathered in Jerusalem on the day of Pentecost. The word 'pentecost' means 'fifty'. Pentecost was the fiftieth day of the Jewish celebration of Shavu'ot, the annual celebration of the Jewish Feast of Weeks which occurred after Passover. During Shavu'ot in Jesus' time the Jewish people remembered and celebrated the harvesting of the first fruits, the bringing of them to the Temple in Jerusalem and the giving of the Torah at Mount Sinai to Moses.

The Holy Spirit came like 'the rush of a violent wind' and filled the entire house. 'Divided tongues, as of fire, appeared among them, and a tongue rested on each of them. All of them were filled with the Holy Spirit and began to speak in other languages, as the Spirit gave them ability' (Acts of the Apostles 2:2–4). The disciples, led by Peter, then left the security of the upper room, went out into the marketplace and boldly shared the news of 'God's deeds of power' (Acts of the Apostles 2:11) with the Jews who had come 'from every nation under heaven' to celebrate Shavu'ot in Jerusalem. All who heard them were astounded to hear the good news in their native languages.

FAITH WORD

Pentecost

The 'fiftieth day' at the end of the seven weeks following Passover (Easter in the Christian dispensation). At the first Pentecost after the Resurrection and Ascension of Jesus, the Holy Spirit was manifested, given and communicated as a divine Person to the Church, fulfilling the paschal mystery of Christ according to his promise.

—CCC, Glossary

If you were among the first disciples, what might have been some of your questions and fears about your future?

OVER TO YOU

- Reread Acts of the Apostles 2:1–12.
- What stands out for you now from this story of Pentecost?

DO NOT LET YOUR HEARTS BE TROUBLED

Between the Ascension and Pentecost the disciples were undoubtedly at a crossroads, trying to decide how to move forward. They no doubt were wondering when the Holy Spirit would come to them as Jesus had promised. How did they handle that time 'in between'? The Acts of the Apostles reveals that this time together was a time of prayer. Luke writes, 'All these were constantly devoting themselves to prayer' (Acts of the Apostles 1:14). It would seem that, while in prayer, they recalled and reflected on Jesus' promise and were awaiting the coming of 'the Advocate' and 'the Helper'.

TALK IT OVER

- What do you think some of the disciples' greatest fears or worries might have been during this time?
- If you were among the first disciples, what might have been some of your questions and fears about your future?

As the first disciples faced their fears and questions, Jesus' words spoken at the Last Supper would certainly have given them courage to face the future.

I have said these things to you while I am still with you. But the Advocate, the Holy Spirit, whom the Father will send in my name, will teach you everything, and remind you of all that I have said to you. . . . Do not let your hearts be troubled, and do not let them be afraid. You heard me say to you, 'I am going away, and I am coming to you.' . . . . And now I have told you this before it occurs, so that when it does occur, you may believe.

—John 14:25–26, 27–29

On that Pentecost, Christ fulfilled his promise. The rushing wind and tongues of fire ignited the disciples' faith. Fire is a biblical symbol of God's energy and the force of God's life-giving action in the world. (See Ecclesiasticus [Sirach] 48:1; 1 Kings 18:38–39; 3:16.) The tongues of fire that rested on each disciple were a visible sign of the Spirit filling them with this burning desire, stirring their passions to motivate them for their mission to share the Good News. The flames

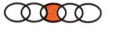

CHAPTER 9: BOUND FOR GLORY | EMBRACE THE VISION | 207

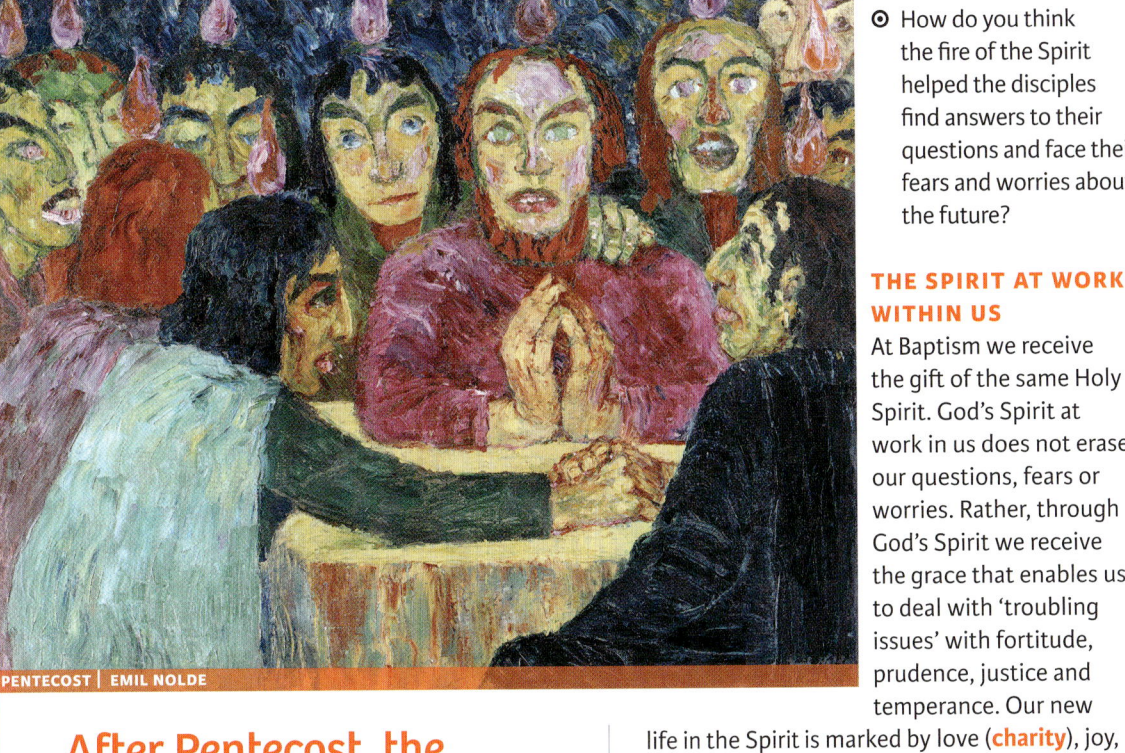

PENTECOST | EMIL NOLDE

TALK IT OVER

- How do you think the fire of the Spirit helped the disciples find answers to their questions and face their fears and worries about the future?

THE SPIRIT AT WORK WITHIN US

At Baptism we receive the gift of the same Holy Spirit. God's Spirit at work in us does not erase our questions, fears or worries. Rather, through God's Spirit we receive the grace that enables us to deal with 'troubling issues' with fortitude, prudence, justice and temperance. Our new life in the Spirit is marked by love (**charity**), joy, peace, patience, kindness, goodness, generosity, gentleness, faithfulness, modesty, chastity and self-control. St. Paul refers to the qualities of a full life in Christ as 'the fruit[s] of the Spirit' (Galatians 5:22–23), which the *Catechism* teaches are 'perfections that the Holy Spirit forms in us as the "first fruits" of eternal glory' (CCC, Glossary). When we experience these twelve perfections, or qualities, in our life, we are experiencing signs of the power of God's Spirit in our lives.

After Pentecost, the disciples were literally 'on fire' with the Spirit

remind us of our passions, our deepest and heartfelt desires that motivate us to engage in the world around us.

At the heart of Jesus' Good News is the unquenchable fire of God's life-giving love for all people. It is that same fire dwelling within us that calls us as disciples of Jesus to love God, neighbors and ourselves as Jesus loved, to live as Jesus lived; 'Just as I have loved you, you also should love one another' (John 13:34). After Pentecost, the disciples were literally 'on fire' with the Spirit. They began boldly to share the Good News of Jesus Christ with the different nations gathered in Jerusalem.

WHAT ABOUT YOU PERSONALLY?

- How can the **Fruits of the Holy Spirit** help you make good decisions?
- Have you ever faced a challenge and struggled with how to move forward? How did your fears and worries play a part in this? Who or what helped you move forward? Might the Holy Spirit have been at work in your life then? Now?

GIFTS FOR BUILDING UP THE BODY OF CHRIST ON EARTH

The New Testament passes on to us the faith of the Church that the Holy Spirit showers the Church with unique gifts, or charisms. A charism

208 | CREDO | THE PROMISED ONE: SERVANT AND SAVIOR

is 'a specific gift or grace of the Holy Spirit which directly or indirectly benefits the Church, given in order to help a person live out the Christian life, or to serve the common good in building up the Church' (CCC, Glossary). In the Letter to the Ephesians, we read:

The gifts he gave were that some would be apostles, some prophets, some evangelists, some pastors and some teachers, to equip the saints for the work of ministry, for building up the body of Christ, until all of us come to the unity of the faith and of the knowledge of the Son of God, to maturity, to the measure of the full stature of Christ.

—Ephesians 4:11–13

The Church, born on the Cross and filled with the Holy Spirit, began her work at Pentecost. The Church, the Temple of the Holy Spirit, has always been and will always be guided by the Spirit to manifest and make present the saving work of God in the world. The Holy Spirit blesses each of the baptized with his gifts and with unique talents to bear fruit in our lives. The grace of the Spirit enables us in our mission to share the Good News of Jesus Christ with those around us.

OVER TO YOU

- ◉ What are your unique and particular gifts? How might the Holy Spirit inspire you to use your gifts to advance the Reign of God?
- ◉ What do you think are the greatest needs in our world? What are the greatest injustices or problems that cry out for God's help? What is the connection between these needs and your gifts?
- ◉ How might you be able to serve and use these gifts for God's glory?

What do you think are the greatest needs in our world? What problems cry out for God's help?

NEARLY 30 PERCENT OF DUTCH COMMUTERS ALWAYS TRAVEL BY BICYCLE; IN THE US ONLY 2 PERCENT OF TRIPS ARE MADE BY BICYCLE

CHAPTER 9: BOUND FOR GLORY | EMBRACE THE VISION | 209

THINK IT THROUGH

A promise fulfilled

OPENING REFLECTION/CONVERSATION

Malvin and his dog, Bandit, had been best friends for years. After Malvin's wife died, Bandit kept him company and helped restore his spirit, as they would sit together day by day on the stoop of their New Orleans home. In August 2005, as Hurricane Katrina threatened their city, Malvin sought refuge from the storm in the Louisiana Superdome, but Bandit was turned away: no dogs were allowed. Heartbroken, Malvin had to leave Bandit behind with a supply of food and water, and hope for the best.

Malvin was evacuated to Houston, but he finally returned to his ravaged home after a few months. He lived in a trailer by his home as he slowly put the pieces of his life back together. But Bandit was gone. Malvin began to search for Bandit in hopes of his rescue.

Animal rescuers eventually found Bandit and he was adopted into a new home in Pennsylvania. In the meantime, Malvin made an unlikely friend, a woman named Sandra who found out about his loss of Bandit on the internet. She promised to do all she could to reunite Malvin and Bandit from her home thousands of miles away in Canada. After months of persistent phone calls, research and legal battles, Sandra succeeded in reclaiming Bandit for Malvin. The joy of a promise fulfilled now fills these new friends with an unforgettable memory.

◉ Have you ever been in a situation where you experienced the joy of a fulfilled promise? If so, share your story.

A PLEDGE OF FUTURE GLORY

The Ascension not only establishes Christ in glory 'at the right hand of God'; it is also a pledge of and the beginning of our glory. The resurrected and ascended Christ fortifies our hope in our ultimate life in God's eternal presence, the fulfillment of God's promise. Out of God's generosity and wisdom, we have another powerful sign to assure us of the fulfillment of God's promise to humankind: the Assumption of Mary. After Jesus, Mary was the first person to experience the total fulfillment of God's promise in eternal life.

TALK IT OVER

◉ Why do you think God granted us another sign to assure us of the promise of Salvation?

210 | CREDO | THE PROMISED ONE: SERVANT AND SAVIOR

THE ASSUMPTION OF MARY

From the very beginning of Mary's life, God showered her with unique graces and privileges that prepared her to be the Mother of Jesus, God's incarnate Son. Among these unique graces are Mary's **Immaculate Conception** and her Assumption. God's grace preserved Mary from all sin—Original Sin and all personal sins—from the moment of her conception and throughout her entire life. Mary's Assumption at the end of her life on earth was God's gift to her, a unique blessing following upon her lifelong union with her Son. St. John of Damascus, also known as St. John Damascene (c. 676–c. 754), one of the Fathers of the Church in the East, wrote three sermons on the Assumption. In Sermon II he taught:

ASSUMPTION OF THE VIRGIN MARY | 16TH-CENTURY PORTUGUESE

> It was fitting that she, who had kept her virginity intact in childbirth, should keep her own body free from all corruption even after death. It was fitting that she, who had carried the Creator as a child at her breast, should dwell in the divine tabernacles. It was fitting that the spouse, whom the Father had taken to himself, should live in the divine mansions. It was fitting that she, who had seen her Son upon the cross and who had thereby received into her heart the sword of sorrow which she had escaped in the act of giving birth to him, should look upon him as he sits with the Father. It was fitting that God's Mother should possess what belongs to her Son, and that she should be honored by every creature as the Mother and as the handmaid of God.

The Assumption of Mary names the Tradition of the Church that, at the end of her life on earth, Mary was assumed, or taken up, into heaven, body and soul. Mary did not experience the bodily decay of death; from the moment of the end of her life, she has lived in the glory of the Resurrection, body and soul, in the presence of God.

The Assumption of Mary, however, is not the same as the Ascension of Jesus. Jesus ascended out of his own divine power, while Mary was taken up by the grace of God. In her Assumption, Mary was given the unique grace to participate fully in the joy of her Son's Resurrection and in the new order of creation that it inaugurated; she did not have to wait until the 'resurrection of her body' when Christ would come again in glory to judge the living and the dead.

On November 1, 1950, Pope Pius XII, who was Pope from 1939 to 1958, honored this long-standing Tradition of the Church. In the Apostolic Constitution *Munificentissimus Deus* (The Most Bountiful God), the Pope pronounced the Assumption of Mary to be a dogma of Catholic faith. This means that the Assumption of Mary is a truth of faith contained in **divine Revelation** and defined by the **Magisterium**, which the faithful are obliged to believe. Pope Pius XII taught:

CHAPTER 9: BOUND FOR GLORY | *THINK IT THROUGH* | 211

THE ASSUMPTION OF THE VIRGIN MARY | P.J. BREPOLS

REFLECT AND DISCUSS

◉ Compare the Ascension and the Assumption. Why do you think it is important to distinguish between them?

◉ The distinction between the Ascension and the Assumption praises the power of God in all good things. Why do you think it is important to recognize good things as God's gifts? What may happen if one forgets God as the source of all goodness and hope?

PRAY FOR US NOW

As one of the last actions of his life on earth, Jesus entrusted his mother and 'the disciple whom he loved' to each other. (Read John 19:25–27.) This union between Mary and 'the disciple whom [Jesus] loved' symbolizes the relationship binding Mary and the Church and her lifetime of dedication to her Son and his mission. Jesus gave us his own mother to be our Mother in faith. Mary, who accepted 'the disciple whom [Jesus] loved' into her care, continues to care for all the disciples of Jesus.

Mary's presence in heaven amplifies her role as Mother of the Church. She is in the presence of God and in the company of her Son, interceding on behalf of the whole Church. The Church's trust and faith in her role in the divine plan of Salvation is expressed in the Hail Mary when we pray:

Holy Mary, Mother of God,
pray for us sinners,
now and at the hour of our death.

Mary trustingly brings our prayers and hopes to her glorified Son, Jesus Christ, as she brought the needs of the newlyweds at Cana in Galilee. The intercession of the Mother of Jesus on our behalf, who are also her children in faith, reflects our bond to Christ and surrounds our prayers with hope and compassion.

By the authority of our Lord Jesus Christ, of the Blessed Apostles Peter and Paul, and by our own authority, we pronounce, declare, and define it to be a divinely revealed dogma: that the Immaculate Mother of God, the ever Virgin Mary, having completed the course of her earthly life, was assumed body and soul into heavenly glory.
—*Munificentissimus Deus,* no. 44

While the Assumption was named a dogma of the Church in 1950, Christians have celebrated the miraculous end to Mary's life for centuries. Mary's Assumption is a sign of hope for all people. In her faith and dedication to her Son, Mary's life was already a sign of the new order of creation that would be accomplished by the Death and Resurrection of Jesus. Both her Immaculate Conception and Assumption help us understand this. Mary invites us to follow her in the way she followed her Son. Her relationship with the Lord can shape and deepen ours.

212 | CREDO | THE PROMISED ONE: SERVANT AND SAVIOR

OVER TO YOU

- Have you ever prayed for a friend or relative? How did praying for this person reflect your relationship with them? With God? How did it shape your relationship with them? With God?
- Why do you think it is important to pray for one another? What does praying for another person accomplish?
- When and how can you ask Mary to pray for you?

The Assumption of Mary is Good News for every person. Her place in heaven, living in the eternal presence of God and in the company of her glorified Son, is a blessing to us. She continues to pray and care for 'those whom he loves' and for the final fulfillment of Jesus' mission as it unfolds in the Church. The Assumption is also Good News because it reveals, in a different way, the fulfillment of God's promise of Salvation for all humankind. Mary in heaven, body and soul, whom the Church honors as the Queen of Heaven and Earth, amplifies the hope of all Christians for our eternal life with God, with Mary and with the angels and all the saints.

A PIONEER IN FAITH: EXEMPLAR DISCIPLE

Mary is honored and revered as the Mother of all Christians and as the exemplar disciple in all the cultural families that make up the Church across the world. While Mary was a first-century Jewish woman, the statues and images of Mary and the Marian devotional practices around the world that match her many titles often take the form of the particular culture that honors her. Mary's skin, her features and her clothing tend to resemble those of the local people who are devoted to her. Throughout Christian history, Mary has also been honored with many titles that indicate her universal appeal and the trust in her intercession for us with her Son. For example, Catholics pray to Mary as Our Lady of Guadalupe (Mexico), Our Lady of Częstochowa (Poland), Our Lady of Lourdes (France), Our Lady of Knock (Ireland), Our Lady of Lavang (Vietnam) and Our Lady of Kibeho (Rwanda). Christians around the world have truly responded to their dying Savior's request, 'Here is your mother'.

CELEBRATION OF THE VIRGIN MARY PILGRIMAGE, ROMERIA, BENALMADENA, SPAIN

TALK IT OVER

Brainstorm and discuss responses to the following:

⊙ What other titles do people use to address Mary or to ask for her prayers?

⊙ Why do you think the various depictions of Mary adopt the features of the people from the cultures in which they originate? What does this communicate about Mary's role as Mother of all Christians? How would you depict Mary as Mother to your community? What title would you give her? How is she a sign of hope for you? What is the greatest need you have for Mary's intercession at this time?

Every year since the seventh century the Catholic Church around the world joins in celebrating the Solemnity of the Assumption. By declaring the Assumption a Solemnity, the Church asserts her belief in the importance of the Assumption in the Christian life. In the United States, the Solemnity of the Assumption is a holy day of obligation, which the Church celebrates on August 15.

OVER TO YOU

Blessed Pope John Paul II often urged Christians to 'learn from Mary'. This metaphor depicts the Mother of Jesus as a teacher. Indeed, as Jesus' earthly mother, Mary was his first teacher. Mary taught us a profound lesson about God's promise and fulfillment. Her whole life, from her Immaculate Conception to her Assumption, spoke of promise and fulfillment.

⊙ Have you ever thought of Mary as a teacher? Why is this a fitting metaphor?

⊙ What can you learn from Mary for your life in faith today?

DECIDE FOR YOURSELF

⊙ How does the life and Assumption of Mary offer you hope for your own life as a disciple of Jesus?

⊙ Will you ask Mary to pray for you?

PILGRIMS AT THE SANCTUARY OF OUR LADY IN LOURDES, FRANCE, DURING THE FEAST OF THE ASSUMPTION, 2011

JUDGE AND ACT

REFLECT ON WHAT YOU HAVE LEARNED

In this chapter we learned about the Ascension, Pentecost and the Assumption of Mary, all signs of the triumph of Christ. They signal the Reign of God, the new order of creation that he ushers in. These glorious events strengthen both our commitment to live as disciples of Jesus now and our hope in eternal life with him. The mysteries of faith also invite us to be agents of God's Reign around us, to work to realize God's Kingdom now, with the help of God's grace, through our good words and deeds.

- ⊙ Reflect for a moment on what you have learned in this chapter.
- ⊙ What real difference will your faith make to your everyday life from here on?
- ⊙ Think of someone with whom you can share your faith, perhaps a person who needs a bit of reassurance and encouragement.

LEARN BY EXAMPLE

The story of St. Lucy

From her earliest days, the Church has seen herself as a pilgrim people, a people on a journey. The hope of sharing in the glory of Christ has given Christians not only the vision to see their suffering in this life as a sharing in the suffering of Christ, but also the courage and the perseverance to cope with suffering and sacrifice as the road to sharing in the glory of their Lord. The life, suffering and death of St. Lucy is a model for us of that faith and hope.

   The name 'Lucy' means 'light'. And the bravery of Lucy gave rise to many legends that inspire Christians to keep their eye on the eternal destination. One of those legends tells of the attempt of a Roman official to force Lucy into a life of prostitution, which she resisted. The legend goes on to claim that when the guards came to carry her to her death, Lucy was so heavy they could not move her. The manner of Lucy's martyrdom is uncertain; some say she was burned to death; others say her throat was cut with a sword. Whatever the means of her death, she was

ST. LUCY WITH ST. ELIZABETH OF HUNGARY

killed in 304 during the persecution by the Emperor Diocletian, a persecution marked by the torture of Christians.

   St. Lucy's life and death is a profession of her faith and the faith of the Church that our sharing in the sufferings of Christ is founded in our hope of sharing in the glory of Christ. The Catholic Church remembers the life of St. Lucy each year on December 13.

CHAPTER 9: BOUND FOR GLORY | JUDGE AND ACT | 215

TALK IT OVER

- Have you ever been in a situation where it was difficult for you to stand up for your faith in Christ? How did you respond? What gave you the vision and strength to meet that challenge?
- How might the wisdom you have learned in this chapter help you to respond to similar situations in the future?

OVER TO YOU

- What can be some of the risks of giving real witness to your faith?
- What are the benefits?
- How can your faith in the Glorified Christ and in the Holy Spirit help you to speak the truth, even in difficult circumstances?

- How will you apply this wisdom in your life from here on?

RESPOND WITH YOUR FAMILY

- Reflect on and talk with your family about:
  - Where do you find reflected in your family the Good News of the Ascension of Christ Jesus and the presence of the Holy Spirit in your life?
  - Where do you see our world still struggling against God's Reign? How can you as a family bring hope to those situations?

WHAT WILL YOU DO NOW?

- Decide on one thing you will commit to do to help advance the coming of God's Reign 'on earth as it is in heaven'.

LEARN BY HEART

Divided tongues, as of fire, appeared among them, and a tongue rested on each of them. All of them were filled with the Holy Spirit.

ACTS OF THE APOSTLES 2:3–4

216 | CREDO | THE PROMISED ONE: SERVANT AND SAVIOR

PRAYER REFLECTION

The Glorious Mysteries of the Rosary

Pray the Glorious Mysteries of the Rosary together. Directions for praying the Rosary may be found in the section 'Catholic Prayers, Devotions and Practices' at the back of this text. Begin the praying of each decade by reflecting on each of the Glorious Mysteries.

THE FIRST GLORIOUS MYSTERY: THE RESURRECTION

After the sabbath, as the first day of the week was dawning, Mary Magdalene and the other Mary went to see the tomb. And suddenly there was a great earthquake; for an angel of the Lord, descending from heaven, came and rolled back the stone and sat on it. His appearance was like lightning, and his clothing white as snow. For fear of him the guards shook and became like dead men. But the angel said to the women, 'Do not be afraid; I know that you are looking for Jesus who was crucified. He is not here; for he has been raised, as he said. Come, see the place where he lay. Then go quickly and tell his disciples, "He has been raised from the dead, and indeed he is going ahead of you to Galilee; there you will see him." This is my message for you.' So they left the tomb quickly with fear and great joy, and ran to tell his disciples.

—Matthew 28:1–8

THE SECOND GLORIOUS MYSTERY: THE ASCENSION

Then [Jesus] led them out as far as Bethany, and, lifting up his hands, he blessed them. While he was blessing them, he withdrew from them and was carried up into heaven. And they worshipped him, and returned to Jerusalem with great joy; and they were continually in the temple blessing God.

—Luke 24:50–53

THE THIRD GLORIOUS MYSTERY: THE COMING OF THE HOLY SPIRIT

When the day of Pentecost had come, they were all together in one place. And suddenly from heaven there came a sound like the rush of a violent wind, and it filled the entire house where they were sitting. Divided tongues, as of fire, appeared among them, and a tongue rested on each of them. All of them were filled with the Holy Spirit and began to speak in other languages, as the Spirit gave them ability.

—Acts of the Apostles 2:1–4

THE FOURTH GLORIOUS MYSTERY: THE ASSUMPTION OF MARY

Therefore my heart is glad, and my soul rejoices;
    my body also rests secure.
For you do not give me up to Sheol,
    or let your faithful one see the Pit.
You show me the path of life.
    In your presence there is fullness of joy;
    in your right hand are pleasures for
      evermore.

—Psalm 16:9–11

THE FIFTH GLORIOUS MYSTERY: THE CORONATION OF MARY, QUEEN OF HEAVEN

A great portent appeared in heaven: a woman clothed with the sun, with the moon under her feet, and on her head a crown of twelve stars. She was pregnant and was crying out in birth pangs, in the agony of giving birth. Then another portent appeared in heaven: a great red dragon, with seven heads and ten horns, and seven diadems on his heads. His tail swept down a third of the stars of heaven and threw them to the earth. Then the dragon stood before the woman who was about to bear a child, so that he might devour her child as soon as it was born. And she gave birth to a son, a male child, who is to rule all the nations with a rod of iron.

—Revelation 12:1–5

CHAPTER 10

Following the Way of Jesus Christ

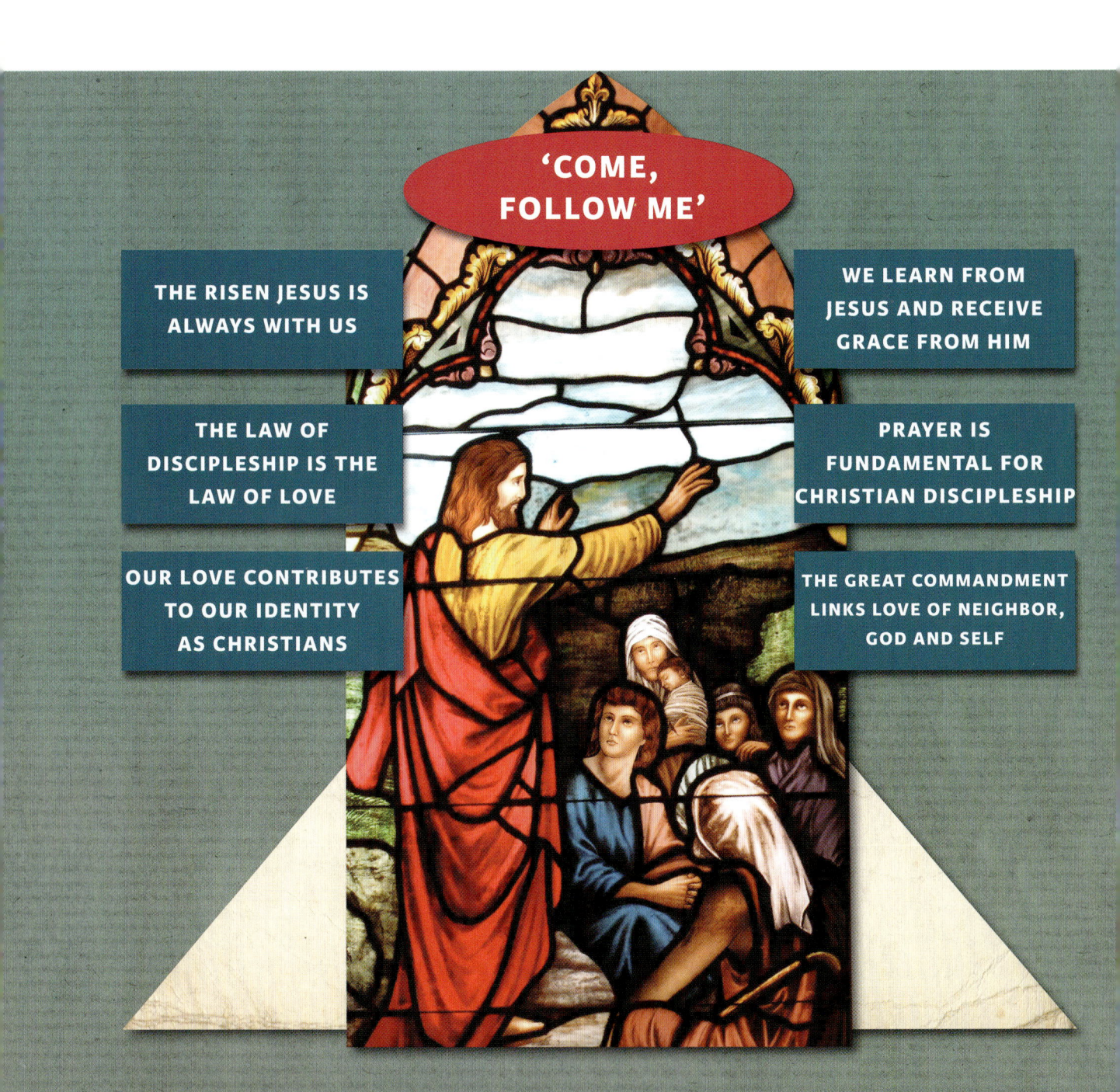

'COME, FOLLOW ME'

THE RISEN JESUS IS ALWAYS WITH US

WE LEARN FROM JESUS AND RECEIVE GRACE FROM HIM

THE LAW OF DISCIPLESHIP IS THE LAW OF LOVE

PRAYER IS FUNDAMENTAL FOR CHRISTIAN DISCIPLESHIP

OUR LOVE CONTRIBUTES TO OUR IDENTITY AS CHRISTIANS

THE GREAT COMMANDMENT LINKS LOVE OF NEIGHBOR, GOD AND SELF

THIS CHAPTER EXPLORES THE DEPTH AND MEANING OF the commitment to follow Christ. Being a Christian is not just a cultural label; it is a specific way of living in the world shaped by faith in Jesus Christ. Christian discipleship means following 'the way' of Christ in our everyday life. Being a disciple of Christ must trump every other aspect of our identity—our nationality, politics, gender and so on. It is a 365/24/7 commitment. Love of God and love of neighbor as oneself is the most defining aspect of Christian discipleship—our 'greatest commandment'.

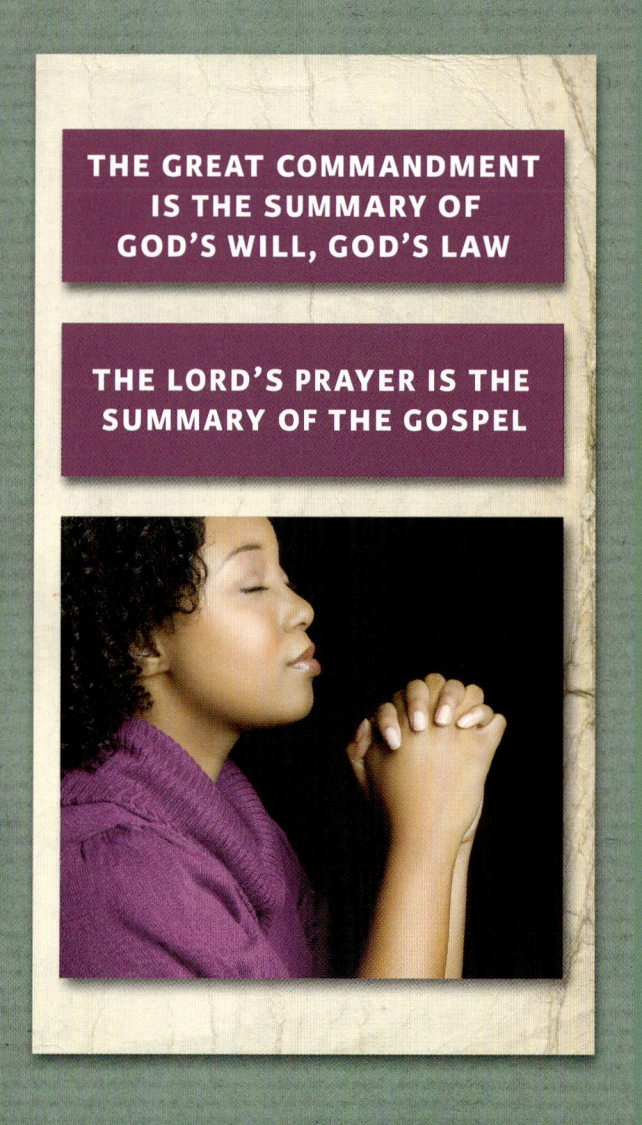

THE GREAT COMMANDMENT IS THE SUMMARY OF GOD'S WILL, GOD'S LAW

THE LORD'S PRAYER IS THE SUMMARY OF THE GOSPEL

LEARNING OUTCOMES

As a result of studying this chapter and exploring the issues raised, you should be able to:

- ⊙ explore what it means to bear the name 'Christian';
- ⊙ explore the centrality of the life and teachings of Jesus for Christians today;
- ⊙ realize the centrality of 'love' in the life of a Christian;
- ⊙ explore the biblical image of Jesus as 'a shepherd' and its implications for Christians;
- ⊙ explore Christian discipleship in the context of the Lord's Prayer;
- ⊙ understand the significance of the Mezuzah for the Jewish people;
- ⊙ understand the implications of the teaching of Jesus in the parable of the Good Samaritan;
- ⊙ know the meaning of the faith words 'disciple' and 'charity';
- ⊙ recall the story of St. Paul's conversion;
- ⊙ understand more fully that 'the way' of Jesus includes working toward justice and freedom for all.

FAITH-FORMATION OUTCOMES

As a result of studying this chapter and exploring the issues raised, you should also:

- ⊙ reflect on how you would be recognized by an observer as a Christian;
- ⊙ articulate the challenges underlying Jesus' invitation to 'Come, follow me';
- ⊙ explore ways Jesus can inspire you to face the challenge of embracing the great commandment of love;
- ⊙ improve your practice of prayer;
- ⊙ understand prayer as spending time in the presence of God;
- ⊙ articulate the challenges you face as you embrace God's commandment to love all people;
- ⊙ identify the full meaning of 'love of self' as including respecting our whole person, body, mind and spirit;
- ⊙ express ways you can bring good news to people who experience injustice and oppression in the world today;
- ⊙ reflect on and put into practice the message and challenge of the Lord's Prayer.

FAITH WORDS: Disciple; Mezuzah; Charity (Love)

LEARN BY HEART: 1 John 4:21

LEARN BY EXAMPLE: The witness and discipleship of St. Paul

ATTEND AND REFLECT

What's in a name?

OPENING REFLECTION/ACTIVITY

Many Christians wear crosses to signal their identity, or as a way to remind themselves to follow Jesus in their everyday life. However, Christian identity goes far deeper than wearing a symbol or piece of jewelry.

⊙ When you hear the name 'Christian', what images immediately come to mind? What people immediately come to mind?

⊙ Brainstorm a list of your own, and then combine your ideas with those of other students, under the heading 'What's in a Name?'

⊙ What are the most positive images on the total list? Any there any negative images?

WHAT ABOUT YOU PERSONALLY?

⊙ What is your personal favorite from the list of images and names? Explain your choice.

⊙ Now, identify some things or symbols that help to remind you of your Christian identity.

Hearing the name 'Christian' can also bring to mind particular people whom the Church honors because of their fidelity to living as followers of Christ; for example, St. Francis of Assisi or St. Teresa of Ávila, or more recent Catholic heroes, such as Blessed Mother Teresa of Calcutta, Blessed John Paul II and Archbishop Oscar Romero. We may think of the Pope or of a local bishop or priest, or of people from our own family, or people who work or volunteer at our school or parish. The people we think of as Christians will always be people who live the Gospel by loving God and by loving their neighbor as themselves, which the Scriptures tell us is the heart of living as Jesus' disciples.

THINK, PAIR AND SHARE

⊙ Imagine you are spending time with a group of friends who know very little about Christianity, and they ask you to tell them about 'being Christian'. To explain your faith, you decide to list some of the best representative examples of Christians that you can think of and you outline why you have selected these 'Christians'.

⊙ Share your list with a partner. See if you can agree on one definitive list. When you have completed this task, check in with another group.

SO, WHAT'S IN A NAME?

The name 'Christian' contains 'Christ'. 'Christ' is not the last, or family, name of Jesus. It is the central title the Scriptures use to reveal the

220 | CREDO | THE PROMISED ONE: SERVANT AND SAVIOR

Do you think people identify you as a religious person? As a Christian? As a Catholic?

ASH WEDNESDAY SERVICES AT ST. PATRICK'S CATHEDRAL, NEW YORK CITY

mission of Jesus. 'Christ' means 'Messiah' or 'Anointed One of God'. Jesus is the Anointed One, the Messiah, whom God promised to send to save his people. He is the One God sent to bring all people and all nations back into full relationship with God and into right relationship with one another. By bearing the name 'Christian', all the baptized share in and continue this mission of Jesus, the Christ.

What ultimately defines a person's identity as 'Christian' is their adherence to Jesus Christ. We are called Christians, not 'Biblians', 'Churchians' or 'Sacramentians'. Although the Bible, the Church and the Sacraments are all central and vital elements of the Christian faith and life, Jesus Christ is the center of that life. The *Catechism of the Catholic Church* states: 'At the heart [of the Christian faith] we find a Person, the Person of Jesus of Nazareth, the only Son from the Father' (CCC, no. 426). Jesus Christ—and communion with him—the Father and the Holy Spirit define who we are as disciples of the Christ.

OVER TO YOU

⊙ Do you think people identify you as a religious person? As a Christian? As a Catholic? Explain.

THE JESUS OF HISTORY AND THE CHRIST OF FAITH

Jesus was certainly recognized as a 'man of God'. Faithful to his religion and heritage, he walked the roads of Palestine, inviting people to 'Come, follow me'. He taught and lived the divinely revealed Law of Love to the fullest, and he commanded his followers to live as he lived. He loved his Father, his family and friends, and those who considered themselves his enemies. He showed his love, God's love, for people in need, bringing good news to the poor, liberty to captives and sight to the blind. He ate with sinners and set the oppressed free; he fed the hungry, cured the sick and invited Jew and Gentile.

Gradually, but with certitude, Jesus' disciples and others came to believe that this Messiah was more than a 'son of man'; he was truly the Son of God. He was indeed true God and true man. The Jesus of History is also the Christ of Faith. Incarnate of the Blessed Virgin Mary, Jesus is Lord and Savior. By his life, Passion (suffering and Death), Resurrection and Ascension, he, who is full of grace and truth, released the abundance of God's grace that makes it possible for us to live as children of God and disciples of Jesus now and for ever, when our life and mission on earth as bearers of Christ's name is completed.

TALK IT OVER

⊙ What is your own essential understanding of what it means to follow Jesus?
⊙ Do you believe that it is really possible to live as a disciple of Jesus in today's world? Why or why not?

CHAPTER 10: FOLLOWING THE WAY OF JESUS CHRIST | ATTEND AND REFLECT | 221

At the core of our Christian faith is our relationship with Jesus Christ, who is 'the way, and the truth, and the life' (John 14:6). Everything else has been given to us—rules or regulations, teachings and practices—to deepen our knowledge of Christ and grow in intimacy and communion (friendship) with him. All that we do, teach and practice as Catholics flows from and builds up our communion with him and strengthens us to live as his disciples.

PETER AND JOHN AT THE GATE OF THE TEMPLE | REMBRANDT

BOLD WITNESSES

In the Acts of the Apostles Luke tells us that soon after Pentecost, Peter and John healed a beggar who was 'lame from birth'. The beggar was sitting near the entrance to the Temple grounds, known as the Beautiful Gate. Peter and John moved on to another part of the Temple, the Portico of Solomon, where they continued to preach and teach about Jesus. No doubt, many people witnessed them. Among these people were Pharisees, Temple priests and other leaders of the Jews who, suspicious of Peter and John as they were of Jesus, brought Peter and John before the Trial Council to defend their actions. Not knowing the outcome of their hearing, Peter said:

This Jesus is
> 'the stone that was rejected by you, the builders;
> it has become the cornerstone'.

There is salvation in no one else, for there is no other name under heaven given among mortals by which we must be saved.
> —Acts of the Apostles 4:11–12

John and Peter's bold profession of faith amazed the Trial Council, who held their lives in their hands. John and Peter left not knowing the outcome of their testimony. Would it be freedom? Would it be death? (Read the entire episode in Acts of the Apostles 4:1–22.)

REFLECT AND DISCUSS

Jesus is the cornerstone of the Church and of the life of every Christian. Peter and John boldly gave witness to this faith.

- When building a house, the cornerstone is essential to the foundation, as it supports and determines how the other stones will be laid. With a partner, explore the image of Christ as the cornerstone. Imagine you are constructing a house, your life, built on Christ. Use your imagination to think about the elements of this 'house', the location, the residents, the neighborhood, and so on; in other words, the things and people you will need to make Jesus the cornerstone of your life.
- What other blocks may be necessary for raising the walls?
- What may the doors and windows stand for?
- What kind of rooms will be inside?
- When you have completed the task, share your 'house' with the rest of the class.

222 | CREDO | THE PROMISED ONE: SERVANT AND SAVIOR

THEY WILL KNOW WE ARE CHRISTIANS BY OUR LOVE

The Trial Council recognized Peter and John as companions of Jesus. Those who listened to them and saw them in action could tell that, even after Jesus' Death, they were dedicated to being his companions. They continued to follow the life, teachings and mission of Jesus, 'the stone that was rejected'.

A popular hymn repeats the refrain 'And they'll know we are Christians by our love, by our love. They will know we are Christians by our love'. We show that we are Jesus' disciples when we put into practice his command, 'Just as I have loved you, you also should love one another. By this everyone will know that you are my disciples, if you have love for one another' (John 13:34–35). Any cross we wear around our neck, display on the rear bumper of our car, or display in our home or classroom, means little or nothing without this love. St. Paul made this very clear when he taught:

If I speak in the tongues of mortals and of angels, but do not have love, I am a noisy gong or a clanging cymbal. And if I have prophetic powers, and understand all mysteries and all knowledge, and if I have all faith, so as to remove mountains, but do not have love, I am nothing. If I give away all my possessions, and if I hand over my body so that I may boast, but do not have love, I gain nothing.

—1 Corinthians 13:1–3

Our loving words, actions, gestures, choices and relationships, made in the name of Christ, contribute to making us who we are— 'Christians', faithful and loyal followers of the One whose name we bear.

LET'S PROBE DEEPER

Read Paul's full description of Christian love in 1 Corinthians 13:4–13. Keep in mind, as you read the passage, that many Christians in the early Church read or heard the name 'Christ' when they read or heard the word 'love'. Also notice that the passage ends: 'Now faith, hope and love abide . . . and the greatest of these is love.' Love is indeed the gift from God that not only identifies us as Christians but enables us to live as one with

God the Holy Trinity, who is Love, and with other people and all creation.

TALK IT OVER

⊙ With a partner, recall your list of people whom you think are among the best examples of people living as disciples of Christ. How do they demonstrate the true love that Paul describes? What are some of the words and actions that show the love of a follower of Christ?

REFLECT

⊙ Think about someone observing your own life. Do you think they might immediately recognize you as a Christian based on your words, actions, gestures, choices and relationships?

JOURNAL EXERCISE

⊙ Christ is your companion! Reflect on how your love for Christ and his love for you can sustain you each day of your life. Write your thoughts on this in your journal.

HEAR THE STORY

Come, follow me

THE GOOD SHEPHERD | WOODCUT AFTER JULIUS SCHNORR VON CAROLSFELD

OBSERVE AND RESPOND

⊙ Look carefully at the picture of the Good Shepherd.
⊙ What stands out for you about it?
⊙ Which lamb do you think the Good Shepherd is carrying?
⊙ When do you most need to be 'carried' by Jesus, the Good Shepherd?

Sheep are born with a strong instinct to follow. In fact, sheep have a keen memory for human faces and voices; they really do know their shepherd. Shepherds rely on this flocking instinct to keep their sheep safe, healthy and well nourished. (This instinct has erroneously given rise to the adjective 'sheepish', a pejorative label meaning 'meek, stupid or timid'.)

OPENING REFLECTION

A favorite image of God in the Old Testament is that of a good shepherd. For example, Isaiah wrote:

[The Lord God] will feed his flock like a shepherd;
   he will gather the lambs in his arms,
and carry them in his bosom,
   and gently lead the mother sheep.
                 —Isaiah 40:11

Jesus also said of himself, 'I am the good shepherd.' He then added, 'The good shepherd lays down his life for the sheep' (John 10:11). Jesus' first hearers would easily have made the connection between Jesus' words and the words of Isaiah and other passages in the Scriptures of ancient Israel.

THINK, PAIR AND SHARE

⊙ Imagine you are among the first of Jesus' disciples to hear him say, 'I am the good shepherd. My sheep hear my voice. I know them, and they follow me' (John 10:11, 27).
⊙ Reflect with a partner on these words of Jesus. Use these questions to guide your reflection:
  – What do you think Jesus meant by these words?
  – How does this make you feel?
  – What are some implications of these words for your life?
  – What are some of the positives of thinking about your relationship with Jesus as like a sheep with a shepherd?
  – What are some of the limitations that come to mind when you consider such a relationship?

224 | CREDO | THE PROMISED ONE: SERVANT AND SAVIOR

FAITH WORD

Disciple

Name given in the New Testament to all those men and women who followed Jesus and were taught by him while he was alive, and who, following Jesus' death, Resurrection, and Ascension, formed the Church with the Apostles and helped spread the Good News, or Gospel message. Contemporary members of the Church, as followers of Jesus, can also be referred to as disciples.

—*United States Catholic Catechism for Adults* [USCCA], 509

JESUS TEACHING | ST. MATTHEW'S CHURCH, CHARLESTON, SOUTH CAROLINA

COME, FOLLOW ME

Discipleship begins with an invitation. The most common invitation of Jesus in the Gospels is 'Come, follow me'. People were free to choose to follow him or not. Some did and others did not. Upon hearing Jesus' invitation, for example, Peter, Andrew, James and John immediately left their fishnets, their families and career and followed Jesus to become fishers of people with him. (Read Matthew 4:18–22.) Matthew the tax-collector did the same. (Read Matthew 9:9.)

On the other hand, not everyone chose to follow Jesus or remained with him after initially following him. The rich young man and the disciple who sought to bury his father resisted Jesus' invitation to follow. They were too attached to their goods and obligations. (Read Matthew 19:22 and Luke 9:59.) On another occasion, Jesus had preached, 'I am the living bread that came down from heaven. Whoever eats of this bread will live for ever; and the bread that I will give for the life of the world is my flesh' (John 6:51). Many of those who followed Jesus found his teachings too 'difficult', and 'turned back and no longer went about with him'. (Read this story in John 6:60–71.)

WHAT ABOUT YOU PERSONALLY?

⊙ Imagine yourself being in a crowd of curious listeners surrounding Jesus as he preaches in a public place. This is the first time you have been in the presence of Jesus. At the end, he turns to you and says, 'Come, follow me.'

⊙ What would be your initial reaction to his words?

⊙ What would you do?

The costs and rewards of living as a committed disciple and apprentice of Jesus are great. But there is no better way to live one's life than by accepting and living the demands of Jesus' invitation, 'Come, follow me'. Just imagine how loving, faithful and hopeful we can be, the more we follow 'the way' of Jesus and continue his work.

The more the first disciples came to be with Jesus, to listen to him and watch him, the more they appreciated that there was a cost, 'a cross', to following their Master. Perhaps, most challenging of all for his disciples was Jesus' teaching that living as his disciples would include similar suffering. (Read Matthew 10:38, 16:24; Mark 8:34; Luke 9:23, 14:27.) They slowly came to grasp that

CHAPTER 10: FOLLOWING THE WAY OF JESUS CHRIST | HEAR THE STORY | 225

Much of the media and product marketing encourages us to give in and indulge

the way of life they were being apprenticed in was one that could easily cost them their lives, as it would cost their Master his life.

We, Jesus' apprentices, both learn from him and receive the grace from him to rise above any trials and sufferings that come our way. While we cannot escape the hardships in life, we trust that, with the help of the Holy Spirit, we will have the strength to handle whatever challenges we meet.

OVER TO YOU

⊙ Have you ever questioned why God the Father allowed his Son, Jesus, to suffer and die the way he did? Explain.

After his Ascension Jesus, our Good Shepherd, did not leave us on our own. We know that he is always present to us, showing us the path and sustaining us along the way.

THINK, PAIR AND SHARE

Giving into one's weaknesses is a commonplace temptation that seems to be endorsed by the world around us. Much of the media and product marketing encourages us to give in and indulge.

⊙ With a partner, brainstorm and discuss examples of the way the media and advertising agents encourage young people to give in to desires that keep them from living as disciples of Jesus. Showcase your examples for the rest of the class.

⊙ Why might a measure of self-denial be a good thing?

⊙ Neither extreme self-indulgence nor extreme self-denial is life-giving. How can your faith help you find a life-giving balance in your life? How can the example and teaching of Jesus inspire you?

226 | CREDO | THE PROMISED ONE: SERVANT AND SAVIOR

QUO VADIS DOMINE?

'Come, follow me.' To where is Jesus asking us to follow him? There is a well-known legend of St. Peter that helps us answer this question. The Latin phrase *Quo vadis Domine?* translates as 'Lord, where are you going?' According to the legend, St. Peter was fleeing from Rome to avoid persecution when he had a vision of Jesus Christ trudging toward the city carrying a cross. Astonished, Peter asked Jesus, '*Quo vadis Domine?*' Jesus replied, '*Eo Romam iterum crucifigi*' ('I am going to Rome to be crucified again'). As a result of this experience, Peter changed direction and courageously returned to Rome to face persecution—and possible martyrdom—in order to shepherd the fledging Church in Rome.

The *Quo Vadis* legend is all about faith and courage, or fortitude. It tells us what it means to accept the demands of following Jesus. Followers of Christ join their sufferings to those of Christ and know that their accepting suffering, as Christ did, is never in vain. We have his word that he will strengthen and sustain us in times of suffering, and we respond to the voice of the Good Shepherd and follow him.

WHAT ABOUT YOU PERSONALLY?

⊙ How might Jesus' solidarity with you sustain you, especially when your cross feels really heavy?

REFLECT

Living for others entails a life marked by good deeds, great and small. Think about your past week and the many times you may have encountered people in need.

⊙ Were you able to respond to people in need? Who was easiest to address? Who was most difficult?
⊙ Was there much sacrifice needed on your part? Explain.
⊙ How willing and ready were you to make that sacrifice?
⊙ If you feel comfortable doing so, share your thoughts on these questions with a friend.

JUDGE AND DECIDE

God has blessed us, all of us, with special gifts for helping others.

⊙ What do you think are your best gifts for love and service to others?
⊙ How will you put them to work today?

Followers of Christ join their sufferings to those of Christ and know that their accepting suffering, as Christ did, is never in vain

QUO VADIS? | ST. PETER'S CHURCH, WESTUM, GERMANY

EMBRACE THE VISION

The 'way' of discipleship

live in 'right relationship' with others and with ourselves. Personal prayer helps us clarify how to follow Jesus Christ in everyday life. Prayer also unites us to those around us, because in prayer we are able to embrace the joys and sorrows of others in the presence of God.

The four accounts of the Gospel are full of examples of Jesus praying. Jesus prayed many times in order to think about his mission and simply to spend time in conversation with the Father (see John 17). Sometimes, Jesus spent time alone in nature when he prayed; for example, Jesus prayed by the lakeshore (Matthew 13:1), on the mountain (Luke 6:12), in a deserted place (Mark 1:35), in the garden of Gethsemane (Matthew 26:36) and on the Mount of Olives (Luke 21:37).

When Jesus prayed, he showed us how to keep God at the center of our lives. By engaging in prayer, Christians follow Christ and strive to keep God at the center of their lives and to keep their focus on what it means to be and live as a disciple of Jesus.

OPENING CONVERSATION

In school locker rooms around the country, teams gather in the Fall and Winter for final preparations for 'the game'. Coaches summarize final game plans and players focus, and then they quietly 'pray' before heading to the field or court. After warm-ups, all stand, and players, coaches and spectators pause and offer a final prayer before the kickoff or tipoff.

- ⊙ Have you ever participated in such a ritual?
- ⊙ What is the mood like on such occasions—in the locker room? In the gym? Why is this?
- ⊙ How does such a ritual help players, coaches and spectators to focus?

LISTEN TO HIM

Prayer is a fundamental gesture of Christian discipleship. Prayer helps us to focus on who we are and where we are going. Prayer helps us to

WHAT ABOUT YOU PERSONALLY?

- ⊙ How does prayer help you?

SUMMARY OF THE GOSPEL

It is clear that Jesus intended his disciples to pray. When they specifically asked him to teach them to pray, he taught them the Lord's Prayer.

(Read Luke 11:1–4 and Matthew 6:9–13.) The Lord's Prayer is the paradigm of Christian prayer, and deepens our communion with the Father and the Son. In addition to being a prayer it is, in and of itself, a blueprint for living the Gospel. In his teaching of the Lord's Prayer, Jesus also summarized the most basic lessons of Christian discipleship. The Lord's Prayer tells us that Christians must give praise and honor to God and work to bring about God's Reign by doing God's will on earth. Praying the Lord's Prayer reminds us of our total dependence on God; he alone is the source of our 'daily bread'. It calls us to forgive others as we hope to be forgiven, and to avoid temptation and everything that might take us away from God.

THINK, PAIR AND SHARE

- ⊙ With a partner, carefully examine the text of the Lord's Prayer in Matthew 6:9–13.
- ⊙ Then rewrite it in your own words.

The Great Commandment is the summary of God's will, God's Law; and the Lord's Prayer is the summary of the Gospel. The Law of Discipleship is the Law of Love. The Lord's Prayer outlines specific ways disciples of Christ can live the Law of Love—love of God and love for others.

You will recall that when Jesus was asked about what was at the center of living the Covenant, the essence of living as a child of God, he united the teachings of the Law of Love into one two-pronged commandment.

SCRIPTURE EXERCISE

- ⊙ Read and compare Matthew 22:34–40, Mark 12:28–34 and Luke 10:25–28, applying the 'active reading' technique (see instructions in chapter 1).
- ⊙ Share your insights with a partner.

THE GREAT COMMANDMENT/THE LAW OF DISCIPLESHIP

Jesus challenged his disciples to be people of truth, integrity and honesty, to obey the Law and the Prophets and the Ten Commandments, and to live the Great Commandment. We are to love God with our whole mind and heart and soul—everything we've got— and, in the same way, we are to love our neighbors and ourselves. Living as a disciple of Christ must embrace all three dimensions, beginning with love of God. In speaking of the greatest commandment as singular and yet with three mandates, Jesus was intimately linking love of God, of neighbor and authentic love of oneself.

FAITH WORD

Mezuzah

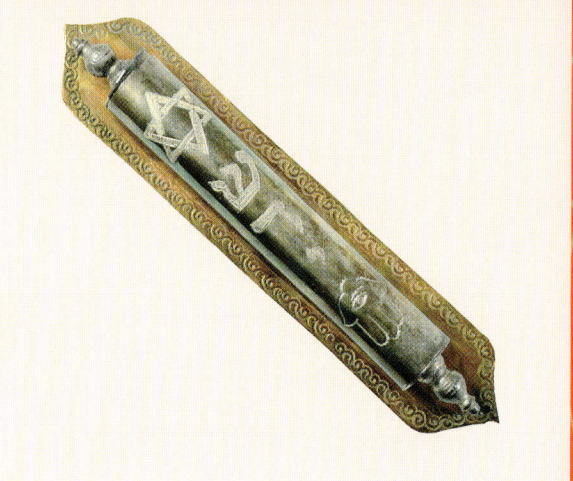

In Jewish homes today, we can often find a small decorative rectangular object nailed to the doorpost. This is called a *mezuzah,* and it contains a tiny scroll. On the scroll are the words of the *Shema,* the Jewish prayer quoting Deuteronomy 6:4–9, which begins: 'Hear, O Israel: The Lord is our God, the Lord alone. You shall love the Lord your God with all your heart, and with all your soul, and with all your might.' Devout Jews observe this tradition, each time they exit and enter their homes, as a reminder to love and honor God above all.

The Mystery of Divine Love is at the heart of the Good News that Jesus preached and lived. One might venture to say that all of Revelation can be summed up as 'The Greatest Love Story'. Jesus made it abundantly clear that we are to respond to this great Mystery by loving God and our neighbor.

St. John explains it well, 'We love because [God] first loved us' (1 John 4:19). Sharing the love of God and returning to God's glory with all of humankind was the foundation, the goal and the mission of Jesus' life. The goal of those who seek to follow Jesus Christ must also be the same: to love and give glory to God in the way we live. We are to discover the presence of God every day, allowing our awareness of God's love to guide our daily decisions and actions. We are to center our life on God, with God as its source and end.

OVER TO YOU

⊙ Does God's unconditional love for you affect the way you love other people? Explain.
⊙ What are some ways in which disciples of Jesus show their faith and trust in God's unconditional love for them?

THE EUCHARIST PROVIDES NOURISHMENT FOR OUR JOURNEY

The Eucharist is 'the source and summit' of the Christian life. The Eucharist nourishes our life as disciples of Jesus. When we gather and worship God at Mass, we listen to the Word of God and receive greater clarity on what it means to live as Christ's disciples. We join with Christ to offer ourselves—our love, our gifts, our lives—to God. We receive the Body and Blood of Christ. The bond of love uniting us with Christ and one another is deepened; and we are nourished to live as Christ's disciples and to continue his mission in the world.

TALK IT OVER

At the conclusion of Mass we are sometimes dismissed with the words, 'Go in peace, glorifying the Lord by your life.'

⊙ Think of some of the many situations that you may routinely face each day. How might your words and actions glorify God in those situations?
⊙ How does praying the Lord's Prayer help you live out that dismissal command?
⊙ How does fully participating in the Mass on a regular basis help you live out that command?

THINK IT THROUGH

Walking the walk

OPENING REFLECTION

Read or listen to these lyrics from Justin Bieber's song 'Pray':

Pray

I just can't sleep tonight,
knowing that things ain't right.
It's in the papers, it's on the TV,
it's everywhere that I go.
Children are crying, soldiers are dying,
some people don't have a home.

I close my eyes, and I can see a better day,
I close my eyes and pray.
I close my eyes and I can see a better day,
I close my eyes and pray.

The words of this song tug at our conscience. It is hard to sleep sometimes, thinking about all the people around the world who are suffering in countless ways. Prayer can help us hold these feelings before God and find strength and courage to do something positive about them.

OVER TO YOU

⊙ Have you ever prayed to see a better day? Did the prayer change the situation? Did it change you?

⊙ Is it enough to pray for change? Why or why not?

⊙ How can prayer help you to make changes in our world?

LIVING OUR NAME: THE PATH OF DISCIPLESHIP

Recall that at the heart of living the Law of Discipleship is giving glory to God by putting into practice, each and every day, both aspects of the Greatest Commandment; namely, 'You shall love the Lord your God with all your heart, and with all your soul, and with all your mind' (Matthew 22:37) and 'You shall love your neighbor as yourself' (Matthew 22:39). Let us focus with more clarity now on what we began to explore on the Great Commandment in the previous section of the chapter.

Throughout his public ministry, Jesus made abundantly clear that loving God and loving others

CHAPTER 10: FOLLOWING THE WAY OF JESUS CHRIST | THINK IT THROUGH | 231

go hand in hand. Jesus' whole life was one of love and compassion for all people, with a special love and favor for those who were looked down upon, excluded or in need. Then, on the night before he died, Jesus revealed that his apprentices and disciples were to follow his example and live the Greatest Commandment as he had done. He told his disciples, 'I give you a new commandment. . . . Just as I have loved you, you also should love one another' (John 13:34). This is the ultimate call to being a Christian—to love like Jesus. The First Letter of John summarizes the centrality of this command to our life as disciples of Jesus:

Those who say, 'I love God', and hate their brothers or sisters are liars; for those who do not love a brother or sister whom they have seen, cannot love God whom they have not seen. The commandment we have from [Christ] is this: those who love God must love their brothers and sisters also.

—1 John 4:20–21

REFLECT AND DISCUSS

⊙ Why do you think living as a disciple of Jesus Christ requires us to love all other people?

⊙ What does living this command demand of you in school? In your neighborhood?

JESUS PROVIDED AN EXAMPLE

In Luke's account of the Greatest Commandment, a lawyer asks Jesus, 'And who is my neighbor?' In response Jesus tells the parable of the Good Samaritan. (You may recall studying this parable in chapter 7 of *God's Word Revealed in Sacred Scripture*, the first book of the *Credo* series.) The main character in the parable, the one whom Jesus holds up for his hearers and for us as an example to imitate, is a Samaritan. Remember, Jews at the time of Jesus despised and looked down upon Samaritans, whom they regarded as outside the 'love of God'.

In the parable a man who was the victim of assault and robbery was left lying by the side of the road leading from Jerusalem to Jericho. A priest and a Levite noticed the injured man lying on the roadside. For reasons the Evangelist does not give, both the priest and the Levite passed by without stopping. Perhaps they thought that the man was dead, and, according to Jewish law, contact with a corpse would defile them and prevent them from performing their ritual

THE GOOD SAMARITAN | JOHANNES ZICK

232 | CREDO | THE PROMISED ONE: SERVANT AND SAVIOR

duties in the Temple. So they crossed to the other side of the road, making sure not to be contaminated. A Samaritan then came along, saw the man and, moved with pity, crossed over to him. After cleaning and bandaging the injured man's wounds, the Samaritan then took him to an inn to recover, paying for any care that the man would need.

Jesus concludes by inviting the lawyer and his disciples to reflect on the meaning of the parable, asking them, 'Which of these was neighbor to the man who fell into the hands of robbers?' The lawyer answered rightly, 'The one who showed him mercy.' Jesus then commanded his listeners, 'Go and do likewise' (Luke 10:37).

OVER TO YOU
- What was Jesus trying to teach his disciples through this parable?
- Where do you see people acting like the priest and the Levite? Like the Good Samaritan?
- What is the best wisdom you can learn about being a disciple of Jesus from the parable of the Good Samaritan?

What separates the Samaritan from the priest and the Levite? One distinguishing characteristic is the Samaritan's ability to see that responding to the genuine needs of another human being outweighs simply obeying a law or the social practice. Jesus taught us this lesson over and over again in the Gospels. For example, he picked grain and healed the sick on the Sabbath (Mark 2:23–28; Mark 3:1–6; Luke 14:1–6); he dined with sinners and tax-collectors (Matthew 9:10); he spoke to the Samaritan woman at the well (John 4:1–42).

Jesus did not come to abolish the laws, rules and commandments that structure our lives of faith. (See Matthew 5:17.) Jesus himself lived by the Torah and integrated the religious practices of the Jews into his life, and revealed the deeper meaning and spirit of the law, namely, that rules, laws and regulations are at the service of God and his people. Jesus fulfilled the Law by showing us that all of life depends on and aims toward giving glory to the Father by living a loving relationship with our God, which overflows into our relationships with one another and with ourselves.

THE GOOD SAMARITAN AT THE INN | ENGRAVING AFTER ALEXANDRE BIDA

CLASS ACTIVITY/DISCUSSION
- Compare the Ten Commandments, the Precepts of the Church, and other Church laws and rules, with the Greatest Commandment— love God and one another as ourselves.
- How is the command to love God and love one's neighbor as oneself reflected in all of these laws and commandments?

WHAT ABOUT YOU PERSONALLY?
- Have you ever struggled with wanting to be loving toward someone who seemed hard to love? What made this situation especially difficult?

LOVE YOURSELF TOO!
All true love flows from our love for God. The Greatest Commandment calls us as disciples of Jesus to a true love and care for ourselves as well as for others. Loving oneself properly does not get in the way of loving God and other people.

CHAPTER 10: FOLLOWING THE WAY OF JESUS CHRIST | THINK IT THROUGH | 233

Jesus repeated what the Torah commanded: 'You shall love your neighbor as yourself' (Matthew 22:39). True human love includes loving God and loving neighbor *and* loving oneself.

We show love for ourselves when we value and respect ourselves as images of God. We show love for ourselves when we acknowledge that our life and all human life is a gift from God; it is a sharing in the very breath (life) of God. Appropriate self-love is not self-indulgence or pampering. Instead, it requires us to accept, care for and keep ourselves safe from sin and from all that might hurt us, physically or spiritually. Such self-love supports our loving our neighbors. Our love for ourselves also overflows into love for our neighbors. When we love ourselves appropriately, we recognize and respect the God-given dignity of all people.

FAITH WORD

Charity (Love)

Charity, or love, is one of the three Theological Virtues by which we give our love to God for his own sake and our love to our neighbor on account of our love of God.

—Based on USCCA, 506

ST. ULRICH SHARES HIS CLOAK WITH A BEGGAR | FRANZ LUDWIG HERRMANN

Every person's life has God-given meaning and purpose. Our bodies, our minds and our spirits all have genuine needs; fulfilling these needs helps us accomplish the very purpose for which God created us. Our basic need is to share in the love of God, to share that love with others, and to give glory to God the Creator in all we say and do. Every person—our neighbor and our self—also has other basic 'corporal' and 'spiritual' needs. Every person needs food, sleep, exercise, rest and health care; we need worship, education and meaningful work; we need family and community, love and friendship. We have the right and the responsibility to seek to fulfill these basic, genuine needs. When we do, we are fulfilling our responsibility to love our self.

To love oneself in a way that honors God also includes discerning our genuine needs from false needs that may arise out of social pressure or selfish desires. Loving ourselves includes avoiding anything that might harm us or bring direct harm to other people.

TALK IT OVER

⊙ Give an example of how you might confuse a genuine need with one that arises from social pressure.

⊙ Why do you think loving yourself appropriately helps you love your family and friends?

⊙ Why do you think loving yourself appropriately gives honor to God?

⊙ What do you think loving yourself appropriately brings to your efforts to live as a disciple of Jesus?

JOURNAL EXERCISE

⊙ Prayer that unites us to God helps us make good decisions about how to love our neighbors as ourselves. Search the Gospels for accounts of Jesus going off to pray before making decisions about fulfilling his mission. What wisdom for your own life does reflection on those passages bring to you? Write your thoughts in your journal.

JUDGE AND ACT

REFLECT ON WHAT YOU HAVE LEARNED

In this chapter we learned what it means for our life to have the name 'Christian'.

- ⊙ What was the most important spiritual wisdom that you learned from exploring the faith concepts in this chapter?
- ⊙ How might that wisdom help you to follow 'the way' of Jesus Christ?

WHAT DIFFERENCE DOES BEING A CHRISTIAN MAKE?

We do not see the exact name 'Christian' used in the New Testament to name the disciples of Jesus. Instead, we read that the members of the early Church defined themselves as followers of 'the Way'. For example, listen to how St. Luke described Paul, just prior to his conversion: 'Meanwhile Saul, still breathing threats and murder against the disciples of the Lord, went to the high priest, and asked him for letters to the synagogues at Damascus, so that if he found any who belonged to the Way, men or women, he might bring them bound to Jerusalem' (Acts of the Apostles 9:1–2).

What is this 'Way' described by Luke? It is the Way Jesus revealed we are to live the Law and the Prophets, which Jesus reminded the lawyer and summarized in the greatest commandment of love. It is the Way of compassion, mercy and justice. It is the Way Jesus proclaimed in the synagogue in his home town of Nazareth at the beginning of his public ministry: 'The Spirit of the Lord is upon me, because [God] has anointed me to bring good news to the poor . . . , to proclaim release to the captives and recovery of sight to the blind, to let the oppressed go free, to proclaim the year of the Lord's favor.' Then he added, 'Today this scripture has been fulfilled in your hearing' (Luke 4:18–21).

JUDGE AND DECIDE

The Letter to James teaches, '[B]e doers of the word, and not merely hearers who deceive themselves' (James 1:22).

- ⊙ Reflect on the passage from James. How is it connected to Jesus' proclamation in the synagogue in Nazareth?
- ⊙ What does it teach about what it means to follow the Way?
- ⊙ What parts of Jesus' teaching do you think James had in mind when he wrote these words?
- ⊙ What does this teaching challenge you to do in your own life?

Be doers of the word, and not merely hearers who deceive themselves

CATHOLIC RELIEF SERVICES PROVIDE FOOD FOR MIGRANTS IN CALAIS, FRANCE

CHAPTER 10: FOLLOWING THE WAY OF JESUS CHRIST | JUDGE AND ACT | 235

LEARN BY EXAMPLE

The witness and discipleship of Paul (CONTINUED)

Recall the story of St. Paul's conversion from chapter 12 of Son of God and Son of Mary *of the* Credo *series. Then read:*

The story of Paul reveals that there was no cost Paul would not pay to follow 'the Way'. Saul, after his conversion to Jesus Christ, would use and be known by his Roman name, Paul, to signal that he had become a disciple. The story of Paul in Acts describes the story of a disciple who would spend the rest of his life evangelizing the Gentiles, proclaiming Jesus Christ throughout the lands along the Mediterranean Sea.

The life of this 'new' disciple was marked by great suffering. For example, Luke tells us in Acts 9:23–30 that very soon after Paul's conversion on the road to Damascus, several Jews tried to arrest and kill him, and other disciples helped him escape by lowering him in a basket through a hole in the wall around Jerusalem (see Acts of the Apostles 9:23–30). On another occasion, Paul and his companion, Silas, were jailed for being rabble-rousers who were 'advocating customs' contrary to Roman law (see Acts of the Apostles 16:16–40). On a return visit to Jerusalem, where Paul was once a respected and zealous rabbi, more that forty people conspired to kill him (see Acts of the Apostles 23:12–22). Paul surely experienced the cost of being a disciple of Jesus Christ.

Then, about three years before the end of his life, the authorities declared Paul to be insane, and ordered him to be sent to Rome along with other prisoners to plead his cause. On his journey he experienced shipwreck, was thrown overboard and washed up ashore (see Acts of the Apostles 24—27). Finally, Paul suffered death during his final stay in Rome because he was zealously 'proclaiming the kingdom of God and teaching about the Lord Jesus Christ with all boldness and without hindrance' (Acts of the Apostles 28:31). The exact date and manner of the Apostle's martyrdom is unknown. But the tradition of the Church says that Paul was beheaded sometime between AD 64 or 68 during the persecution of Nero.

ST. PAUL THE APOSTLE IN PRISON

236 | CREDO | THE PROMISED ONE: SERVANT AND SAVIOR

How can young people today bring good news to the poor, release to captives and freedom to the oppressed?

TALK IT OVER
- How is the life of St. Paul an example of discipleship for young Christians today?
- What other Christian individuals or groups do you know about who proclaim Jesus with 'boldness and without hindrance'?

JUDGE AND DECIDE
Disciples of Jesus give witness to and prepare for the coming of the Kingdom of God—a kingdom of justice where all people live in right relationship, with God, with other people and with all creation.
- What work of justice can you do over the coming days?
- How can young people today bring good news to the poor, release to captives and freedom to the oppressed?

WHAT WILL YOU DO NOW?
- If you had to choose one thing you learned in this chapter and make it a motto for your life at present, what would you choose, and why?
- Better still, how will you try to live it?

RESPOND WITH FAMILY AND FRIENDS
- Share with your family and friends that the Lord's Prayer is a summary of the Gospel. Point out that this means it is a synopsis of the essence of living 'the way' of Jesus.
- Then, using the letters of the title, O-U-R-F-A-T-H-E-R, create an acrostic naming ways that you can live the Our Father.

LEARN BY HEART

The commandment we have from [Christ] is this: those who love God must love their brothers and sisters also.

1 JOHN 4:21

CHAPTER 10: FOLLOWING THE WAY OF JESUS CHRIST | JUDGE AND ACT | 237

PRAYER REFLECTION

LEADER
Sit quietly and remember that you are in the
presence of God. (*Pause*)
In the name of the Father, and of the Son, and of
the Holy Spirit.

ALL
Amen.

LEADER
Lord Jesus Christ, you are the Way;
    you taught us to love and honor God above all,
    and to love our neighbor as ourselves.
This is the greatest of commandments
    and the foundation of our life as your disciples.
Send your Spirit to fill our hearts with the true
        love of God
    so that we may better love and serve those
        around us
    and have true love for ourselves in your name.

ALL
Amen.

LEADER
The Lord's Prayer is the summary of the Gospel;
it is the summary of the way Jesus lived
and the summary of the way the Spirit calls his
        disciples to live.
Let us pray the words that our Lord Jesus Christ
        taught us,
pausing after each line to reflect on the ways
        praying that line
helps us honor our name 'Christian' by living the
        Gospel.

READER
*Read each line and pause after each line to allow
time to reflect on the ways praying this line helps us
honor our name 'Christian' and live the Gospel.*

Our Father who art in heaven, hallowed be thy
        name. (*Pause*)
Thy kingdom come, thy will be done on earth as
        it is in heaven. (*Pause*)
Give us this day our daily bread. (*Pause*)
And forgive us our trespasses, as we forgive those
        who trespass against us. (*Pause*)

**We turn to you in trust
and ask for your
continued grace
to nourish, heal,
    reconcile, and protect us
all**

And lead us not into temptation but deliver us
        from evil. (*Pause*)

LEADER
Loving God,
    through the words your Son taught us,
    we express our love for you;
    for yours indeed is all the power and the glory,
        both now and for ever.
We turn to you in trust and ask for your
        continued grace
    to nourish, heal, reconcile, and protect us all,
    as we wait in hope to share your eternal glory
        in heaven.
We ask this in the name of Jesus Christ your Son,
        who lives and reigns with you and the Holy
        Spirit, one God, for ever and ever.

ALL
Amen.

Pray the Sign of the Cross together.

CHAPTER 11

Jesus: the Way to Holiness

WE ARE CALLED TO LIVE IN FULLNESS OF LIFE BY FOLLOWING THE 'WAY' OF JESUS

GOD'S ALL-ENCOMPASSING LOVE IS OUR MODEL

WE ARE CALLED TO MIRROR GOD'S LOVE FOR US IN OUR LOVE FOR OTHERS AND FOR OURSELVES

GOD'S SANCTIFYING GRACE ENABLES US TO LIVE HOLY LIVES

HOLINESS AND ORDINARY LIFE GO HAND IN HAND

HOLINESS IS FIRST AND FOREMOST THE WORK OF THE HOLY SPIRIT IN OUR LIVES

THE SACRAMENTS ARE OUR PRIMARY SOURCE OF HOLINESS OF LIFE

WE NEED THE ENCOURAGEMENT, GUIDANCE AND SUPPORT OF THE CHURCH TO GROW IN HOLINESS

IN THIS CHAPTER WE WILL EXPLORE THAT EVERYONE is called to holiness of life. Through Baptism every Christian is called to holiness of life in Christ. 'Holiness of life' means seeking and loving what is true and good, and, by so doing, becoming the person God created you to be. Jesus, the Holy One of God, is our model of what it means to live a holy life. We grow in holiness of life through the grace of the Holy Spirit and through our participation in the life, worship and ministry of the Church.

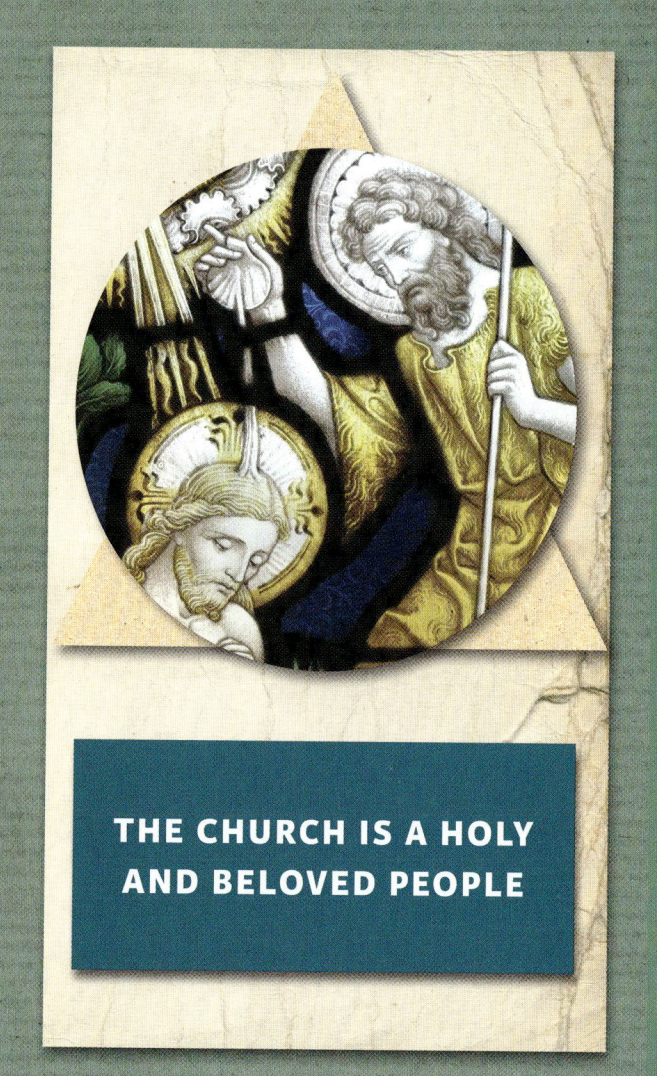

THE CHURCH IS A HOLY AND BELOVED PEOPLE

LEARNING OUTCOMES

As a result of studying this chapter and exploring the issues raised, you should be able to:

- ⊙ understand the Christian meaning of the word 'holy';
- ⊙ describe the characteristics of people whom you believe are 'holy;
- ⊙ understand the meaning of Jesus' words 'Be perfect as your heavenly Father is perfect';
- ⊙ understand the faith term 'sanctifying grace';
- ⊙ understand why 'love' is at the heart of holiness;
- ⊙ discover God's presence in the events of your day-to-day life;
- ⊙ deepen your understanding of the truth and the implications of God creating every human person in the divine image and likeness;
- ⊙ understand more deeply that the Holy Spirit is at work in you as you strive for holiness of life;
- ⊙ understand the role of temptation in your striving for holiness;
- ⊙ recognize that through Baptism a person is joined to Christ and becomes a member of the Church;
- ⊙ explore the faith concept 'communion of saints';
- ⊙ understand the meaning of the biblical phrases 'clothe yourselves' and 'put on the Lord Jesus Christ';
- ⊙ explore Brother Lawrence of the Resurrection as a model of faith.

FAITH-FORMATION OUTCOMES

As a result of studying this chapter and exploring the issues raised, you should also:

- ⊙ articulate ways you can use your gifts and talents to live a life of holiness;
- ⊙ reflect on how a personal role model can help you grow in holiness;
- ⊙ be aware of how you are lured toward false notions of perfection;
- ⊙ reflect on the challenge of Jesus' command to 'love your enemies';
- ⊙ grow in your confidence in God's presence in your life;
- ⊙ identify times in your life when you have experienced your God-given likeness;
- ⊙ name situations in your life in which you need the guidance and support of the Spirit of God to resist temptation;
- ⊙ recognize the importance of being an active member of the Church as you strive to live your faith;
- ⊙ articulate how you will continue to strive toward 'holiness of life'.

FAITH WORD: Sanctifying grace

LEARN BY HEART: Colossians 3:17

LEARN BY EXAMPLE: Brother Lawrence of the Resurrection

ATTEND AND REFLECT

What is holy?

OPENING ACTIVITY

The word 'holy' is much used and has many meanings; for example, a well-known baseball player and manager who became a sportscaster commonly exclaimed 'Holy cow!' when a player made an extraordinary play. Are cows 'holy'?

- Brainstorm what 'holiness' means to you.
- Share your ideas with a partner, and then together see if you can agree on a definition of holiness.

One dictionary defines 'holy' in this way: 'Exalted or worthy of complete devotion as one perfect in goodness and righteousness; Divine; devoted entirely to the deity or the work of the deity; venerated as or as if sacred.' This particular

dictionary definition for 'holy' points us to something greater and beyond our ordinary and everyday life. Perfection in goodness and righteousness is always beyond the reach of human beings. Even the greatest of the saints lamented their lack of perfection and asked for God's mercy for their sins.

The Church defines 'holiness' as 'a state of goodness in which a person—with the help of God's grace, the action of the Holy Spirit, and a life of prayer—is freed from sin and evil. Such a person, when gifted with holiness, must still resist temptation, repent of sins that may be committed, and realize that remaining holy is a lifelong pilgrimage with many spiritual and moral challenges' (*United States Catholic Catechism for Adults* [USCCA], 514).

REVIEW AND DISCUSS

- Work with a partner. Compare your definition of 'holiness' with the dictionary definition and the Church's definition.
- Might you change or add to your own definition of 'holiness' in view of the other definitions you have just read? Why or why not?

OVER TO YOU

- Do you think 'holiness of life' is beyond the reach of ordinary people and removed from our everyday experience? Explain your answer.
- Do you want to be holy? Why or why not?

WHOLENESS OF LIFE/HOLINESS OF LIFE

In this chapter we will explore the connection between 'wholeness' and 'holiness'. Wholeness is about getting your life together, striving to become the best person you can be, the person God created you to be—all across the board. This is an inexhaustible challenge; our striving will

242 | CREDO | THE PROMISED ONE: SERVANT AND SAVIOR

Be who God meant you to be and you will set the world on fire.

ST. CATHERINE OF SIENA

ST. CATHERINE OF SIENA HEALS MATTEO CENNI | VINCENZO TAMAGNI

have its ups and downs, and we may often fall short, and it will always be possible to do even better.

We will also explore what the Church means when she teaches that Christian holiness is the call to live in fullness and perfection of life by following 'the way' of Jesus. Imagine the extraordinary person you can become by following the example of Jesus: how loving, kind and compassionate; how just and peaceful; how faith-filled and hope-filled; how respectful and inclusive, and the list goes on.

TALK IT OVER

⊙ Does the holiness of life—the wholeness of life—that Jesus modeled appeal to you? Why or why not?

Let us now unpack some of the many ways in which the Bible and the Church use the word 'holy'.

HOLY, HOLY, HOLY

'Holy' and 'holiness' are part of common Christian vocabulary that we use to describe the life of a person of faith. In the Bible, God (Exodus 3:6, 12) and his name (1 Chronicles 16:10) alone are holy; Jesus is 'the Holy One of God' (Luke 4:34); and the Spirit of God is the Holy Spirit (Matthew 1:20). But the sacred authors also use the term 'holy' to designate anything or anyone that is 'of God'.

The Old Testament speaks of 'holy ground' (Exodus 3:5); 'holy things of the LORD' (Leviticus 5:15); the 'holy convocation' [of God's people] (Leviticus 23:35); 'holy vessels' (2 Chronicles 5:5); the 'holy city' (Isaiah 52:1) of Jerusalem; the 'holy temple' (Psalm 5:7), and the Holy of Holies in the Temple as the 'most holy place' (1 Kings 7:50). The New Testament speaks of the 'holy covenant' (Luke 1:72); holy prophets (Luke 1:70) and 'holy apostles' (Ephesians 3:5); holy kiss (1 Thessalonians 5:26); holy hands (1 Timothy 2:8); holy scriptures (Romans 1:2); holy laws and commandments (Romans 7:12); and 'holy angels' (Revelation 14:10).

'Holy' is one of the four Marks, or essential characteristics, of the Church founded by Jesus. We profess our faith in one, *holy,* catholic and apostolic Church. The term 'holy' is also used to designate elements of the Catholic life. We speak of the Holy Eucharist, the holy sacrifice of the Mass, Holy Communion, Holy Baptism and Holy Orders. The Sacraments are our primary source of holiness of life, of our living in communion with God. We also speak of holy days of obligation, holy water, the holy Rosary and other sacramentals of the Church as 'holy'. Sacramentals are sacred signs given to us by the Church that help us lead a holy life.

The Preface for Eucharistic Prayer II is addressed to God the 'Father most holy' and speaks of the Church as 'a holy people'. The Preface concludes with the *Sanctus,* or the

CHAPTER 11: JESUS: THE WAY TO HOLINESS | ATTEND AND REFLECT | 243

Think about your gifts and talents. How can you use these gifts to make your life holy?

acclamation 'Holy, Holy, Holy Lord'. The priest then begins Eucharistic Prayer II with the words:

You are indeed Holy, O Lord,
the fount of all holiness.
Make holy, therefore, these gifts, we pray,
by sending down your Spirit upon them. . . .

It is God who shares his life—holiness—with his people, the holy People of God, the Body of Christ. It is God, working through the words and actions of the priest, who 'makes' the bread and wine into the Body and Blood of Christ.

OVER TO YOU
⊙ Think about your gifts and talents. How can you use these gifts to make your life holy?

THE SPIRIT OF HOLINESS
Although the opening definition of 'holiness' might seem to cast 'being holy' as something apart from ordinary life, the opposite is the truth. Holiness and ordinary life go hand in hand. Sacred Scripture and the Church teach that holiness expresses ordinary life in the fullest—in its wholeness. So, do not be

daunted by your call to holiness of life. The truth is that God, the Holy One, created you in the divine image and likeness (see Genesis 1:27) and gave you the gift of life by sharing the divine 'breath' with you (see Genesis 2:7). And Jesus, the Only Begotten Son of God, became one of us 'wanting to make us sharers in his divinity' (*Catechism of the Catholic Church* [CCC], no. 460) and give us the gift of holiness of life.

Holiness of life does not come about just by our own efforts. Holiness of life is first and foremost the work of the Holy Spirit in our lives. The Holy Spirit 'is the sacrament of the Holy Trinity's communion with men' (CCC, no. 747). Regular participation in the Eucharist is essential to striving for holiness of life. In the Eucharist we offer the most ordinary of gifts and, through the work of the Holy Spirit and the words of the priest, the bread and wine become the very Body and Blood of Christ. In the Eucharist, joined to Christ, the Holy One, we offer all the ordinary details of our life—including our shortcomings and faults —to the Father.

Instead of something set apart from ordinary life, holiness is better understood as taking ordinary life and letting the Spirit of God fill it through and through, so that our life's full potential shines forth as a light in the world. Holiness understood in this way means to live into wholeness of life.

THINK, PAIR AND SHARE
⊙ Think about someone who is part of your life whom you consider to be truly 'holy'. What are the characteristics that make this person holy? Describe this person to your partner.
⊙ Share your reflections on how the person each of you named can be a model for your own growth into holiness of life.

HEAR THE STORY

Be perfect

OPENING CONVERSATION

Though we always fall short of it, everyone has an innate desire for perfection. This is why advertising is so effective; it creatively promises people something (whether they really need it or not) that will bring perfection—perfect teeth, perfect appearance, perfect weight, a perfect night's sleep . . . and the list goes on and on.

⊙ What models of perfection of body and mind are prescribed by advertising?

⊙ Have you ever felt pressured to conform to any of these? Talk with a partner about why this was so.

BE PERFECT AS GOD IS PERFECT

While seeking perfection of our body and mind is an important part of striving for holiness of life (it is commanded by the Fifth Commandment), this is far from the whole picture. Amidst all this pressure for perfection, we can hear another invitation, to a very different kind of perfection.

In the Gospel according to Matthew, Jesus gathers all of his disciples on a mountainside, and teaches them the core values by which they are to live. We hear Jesus' command: 'Be perfect, therefore, as your heavenly Father is perfect' (Matthew 5:48). To gain some insight into what Jesus' command to be perfect included, we need to read the words of Jesus that immediately preceded his command:

But I say to you, Love your enemies and pray for those who persecute you, so that you may be children of your Father in heaven; for he makes his sun rise on the evil and on the good, and sends rain on the righteous and on the unrighteous.

—Matthew 5:44–45

Jesus was commanding his disciples to imitate both the perfection of God and the way he himself lived his life by making the path to perfection—to holiness of life—include even one's enemies. What a stunning challenge! How can humankind 'be like' the love of God, the All-Powerful, All-Knowing and eternal Creator of heaven and earth? Fulfilling Jesus' command can seem so out of reach and so far removed from our imperfect selves that we are already set up for failure.

Jesus, of course, did not ask us to be God; he commanded us to be *like* God, in whose image God created us. We are to strive, each and every

day, to mirror God's love for us in our love for others and for ourselves. St. Gregory of Nyssa (c. 330–c. 395) summarized the challenge of seeking perfection and holiness of life. He wrote, 'Christian perfection has but one limit, that of having none' (quoted in CCC, no. 2028).

GROUP EXERCISE

⊙ Work in small groups and describe what is involved in striving for the kind of perfection to which Jesus invites his disciples. Try to agree on the six most important steps you should take to strive for that perfection.

COMMUNION WITH GOD

These words from the Fourth Gospel are part of Jesus' prayer to his Father in his Farewell Discourse to his disciples; they succinctly state the goal of perfection and holiness of life:

As you, Father, are in me and I am in you, may they also be in us, so that the world may believe that you have sent me. The glory that you have given me I have given them, so that they may be one, as we are one, I in them and you in me, that they may become completely one, so that the world may know that you have sent me and have loved them even as you have loved me.

—John 17:21–23

Our path to perfection, as unachievable as it may seem, is to try to live in loving communion with God and with one another. The more we strive to live 'the way' that Jesus lived, the more we will come into fullness, or holiness, of life. God's all-encompassing love is the model for us. While it may not be easy to strive to love as God loves, that is what striving for Christian perfection (indeed, human perfection) is all about. What makes all this possible is God empowering us, or giving us the grace, to seek perfection and holiness of life. We call God's gift of love 'sanctifying grace', or grace that 'makes us holy'. The Holy Spirit continuously fills our lives with 'sanctifying grace', which enables us to live holy lives in imitation of Jesus Christ.

FAITH WORD

Sanctifying Grace

Sanctifying grace is a habitual gift of God's own divine life, a stable and supernatural disposition that enables us to live with God and to act by his love.

—USCCA, 514

> **You are the salt of the earth; but if salt has lost its taste, how can its saltiness be restored? It is no longer good for anything, but is thrown out and trampled under foot.**
>
> **MATTHEW 5:13**

MEN BOILING SEA WATER TO OBTAIN SALT

LOVE IS AT THE HEART OF HOLINESS

The perfection of Christian life is a great challenge, but it is never that far out of reach if we see it as the increasing ability to reflect God's love to those around us. Jesus taught that central to the life of his disciples is the vocation to be 'salt of the earth' and 'light of the world'. (Read Matthew 5:13–16.) The life and example of Jesus Christ teach us about this road to Christian perfection and holiness of life.

But Jesus did not only hold up this task and challenge; he promised that he and the Father would send the Holy Spirit to help and guide us. The Holy Spirit gives us the graces to be able to travel that road and to share God's love with everyone, including those who claim to be our enemies and those whom we find difficult

to love. Love for all without exception is the Christian way to perfection and fullness of life. As God loves all, so God's own people must be 'lights in the world' of this love and bring Christ, the Light of the world, to all people.

JUDGE AND DECIDE

The written Gospels tell us that Jesus had compassion for those who were suffering; served those around him; had authority and integrity; and, ultimately, gave his life for the love of all people.

- ⊙ What do you think the life of Jesus teaches us about perfection?
- ⊙ How do you think you could emulate some of the aspects of Jesus' life right now?

EMBRACE THE VISION

Grounded in the image of God

OPENING REFLECTION

Consider this excerpt from the poem 'The Inner History of a Day'. Notice that the words call attention to the holiness of each day and the ordinary moments that reveal God's presence to us in countless ways.

The Inner History of a Day

We seldom notice how each day is a holy place
Where the eucharist of the ordinary happens,
Transforming our broken fragments
Into an eternal continuity that keeps us.

Somewhere in us a dignity presides
That is more gracious than the smallness
That fuels us with fear and force,
A dignity that trusts the form a day takes.

WHAT ABOUT YOU PERSONALLY?

- Think of the most mundane moments of your life—the moments you repeat daily or even several times a day.
- Where do you see God's presence in such moments?

LET'S PROBE DEEPER

- How do you think confidence in God's presence can help us overcome the 'smallness that fuels us with fear and force'?

N THE IMAGE OF GOD

God's own breath of life is the divine seed
anted within each of us. God's own image is
ecially reflected in our unique spirit and soul.
hen we long for God, when we are aware of the
mpleteness of our present life, when we try
ve truly, we are experiencing our God-given
ess and dignity. Our confidence and sense
nity, which are greater than fear and force,

come from God. When we have the creativity and the passion to try to make the world around us a better place, and when our imagination is full of hope and possibility, we are experiencing God calling us to holiness of life.

JOURNAL EXERCISE

- Take a few minutes to write about a time when you have felt especially creative, imaginative and loving, and have been aware of your closeness to God.

Being created in the image of God also means that our journey through life leads to our return to God, the divine source from whence we came forth. Because we bear God's divine fingerprints, we belong to God. If godliness is another way to describe holiness, then being made in God's image is the foundation of being godly. However, this holiness, this godliness, does not come automatically. We still need to cooperate with

THE PROMISED ONE: SERVANT AND SAVIOR

God's grace and make every good effort to follow Jesus Christ and his greatest commandment to love God by loving our neighbors as ourselves. The Holy Spirit inspires and sustains our efforts to live into holiness of life after 'the way' of Jesus.

Our being created in the image of God and alive by the divine breath of life also means that God has blessed us with the gifts of creativity and imagination. Our ability to create, invent and imagine recalls God's creation of the world. This is why every good human creation ultimately honors God. At the same time, God has granted us the gift of free will, which means that we are able to choose between using our creativity and imagination for good or for evil. While we are created in the image and likeness of God, we can obscure this image by choosing to use our creativity in harmful or selfish ways. This is why we need to strive to form our conscience well. We need to reflect regularly on our lives and strive each and every day for a true conversion of heart and life.

GROUP ACTIVITY

⊙ Work in small groups to think of examples of situations where people chose to use their God-given creativity and imagination in destructive and harmful ways.
⊙ Share your examples with the class.

THE GUIDANCE OF THE SPIRIT

Job compared our own breath of life with the Spirit of God at work within us (Job 27:3). In the language of the Old Testament, the Spirit of God is often synonymous with the breath of God, which God breathes into the 'earth person', who then becomes alive with the very life of God. (See Genesis 2:7.)

In growing into a life of holiness, we often struggle with the freedom of our will. Choosing between good and evil can be difficult. Evil is powerful because it can tempt us and appeal to our

desires. But let us be clear; to be tempted is not a sin. Temptation becomes a sin only when we knowingly and freely give in to it.

Remember that Jesus himself struggled with temptation. (Reread the account of the Temptation of Jesus in Matthew 4:1–11 or Luke 4:1–13). The Gospel tells us that after Jesus was baptized in the river Jordan he went out into the wilderness, where he remained for forty days, fasting and preparing for his great public ministry. During this time he was tempted by the Devil to give up, go home and eat some food, and to take the easy way out of his mission. Jesus' response to temptation is the model for us when we are tempted.

OVER TO YOU

⊙ Temptations are a fact of life. Think of times when you have been tempted to do something wrong. What was it that tempted you?

THE TEMPTATION OF CHRIST | SAGRAD COR DE JESUS, BARCELONA

⊙ Pause and pray this petition from the Lord's Prayer: 'Lead us not into temptation.'

The Letter to the Hebrews, which was written to Christians who were being tempted to abandon the way of Jesus, offers us this consoling thought: 'For we do not have a high priest who is unable to sympathize with our weaknesses, but we have one who in every respect has been tested [tempted] as we are, yet without sin' (Hebrews 4:15). Jesus knew well what it is like to be tempted away from holiness of life. And the Risen Jesus will come to our aid as needed and will understand all of our temptations, and send the Holy Spirit to help us resist them.

The Holy Spirit accompanied Jesus into the wilderness and was with him as he resisted temptation. In the same way, the Holy Spirit is with us in times of temptation. We, disciples of Jesus Christ, are temples of the Holy Spirit and are in the constant company of the Holy Spirit. The Spirit guides our reasoning and graces us with his sevenfold gift of wisdom and understanding, counsel (right judgment) and fortitude (courage), knowledge and piety (reverence), and fear of the Lord (wonder and awe). These **Gifts of the Holy Spirit** help us to know and to choose good over evil, and so grow in holiness.

REFLECTIVE EXERCISE

⊙ Spend a few minutes paying attention to your breathing in and breathing out, slowly and deeply. As you breathe, imagine what it would be like if you could no longer breathe.
⊙ Next, think about each breath as the Spirit of God, entering your body to keep you alive. Imagine you are breathing in God's life and breathing out God's love. With each slow breath, invite the Spirit in to fill you, guide you and give you life.
⊙ Then reflect on these questions:
  – Where do you need the Spirit's guidance the most?
  – Where and when do you need wisdom and courage to resist temptation?
  – How will you allow the Spirit to guide you today?

The Holy Spirit accompanied Jesus into the wilderness and was with him as he resisted temptation

THINK IT THROUGH

Called to be holy together

OPENING REFLECTION/ CONVERSATION

Teams are more than just a collection of people with a purpose. Being part of a team shapes a member's identity, and each member shapes the collective identity of the team as well. No team would be what it is without each member contributing his or her unique gifts and talents. At the same time, being part of the team adds something to the life of each member; for example, social support, a sense of belonging, and greater mission and achievement than would be possible individually.

- When have you ever been on a team?
- How was it different than engaging in an activity by yourself?
- What did you contribute to the team?
- What did the team add to your life?

LET'S PROBE DEEPER

- The Church could be described as the 'team of disciples' of the Risen Jesus. How might being a member of this team help you to grow in holiness of life?

WE ARE A HOLY AND BELOVED PEOPLE

God did not create the human person to live alone. He did not create us to be solitary beings; he created us to live in community. The Christian call to grow in holiness is a communal and not a private effort. As disciples of Jesus Christ, we are part of the greater body of the People of God, past and present, those living and those who have died. We are a holy people called together by God. We are a people who encourage and support one another on our journey to holiness.

Baptism is the doorway to the Christian life and to this great company of people and community of support. In Baptism we become members of the Body of Christ and the Communion of Saints, the holy People of God. Joined to Christ through Baptism, we become adopted children of the Father and brothers and sisters in Christ. We are made sharers in the divine life, receive the gift of the Holy Spirit and become temples of the Holy Spirit. As members of the Church, the Holy Spirit is present within each of us, affirming us in countless ways to be beloved children of God.

Through Baptism we live in an intimate, familial relationship with the Holy Trinity. The members of the Church are indeed God's beloved children. God loves, supports, animates, guides and strengthens the Church. As members of the Church, we have the guidance of the Spirit to choose what is good, to choose to respond faithfully to Jesus' command to strive to be perfect as God is perfect.

CHAPTER 11: JESUS: THE WAY TO HOLINESS | THINK IT THROUGH | 251

To become the whole people whom God desires and created us to be requires living in relationship with God and with others

PAIR TEACHING

◉ Father, Son, Spirit, Church, Member, Holiness. Spend a few minutes thinking about how these six words stand in relationship to one another. (You might draw a concept map to help.)

◉ Pair up and explain to your partner the relationship between Father, Son, Spirit, Church, Member and Holiness as you see it.

◉ Next, listen to your partner's explanation.

◉ Share your best insights with the class.

THE COMMUNION OF SAINTS

We cannot become fully alive humans in isolation. To become the whole people whom God desires and created us to be requires living in relationship with God and with others. Becoming whole and becoming holy are two sides of the same coin. It requires a community of support. The Church is that community. The Church is the People whom God has called together in the name of Christ. The Church is 'the assembly of those whom God's Word "convokes" ' (CCC, no. 777) and the 'visible plan of God's love for humanity' (CCC, no. 776).

God's Spirit works most effectively through the whole Church, especially through the Sacraments, to lead all her members into holiness of life. We are also nourished by Sacred Scripture, by the Church's teachings and by her many spiritual traditions. In the Church, too, we find inspiring models of holiness, around us and among the saints who have gone before us. Through their example we learn to live a life of faith, hope and charity (love) and develop and practice the moral virtues.

The Church encourages, guides and supports us to join in works of compassion and justice, mercy and forgiveness that enable us to grow in holiness. The Holy Spirit guides and inspires all of these aspects and spiritual resources of the Church. In the Letter to the Colossians, St. Paul

252 | CREDO | THE PROMISED ONE: SERVANT AND SAVIOR

offers us a vision of the Church living in peace and harmony:

> As God's chosen ones, holy and beloved, clothe yourselves with compassion, kindness, humility, meekness, and patience. Bear with one another and, if anyone has a complaint against another, forgive each other; just as the Lord has forgiven you. . . . Above all, clothe yourselves with love, which binds everything together in perfect harmony. And let the peace of Christ rule in your hearts, to which indeed you were called in the one body. And be thankful. Let the word of Christ dwell in you richly; teach and admonish one another in all wisdom; and with gratitude in your hearts sing psalms, hymns, and spiritual songs to God. And whatever you do, in word or deed, do everything in the name of the Lord Jesus, giving thanks to God the Father through him.
>
> —Colossians 3:12–17

The Church is a 'holy' and a 'whole community' which gives witness to the presence of God in the world. However, Paul found disharmony and disunity at work in the early Church. In response to this he wrote some of the letters we find in the New Testament. In our world today, there are also many examples of disharmony and disunity. Yet Paul's vision is indeed possible because such harmony and peace is the work of the Holy Spirit.

As members of the Church, it is our challenge to bring about this harmony and unity.

LET'S PROBE DEEPER

- Work with a partner. Read Colossians 3:12–17 slowly, dwelling on all the characteristics it lists that should mark the life of the Church and her members.
- Are these characteristics simply ideals and impossible to achieve? Share your views.
- Discuss how you could help to bring a little of these characteristics to the communities to which you belong, to family or friends, to school or neighborhood.

WHAT ABOUT YOU PERSONALLY?

Notice how often the Colossians passage uses the phrase 'clothe yourselves' when suggesting to take on a certain behavior or characteristic. This phrase recalls that in Baptism we 'put on the Lord Jesus Christ' (Romans 13:14). What you wear is unmistakably visible to those around you. In fact, often the first thing that people notice about others is what they are wearing. Clothing can define for others one's attitude, status, personality and values.

- How might compassion, kindness, humility and justice be the first things that people notice about you?
- What can you do to clothe yourself in these characteristics?

How might compassion, kindness, humility and justice be the first things that people notice about you?

CHAPTER 11: JESUS: THE WAY TO HOLINESS | THINK IT THROUGH | 253

JUDGE AND ACT

REFLECT ON WHAT YOU HAVE LEARNED

◉ Looking back over this chapter, what are some of the best truths and wisdom that you have learned about striving for holiness of life? Make a list, and share your list with a partner.

◉ When have you experienced the Holy Spirit motivating you to strive for holiness of life?

◉ What might be your own next step on the journey into holiness of life?

LEARN BY EXAMPLE

The story of Brother Lawrence of the Resurrection (1614–91)

Born in the Lorraine region of eastern France, Nicolas Herman entered the Carmelite priory in Paris as a lay brother and took the religious name 'Lawrence of the Resurrection'. Brother Lawrence is an example for us of someone who discovered the path toward holiness of life in the routine of daily life.

Brother Lawrence spent almost all of the rest of his life within the walls of the priory, working in the kitchen and, in his later years, as a cobbler repairing sandals. His daily routine was, to say the least, mundane: scrubbing pots and pans, peeling and chopping food, preparing meals and cleaning up after others. Despite Brother Lawrence's 'ordinary' position in the priory, his character attracted many to him. He had a reputation for experiencing profound peace. He became well-known for his thoughts about finding the presence of God in the most ordinary and everyday experiences of daily life, and visitors came to seek spiritual guidance from him.

An abbot of Brother Lawrence's religious community has gathered his thoughts and reflections in a spiritual classic, *The Practice of the Presence of God*. Brother Lawrence's words reveal that even though he spent his life in the kitchen, being mindful of God's presence allowed him to live his life to the fullest. He grew in holiness of life by doing very ordinary things with a sense of God's presence. Brother

"The Lord walks among the pots and pans"

BROTHER LAWRENCE | REBECCA LACHANCE

Lawrence can help us discover that in peeling a potato, scrubbing a pot, drying a dish, God is there. In riding to school, taking notes in class, doing chores, walking the dog, God is there. (Can you think of other examples?) Being aware of God like this is the simplest form of prayer. It opens the door to making holy every aspect of our lives.

254 | CREDO | THE PROMISED ONE: SERVANT AND SAVIOR

JUDGE AND DECIDE

St. Ignatius of Loyola, a contemporary of Brother Lawrence, wrote that we can come to see God in all things.

- How can the wisdom of Brother Lawrence help you grow in holiness?
- What do you think might happen if you looked for the presence of God in the most boring and tiresome activities you have to do? Imagine finding God's presence in loading the dishwasher or taking out the garbage. Do you think this is possible?

RESPOND WITH FAMILY AND FRIENDS

- Decide how you and your friends, family, team and parish can help one another to respond to the Holy Spirit and grow in holiness of life.
- Consider the lives of those around you: for many people, everyday life is burdensome, boring and without meaning. Many people suffer from the ordinariness of their lives, searching for something better but not sure where to turn. Do you recognize people like this around you? Discuss with your family and friends how you can point others toward the fullness of life.

JOURNAL EXERCISE

- Think about the times you might have felt the presence of God or the movement of the Holy Spirit in your life. Perhaps you were aware of your conscience in deciding for something good. Maybe you felt creative and excited about something new. You might have sensed the presence of God in an otherwise ordinary moment. How do these encounters with God fill you with hope? How do they bring you closer to God and to others around you? Write your reflections in your journal.
- Now think back also on the times when you were uneasy and felt distant from God. Maybe you made a poor decision. Perhaps you felt overwhelmed by life, by boredom or by a sense of meaninglessness. Where do you need God the most in your life? Again, write your reflections in your journal.
- Keep these hopes and needs in mind as we move on to the Prayer Reflection.

LEARN BY HEART

Whatever you do, in word or deed, do everything in the name of the Lord Jesus, giving thanks to God the Father through him.

COLOSSIANS 3:17

CHAPTER 11: JESUS: THE WAY TO HOLINESS | JUDGE AND ACT | 255

PRAYER REFLECTION

LEADER

Sit quietly and remember that you are—as always—in the presence of God. (*Pause*)
In the name of the Father, and of the Son, and of the Holy Spirit.

ALL

Amen.

LEADER

Creator God, you created all human beings in your image;
  you implant in each of us a divine seed of life, dignity and stillness.
Send your Holy Spirit to be with us now
  as we seek your presence in this otherwise ordinary moment,
  to make our lives holy so that we may share God's love with those around us.
We ask this in the name of Jesus the Lord.

ALL

Amen.

READER

Read aloud Colossians 3:12–17.
The word of the Lord.

ALL

Thanks be to God.

LEADER

Loving God, you keep us company day and night, filling our lives with your presence
  so that we may grow in holiness and share your love with those around us.
We look back now and think about your presence in our lives,
  seeking your face, especially in the ordinary and mundane.
Send your Holy Spirit
  to help us bring to mind moments of fullness and joy,

when we were in step with your Spirit,
  as we praise you for these moments in our hearts. (*Pause*)

All pray silently about these moments.

LEADER

Lord God, always present with us,
  help us also to recall moments when our longing for you was deep, and we felt dry, empty and bored.
We ask you especially to fill these moments with your life-giving breath. (*Pause*)

All pray silently about these moments.

LEADER

Gathering all these highs and lows of our life into one prayer,
we offer you the words your Son Jesus taught us.

ALL

Our Father. . . .

LEADER

Holy God, loving Father,
  we trust you to guide us in our own journey toward holiness.
 Come, Holy Spirit,
  keep our hearts attuned to your movement in our lives,
  so that we may follow your call
  and reveal to those around us the full potential of life that you promise to every person.
We ask this in the name of Jesus the Lord.

ALL

Amen.

Pray the Sign of the Cross together.

CHAPTER 12

Lord, Teach Us to Pray

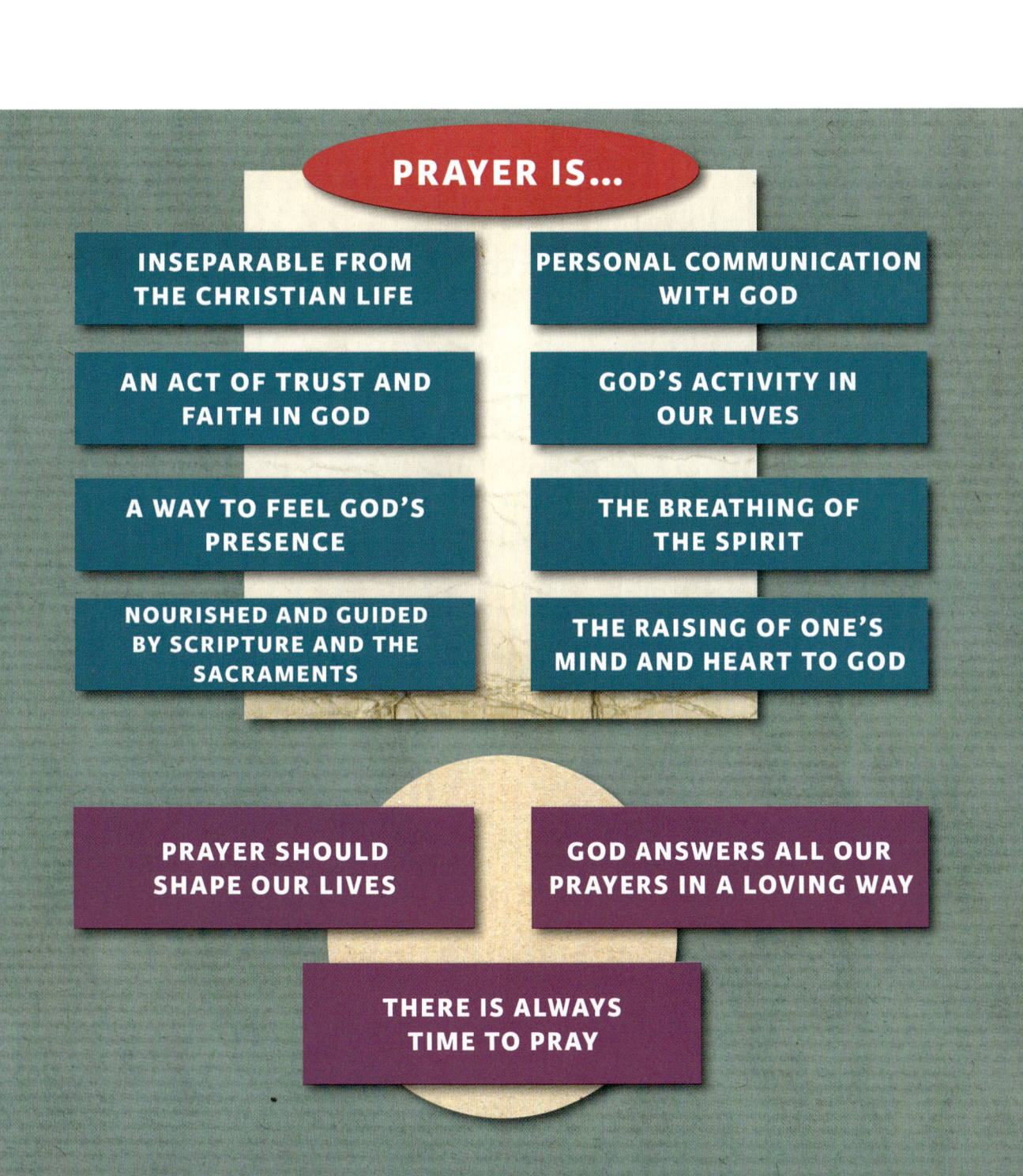

PRAYER IS...

INSEPARABLE FROM THE CHRISTIAN LIFE

PERSONAL COMMUNICATION WITH GOD

AN ACT OF TRUST AND FAITH IN GOD

GOD'S ACTIVITY IN OUR LIVES

A WAY TO FEEL GOD'S PRESENCE

THE BREATHING OF THE SPIRIT

NOURISHED AND GUIDED BY SCRIPTURE AND THE SACRAMENTS

THE RAISING OF ONE'S MIND AND HEART TO GOD

PRAYER SHOULD SHAPE OUR LIVES

GOD ANSWERS ALL OUR PRAYERS IN A LOVING WAY

THERE IS ALWAYS TIME TO PRAY

IN THIS CHAPTER WE EXPLORE CHRISTIAN PRAYER. Jesus prayed, and prayer was a vital component in his fulfilling his mission. Prayer is also a vital component of the life of a disciple of Jesus. Prayer is spending time with God, talking with and listening to God. There are many ways to be present with God in prayer. Prayer is both communal and personal; we pray as individuals and also with the Church. The Church's many traditions and practices of prayer help us pray 'always' and in 'all ways'.

LEARNING OUTCOMES

As a result of studying this chapter and exploring the issues raised, you should be able to:

- ⊙ explore prayer as a means of nurturing and deepening your relationship with God;
- ⊙ name and describe the five forms of prayer that are part of the Tradition of the Church;
- ⊙ understand that when we pray for others we bring them with us into the presence of God;
- ⊙ discover more about prayer in the life of Jesus;
- ⊙ understand the Mass as the greatest prayer of the Church;
- ⊙ explore the many prayer traditions within the Catholic Church;
- ⊙ identify the benefits of praying frequently and using repetitive prayer formats;
- ⊙ recognize that life can challenge your faith, your efforts and even your desire to pray;
- ⊙ reflect on the impact prayer might have in difficult situations;
- ⊙ understand that God answers all our prayers in a loving and life-giving way;
- ⊙ research one of the schools of spirituality that enrich the Church;
- ⊙ explore the prayers of meditation and contemplation;
- ⊙ understand regular prayer as a practice that sustains one's commitment to justice and compassion.

FAITH-FORMATION OUTCOMES

As a result of studying this chapter and exploring the issues raised, you should also:

- ⊙ reflect on your own practice of prayer;
- ⊙ renew your commitment to include prayer in your busy life;
- ⊙ recall times in your life when you have turned to God in crisis;
- ⊙ identify the people in your life whom you would like to bring into the presence of God through prayer;
- ⊙ value how the Mass nurtures your prayer life;
- ⊙ use different prayer forms;
- ⊙ identify times when you felt that God responded or didn't respond to your prayers;
- ⊙ pray with your class using the *lectio divina* format.

FAITH WORD: Prayer

LEARN BY HEART: 1 Thessalonians 5:16–18

LEARN BY EXAMPLE: Frère Roger and the Taizé Community

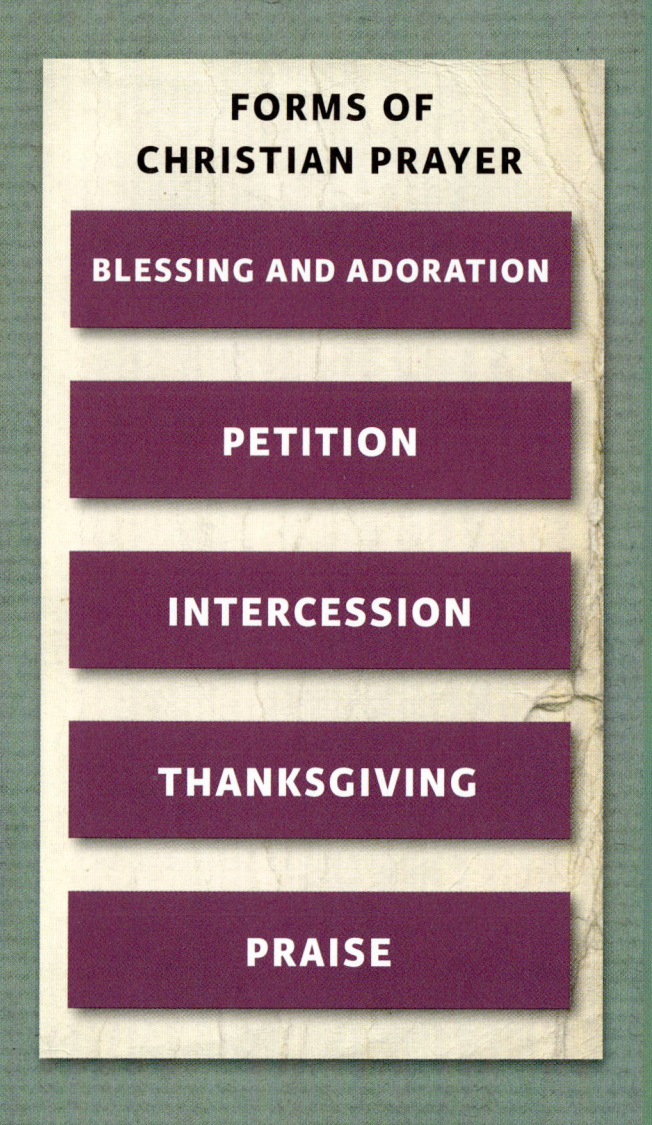

FORMS OF CHRISTIAN PRAYER

- BLESSING AND ADORATION
- PETITION
- INTERCESSION
- THANKSGIVING
- PRAISE

ATTEND AND REFLECT

Too busy to pray?

A Childhood Prayer

Randy grew up with this poem engraved on a wooden plaque on his bedroom wall. Years later he heard it prayed at church one Sunday.

I got up early one morning
And rushed right into the day!
I had so much to accomplish
That I didn't have time to pray.

Problems just tumbled about me,
And heavier came each task.
'Why doesn't God help me?' I wondered.
He answered, 'You didn't ask!'

I tried to come into God's presence;
I used all my keys at the lock.
God gently and lovingly chided,
'Why, child, you didn't knock!'

I wanted to see joy and beauty,
But the day toiled on, gray and bleak.
I wondered why God didn't show me.
He said, 'But you didn't seek.'

I woke up early this morning,
And paused before entering the day.
I had so much to accomplish
That I had to take time to pray!

After hearing the poem, Randy realized how much these simple verses meant to him as a child. He learned once again the poem's message: we have to make time for prayer.

TALK IT OVER
- Do you find time for prayer, especially on busy days? Why or why not?
- What are some of the first things that come to mind for you when you think of prayer?

PRAYING ALL WAYS
In seeking to describe what prayer means to you, you may think of spending time in church, kneeling before your bed at nighttime, saying grace before a meal in a restaurant or at the family dinner table, or holding hands with the people next to you in the stands just before the beginning of a game or match. Maybe the word 'Amen' or blessing yourself and making the sign of the cross comes to mind. Prayer takes many forms and means different things to different people, but what all descriptions of prayer have in common is God. Here are some descriptions of prayer:

260 | CREDO | THE PROMISED ONE: SERVANT AND SAVIOR

- Prayer is a reverent petition made to God.
- Prayer is personal communication with God.
- Prayer is God's activity in our lives.
- Prayer is a search to fill our deepest hungers.
- Prayer is a way to make contact with God and to feel his presence in one's life.
- Prayer is the solution to all our problems.
- Prayer is the breathing of the Spirit.

JOURNAL EXERCISE
- Compare your thoughts on prayer with these descriptions.
- Now write your own description of prayer. Be specific.

CHRISTIAN PRAYER: COMMUNION AND COMMITMENT

Prayer is spending time with God and sharing with him whatever is on our mind or in our heart. Here is how three saints of the Church described prayer. St. Thérèse of Lisieux (1873–97) wrote: 'For me, prayer is a surge of the heart; it is a simple look turned toward heaven, it is a cry of recognition and of love, embracing both trial and joy' (quoted in *Catechism of the Catholic Church* [CCC], no. 2558). St. John Damascene (c. 676–c. 749), a Doctor of the Church and patron saint of Christian artists, described prayer this way: 'Prayer is the raising of one's mind and heart to God or the requesting of good things from God' (quoted in CCC, no. 2590). St. Teresa of Ávila (1515–82), a Doctor of the Church and Spanish mystic, offers us another description of prayer as 'nothing else than a close sharing between friends; it means taking time frequently to be alone with him who we know loves us' (quoted in CCC, no. 2709).

Spending time together frequently and communicating openly and honestly is vital to deepening one's relationship with another person. The same is true of our relationship with God. Think about a best friend and recall the time when you were just getting to know each other. What kinds of activities helped you grow in friendship? You spend time with your friend primarily because you enjoy each other's company.

Prayer is enjoying God's company regularly so that your relationship deepens. The amazing truth about prayer is that 'God tirelessly calls each person to this mysterious encounter with Himself' (CCC, no. 2591). It is God who always initiates the conversation. Prayer is a gift. God so enjoys our company that he is the one who invites us to be with him in prayer. It is the Holy Spirit in the Church who invites and teaches the children of God to pray.

OVER TO YOU
- What might happen when friends do not spend much time together?
- Do you think the same is true of your friendship with God? Explain.

ST. THÉRÈSE OF LISIEUX

CHAPTER 12: LORD, TEACH US TO PRAY | ATTEND AND REFLECT | 261

Having a friend involves a commitment. We need to invest time in a relationship if it is to survive and grow. Sometimes your friend needs your help and support, so you may give them a ride, listen to their troubles, lend them your phone, or help them with projects, chores or homework. Would you really be good friends if you could not count on each other for help and support? Friends have an understanding that they can turn to and rely on one another.

Likewise, God relies on us. God is always loyal and faithful to us; we, too, are to be loyal and faithful to God. Spending time with God is a sign of our commitment to him. In biblical terms, prayer is an expression of our Covenant with God. Prayer should shape our lives, our attitudes, our habits and our choices. Like your friend who can count on you, God also counts on you to share his love with those around you, especially those who seem to need it most. Prayer helps us live out our commitment to be disciples of Jesus.

REFLECT AND DISCUSS
⊙ How would you describe a friendship in which so-called friends never had or were willing to make time for one another?
⊙ Using the same criteria, describe a disciple of Christ who seems to make little time for God?
⊙ What are some ways in which a busy young Christian might regularly make time for God throughout the day?

THERE IS ALWAYS TIME TO PRAY
Recall the story of Brother Lawrence of the Resurrection in chapter 11. Brother Lawrence found the presence of God in the midst of his everyday chores. He did not see prayer as something that had to be added to his daily routine. Prayer was the foundation for his way of being in the world. For him, peeling and chopping vegetables was a prayer; setting and clearing the table was another prayer; scrubbing pots and pans was yet another, just as was gathering in the

VOLUNTEERS IN SEATTLE CONSTRUCT A TRANSITIONAL HOUSING COMPLEX FOR THE HOMELESS

chapel to join the other members of his religious community for communal prayer.

'Prayer and the Christian life are inseparable' (CCC, no. 2745). Prayer is as vital for our spiritual wholeness and wellbeing as sleeping, eating and exercising are for our physical wellbeing. But, we know well enough that when we get busy with other things, sleeping, eating and exercising can easily fall by the wayside. Sadly, the same can happen with prayer. Perhaps we do not include prayer in our busy lives because we are distracted by other things, erroneously thinking that prayer has to be long and time-consuming. It's true, there are many reasons why we can put praying aside. But prayer does not depend on the length of time we spend. We can turn our mind and heart to God in a few seconds if we like, and God welcomes even the shortest prayers. In commenting on St. Paul's words 'Pray without ceasing' (1 Thessalonians 5:17), Origen (c.185–254), a scholar and theologian from Alexandria in North Africa, wrote:

He 'prays without ceasing' who unites prayer to works and good works to prayer. Only in this way can we consider as realizable the principle of praying without ceasing.

—quoted in CCC, no. 2745

JOURNAL EXERCISE

Write your reflections on these questions in your journal.

- ⊙ What wisdom have you learned from the poem or from Brother Lawrence's example about the role of prayer in our busy lives?
- ⊙ In what ways do you pray? What is your favorite prayer, or way of praying?

FROM FAITH TO LIFE

- ⊙ Renew your commitment to include prayer in your busy life. Consider making some of your everyday actions a form of prayer.

CHAPTER 12: LORD, TEACH US TO PRAY | ATTEND AND REFLECT | 263

HEAR THE STORY

Being prayerful

MICHAEL CONNER HUMPHREYS AS FORREST AND HANNA R. HALL AS JENNY IN *FORREST GUMP*

OPENING REFLECTION/CONVERSATION

In the popular film *Forrest Gump* (1994), we see Jenny and Forrest as children, running through a field to hide from Jenny's father, who is drunk and angry and pursuing them. Jenny drops to her knees and repeats the prayer, 'Dear God, make me a bird. So I could fly far. Far, far away from here.' Jenny escapes from her father that day.

The depiction of prayer in *Forrest Gump* is of an activity associated with urgency and desperation—Jenny and Forrest are in trouble; Jenny's response is to pray.

⊙ Do you find that there are certain times or circumstances when you are more likely to turn to God? Explain.

⊙ Talk about other examples of prayer in film and television.

A HEAVENLY HELPLINE—AND MUCH MORE

In such films as *Forrest Gump,* prayer is often associated with a person needing and seeking God's help in times of trouble. In our own lives, too, we seem almost spontaneously to turn to God when we face difficult situations. We seek both comfort and courage and wisdom to face situations that seem too much for us to handle. Recall Jesus' prayer to his Father in the Garden of Gethsemane as he was about to face his arrest, his denial by Peter, his trial and scourging, his abandonment by many of his disciples, and his Crucifixion (see Matthew 26:36–46). We, too, trust that we are not alone and helpless, even in the most difficult times of our lives; and we reach out to God in prayer.

At such times, prayer is an act of trust. It is an expression of our faith that God, who desires for us to live an abundant life, life to its fullest, is always present with us, providing and caring for us. That is what he clearly revealed to us when the Son of God took on flesh and lived among us. It is God's commitment to us, his Covenant with us.

WHAT ABOUT YOU PERSONALLY?

⊙ Have you ever turned to God in difficult times? How was God there for you in your need?

We limit our understanding of prayer when we focus on only one dimension, or form, of prayer. Prayer, like communication between friends, is about far more than asking for help in difficult times. It is acknowledging and celebrating that God is part of and present in our whole life, in our good and bad times. Think for a moment of all the dimensions that bind and deepen your true friendships. There are times of praising one another, times of thanking one

264 | CREDO | THE PROMISED ONE: SERVANT AND SAVIOR

another and times of figuring out how you can help one another. And, above all, there are those high-five moments, those times when you share with another that your relationship is central to your life. Prayer takes all those forms too. Indeed, we can pray in 'all ways'. Here is how the Church describes the various forms of Christian prayer:

Prayer of Blessing and Adoration: When we pray a prayer of blessing and adoration we acknowledge that God is the center of our life. We 'bless the One who is the source of every blessing' (CCC, no. 2626), we acknowledge that God alone is the Creator and we 'exalt the greatness of the Lord who made us and the almighty power of the Savior who sets us free from evil' (CCC, no. 2628). 'Because God blesses the human heart, it can in return bless him who is the source of every blessing' (CCC, no. 2645).

Prayer of Petition: By the prayer of petition we express our awareness of our relationship with God. 'We are creatures who are not our own beginning, not the masters of adversity, not our own last end. We are sinners who as Christians know that we have turned away from our Father. Our petition is already a turning back to him' (CCC, no. 2629).

Prayer of Intercession: The prayer of intercession is the 'asking on behalf of another'. 'Intercession is a prayer of petition which leads us to pray as Jesus did' (CCC, no. 2634).

Prayer of Thanksgiving: St. Paul summed up the life of a disciple of Christ, saying, 'Give thanks in all circumstances' (1 Thessalonians 5:18). Our whole life, our good times and bad times, glorifies God. 'Every joy and suffering, every event and need can become the matter of thanksgiving which, sharing in that of Christ, should fill one's whole life' (CCC, no. 2648).

Prayer of Praise: 'Prayer of praise is entirely disinterested and rises to God, lauds him, and gives him glory for his own sake, quite beyond what he has done, but simply because HE IS' (CCC, no. 2649).

The Holy Spirit 'who teaches the Church and recalls to her all that Jesus said, also instructs her in the life of prayer, inspiring new expressions of these same basic forms of prayer' (CCC, no. 2644)

REFLECT AND DISCUSS

- ⊙ What is different about prayers of need and prayers of joy, prayers of petition and prayers of thanks? Recall and compare your emotions and particular words or expressions of prayer at these times.
- ⊙ Why might it be important to pray about both our trials and our joys? What do you think we might miss out on if we forget about one or the other?

FAITH WORD

Prayer

The raising of one's mind and heart to God in thanksgiving and in praise of his glory. It can also include the requesting of good things from God. It is an act by which one enters into awareness of a loving communion with God.

—*United States Catholic Catechism for Adults* [USCCA], 523

LORD, HEAR OUR PRAYER

There are twenty-one letters in the New Testament. St. Paul the Apostle and other leaders wrote these letters to the members of the early Church scattered around the Mediterranean Sea. These letters, which reveal the cares and concerns of the Apostles for those to whom they were writing, usually include a prayer in the salutation or conclusion of the letter. For example, in Romans Paul begins, 'Grace to you and peace from God our Father and the Lord Jesus Christ' (Romans 1:7); and in the First Letter to the Thessalonians, he concludes, 'The grace of our Lord Jesus Christ be with you' (1 Thessalonians 5:28).

Through prayer, through open and honest communication, we grow in our loving relationship with God. 'Prayer is the living relationship of the children of God with their Father who is good beyond measure, with his Son Jesus Christ and with the Holy Spirit' (CCC, no 2565). Prayer also deepens and enriches our relationships with our family, friends, neighbors and even people we do not know by name. Prayer connects us with one another through God's presence, even if we are otherwise far away. When we bring other people with us into the presence of God by raising them up through prayer, we strengthen the Body of Christ, the People whom God has gathered in Christ's name.

OVER TO YOU

⊙ Compare the way you stay in contact with your friends each day and the way you stay in contact with God. Which of the two are you more regularly in contact with? Why might that be so?

REFLECT AND DISCUSS

⊙ When are the times you pray for others?

⊙ Have you ever prayed for an enemy, following Jesus' teaching in Matthew 5:44; for example, for a person or group of people who showed disrespect for you, or bullied you, or spread rumors about you? What moved you to pray for this person or group of people?

⊙ Did your praying for this person or group of people affect the way you behaved toward them? Explain.

JOURNAL EXERCISE

⊙ Think about the people in your life that you most want to bring into the presence of God through prayer. What is your greatest hope for each of these people? Listen to God speaking to your heart. Reflect on what you can do for these people here and now to share God's love with them. Write your reflections in your journal.

EMBRACE THE VISION

Praying with the Church

OPENING REFLECTION

Jesus was true God and true man. He was like us in all ways except sin. In speaking of the prayer of Jesus, the *Catechism* teaches:

The Son of God who became Son of the Virgin also learned to pray according to his human heart. He learns the formulas of prayer from his mother, who kept in her heart and meditated upon all the 'great things' done by the Almighty [see Luke 1:49; 2:19; 2:51]. He learns to pray in the words and rhythms of the prayer of his people, in the synagogue at Nazareth and the Temple at Jerusalem. But his prayer springs from an otherwise secret source, as he intimates at the age of twelve: 'I must be in my Father's house' [see Luke 2:49].

—CCC, no. 2599

Jesus' prayer to his Father 'is the perfect model of prayer in the New Testament' (CCC, no. 2620).

SCRIPTURE EXERCISE

⊙ Work with a partner. Page through the four accounts of the Gospel to find passages that speak of Jesus at prayer. Describe the form of prayer that Jesus is engaged in. Here are a few passages to get you started:
  – Matthew 6:9–13, 21; 6:33; 11:25–27
  – Mark 1:32–35; 14:32–36
  – Luke 3:21; 4:16–19; 6:12–15; 9:18–20; 9:28–31; 10:21; 22:32–34; 22:41–44; 23:46
  – John 11:41–42

THINK, PAIR AND SHARE

⊙ Think about the ways you like to pray. Maybe you enjoy visiting the Blessed Sacrament, praying the Rosary, journaling, spending time with nature, engaging with traditional devotions, reading Scripture, or listening to music as you raise your mind and heart to God.
⊙ How do your gestures and habits of prayer connect you to a greater community of faith?
⊙ Share your thoughts on this with a partner.

THE PRAYER OF THE CHURCH/THE PRAYER OF CHRIST

The four accounts of the Gospel clearly portray Jesus joining with his fellow Jews for formal prayer. He prayed in the Temple; he celebrated Jewish feasts, such as Passover; and he prayed in the synagogue. Jesus prayed alone as well as with his disciples and others. He prayed for himself and for others.

CHAPTER 12: LORD, TEACH US TO PRAY | EMBRACE THE VISION | 267

THE LAST SUPPER OF CHRIST STAINED GLASS WINDOW

Every liturgical action, especially the celebration of the Eucharist and the Sacraments, is an encounter between Christ and his Church

Catholics and other Christians pray as Jesus did. 'There is no other way of Christian prayer than Christ. Whether our prayer is communal or personal, vocal or interior, it has access to the Father only if we pray "in the name" of Jesus' (CCC, no. 2664). As Jesus learned the formulas and rhythms of the prayer of his people, we learn to pray from the Church. Our prayers include morning and evening prayer, grace before and after meals, the Liturgy of the Hours, and, most importantly, regular Sunday participation in the Eucharist.

TALK IT OVER

⊙ Do you model your prayer life on Jesus' life of prayer? Explain.
⊙ Do you feel connected to Jesus every time you pray? Why or why not?

WORD AND SACRAMENT

'The Word of God, the liturgy of the Church, and the virtues of faith, hope, and charity are sources of prayer' (CCC, no. 2662). The Church is a people of prayer, and she invites us to pray regularly: daily prayers, the Liturgy of the Hours, Sunday Eucharist, the feasts of the liturgical year and many other ways. The Liturgy of the Church is the center of the Church's prayer. The celebration of the Eucharist, the Church's great prayer of thanksgiving, is the center of the Liturgy and the Sacraments. 'The prayer of the Church, nourished by the Word of God and the celebration of the liturgy, teaches us to pray to the Lord Jesus' (CCC, no. 2665).

The Church's sacramental Liturgy focuses on both the proclamation of the Word and the celebration of the Sacrament. This structure 'was prefigured in the Old Covenant' (CCC, no. 1093).

268 | CREDO | THE PROMISED ONE: SERVANT AND SAVIOR

A brief look at the structure of the Mass reveals this. The Mass has two main parts, the Liturgy of the Word and the Liturgy of the Eucharist. During Mass we first spend time proclaiming, listening to, reflecting on and responding to the Word of God. We then celebrate the Liturgy of the Eucharist, remembering and being made sharers in God's saving events among us 'which have found their fulfillment in the mystery of Christ' (CCC, no. 1093).

Hearing the Word of God and receiving the Eucharist help to nourish and sustain us in our mission to share God's love with those around us. The Second Vatican Council well described the Mass as 'the summit and source' of the whole Christian life (*Constitution on the Sacred Liturgy*, no. 10). The Mass and the other Sacraments are like a great lexicon of Catholic prayer that brings together a multitude of expressions of God and the People of God in loving relationship.

REFLECT AND DISCUSS

- ◉ How do you think the Mass can support and inform your individual prayer life?
- ◉ Why do you think the proclamation of the Word of God is part of the celebration of every Sacrament?

LET'S PROBE DEEPER

Scripture is both a source and guide for prayer. 'Prayer unfolds throughout the whole history of salvation as a reciprocal call between God and man' (CCC, no. 2591). Through the proclamation of Scripture during the Liturgy, we can learn from the wisdom of the community of God's people who have sought to spend time with God in prayer throughout the history of Salvation. For example, from the faith stories of Abraham and Moses, David and Solomon, Elijah and the other prophets, Mary and Zechariah and so many others, we discover the importance of prayer.

- ◉ Work alone, with a partner or in small groups to research the role of prayer in the lives of the people of faith named above. (*Clue*: See *Catechism*, nos. 2570–2589 and 2617–2619, and Scripture passages referenced in the *Catechism*.)

DAILY PRAYER OF THE CHURCH

The prayer life of the Church flows from and mirrors the prayer tradition found in both the Old Testament and the New Testament. Many prayers of the Catholic Church, such as the Lord's Prayer, the Hail Mary, the Rosary, the *Angelus*, the *Magnificat* (Canticle of Mary), the *Benedictus* (Canticle of

The Mass has two main parts, the Liturgy of the Word and the Liturgy of the Eucharist

Zechariah) and the Psalms, are rooted in the Bible. (See these prayers in the section 'Catholic Prayers, Devotions and Practices' at the back of this text.)

From the early days of the Church, the disciples of Jesus, like their Jewish brothers and sisters, set aside time every day to pray. This practice developed over time into the unique format that we know today as the Liturgy of the Hours. The origins of the Liturgy of the Hours can be found in the monastic communities of men and women that began to emerge. People in those communities lived, worked and prayed together. They followed a structured life and they desired to grow in holiness through the simplicity of their lifestyle and their shared work and prayer.

In response to their living out this commitment, some monastic communities invented a regular schedule of prayer, gathering up to five times a day to pray the psalms: morning, noon, night, and sometimes in between. Some monks organized the psalms in a special order to fit this schedule; this came to be known as the Psalter. The Liturgy of the Hours is the Church's inheritance from this monastic tradition of praying the psalms and reading the Scriptures together at certain times throughout the day. In those communities, members who could not read substituted the praying of the Lord's Prayer at the times of the day when the community gathered for prayer.

RESEARCH, REFLECT AND SHARE

Praying the psalms is not only central to the Liturgy of the Hours but also to the prayer life of the People of God, the Church.
⊙ Scan the Book of Psalms. Select one psalm that particularly appeals to you.
⊙ Take turns sharing your selected psalm and the reasons you chose it with a partner.

Right now, there are Catholics praying the Liturgy of the Hours somewhere in the world, sharing in the same prayer designated for this day. By praying the Liturgy of the Hours we can join our prayer to the prayer of millions of people around the world at that time: praying in church, sitting on a bus, waiting at the airport, waiting for the dryer at the laundromat, sitting in a coffee shop, taking a break at the library, on a retreat, in a monastery— anywhere you can think of. Praying the Liturgy of the Hours is one more way to join in prayer with the greater Body of Christ around the world, to join the Church in praying ceaselessly.

OVER TO YOU

⊙ What difference might it make knowing that you are united in prayer to so many people around the world?

THINK IT THROUGH

Lord, teach us to pray

OPENING REFLECTION

When the disciples of Jesus learned that John the Baptist had taught his followers a special way to pray, they wanted Jesus to do the same for them. They approached Jesus and asked him, 'Lord, teach us to pray, as John taught his disciples' (Luke 11:1). Jesus responded by teaching them the Lord's Prayer. He then continued:

Suppose one of you has a friend, and you go to him at midnight and say to him, 'Friend, lend me three loaves of bread; for a friend of mine has arrived, and I have nothing to set before him.' And he answers from within, 'Do not bother me; the door has already been locked, and my children are with me in bed; I cannot get up and give you anything.' I tell you, even though he will not get up and give him anything because he is his friend, at least because of his persistence he will get up and give him whatever he needs.

So I say to you, 'Ask, and it will be given to you; search, and you will find; knock, and the door will be opened for you. For everyone who asks receives, and everyone who searches finds, and for everyone who knocks, the door will be opened.'

—Luke 11:5–10

Just as Jesus was confident and trusted in his Father, we, his disciples, are confident that God hears and responds to all of our prayers. But sometimes we may be tempted to wonder, 'Will God really respond?' At times it may be hard to believe that God is responding to our prayers of petition and intercession—especially if God does not answer exactly as we request. When this happens we may be tempted not to persevere in our prayer. But we can be sure that God hears and does respond to all of our prayers. Let us explore this mystery a little more.

OVER TO YOU

- What is your first reaction to what Jesus says here about prayer?
- What do you think Jesus is trying to tell us?
- Can you believe what he is saying? Why or why not?
- How have you experienced God's response to your prayers? Do you think God answers all of our prayers? Why or why not?

JESUS PRAYS WITH HIS DISCIPLES | ENGRAVING AFTER ALEXANDRE BIDA

CHAPTER 12: LORD, TEACH US TO PRAY | THINK IT THROUGH | 271

ST. JOHN CHRYSOSTOM | PEDRO ORRENTE

works. When we turn to God with trust, openness and perseverance, something always happens. God listens and responds to our needs. When we leave an opening for God to come into our lives, the movement of God's Spirit brings faith, hope, love, courage, strength and guidance to those areas where we need these the most.

The gifts of grace that God gives us are specific to each life and circumstance, but through our prayer we will experience change. It may be a change in our circumstances, change in the lives and actions of those around us, or an interior change in our understanding and heart.

REFLECT AND DISCUSS

Many people who have been diagnosed with a terminal illness pray that they may be cured of their illness, and their family and friends also pray for their return to good health. We often pray for such people at Mass. Yet, some of these people still suffer and die.

◉ Why do people pray when the odds of recovery are stacked against them?

◉ What can happen when people's prayers seem to fail? How might this change a person's faith and trust in God?

THE POWER OF PRAYER

The Bible is full of God's responses to the prayers of people in need. St. John Chrysostom reminds us that:

> The potency of prayer has subdued the strength of fire; it has bridled the rage of lions, hushed the anarchy to rest, extinguished wars, appeased the elements, expelled demons, burst the chains of death, expanded the gates of heaven, assuaged diseases, repelled frauds, rescued cities from destruction, stayed the sun in its course, and arrested the progress of the thunderbolt.

Through his words in Luke's Gospel, Jesus teaches us something very important: prayer

The mystery of prayer often invites us beyond the limits of our understanding; God sees the big picture, but often we do not. Prayer is an act of faith, of openness and trust in God; we accept that the answer to our prayers is ultimately in God's hands. In prayer we express that we trust in God's love and care for us. We can even pray for miracles, but we cannot feel entitled to them. Typically, God does not intervene and suspend the dynamics of nature. When those dynamics bring harm or even death to us, we can be sure that God is there with us. God's own Word to us in Scripture has revealed this over and over again.

God always hears our prayers. Sometimes God's response, God's grace, comes to us in earth-shattering ways, and sometimes in a quiet

272 | CREDO | THE PROMISED ONE: SERVANT AND SAVIOR

sense of peace, hope and stillness. So, if a loved one has terminal cancer and does not recover, we can be sure that our prayer helps him or her. God is with our loved one, preparing him or her for death and new life. We pray with Jesus as he taught us and as he himself did. We can always count on our loving God to hear our prayers and respond to them in a loving and life-giving way.

WHAT ABOUT YOU PERSONALLY?

◉ Have you ever persisted in your praying but truly felt your prayers were not answered? If so, how did you respond to that feeling?

THE PERFECT PRAYER

'Prayer is primarily addressed to the Father' (CCC, no. 2680). In response to his disciples' request to teach them to pray, Jesus replied, 'When you pray, say, "Father, hallowed be your name. . . ." ' (Luke 11:2). The Lord's Prayer is the fundamental prayer of the Church. In the third century, Tertullian described the importance of praying the Lord's Prayer in the life of a Christian. He taught that the Lord's Prayer 'is truly the summary of the whole gospel' (*On Prayer*, quoted in CCC, no. 2761). In the same treatise Tertullian later wrote:

Since the Lord . . . after handing over the practice of prayer, said elsewhere, 'Ask and you shall receive', and since everyone has petitions which are particular to his circumstances, the . . . appropriate prayer [the Lord's Prayer] is said first, as the foundation of further desires.

—quoted in CCC, no. 2761

In the twelfth century, St. Thomas Aquinas taught:

The Lord's Prayer is the most perfect of prayers. . . . In it we ask, not only for all the things we can rightly desire, but also in the sequence that they should be desired. This prayer not only teaches us to ask for things, but also in what order we should desire them.

—*Summa Theologiae*, II–II, 83, 9

We, the Church, continue to live this tradition today. We pray the Lord's Prayer daily and in every celebration of the Liturgy. We call upon

the Father because Jesus, the Son of God made man, has revealed him to us and invited us to do so. In so doing, we grow in our intimacy and communion with the Father and his Son, Jesus Christ.

READ AND DISCUSS

◉ With a partner read the petitions of the Lord's Prayer. Then discuss the teachings of St. Thomas when he said that the Lord's Prayer shows us the sequence in which we should petition God.

OVER TO YOU

◉ Consider praying the Lord's Prayer more often.

The Lord's Prayer is the most perfect of prayers.

ST. THOMAS AQUINAS

ST. THOMAS AQUINAS | 15TH-CENTURY WOODCUT

JUDGE AND ACT

REVIEW WHAT YOU HAVE LEARNED

In this chapter we explored the mystery of Christian prayer. We deepened our understanding of the role of prayer in the life of Jesus and in the life of his disciples. We learned that we can pray alone and with others; we can pray always and in 'all ways'; we can pray anytime, anywhere.

⊙ Identify one thing you have learned about prayer from studying this chapter that you want to bring with you throughout your life.

⊙ Work with a partner to compose a prayer asking God for guidance in making a good choice.

LEARN BY EXAMPLE

The story of Frère Roger and the Taizé Community

Blessed Pope John Paul II, during one of his many journeys outside Rome, took the time to make a stop in Taizé, France, and visit with Frère Roger and the Taizé community. Several thousand youth were present on the day of the Pope's visit. They had been praying in silence throughout the night, and at 8:30 in the morning Frère Roger, the other brothers and many young people came to greet the Pope. The Pope welcomed them, saying:

> Like you, pilgrims and friends of the community, the Pope is only passing through. But one passes through Taizé as one passes close to a spring of water. The traveler stops, quenches his thirst and continues on his way. The brothers of the community, you know, do not want to keep you. They want, in prayer and silence, to enable you to drink the living water promised by Christ, to know his joy, to discern his presence, to respond to his call, then to set out again to witness to his love and to serve your brothers and sisters in your parishes, your schools, your universities, and in all your places of work.

Frère Roger lived out Paul the Apostle's teaching, 'Rejoice always, pray without ceasing, give thanks in all circumstances; for this is the will of God in Jesus Christ for you' (1 Thessalonians 5:16–18). On August 16, 2008, Frère Roger was stabbed and killed by a woman who was probably mentally disturbed. On hearing the news, Pope Benedict XVI said:

> Frère Roger is in the hands of eternal goodness, of eternal love. He invites and exhorts us to be faithful laborers in the vineyard, even in sad situations, certain that the Lord accompanies us and gives us his joy.

274 | CREDO | THE PROMISED ONE: SERVANT AND SAVIOR

TALK IT OVER

- What can you learn from the example of Frère Roger and the Taizé community about the importance of prayer in the life of a disciple of Jesus?

LET'S PROBE DEEPER

There are many different schools of spirituality that share in the living tradition of prayer and are guides for the spiritual life. Some of the schools of spirituality are Benedictine, Dominican, Franciscan and Ignatian.

- Work with a partner and research one of the schools of spirituality that enrich the Church. If your school is served by a religious community, be sure to research the spirituality that is at the heart of that community.
- Share your findings on your school website.

HEART TO HEART WITH GOD

While we, perhaps, most often use vocal prayer, or words, to communicate with God, the Taizé community builds its prayer on the three traditional expressions of prayer; namely, vocal prayer, meditation and contemplation. Both meditation and contemplation are like a 'heart to heart' with God. Meditation is silent listening and responding to God in one's own words. 'Meditation is above all a quest. . . . Meditation engages thought, imagination, emotion, and desire . . . in order to deepen our convictions of faith, prompt the conversion of our heart, and strengthen our will to follow Christ' (CCC, nos. 2705, 2708).

A favorite way to mediate is to take a passage of Scripture, to read it slowly, and then to listen carefully to God's Word to discover how it relates to one's own life. Some people find it helpful to meditate before a holy icon. An icon is a painted panel with some representation of God, of Jesus Christ or an event from his life, or of the Blessed Mother Mary or a saint. The icon functions as a window into the mystery of faith that it represents, and helps those who pray to focus their prayer, to look through the icon into the realm of God.

The *Catechism* reminds us that, besides Scripture and holy icons, we can meditate on 'the great book of creation, and that of history—the page on which the "today" of God is written' (CCC, no. 2705). We can take any event or happening that comes our way in daily life, or the beauty of nature, and use it to focus our conversation with God.

OVER TO YOU

- Do you think Jesus ever expressed his prayer through meditation? Explain.
- When have you expressed your prayer through meditation? Was your meditation planned? Or did it come about spontaneously?
- How might you include a simple prayer of meditation in your daily prayer? What difference might that make in helping you to 'pray without ceasing' and 'give thanks in all circumstances' as Paul taught us to do?

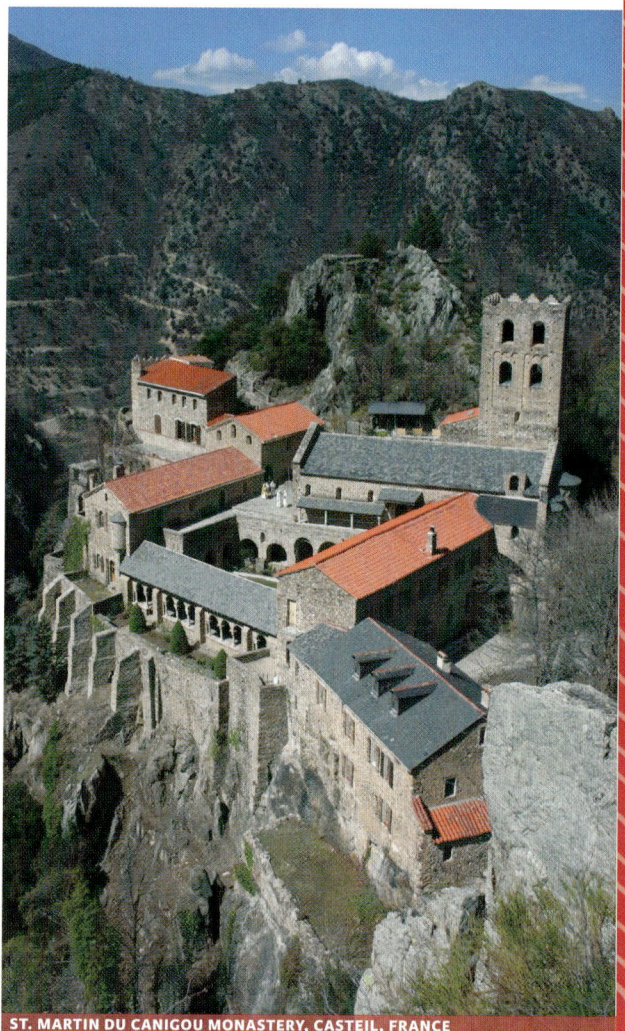

ST. MARTIN DU CANIGOU MONASTERY, CASTEIL, FRANCE

CHAPTER 12: LORD, TEACH US TO PRAY | JUDGE AND ACT | 275

There is another wordless prayer that God invites us to take part in. This is the prayer of contemplation. 'Contemplative prayer is the simplest expression of the mystery of prayer' (CCC, no. 2713). In contemplation we simply respond to God's invitation and gift to be with him. In silence we open ourselves to his presence. St. Teresa of Ávila described contemplation as 'a close sharing between friends', and said that she often contemplated simply by sitting, saying nothing, but imagining God looking upon her with great love. For example, you can contemplate by paying attention to your breathing, imagining yourself breathing in God's life and breathing out God's love. As we said at the beginning of this chapter, we can pray 'always' and in 'all ways'.

WHAT WILL YOU DO NOW?

- Are you willing to volunteer to be a prayer partner with children in your parish school or religious education program who are preparing for First Holy Communion?
- What is the most important thing you would want these younger children to understand about prayer?
- What vocal prayers would you help them to learn by heart? (*Suggestion*: Check the back of the text they are using.)

RESPOND WITH FAMILY AND FRIENDS

There is a Catholic adage that says 'We must be willing to work for what we pray for'. In other words, it is not enough simply to pray for justice or to pray for those who are in need. Our prayer should prompt us to do works of justice and compassion, as Frère Roger did and the Brothers of Taizè continue to do.

- When you think about praying for the needs of those around you, what might you also do to help them in their need? How do your prayers encourage you to take action? What prayer might you say to God to sustain your commitment to justice and compassion?
- Talk to your friends and family about prayer and its relationship to good works.

JOURNAL EXERCISE

- What commitment are you willing to make to try to follow the example of Jesus, the Master Pray-er, in your day-to-day life, in your interactions with your family and friends? Write your reflections in your journal.

LEARN BY HEART

Rejoice always, pray without ceasing, give thanks in all circumstances; for this is the will of God in Christ Jesus for you.

1 THESSALONIANS 5:16—18

276 | CREDO | THE PROMISED ONE: SERVANT AND SAVIOR

PRAYER REFLECTION

LEADER

Sit quietly and remember that you are—as always— in the presence of God. *(Pause)*
In the name of the Father, and of the Son, and of the Holy Spirit.

ALL

Amen.

LEADER

For our prayer reflection today we will use the *lectio divina* prayer method, which you may recall from *Son of God and Son of Mary*, the second text in the *Credo* series. *Lectio divina* is a way of praying the Word of God through meditating on a passage from Scripture. As with all prayers of meditation, *lectio divina* leads us to putting God's Word into action.

Lectio (Read)

LEADER

Recall that we live in the presence of God. Jesus told us that he is always with us when we gather to pray. *(Pause)* Open your Bible to the eleventh chapter in Matthew's Gospel. Read verses 25–30 slowly, expecting that there might be a Word of God's wisdom there for your life. Notice what word or image stands out for you; what words of Jesus resonate for you in your life right now.

All read the passage and pause for reflection (and perhaps some sharing of thoughts on what was read).

Meditatio (Meditate)

LEADER

Reread the passage. This time as you read, pause and imagine the scene; place yourself within it as an observer. Talk to God about what you are seeing, hearing, noticing as Jesus prays. *(Pause)*

Contemplatio (Contemplate)

LEADER

Read the passage once again. Now listen in silence for what God may be saying to you. It may help to focus on the particular word or image that seems most significant. Rest in the loving presence of God. *(Pause)*

Oratio (Pray)

LEADER

Slowly come out of contemplation. Look into your own heart for the personal prayer you might say. *(Pause)* Now raise your prayer up to God, aloud or in the quiet of your heart.

Actio (Act)

LEADER

Ask yourself, 'What decision is God inviting me to make?', 'What is God calling me to do?' *(Pause)*

All share decisions or overall responses to the experience. Then silently pray the words 'Thy kingdom come; thy will be done' over and over again in the form of a mantra prayer.

LEADER

Let us glorify God by our lives.

Pray the Sign of the Cross together.

CHAPTER 13

Jesus Christ, the Lord of Eternal Life

JESUS WILL COME AGAIN IN GLORY TO JUDGE THE LIVING AND THE DEAD

GOD WILL JUDGE US ON HOW WELL WE HAVE LOVED AND LIVED AS JESUS MODELED

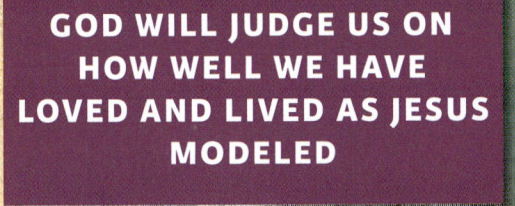

OUR LIFE ON EARTH IS A PREPARATION FOR DEATH AND LIFE AFTER DEATH

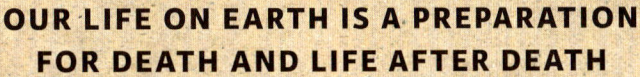

WE BELIEVE AND HOPE THAT WE WILL LIVE A LIFE EVERLASTING WITH THE HOLY TRINITY, THE ANGELS, MARY AND ALL THE SAINTS

THINKING ABOUT THE LAST THINGS CAN ENRICH OUR FAITH AND HOPE AND ENCOURAGE US TO LOVE GOD, OTHER PEOPLE AND OURSELVES

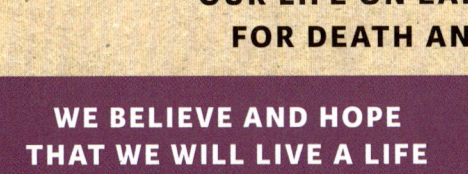

IN THIS CHAPTER WE EXPLORE MORE DEEPLY THE teachings of the Catholic Church on death and life after death. Catholics believe that all of our life on earth is a preparation for death and life after death. We live in the hope that God's final desire for us, as revealed in Jesus Christ, is that we come home to God to share in eternal life. This hopeful attitude toward death can shape everything we do now as we strive to live as disciples of Jesus Christ.

THE LAST THINGS

HEAVEN

HELL

PURGATORY

PARTICULAR JUDGMENT

FINAL (LAST) JUDGMENT

RESURRECTION OF THE BODY

LEARNING OUTCOMES

As a result of studying this chapter and exploring the issues raised, you should be able to:

- articulate your understanding of and attitude toward death;
- explore the depiction of the Last Judgment at the Cathedral of Chartres, France;
- explore the persecution of Christians in the Roman Empire;
- understand the meaning of the faith word 'martyr';
- understand the teaching of the Catholic Church on the Last, or Final, Judgment;
- respond to the image of God as judge, in particular in Exodus 34:6–7 and Matthew 25:31–46;
- reflect on Jesus' teaching in Matthew 7:3–5;
- explore Jesus' teaching in the parable of the Rich Man and Lazarus;
- understand heaven to be the fulfillment of all our life's questions and deepest longings;
- understand hell as choosing to live for eternity apart from God's love;
- understand the Church's teaching on Purgatory;
- discover the importance of developing virtues as you strive for life everlasting in heaven;
- explore St. Paul's teaching on love;
- identify the interconnectedness of the theological virtues of faith, hope and love;
- learn more about the first Christian community of believers.

FAITH-FORMATION OUTCOMES

As a result of studying this chapter and exploring the issues raised, you should also:

- deepen your relationship with God through a heightened sense of what really matters in life;
- resolve to integrate Jesus' teaching in Matthew 7:1–2 into your life;
- describe the impact the concept of heaven has on your striving for holiness of life;
- articulate how or why someone might refuse God's loving relationship and invitation to heaven;
- reflect on ways you can put God first every day;
- describe situations where you could make love a habit, or 'virtue';
- consider how you might best reveal God's peace, fulfillment and joy to others;
- identify where you need God's grace to develop good habits of faith, hope and love.

FAITH WORD: Martyr

LEARN BY HEART: Matthew 7:1–2

LEARN BY EXAMPLE: The early Church

ATTEND AND REFLECT

What do you think about life after death?

OPENING REFLECTION

Have you ever heard the saying 'Only two things in life are for sure—death and taxes'? Indeed, there are very few people who escape paying taxes of some kind, and no one escapes death. You may find it difficult to accept that truth now, in the prime of your youth, but your life on earth will end someday—even if you are blessed to live to a ripe old age. A true understanding of the meaning of death that God has revealed can help you live your life all the more abundantly and embrace every day as a gift. Our Catholic faith, our families and friends, indeed all people, can help us come to a true understanding of death, which, in turn, can help us not only to live well but to die well.

THINK, PAIR AND SHARE

In the Apostles' Creed, Catholics confess their belief both that Jesus 'will come to judge the living and the dead' and in 'the resurrection of the body and life everlasting'. In the Nicene Creed, the Profession of Faith prayed most often at Sunday Mass, we confess that Jesus 'will come again in glory to judge the living and the dead' and that we 'look forward to the resurrection of the dead and the life of the world to come'.

⊙ What do you think happens after the death of your body? Share your ideas with a partner.
⊙ Then turn to another pair and all four of you share your views.

JOURNAL EXERCISE

Complete these sentences:
⊙ My attitude toward death is . . . .
⊙ I hold this attitude because . . . .
⊙ My understanding of death helps me to live each day by . . . .

FAITH THROUGH ART

Christian artists express the truths of faith in many forms, and this is wholly in keeping with the teaching of the Catholic Church, which states:

Truth is beautiful in itself. Truth in words, the rational expression of the knowledge of created and uncreated reality, is necessary to man, who is endowed with intellect. But truth can also find other complementary forms of human expression, above all when it is a matter of evoking what is beyond words: the depths of the human heart, the exaltations of the soul, the mystery of God.

—*Catechism of the Catholic Church (CCC)*, no. 2500

CATHEDRAL OF OUR LADY OF CHARTRES, NORTH FAÇADE

The millions of pilgrims who travel each year to view works of Christian art attest to the power of art to express visually the faith of Christians.

Try to imagine yourself as a pilgrim who has come to see the newly built Cathedral of Chartres, France. It is about the year 1200 and you have traveled far to worship God in this magnificent new building. You are awestruck as you reverently approach the Cathedral with a crowd of other pilgrims. As you enter the doors, a forest of stone columns draws your eyes upward toward brilliant, colorful stained-glass windows that embrace you in their light bursting through their panes.

Your eyes remain on the nearest windows, as you notice detail after detail. Some of the sacred images look familiar—the beautiful woman holding a child must be the Blessed Mother! The three kings kneeling before her and the child in another window must be the Magi! Stories of the faith that you have often heard now come to life in a new way.

The millions of pilgrims who travel each year to view works of Christian art attest to the power of art to express visually the faith of Christians

Then, above the main portal, you see a large round window, the most breathtaking and awe-inspiring window of all. It looks like a starburst or a rose, with many scenes and panels circulating out from the center. In the very center you see Christ. You know it is him because he radiates light and his halo has a cross in it. He is majestic, seated with his arms open; the image is powerful, serene, inviting. Images of angels and saints

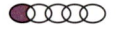

CHAPTER 13: JESUS, THE LORD OF ETERNAL LIFE | ATTEND AND REFLECT | 281

surround the Christ figure in smaller scenes. One image catches your eye and makes you pause a while; it is the depiction of an angel holding a balance scale with tiny people in it, as the angel fends off a green devil who is trying to tip the scale toward himself.

As your eyes move on, you notice more figures of ordinary people: no crowns, no halos like most of the other characters. Some are climbing out of open graves. Some are embraced by angels and carried upward to the lap of an old prophet . . . you think it might be Abraham. These images are serene, comforting. Some other scenes are less so. You notice some people falling into the mouth of a large monster; others are being grabbed by a green-faced devil. From these disturbing images, your eyes draw back toward the scene of the angel with the balance scale; then to Christ in the center.

TALK IT OVER

◉ Why do you think the designers of Chartres Cathedral placed the **Last Judgment** Window where it would be the last thing people would see upon exiting the cathedral?

WHAT ABOUT YOU PERSONALLY?

◉ Which of these images comfort you? Disturb or worry you? Why?

THE LAST THINGS

Heaven, **hell**, Purgatory, particular judgment, Final (Last) Judgment, and resurrection of the body are referred to as 'The Last Things'. These realities typically hover at the edge of people's consciousness, even when they are focusing on following Jesus in their everyday life. Though we recall some of these realities regularly when praying the Nicene Creed and the Apostles' Creed, they can seem abstract and far away. The fact is that none of us likes to think about our own mortality, let alone think about the end of all time. Life keeps us busy, too occupied in the present moment to focus much on such things. In short, we think about these 'Last Things'—if we think about them at all—as being relevant for

282 | CREDO | THE PROMISED ONE: SERVANT AND SAVIOR

us only sometime in our future. But maybe we are missing out on something. Many of history's great thinkers, both Christian and non-Christian, have argued that thinking about death can help us to live more fully alive in the present.

During this course of study you have explored the meaning of Jesus' life, Death and Resurrection for your own life—Jesus has conquered death and given you and all people hope in eternal life. Catholics profess this truth, over and over again, each time we celebrate the Funeral Mass. In one of the Prefaces, the priest proclaims boldly, 'for your faithful, Lord, life is changed not ended'. United with Christ through Baptism, we both die with him and rise with him to new life. We believe and hope that we will eventually live a life everlasting with the Holy Trinity, the angels, Mary and all the saints.

OVER TO YOU

⊙ Think about your past few days: how many times have you thought about heaven, hell, Purgatory, the Final Judgment or the resurrection of the dead? Should we think of these more often? Why or why not?

⊙ What difference might it make to our daily outlook if we believed that Jesus has conquered death and won the possibility for us of eternal life with God?

Knowledge of the 'Last Things' is not an end in and of itself. We might avoid being trapped by this temptation by renaming 'The Last Things' as 'The Eternal and Final Human Experience'. The Last Things point to something that is fundamental about God's relationship with his people, and about our relationship with God. Thinking about heaven, hell, Purgatory, one's particular judgment, the Final Judgment and the resurrection of our body can enrich our faith and hope and encourage us to love God, other people and ourselves. Instead of being far-away concepts, the Last Things can help us recognize and value what really matters in life and deepen our loving relationship with God in this present moment.

CREATIVE ACTIVITY

⊙ Work in groups to create a rose window depicting life, judgment and eternity in

God's company. The window may be similar to a medieval rose window, like the one at Chartres; or it may be a modern interpretation in the form of a collage, a digital slideshow or animation. Be creative! Before you begin, take a close look at the details of the Last Judgment in the Chartres Cathedral window.

REFLECT AND DECIDE

Christian artists have sometimes depicted themselves, or the patron who commissioned their work of art, humbly in the corner of their creation, as if he or she were part of the scene.

⊙ Where would you place yourself in the rose window that you created?

⊙ What might your choice of location express about your faith and hope in eternal life?

MADONNA WITH CHILD AND TWO DONORS | GENTILE BELLINI

CHAPTER 13: JESUS, THE LORD OF ETERNAL LIFE | ATTEND AND REFLECT | 283

HEAR THE STORY

Convicted of Christianity

PLAQUE AT THE TYBURN CONVENT, LONDON, ENGLAND

OPENING CONVERSATION

You have probably heard stories of the ancient martyrs, people who were judged and who died giving witness to their faith in Christ. The story of the martyrs is still being written today and, no doubt, will be written until Christ comes again in glory to judge the living and the dead. In fact, seventy-five percent of people who suffer for their faith today are Christians.

⊙ Why do you think Christians are still being persecuted in some parts of the world today?

⊙ What aspect, belief or practice of Christian faith would you be willing to suffer—even die—for?

THE WITNESS OF MARTYRS

Christians from the beginning of the Church have been willing to make sacrifices, accept pain and suffering, even death itself, in witness to Christ and their faith. The days of the early Church have been described as the 'Age of Martyrs'. Christians in the great and sprawling Roman Empire lived in expectation of dying for their faith. Christians were often considered to be insurrectionists who steadfastly refused to worship the pantheon of Roman gods and to acknowledge the Emperors, living and dead, to be 'gods'. To the Romans, the Christian worship of Jesus as their only Lord was an act of treason, deserving of death.

These would-be martyrs knew they were following the example of Jesus himself, who suffered and died for their sins. They knew Jesus had predicted that his disciples would also suffer for their faith, and they trusted in his promises that he would be with them in their suffering. They believed and trusted that the Holy Spirit, as Jesus promised, would be their Advocate and give them the courage to face their pain, suffering and death. They believed that in their suffering and death they were joined to Christ, whose suffering and Death on the Cross gave new meaning to suffering. They believed their suffering and death would not be in vain and they looked beyond their suffering to the promise of eternal life with God in heaven.

This witness of the martyrs filled the early Church with hope. The more Christians were persecuted, the more people, inspired by the witness of the martyrs, wanted to become Christian. This witness of the martyrs gave rise to the saying, 'The blood of martyrs is the seed of the Church.'

284 | CREDO | THE PROMISED ONE: SERVANT AND SAVIOR

TALK IT OVER

- Do you know the story of any Christians who have suffered and even died for their faith in Christ? Share that story with a partner.
- Do you know of any Christians who are suffering today because they are giving witness to Christ and their faith? Share that story with a partner.

CLASS DEBATE

Debate the following motion: 'It is better to live for your faith than to die for it.'

GOD OF JUSTICE

Each time we pray the Nicene Creed, we profess, 'I believe in one Lord Jesus Christ . . . He will come again in glory to judge the living and the dead. . . .' The *Catechism of the Catholic Church* summarizes this teaching:

Christ is Lord of eternal life. Full right to pass definitive judgment on the works and hearts of men belongs to him as redeemer of the world. He 'acquired' this right by his cross. The Father has given 'all judgment to the Son' [see John 5:22, 27; Matthew 25:31; Acts of the Apostles 10:42, 17:31; and 2 Timothy 4:1]. Yet the Son did not come to judge, but to save and to give the life he has in himself [see John 3:17, 5:26].
—CCC, no. 679

What we say about Jesus, we indeed say about God the Holy Trinity. God will judge the conduct of each of our lives, and the secrets of our life will be brought to light. (Read Mark 12:38–40;

Luke 12:1–3; John 3:20–21; Romans 2:16 and 1 Corinthians 4:5.) Throughout the Bible the sacred authors often speak of God the Judge.

For example, in the Book of Exodus we read the story of Moses coming down from Mount Sinai with the Ten Commandments, only to find his people worshiping a golden calf. He smashes the stone tablets on which the Commandments were written. The people repent and plead with Moses to return to God on the mountain to renew their Covenant. To his amazement, Moses hears God say, 'The LORD, the LORD, a God merciful and gracious, slow to anger, and abounding in steadfast love and faithfulness, keeping steadfast love for the thousandth generation, forgiving iniquity and transgression and sin, yet by no means clearing the guilty' (Exodus 34:6–7). The Old Testament reveals God as the one who insures final justice, promoting good and condemning evil. It is a longing of every human heart that all evil will be punished and all good will be rewarded. Our faith is that

FAITH WORD

Martyr

From the Greek word *martyr*, which means 'witness'. In a Christian context, a martyr is 'one who witnesses to Christ and the truth of faith, even to the point of suffering' (*United States Catholic Catechism for Adults* [USCCA], 519).

ST. MAXIMILIAN KOLBE, A TWENTIETH-CENTURY MARTYR

God will see to such 'final' judgment.

OVER TO YOU

⊙ How do you respond to the image of God as Judge?

In the New Testament, Jesus says of himself, 'I came not to judge the world, but to save the world' (John 12:47). Jesus revealed God to be a Loving Judge, and a Judge who will judge us precisely on how well we have loved like our God and as Jesus modeled.

Recall the well-known parable of the Judgment of Nations in Matthew 25:31–46. Christ the triumphant King of all creation will preside at the Final Judgment of all humankind. He will separate people into those who have cared for others, especially those in need, and those who have not done so. The mystery of divine Love is such that Christ will honor the choices each person has made in either showing compassion or ignoring those in need. The Loving Judge will judge us on how well we have loved God by loving our neighbor as ourselves. He will judge us in so far as we have willingly chosen to work for the restoration of the divine plan of justice according to which he first created the world. 'At the end of time, the Kingdom of God will come in its fullness. Then the just will reign with Christ for ever, glorified in body and soul, and the material universe will be transformed. God will then be "all in all" in eternal life' (CCC, no. 1060).

THINK, PAIR AND SHARE

⊙ Work with a partner. Compare God the Judge revealed in Matthew 25:31–46 with the image of God the Judge in Exodus 34:6–7.

⊙ Share the results of your comparisons with the whole class.

GOD ALONE IS JUDGE

The heart of Jesus' mission was forgiveness and reconciliation, not revenge or punishment. Jesus often warned his disciples not to rush to judgment of other people and seek revenge. God certainly did not, and does not! Rather, God sent his Son, Jesus Christ, who commanded us, 'Do

DAY OF JUDGMENT | CHURCH OF THE HOLY SAVIOUR, CHORA, TURKEY

Why is it so difficult to resist the temptation to judge others?

not judge, so that you may not be judged. For with the judgment you make you will be judged, and the measure you give will be the measure you get' (Matthew 7:1–2).

Only God knows the inner workings of the human heart. Unlike God, we simply do not have the insight and knowledge of someone else's heart. We do not know the full circumstances surrounding their actions to judge them fairly. Indeed, we need to resist the temptation to judge others and make this an aspect of living the greatest commandment—to love God by loving one's neighbor as oneself. Christian faith should prevent us from making harsh judgments on any basis. 'Christ is Lord of eternal life. Full right to pass definitive judgment on the works and hearts of men belongs to him as redeemer of the world' (CCC, no. 679).

TALK IT OVER

⊙ Why is it so difficult to resist the temptation to judge others?
⊙ How can Christian faith help us to avoid harsh judgments of others?

When tempted to judge someone quickly, remember these words of Jesus, the carpenter and carpenter's son:

Why do you see the speck in your neighbor's eye, but do not notice the log in your own eye? Or how can you say to your neighbor, 'Let me take the speck out of your eye', while the log is in your own eye? You hypocrite, first take the log out of your own eye, and then you will see clearly to take the speck out of your neighbor's eye.

—Matthew 7:3–5

CHAPTER 13: JESUS, THE LORD OF ETERNAL LIFE | HEAR THE STORY | 287

Can we really have a log stuck in our eye? Of course not. Jesus used exaggerated language here to make a point. The fact is that we can be terribly unaware of our own faults, but very quick to point out the faults in others. It is better for us to judge ourselves before we judge others and to treat others with understanding and compassion as Jesus did and commanded us to do.

REFLECT AND SHARE
⊙ Can you tell of an experience when you had 'a speck in your eye' but someone with 'a log in their own eye' saw it?
⊙ Or the reverse: might you ever have 'a log in your own eye' but notice 'the speck in another's eye'? Give examples.

LET'S PROBE DEEPER
⊙ When something is in our eye, we cannot see it with that same eye. The only way to figure out the obstruction is by looking in a mirror. Think about those persons or things in your life that help you to see your true self. Why are these 'mirrors' so valuable to us?
⊙ After we have faced our own mirrors, Jesus calls us to hold up a mirror to those around us so that they can remove their own 'specks'. What do you think is the best way to go about this? How can we avoid judgment and show compassion instead?

WHAT ABOUT YOU PERSONALLY?
⊙ What particular decision about living your faith emerges for you from these reflections about judgment?

EMBRACE THE VISION

Our journey to eternal life

OPENING ACTIVITY/ CONVERSATION

In addition to Matthew 25 there are many other Gospel stories about judgment of people after their death. A much quoted parable is the parable of the Rich Man and Lazarus in Luke 16:19–31. Take a moment to read this parable. Then discuss:

- ⊙ What is the main message of this parable of Jesus?
- ⊙ Why does God judge the rich man so harshly?
- ⊙ Why does God judge Lazarus so kindly?
- ⊙ Is this a fair judgment? Why or why not?

JESUS TELLING THE PARABLE OF THE RICH MAN | ENGRAVING AFTER ALEXANDRE BIDA

A PARABLE FOR OUR TIME

The rich man in the parable of the Rich Man and Lazarus was given the name Dives (a word meaning 'rich') sometime during the Early Middle Ages. The parable warns that excessive attachment to wealth can tempt us to make very bad judgments. The blind pursuit of wealth can, in turn, blind us to the needs of others, especially the poor and those whom society marginalizes, or refuses even to 'see'.

Jesus' lead-in to this parable is very telling, 'You cannot serve God and wealth' (Luke 16:13). (See also Matthew 6:24.) Jesus was referring to much more than placing the pursuit of economic wealth at the center of our lives. By 'wealth' Jesus meant any kind of 'false god'—power or pleasure, fame or fortune—anything with which

we choose to replace God in our lives. We are to keep God as the center of our lives as the First Commandment commands.

TALK IT OVER

- ⊙ What are some of the 'false gods' that people follow today?
- ⊙ Why does following 'false gods' have disastrous consequences for one's self? For others? For the earth?
- ⊙ What else does the parable of the Rich Man and Lazarus reveal about life after death?

GROUP ACTIVITY/DISCUSSION

- ⊙ Role-play the parable of the Rich Man and Lazarus.
- ⊙ How might the rich man have acted differently?
- ⊙ How can the hope of heaven shape our lives here on earth?

CHAPTER 13: JESUS, THE LORD OF ETERNAL LIFE | EMBRACE THE VISION | 289

WHAT ABOUT YOU PERSONALLY?

- When have you been tempted to act like the rich man in the parable?
- What do you think are the consequences of acting in this way?
- How do you think you will be accountable for the consequences of your bad judgments?

LET'S PROBE DEEPER

In the parable, God points out to the rich man the consequences of his choice. While the rich man suffers in torment, Lazarus lives in the company of angels and great holy people of the past. The separation of Lazarus and the rich man after their deaths reflects the separation and distance that the rich man put between himself and Lazarus on earth. Lazarus lives in a state of eternal happiness—heaven. Dives lives in a state of tormenting unhappiness—hell.

THE BEATIFIC VISION | WILLIAM BLAKE

HEAVEN, OUR ETERNAL HOME

God's desire for us is eternal life with him in heaven. While we often think of heaven as a place, it is more accurately described as living in an eternal and loving relationship with God. We simply cannot imagine what this really means. In the third century, St. Cyprian, Bishop of Carthage (modern Tunis) in Northern Africa, wrote:

How great will your glory and happiness be, to be allowed to see God, to be honored with sharing the joy of salvation and eternal light with Christ your Lord and God . . . to delight in the joy of immortality in the Kingdom of heaven with the righteous and God's friends.
—Quoted in CCC, no. 1028

The Church uses the term 'Beatific Vision', seeing God face to face, to express the awe and depth of the happiness of heaven. 'Those who die in God's grace and friendship and are perfectly purified live for ever with Christ. They are like God for ever, for they "see him as he is", face to face' (CCC, no. 1023). Of course, the Church is using very human language here, just as the sacred authors did in writing Sacred Scripture. There is no intention to suggest that God has a physical 'face' as we do. The words simply seek to express the intimacy of the relationship with God that we will experience for ever, the very love with which God created us.

But heaven is not only between 'you' and 'God'. Heaven is also living in undisturbed harmony and peace with others. The promise of heaven includes enjoying for ever the love of all those who have loved us and of all those whom we have loved on earth.

The Church uses the term 'Beatific Vision' to express the awe and depth of the happiness of heaven

REFLECT

⦿ Think about the moments in your life when you were most at peace and felt true joy and satisfaction; these moments provide a faint glimpse of what heaven will be like.

PURGATORY: HOPE AND MERCY AFTER DEATH

Recall the teaching of the Church that you read above: 'Those who die in God's grace and friendship and are perfectly purified live for ever with Christ' (CCC, no. 1023). Jesus taught that we are to be 'as perfect as God is perfect'. But what happens if we die before we reach that 'perfection'? What happens should we die while we are still a work-in-progress, still striving to fulfill Jesus' command? The Catholic Church's teaching on Purgatory addresses these questions.

The Church's teaching on Purgatory is a message of hope, a message that proclaims the mystery of divine mercy. 'All who die in God's grace and friendship, but still imperfectly purified, are indeed assured of their eternal salvation; but after death they undergo purification, so as to achieve the holiness necessary to enter the joy of heaven' (CCC, no. 1030). Purgatory speaks to the depths of God's love and the divine desire that we live in communion with the Holy Trinity for ever. (Recall the parable of the Prodigal Son/Loving Father in Luke 15:11–32.)

God's love is always at work, even after our soul separates from our body at the moment of our death, drawing all those who are seeking him with a sincere heart into his eternal presence. But if we die before we are completely ready for God's presence, God's transforming love remains at work in our life after death. Even if we do not have it 'all together' at the end of this life on earth, Purgatory offers us the assurance that God still gives us a chance and wants us to do so even after death.

The souls in a state of Purgatory, or purification after death, are among the faithful who make up the Communion of Saints. So, we maintain a living relationship with the souls in Purgatory. Our love and concern and care for the souls in Purgatory does not end with the death of their bodies. This is why the Church prays for the souls in Purgatory.

CHAPTER 13: JESUS, THE LORD OF ETERNAL LIFE | EMBRACE THE VISION | 291

From the beginning the Church has honored the memory of the dead and offered prayers in suffrage for them

From the beginning the Church has honored the memory of the dead and offered prayers in suffrage for them, above all the Eucharistic sacrifice, so that, thus purified, they may attain the beatific vision of God. The Church also commends almsgiving, indulgences and works of penance undertaken on behalf of the dead.

—CCC, no. 1032

Growing in the love of God and neighbor is a lifelong process—and, for some, a process that continues after death. Through Purgatory we can finally triumph over undue worldly attachments that draw us away from God's love and may stand in the way of our loving relationship with God. Purgatory gets us ready for the Beatific Vision—for seeing and being with God, 'face to face'.

TALK IT OVER

What does the Church's teaching on Purgatory mean for you?

HELL: A TERRIBLE PRICE TO PAY

God's own Word to us is that he invites and desires us to live in a loving, eternal relationship with him. For this reason, God sent his Son. (Read John 20:31.) Sadly and tragically, some may totally reject that invitation and spurn God's desire. While some may reject the offer of divine love, over and over again, God never stops extending that offer. There is a possibility that a person, despite his or her knowledge of God and God's love for him or her, may say, 'No thanks!', and choose to turn his or her back on God's love and instead try to find happiness outside that love.

Hell is freely and knowingly choosing to live for all eternity refusing God's love. Hell is the eternal torment of knowing that we have chosen to leave our deepest desires and hopes unmet and unfulfilled. Hell is living in eternal exile, a self-imposed, tormenting exile into an abyss that lasts for ever.

We have glimpses into the reality of hell in those moments of restlessness, need, lack,

292 | CREDO | THE PROMISED ONE: SERVANT AND SAVIOR

emptiness, isolation, meaninglessness, violence, hatred, shame and embarrassment that we have all experienced. God always continues to reach out to us in our lives and extends an invitation to loving relationship.

Remember the good thief who died alongside Jesus on Calvary. Human judgment sentenced him to capital punishment. At the very last moment of his life, he repented and Jesus promised him, 'Truly I tell you, today you will be with me in Paradise' (Luke 23:43). Eternal punishment is never the desire of God. God is always offering us the grace to repent, until the very end.

OVER TO YOU

- ⊙ Do you think it is possible for someone ultimately (eternally) to reject God's love and friendship?
- ⊙ Do you think that hell means God gives up on some people? Explain.

REFLECT AND DISCUSS

- ⊙ Why do you think Catholics do not proclaim any one particular person to be in hell? As you

reflect on this, think about Christ's teaching on judgment, as well as the role of hope in Christian life. Take a moment to organize your thoughts and then discuss it as a class.

Although the possibility of hell is entirely real, Catholic teaching stops short of labeling anyone as hell-bound, even people who have harmed others and committed great evil in their lifetime. By contrast, there are thousands of people whom the Catholic Church proclaims to be in heaven. Then add all the unnamed saints that we celebrate on November 1 each year. These are the countless 'ordinary' good people who sincerely did their best to live good lives—to seek holiness of life—and who are now seeing God face to face in heaven.

JUDGE AND DECIDE

- ⊙ What are some of the ways in which you can say yes to God's invitation to love, peace, joy and fulfillment through interacting with the people around you? Be specific.

Truly I tell you, today you will be with me in Paradise.

LUKE 23:43

CHRIST AND THE GOOD THIEF | TITIAN

THINK IT THROUGH

Making virtue a habit

Christians, this means to love as Jesus loved. With the help of God's grace and through Jesus' life, Death, Resurrection and Ascension, we have been made sharers in the 'abundant' life that he promised and earned for us. But, we need to develop the habit of cooperating with God's grace; we need to practice and practice and practice some more.

OVER TO YOU

⊙ How consciously and sincerely do you seek to live the Great Commandment?
⊙ Do you do so regularly or in spurts? Explain.

A habit is a habitual and firm disposition to do something. We can develop good habits, or virtues, and, of course, we can develop bad habits. Habits, both good and bad, become part of who we are. Have you ever tried to break a bad habit, such as biting your nails? When you do, you discover how strong our habits are. It can take weeks of vigilance to stop a bad habitual action. What about good habits, such as practicing honesty and telling the truth even when it is embarrassing?

Making good habits part of the way you 'normally' act does not just happen. Such a 'way of acting' comes about only with effort, with practice. One author observed this about habits: 'Habits are safer than rules; you don't have to watch them. And you don't have to keep them either. They keep you.' The author's point here is that our habits help us express who we are and shape our way of 'being' in the world.

OPENING REFLECTION/CONVERSATION

Think for a moment about how effortlessly 'superstars' seem to use their skills to achieve success—whether they be in athletics or in the performing arts or in technology or in academics and so on. The secret, of course, is the hidden hours of practice, practice and more practice that went into the development of those skills.

⊙ What skills do you excel at?
⊙ What part did practicing those skills play in your excelling at them?

GETTING INTO THE HABIT

The Word of God leaves us in no doubt! The 'only' way to prepare for God's judgment on our lives is to live a 'good life', to seek holiness of life. We are to strive to live the Great Commandment with our whole heart and our whole mind. For

294 | CREDO | THE PROMISED ONE: SERVANT AND SAVIOR

To live a life rooted in virtue is at the heart of our response to Jesus' invitation to 'Come, follow me'

JESUS CALLS MATTHEW | ENGRAVING AFTER ALEXANDRE BIDA

REFLECT AND SHARE

- What do you think of the statement that 'Habits keep you'?
- What would you name as some of your own best habits?
- How does your Christian faith shape your habits?

VIRTUES

No matter what our age, we need to develop the good habit of living for the Kingdom of God by cooperating with the Holy Spirit and accepting the grace of Redemption. We call these good habits 'virtues'. To live a life rooted in virtue is at the heart of our response to Jesus' invitation to 'Come, follow me'. Living the virtues keeps us in loving relationship with God and gives us a taste of the 'abundance of life' that Jesus promised. Living a virtuous life is the way Christians prepare to hear Christ's welcoming words, 'Come, you that are blessed by my Father, inherit the kingdom prepared for you from the foundation of the world' (Matthew 25:34).

A virtue is 'a habitual and firm disposition to do good' (CCC, no. 1833). In describing the virtuous life, the Church speaks of 'human virtues' and 'theological virtues'. 'Human virtues acquired by education, by deliberate acts and by perseverance ever-renewed in repeated efforts are purified and elevated by divine grace. With God's help, virtues forge character and give facility in the practice of the good' (CCC, no. 1810). The human virtues can be grouped around the four cardinal virtues: prudence, justice, fortitude and temperance.

The human virtues are rooted in the theological virtues of faith, hope and charity (love). These three virtues are gifts from God which 'dispose Christians to live in a relationship with the Holy Trinity. They have the One and Triune God for their origin, motive, and object. . . . They are infused by God into the souls of the faithful to make them capable of acting as his children and of meriting eternal life'. The gifts of faith, hope and charity are the pledge of God's 'presence and action in the faculties of the human being' (CCC, nos. 1812–1813).

TALK IT OVER

- Where do you see people in the world today living the human virtues or the theological virtues? Give a brief but specific description.

CHAPTER 13: JESUS, THE LORD OF ETERNAL LIFE | THINK IT THROUGH | 295

WHAT ABOUT YOU PERSONALLY?

- Where do you see these virtues at work in your own life?
- How might they become a more regular part of your life?

THE GREATEST VIRTUE OF ALL

The virtues are always at work in building up the Church, the Body of Christ, in the world. The Acts of the Apostles and the New Testament Letters give evidence of this. Paul's First Letter to the Corinthians speaks to the role of the human and theological virtues in the life of Christ's disciples.

The Church in the Greek city of Corinth was in conflict when Paul wrote the First Letter to the Corinthians. The efforts to live a life of virtue had become a bone of contention. Some disciples stood out as really smart and knowledgeable about faith. Others stood out for having the gift of prophecy. Then there were some who had the mysterious gift of being able to speak in 'tongues', and those who heard them were moved in faith. Eventually, following either one gifted person or another led to divisions in the Church at Corinth. Finally, one concerned person sent a letter to Paul, asking him for help. Part of Paul's reply, 1 Corinthians 13:1–13, contains one of the best known passages in the New Testament. It concludes that love is the greatest virtue of all.

REFLECT AND DISCUSS

- Work with a partner and read 1 Corinthians 13:1–13.
- What is the main point Paul was trying to communicate to the Corinthians—and to us?

Clearly St. Paul was both admonishing the Church in Corinth and encouraging them to refocus on the fundamental habit, or virtue, of the Christian life, namely, love.

OVER TO YOU

- Read this teaching from the *Catechism*:

  The practice of all the virtues is animated and inspired by charity, which 'binds everything together in perfect harmony' [see Colossians 3:14]; it articulates and orders them among themselves; it is the source and the goal of their Christian practice.

  —CCC, no. 1827

- How do you think this statement is supported by 1 Corinthians 13:1–13? Discuss your response with a partner.

Faith, hope and love lead the way to many other virtuous habits: compassion, kindness, gentleness, a positive attitude, encouragement of others, patience, honesty. But love is the greatest of all the virtues, just as love is the greatest of all the Commandments. Making a habit of responding to the gifts of faith, hope and love gives us the foundation to live our lives as children of God and disciples of Christ.

JOURNAL EXERCISE

- Keeping in mind Paul's description of the virtues, how might you act from day to day so that love becomes ingrained as a habit in your heart and lifestyle? What are some of the things you might do to grow in this great virtue? Be specific.

JUDGE AND ACT

REVIEW WHAT YOU HAVE LEARNED

Jesus is the Lord of eternal life. His life, Death, Resurrection and Ascension revealed the path to eternal life and made it possible for us to undertake that journey.

◉ If you had to choose one thing you learned from studying this chapter that you feel could make a difference for your life, what would it be? And how might you make it part of your life?

LEARN BY EXAMPLE

The story of the early Church

The members of the early Church certainly lived in expectation of the return, or Second Coming, of Christ. They lived in the hope that they would soon be reunited with him as he had promised. After encouraging the Church in Thessalonia 'to live and to please God (as, in fact, you are doing), you should do so more and more' (1 Thessalonians 4:1), St. Paul wrote:

For the Lord himself, with a cry of command, with the archangel's call and with the sound of God's trumpet, will descend from heaven, and the dead in Christ will rise first. Then, we who are alive . . . will be caught up in the clouds together with them to meet the Lord in the air; and so we will be with the Lord for ever. Therefore, encourage one another with these words.

—1 Thessalonians 4:16–18

In the Acts of the Apostles, which was written after the Letter to the Thessalonians, we catch a glimpse of how the early Church 'lived to please God' in their hope of eternal life. (With a partner, read Acts of the Apostles 2:43–47. Try to imagine being among the first Christians.) We discover that the early Church in Jerusalem lived as 'one'. They shared all their possessions in common, and they helped those around them who were in need. They studied the teachings of the Apostles, shared meals together and worshiped in the Temple. (Remember, they saw themselves as Jews who were following the 'way' of Jesus.)

EARLY CHRISTIANS IN AD 50 | 19TH-CENTURY ENGRAVING

Their lifestyle, which was based on the Great Commandment and the New Commandment, caught the attention of those living around them. People sensed that the community of Jesus' followers was up to something good, and they wanted to be part of it. Sharing all of one's things and giving them to people in need was as radical back then as it is today. Many people, Jews and Gentiles, more than likely would have wondered and asked themselves and one another, 'How can these followers of Christ risk their own security in this way?'

There was something so irresistible and attractive about 'the way' the members of the early Church were living that, Luke tells us, 'day by day the Lord added to their number' (Acts of the Apostles 2:47). In their witnessing to their faith in Christ, they were also giving a glimpse of the Kingdom of Heaven to those around them.

TALK IT OVER

◉ Work with a partner. Brainstorm a list of the faith-based communities to which you belong, for example, church youth group, school service group and so on.

◉ Compare those communities to the early Church described by Luke in the Acts of the Apostles.

◉ Why do you think someone might wish to be part of your community?

◉ What can you do to make your community reveal more clearly signs of peace, fulfillment and joy in God's company?

JUDGE AND DECIDE

◉ Where do you need God's help the most to develop good habits of faith, hope and love in your relationship with God and others?

RESPOND WITH FAMILY AND FRIENDS

◉ The world needs people of faith, hope and love. The world needs people to witness to the abundance of life promised by Jesus. Families and friends whose lives give witness to the coming of the Kingdom of Heaven do just that. Think about ways that you can be this kind of person with your friends and with your family.

LEARN BY HEART

Do not judge, so that you may not be judged. For with the judgment you make you will be judged, and the measure you give will be the measure you get.

MATTHEW 7:1–2

298 | CREDO | THE PROMISED ONE: SERVANT AND SAVIOR

PRAYER REFLECTION

LEADER

Sit quietly and remember that you are—as always—in the presence of God. (*Pause*)
In the name of the Father, and of the Son, and of the Holy Spirit.

ALL

Amen.

LEADER

Emmanuel, God-with-us,
   you came to us as Jesus Christ,
   so that experiencing the love of your Son,
   we may fall even deeper in love with you, our
      God and Creator of all, seen and unseen.
Send us your Holy Spirit now,
   as we celebrate your love for all people.
Help us to respond with faith and hope to your
      invitation
   to share in your love, now and for ever.
We ask this through Christ's holy Name.

ALL

Amen.

LEADER

Search me, O God, and know my heart;
   test me and know my thoughts.
See if there is any wicked way in me,
   and lead me in the way everlasting.

GROUP 1

O LORD, you have searched me and known me.
You know when I sit down and when I rise up;
   you discern my thoughts from far away.
You search out my path and my lying down,
   and are acquainted with all my ways.

GROUP 2

Even before a word is on my tongue,
   O LORD, you know it completely.
You hem me in, behind and before,
   and lay your hand upon me.

Such knowledge is too wonderful for me;
    it is so high that I cannot attain it.

ALL
Search me, O God, and know my heart. . . .

GROUP 1
Where can I go from your spirit?
    Or where can I flee from your presence?
If I ascend to heaven, you are there;
    if I make my bed in Sheol, you are there.

GROUP 2
If I take the wings of the morning
    and settle at the farthest limits of the sea,
even there your hand shall lead me,
    and your right hand shall hold me fast.
If I say, 'Surely the darkness shall cover me,
    and the light around me become night',
even the darkness is not dark to you;
    the night is as bright as the day,
    for darkness is as light to you.

ALL
Search me, O God, and know my heart. . . .

GROUP 1
For it was you who formed my inward parts;
    you knit me together in my mother's womb.
I praise you, for I am fearfully and wonderfully
        made.
    Wonderful are your works;
that I know very well.
    My frame was not hidden from you,
when I was being made in secret,
    intricately woven in the depths of the earth.
    Your eyes beheld my unformed substance.

GROUP 2
In your book were written
    all the days that were formed for me,
    when none of them as yet existed.
How weighty to me are your thoughts, O God!
    How vast is the sum of them!

I try to count them—they are more than the
        sand;
    I come to the end—I am still with you.

ALL
Search me, O God, and know my heart. . . .
                                —Psalm 139:1–18, 23–24

Reflection on the Word of God

LEADER
Ponder the words of the psalm. What word or
phrase catches your attention? Think about
why this word or phrase stands out for you as
meaningful. How might God be speaking to you
now?

All spend a few minutes in silent reflection.

LEADER
Loving God,
you surround us with your love, and know
        us more intimately than we even know
        ourselves.
Your greatest desire is for us to live in right and
        loving relationship with you,
    here and for all eternity.
 Send your Holy Spirit
    so that we may live a life of faith, hope and
        love with those around us in response to
        your invitation.
We ask this in the name of Jesus Christ your Son,
        who lives and reigns with you and the Holy
        Spirit, one God, for ever and ever.

ALL
Amen.

Pray the Sign of the Cross together.

CATHOLIC PRAYERS, DEVOTIONS AND PRACTICES

SIGN OF THE CROSS
In the name of the Father,
and of the Son,
and of the Holy Spirit. Amen.

OUR FATHER (LORD'S PRAYER)
Our Father who art in heaven,
hallowed be thy name;
thy kingdom come,
thy will be done
on earth as it is in heaven.
Give us this day our daily bread,
and forgive us our trespasses,
as we forgive those who trespass against us;
and lead us not into temptation,
but deliver us from evil. Amen.

GLORY PRAYER (DOXOLOGY)
Glory be to the Father,
and to the Son,
and to the Holy Spirit;
as it was in the beginning
is now, and ever shall be,
world without end. Amen.

PRAYER TO THE HOLY SPIRIT
Come, Holy Spirit, fill the hearts of your faithful.
And kindle in them the fire of your love.
Send forth your Spirit and they shall be created.
And you shall renew the face of the earth.

O God, by the light of the Holy Spirit you have
    taught the hearts of your faithful.
In the same Spirit, help us to know what is truly
    right and always to rejoice in your consolation.
We ask this through Christ, our Lord. Amen.

HAIL MARY
Hail Mary, full of grace,
the Lord is with thee.
Blessed art thou among women
and blessed is the fruit of thy womb, Jesus.
Holy Mary, Mother of God,

pray for us sinners,
now and at the hour of our death. Amen.

APOSTLES' CREED
I believe in God,
the Father almighty,
Creator of heaven and earth,
and in Jesus Christ, his only Son, our Lord,
who was conceived by the Holy Spirit,
born of the Virgin Mary,
suffered under Pontius Pilate,
was crucified, died, and was buried;
he descended into hell;
on the third day he rose again from the dead;
he ascended into heaven,
and is seated at the right hand of God the Father
    almighty,
from there he will come to judge the living and
    the dead.

I believe in the Holy Spirit,
the holy catholic Church,
the communion of saints,
the forgiveness of sins,
the resurrection of the body,
and life everlasting. Amen.

NICENE CREED
I believe in one God,
the Father almighty,
maker of heaven and earth,
of all things visible and invisible.

I believe in one Lord Jesus Christ,
the Only Begotten Son of God,
born of the Father before all ages.
God from God, Light from Light,
true God from true God,
begotten, not made, consubstantial with the
    Father;
through him all things were made.
For us men and for our salvation
he came down from heaven,

and by the Holy Spirit was incarnate of the Virgin Mary,
and became man.

For our sake he was crucified under Pontius Pilate,
he suffered death and was buried,
and rose again on the third day
in accordance with the Scriptures.
He ascended into heaven
and is seated at the right hand of the Father.
He will come again in glory
to judge the living and the dead,
and his kingdom will have no end.

I believe in the Holy Spirit, the Lord, the giver of life,
who proceeds from the Father and the Son,
who with the Father and the Son is adored and glorified,
who has spoken through the prophets.

I believe in one, holy, catholic and apostolic Church.
I confess one Baptism for the forgiveness of sins
and I look forward to the resurrection of the dead
and the life of the world to come. Amen.

JESUS PRAYER

Lord Jesus Christ, Son of God, have mercy on me, a sinner. Amen.

ACT OF FAITH

O my God, I firmly believe that you are one God in three divine Persons, Father, Son, and Holy Spirit. I believe that your divine Son became man and died for our sins and that he will come to judge the living and the dead. I believe these and all the truths which the Holy Catholic Church teaches because you have revealed them, who are eternal truth and wisdom, who can neither deceive nor be deceived. In this faith I intend to live and die. Amen.

ACT OF HOPE

O Lord God, I hope by your grace for the pardon of all my sins and after life here to gain eternal happiness because you have promised it, who are infinitely powerful, faithful, kind, and merciful. In this hope I intend to live and die. Amen.

ACT OF LOVE

O Lord God, I love you above all things and I love my neighbor for your sake because you are the highest, infinite and perfect good, worthy of all my love. In this love I intend to live and die. Amen.

PRAYER FOR VOCATIONS

Loving Mother, Our Lady of Guadalupe,
you asked Juan Diego to help build a Church that would serve a new people in a new land.
You left your image upon his cloak as a visible sign of your love for us,
so that we may come to believe in your Son, Jesus the Christ.
Our Lady of Guadalupe and St. Juan Diego,
help us respond to God's call to build your Son's Church today.
Help us recognize our personal vocation to serve God as married or single persons or priests, brothers or sisters as our way to help extend the Reign of God here on earth.
Help us pay attention to the promptings of the Holy Spirit.
May all of us have the courage of Juan Diego to say 'Yes' to our personal call!
May we encourage one another to follow Jesus, no matter where that path takes us. Amen.

Daily Prayers

Morning Prayer
CANTICLE OF ZECHARIAH (THE *BENEDICTUS*)

Blessed be the Lord, the God of Israel;
for he has come to his people and set them free.
He has raised up for us a mighty Savior,
born of the House of his servant David.
Through his prophets he promised of old
that he would save us from our enemies,
from the hands of all who hate us.
He promised to show mercy to our fathers
and to remember his holy covenant.
This was the oath he swore to our father Abraham:
to set us free from the hand of our enemies,
free to worship him without fear,
holy and righteous in his sight
all the days of our life.

CATHOLIC PRAYERS, DEVOTIONS AND PRACTICES | 303

You, my child, shall be called the prophet of the
    Most High,
for you will go before the Lord to prepare his way,
to give his people knowledge of salvation
by the forgiveness of their sins.
In the tender compassion of our God
the dawn from on high shall break upon us,
to shine on those who dwell in darkness and the
    shadow of death,
and to guide our feet into the way of peace.
Amen.

MORNING OFFERING

O Jesus, through the Immaculate Heart of Mary,
I offer you my prayers, works, joys and sufferings
    of this day
for all the intentions of your Sacred Heart,
in union with the Holy Sacrifice of the Mass
    throughout the world,
for the salvation of souls, the reparation for sins,
    the reunion of all Christians,
and in particular for the intentions of the Holy
    Father this month. Amen.

Night Prayer
CANTICLE OF MARY (THE *MAGNIFICAT*)

My soul proclaims the greatness of the Lord;
my spirit rejoices in God my savior
for he has looked with favor on his lowly servant.
From this day all generations will call me blessed:
the Almighty has done great things for me
and holy is his name.
He has mercy on those who fear him
in every generation.
He has shown the strength of his arm,
and has scattered the proud in their conceit.
He has cast down the mighty from their thrones,
and has lifted up the lowly.
He has filled the hungry with good things,
and the rich he has sent away empty.
He has come to the help of his servant Israel
for he has remembered his promise of mercy,
the promise he made to our fathers,
to Abraham and his children forever. Amen.

GRACE BEFORE MEALS

Bless us, O Lord, and these your gifts,
which we are about to receive from your bounty,
through Christ our Lord. Amen.

GRACE AFTER MEALS

We give you thanks for all your benefits, almighty
    God, who lives and reigns forever.
And may the souls of the faithful departed,
    through the mercy of God, rest in peace.
    Amen.

PRAYER OF ST. FRANCIS (PEACE PRAYER)

Lord, make me an instrument of your peace:
where there is hatred, let me sow love;
where there is injury, pardon;
where there is doubt, faith;
where there is despair, hope;
where there is darkness, light;
where there is sadness, joy.

O divine Master, grant that I may not so much seek
to be consoled as to console,
to be understood, as to understand,
to be loved as to love.

For it is in giving that we receive,
it is in pardoning that we are pardoned,
it is in dying that we are born to eternal life.
Amen.

Contrition and Sorrow
CONFITEOR

I confess to almighty God
and to you, my brothers and sisters,
that I have greatly sinned,
in my thoughts and in my words,
in what I have done and in what I have failed to
    do,
through my fault, through my fault,
through my most grievous fault;
therefore I ask blessed Mary ever-Virgin,
all the Angels and Saints,
and you, my brothers and sisters,
to pray for me to the Lord our God. Amen.

ACT OF CONTRITION

O my God, I am heartily sorry for having offended
you, and I detest all my sins because of your
just punishments, but most of all because
they offend you, my God, who are all good and
deserving of all my love. I firmly resolve with the
help of your grace to sin no more and to avoid
the near occasion of sin. Amen.

Prayers before the Holy Eucharist

THE DIVINE PRAISES
Blessed be God.
Blessed be his holy name.
Blessed be Jesus Christ, true God and true man.
Blessed be the name of Jesus.
Blessed be his most Sacred Heart.
Blessed be his most precious Blood.
Blessed be Jesus in the most holy Sacrament of
    the altar.
Blessed be the Holy Spirit, the Paraclete.
Blessed be the great Mother of God, Mary most
    holy.
Blessed be her holy and Immaculate Conception.
Blessed be her glorious Assumption.
Blessed be the name of Mary, Virgin and Mother.
Blessed be St. Joseph, her most chaste spouse.
Blessed be God in his angels and in his saints.

ANIMA CHRISTI (SOUL OF CHRIST)
Soul of Christ, sanctify me.
Body of Christ, save me.
Blood of Christ, inebriate me.
Water from the side of Christ, wash me.
Passion of Christ, strengthen me.
O good Jesus, hear me.
Within your wounds hide me.
Permit me not to be separated from you.
From the malicious enemy defend me.
In the hour of my death call me.
And bid me come to you,
that with your saints I may praise you
forever and ever. Amen.

AN ACT OF SPIRITUAL COMMUNION
My Jesus, I believe that you are present in the
    Most Blessed Sacrament.
I love you above all things, and I desire to receive
    you into my soul.
Since I cannot at this moment receive you
    sacramentally, come at least spiritually into
    my heart.
I embrace you as if you were already there and
    unite myself wholly to you.
Never permit me to be separated from you. Amen.

Prayers to Mary, Mother of God

ANGELUS
Verse: The Angel of the Lord declared unto
            Mary.
Response: And she conceived of the Holy Spirit.
            Hail Mary, full of grace,
            the Lord is with thee.
            Blessed art thou among women
            and blessed is the fruit of thy womb,
                Jesus.
            Holy Mary, Mother of God,
            pray for us sinners,
            now and at the hour of our death.
                Amen.
Verse: Behold the handmaid of the Lord.
Response: Be it done unto me according to your
            Word.
            Hail Mary. . . .
Verse: And the Word was made flesh,
Response: And dwelt among us.
            Hail Mary. . . .
Verse: Pray for us, O holy Mother of God,
Response: That we may be made worthy of the
            promises of Christ.

Let us pray. Pour forth, we beseech you, O Lord,
your grace into our hearts: that we, to whom the
Incarnation of Christ your Son was made known by
the message of an Angel, may by his Passion and
Cross be brought to the glory of his Resurrection.
Through the same Christ our Lord. Amen.

MEMORARE
Remember, O most gracious Virgin Mary, that
never was it known that anyone who fled to your
protection, implored your help, or sought your
intercession, was left unaided. Inspired by this
confidence, I fly unto you, O Virgin of virgins, my
mother; to you do I come, before you I stand,
sinful and sorrowful. O Mother of the Word
Incarnate, despise not my petitions, but in your
mercy hear and answer me. Amen.

REGINA CAELI (QUEEN OF HEAVEN)
Queen of Heaven, rejoice, alleluia:
for the Son you were privileged to bear, alleluia,
is risen as he said, alleluia.
Pray for us to God, alleluia.

CATHOLIC PRAYERS, DEVOTIONS AND PRACTICES | 305

Verse: Rejoice and be glad, O Virgin Mary, Alleluia!
Response: For the Lord is truly risen, Alleluia.

Let us pray. O God, who gave joy to the world through the resurrection of your Son, our Lord Jesus Christ, grant, we beseech you, that through the intercession of the Virgin Mary, his Mother, we may obtain the joys of everlasting life. Through the same Christ our Lord. Amen.

SALVE, REGINA (HAIL, HOLY QUEEN)

Hail, holy Queen, Mother of mercy: Hail, our life, our sweetness and our hope. To you do we cry, poor banished children of Eve. To you do we send up our sighs, mourning and weeping in this valley of tears. Turn then, most gracious advocate, your eyes of mercy toward us; and after this our exile show unto us the blessed fruit of your womb, Jesus. O clement, O loving, O sweet Virgin Mary. Amen.

PRAYER TO OUR LADY OF GUADALUPE

God of power and mercy,
you blessed the Americas at Tepeyac
with the presence of the Virgin Mary of
    Guadalupe.
May her prayers help all men and women
to accept each other as brothers and sisters.
Through your justice present in our hearts
may your peace reign in the world. Amen.

THE ROSARY

THE JOYFUL MYSTERIES: Traditionally prayed on Mondays and Saturdays and on Sundays of the Christmas Season.
1. The Annunciation
2. The Visitation
3. The Nativity
4. The Presentation in the Temple
5. The Finding of Jesus after Three Days in the Temple

THE LUMINOUS MYSTERIES: Traditionally prayed on Thursdays.
1. The Baptism at the Jordan
2. The Miracle at Cana
3. The Proclamation of the Kingdom and the Call to Conversion
4. The Transfiguration
5. The Institution of the Eucharist

THE SORROWFUL MYSTERIES: Traditionally prayed on Tuesdays and Fridays and on the Sundays of Lent.
1. The Agony in the Garden
2. The Scourging at the Pillar
3. The Crowning with Thorns
4. The Carrying of the Cross
5. The Crucifixion and Death

THE GLORIOUS MYSTERIES: Traditionally prayed on Wednesdays and Sundays, except on the Sundays of Christmas and Lent.
1. The Resurrection
2. The Ascension
3. The Descent of the Holy Spirit at Pentecost
4. The Assumption of Mary
5. The Crowning of the Blessed Virgin as Queen of Heaven and Earth

How to pray the Rosary

1. Pray the *Sign of the Cross* and pray the *Apostles' Creed* while holding the Crucifix.
2. Touch the first bead after the Crucifix and pray the *Our Father*, pray the *Hail Mary* on each of the next three beads, and pray the *Glory Prayer* on the next bead.
3. Go to the main part of your rosary. Say the name of the Mystery and quietly reflect on the meaning of the events of that Mystery. Pray the *Our Father*, and then, fingering each of the ten beads, pray ten *Hail Marys*. Then touch the next bead and pray the *Glory Prayer*. (Repeat the process for the next four decades.)
4. Pray the *Salve Regina (Hail, Holy Queen)* and conclude by praying:
   Verse: Pray for us, O holy Mother of God.
   Response: That we may be made worthy of the promises of Christ.
   Let us pray. O God, whose only-begotten Son, by his life, death and Resurrection, has purchased for us the rewards of eternal life, grant, we beseech you, that meditating on these mysteries of the most holy rosary of the Blessed Virgin Mary, we

may imitate what they contain and obtain what they promise, through the same Christ our Lord. Amen.

5. Conclude by praying the *Sign of the Cross*.

STATIONS, OR WAY, OF THE CROSS

The tradition of praying the Stations, or Way, of the Cross dates from the fourteenth century. The tradition, which is attributed to the Franciscans, came about to satisfy the desire of Christians who were unable to make a pilgrimage to Jerusalem. The traditional Stations of the Cross are:

FIRST STATION: Jesus is condemned to death
SECOND STATION: Jesus is made to carry his Cross
THIRD STATION: Jesus falls the first time
FOURTH STATION: Jesus meets his mother
FIFTH STATION: Simon helps Jesus to carry his Cross
SIXTH STATION: Veronica wipes the face of Jesus
SEVENTH STATION: Jesus falls the second time
EIGHTH STATION: Jesus meets the women of Jerusalem
NINTH STATION: Jesus falls the third time
TENTH STATION: Jesus is stripped of his garments
ELEVENTH STATION: Jesus is nailed to the Cross
TWELFTH STATION: Jesus dies on the Cross
THIRTEENTH STATION: Jesus is taken down from the Cross
FOURTEENTH STATION: Jesus is laid in the tomb.

In 1991 Blessed Pope John Paul gave the Church a scriptural version of the Stations. The individual names given to these stations are:

FIRST STATION: Jesus in the Garden of Gethsemane—Matthew 25:36–41
SECOND STATION: Jesus, Betrayed by Judas, Is Arrested—Mark 14:43–46
THIRD STATION: Jesus Is Condemned by the Sanhedrin—Luke 22:66–71
FOURTH STATION: Jesus Is Denied by Peter—Matthew 26:69–75
FIFTH STATION: Jesus Is Judged by Pilate—Mark 15:1–5, 15
SIXTH STATION: Jesus Is Scourged and Crowned with Thorns—John 19:1–3
SEVENTH STATION: Jesus Bears the Cross—John 19:6, 15–17

EIGHTH STATION: Jesus Is Helped by Simon the Cyrenian to Carry the Cross—Mark 15:21
NINTH STATION: Jesus Meets the Women of Jerusalem—Luke 23:27–31
TENTH STATION: Jesus Is Crucified—Luke 23:33–34
ELEVENTH STATION: Jesus Promises His Kingdom to the Good Thief—Luke 23:39–43
TWELFTH STATION: Jesus Speaks to His Mother and the Disciple—John 19:25–27
THIRTEENTH STATION: Jesus Dies on the Cross—Luke 23:44–46
FOURTEENTH STATION: Jesus Is Placed in the Tomb—Matthew 27:57–60

Some parishes conclude with a prayerful meditation on the Resurrection.

The Way of Jesus: Catholic Practices

THE SEVEN SACRAMENTS
Sacraments of Christian Initiation
BAPTISM: The Sacrament by which we are freed from all sin and are endowed with the gift of divine life, are made members of the Church, and are called to holiness and mission.
EUCHARIST: The ritual, sacramental action of thanksgiving to God which constitutes the principal Christian liturgical celebration of and communion in the Paschal Mystery of Christ. This liturgical action is also traditionally known as the Holy Sacrifice of the Mass.
CONFIRMATION: The Sacrament that completes the grace of Baptism by a special outpouring of the Gifts of the Holy Spirit, which seals and confirms the baptized in union with Christ and calls them to a greater participation in the worship and apostolic life of the Church.

Sacraments of Healing
PENANCE AND RECONCILIATION: The Sacrament in which sins committed after Baptism are forgiven, which results in reconciliation with God and the Church. This Sacrament is also called the Sacrament of Confession.
ANOINTING OF THE SICK: This Sacrament is given to a person who is seriously ill or in danger of death or old age which strengthens the person

with the special graces of healing and comfort and courage.

Sacraments at the Service of Communion

MARRIAGE (MATRIMONY): The Sacrament in which a baptized man and a baptized woman enter the covenant partnership of the whole of life that by its nature is ordered toward the good of the spouses and the procreation and education of offspring.

HOLY ORDERS: The Sacrament in which a bishop ordains a baptized man to be conformed to Jesus Christ by grace, to service and leadership in the Church as a bishop, priest, or deacon.

GIFTS OF THE HOLY SPIRIT

The Seven Gifts of the Holy Spirit are permanent dispositions which move us to respond to the guidance of the Spirit. The traditional list of these Gifts is derived from Isaiah 11:1–3.

WISDOM: A spiritual gift which enables one to know the purpose and plan of God.

UNDERSTANDING: This Gift stimulates us to work on knowing ourselves as part of our growth in knowing God.

COUNSEL (RIGHT JUDGMENT): This Gift guides us to follow the teaching the Holy Spirit gives us about our moral life and the training of our conscience.

FORTITUDE (COURAGE): This Gift strengthens us to choose courageously and firmly the good, despite difficulty, and also to persevere in doing what is right, despite temptation, fear or persecution.

KNOWLEDGE: This Gift directs us to a contemplation, or thoughtful reflection, on the mystery of God and the mysteries of the Catholic faith.

PIETY (REVERENCE): This Gift strengthens us to grow in respect for the Holy Trinity, for the Father who created us, for Jesus who saved us, and for the Holy Spirit who is sanctifying us.

FEAR OF THE LORD (WONDER AND AWE): This Gift infuses honesty in our relationship with God.

FRUITS OF THE HOLY SPIRIT

The Fruits of the Holy Spirit are the perfections that the Holy Spirit forms in us as the 'first fruits' of eternal glory. The Tradition of the Church lists twelve Fruits of the Holy Spirit. They are: love, joy, peace, patience, kindness, goodness, generosity, gentleness, faithfulness, modesty, self-control and chastity.

VIRTUES

The Theological Virtues

Gifts from God that enable us to choose to and to live in right relationship with the Holy Trinity.

FAITH: This virtue by which the believer gives personal adherence to God (who invites his or her response) and freely assents to the whole truth that God revealed.

HOPE: The virtue through which a person both desires and expects the fulfillment of God's promises of things to come.

CHARITY (LOVE): The virtue by which we give love to God for his own sake and love to our neighbor on account of God.

The Cardinal Moral Virtues

The four moral virtues on which all other human virtues hinge.

FORTITUDE: The virtue by which one courageously and firmly chooses the good despite difficulty and also perseveres in doing what is right despite temptation.

JUSTICE: The virtue by which one is able to give God and neighbor what is due to them.

PRUDENCE: The virtue by which one knows the true good in every circumstance and chooses the right means to reach that end.

TEMPERANCE: The virtue by which one moderates the desire for the attainment of and pleasure in earthly goods.

THE NEW LAW

The Great, or Greatest, Commandment

'You shall love the Lord your God with all your heart, and with all your soul, and with all your mind. . . . You shall love your neighbor as yourself.'
Matthew 22:37, 39, based on
Deuteronomy 6:5 and Leviticus 19:18

THE NEW COMMANDMENT OF JESUS

'Love one another. Just as I have loved you, you also should love one another.' John 13:34

THE BEATITUDES

Blessed are the poor in spirit, for theirs is the kingdom of heaven.

Blessed are those who mourn, for they will be comforted.

Blessed are the meek, for they will inherit the earth.

Blessed are those who hunger and thirst for righteousness, for they will be filled.

Blessed are the merciful, for they will receive mercy.

Blessed are the pure in heart, for they will see God.

Blessed are the peacemakers, for they shall be called children of God.

Blessed are those who are persecuted for righteousness' sake, for theirs is the kingdom of heaven.

Blessed are you when people revile you and persecute you and utter all kinds of evil against you falsely on my account. Rejoice and be glad, for your reward is great in heaven, for in the same way they persecuted the prophets who were before you.

– Matthew 5:3–11

SPIRITUAL WORKS OF MERCY

Admonish and help those who sin.
Teach those who are ignorant.
Advise those who have doubts.
Comfort those who suffer.
Be patient with all people.
Forgive those who trespass against you.
Pray for the living and the dead.

CORPORAL WORKS OF MERCY

Feed the hungry.
Give drink to the thirsty.
Shelter the homeless.
Clothe the naked.
Visit the sick and those in prison.
Bury the dead.
Give alms to the poor.

THE TEN COMMANDMENTS, OR THE DECALOGUE

Traditional Catechetical Formula

FIRST: I am the LORD your God: you shall not have strange gods before me.

SECOND: You shall not take the name of the LORD your God in vain.

THIRD: Remember to keep holy the LORD's Day.

FOURTH: Honor your father and mother.

FIFTH: You shall not kill.

SIXTH: You shall not commit adultery.

SEVENTH: You shall not steal.

EIGHTH: You shall not bear false witness against your neighbor.

NINTH: You shall not covet your neighbor's wife.

TENTH: You shall not covet your neighbor's goods.

Scriptural Formula

FIRST: I am the LORD your God, who brought you out of the land of Egypt, out of the house of slavery; you shall have no other gods before me.

SECOND: You shall not make wrongful use of the name of the LORD your God, for the LORD will not acquit anyone who misuses his name.

THIRD: Observe the sabbath day to keep it holy. . . .

FOURTH: Honor your father and your mother. . . .

FIFTH: You shall not murder.

SIXTH: Neither shall you commit adultery.

SEVENTH: Neither shall you steal.

EIGHTH: Neither shall you bear false witness against your neighbour.

NINTH: Neither shall you covet your neighbor's wife.

TENTH: Neither shall you desire . . . anything that belongs to your neighbor.

– From Deuteronomy 5:6–21

PRECEPTS OF THE CHURCH

The Precepts are positive laws made by the Church that name the minimum in prayer and moral effort for the growth of the faithful in their love of God and neighbor.

FIRST PRECEPT: Participate in Mass on Sundays and on holy days of obligation and rest from work that impedes keeping these days holy.

SECOND PRECEPT: Confess sins at least once a year.

THIRD PRECEPT: Receive the Sacrament of the Eucharist at least during the Easter Season.

FOURTH PRECEPT: Fast and abstain on the days established by the Church.

FIFTH PRECEPT: Provide for the materials of the Church according to one's ability.

SOCIAL DOCTRINE OF THE CHURCH

These seven key principles are at the foundation of the Social Doctrine, or Social Teachings, of the Catholic Church:

1. *Life and dignity of the human person.* Human life is sacred and the dignity of the human person is the foundation of the moral life of individuals and of society.

2. *Call to family, community and participation.* The human person is social by nature and has the right to participate in family life and in the life of society.

3. *Rights and responsibilities.* The human person has the fundamental right to life and to the basic necessities that support life and human decency.

4. *Option for the poor and the vulnerable.* The Gospel commands us 'to put the needs of the poor and the vulnerable first'.

5. *Dignity of work and workers.* Work is a form of participating in God's work of Creation. 'The economy must serve people and not the other way around.'

6. *Solidarity.* God is the Creator of all people. 'We are one human family whatever our national, racial, ethnic, economic and ideological differences.'

7. *Care for God's creation.* Care of the environment is a divine command and a requirement of our faith.

FAITH GLOSSARY

'Abba': An Aramaic term of endearment that Jesus used during his agony in the garden (see Mark 14:36) to address God the Father. The term 'Abba' expresses the great intimacy between Jesus, the Son of God, and God the Father. St. Paul teaches that God invites us to address him as 'Abba', as Jesus did.

Agape: In 1 John 4:8, 16 we read: 'God is love.' The Greek word used here for 'love' was *agapē*. The word 'agape' describes God's total 'self-gift' of unconditional and infinite love, both among the Persons of the Blessed Trinity and for each and every one of us.

Apostolic Tradition: Jesus entrusted his revelation and teachings to his Apostles. They passed it on by their preaching and witness. Along with others, they began writing the message down in what became the New Testament. (*United States Catholic Catechism for Adults*, 504)

Ascension: The entry of Jesus' humanity into divine glory to be at the right hand of the Father; traditionally, this occurred forty days after Jesus' Resurrection. (*United States Catholic Catechism for Adults*, 504)

Assumption: The dogma that when the Blessed Virgin Mary's earthly life was finished, because she was sinless, she was kept from corruption and taken soul and body into heavenly glory. (*United States Catholic Catechism for Adults*, 505)

Atonement: By his suffering and death on the Cross, Jesus freed us from our sins and brought about our reconciliation with God the Father. (*United States Catholic Catechism for Adults*, 505)

Canon of Scripture: The canon of Scripture refers to the list of Old Testament and New Testament books that are accepted by the Catholic Church as the inspired Word of God. The Catholic canon lists seventy-three books—forty-six in the Old Testament and twenty-seven in the New Testament.

Charity (Love): Charity, or love, is one of the three Theological Virtues by which we give our love to God for his own sake and our love to our neighbor on account of our love of God. (Based on *United States Catholic Catechism for Adults*, 506)

Chesed: *Chesed* is the Hebrew word for 'commitment'. The sacred authors of the Old Testament often described God's steadfast loyalty and love by using the word *chesed*. *Chesed* is committed love. *Chesed* is a key attribute of God as well as a quality that describes the relationship between God and the human family. *Chesed* is often translated as 'covenant love', a term that describes the nature and depth of the relationship that binds God with people and, in turn, people with God.

Church: This term refers to the whole Catholic community of believers throughout the world. The term can also be used in the sense of a diocese or a particular parish. (*United States Catholic Catechism for Adults*, 507)

Compassion: In the Bible, the English word 'compassion' is a translation of a Greek word meaning 'womb' and of a Hebrew word that is also translated as 'mercy'. Compassion is the quality of a person who so closely identifies with the suffering and condition of another person that the suffering of the other becomes their own, 'enters their womb'. The Latin roots of the English word 'compassion' are *cum* and *passio*, which mean 'suffering with'.

FAITH GLOSSARY | 311

Conscience: 'Moral conscience, present at the heart of the person, enjoins [the person] at the appropriate moment to do good and to avoid evil. It also judges particular choices, approving those that are good and denouncing those that are evil.' When we listen to our conscience, we 'can hear God speaking'. (See *Catechism of the Catholic Church*, no. 1777.)

Conversion: Conversion means turning around one's life toward God and trying 'to live holier lives according to the Gospel' (Vatican II, *Decree on Ecumenism*, quoted in CCC, no. 821).

Covenant: A covenant is a solemn agreement made between human beings or between God and a human being involving mutual commitments or guarantees. The Bible speaks of covenants that God made with Noah and, through him, 'with every living creature' (Genesis 9:10). Then God made the special Covenant with Abraham and renewed it with Moses. The prophets constantly pointed to the New Covenant that God would establish with all humankind through the promised Messiah—Jesus Christ.

Deposit of Faith: The heritage of faith contained in Sacred Scripture and Tradition, handed on in the Church from the time of the Apostles, from which the Magisterium draws all that it proposes for belief as divinely revealed. (*United States Catholic Catechism for Adults*, 509)

Discernment: The practice of looking out for the presence and the workings of the Spirit in our life. It includes trying to understand the promptings of the Spirit and deciding to act in cooperation with the grace of the Holy Spirit.

Disciple: Name given in the New Testament to all those men and women who followed Jesus and were taught by him while he was alive, and who, following Jesus' death, Resurrection, and Ascension, formed the Church with the Apostles and helped spread the Good News, or Gospel message. Contemporary members of the Church, as followers of Jesus, can also be referred to as disciples. (*United States Catholic Catechism for Adults*, 509)

Divine Providence: God's loving care and concern for all he has made; he continues to watch over creation, sustaining its existence and presiding over its development and destiny. (*United States Catholic Catechism for Adults*, 510)

Divine Revelation: God's communication of himself and his loving plan to save us. This is a gift of self-communication, which is realized by deeds and words over time and most fully by his sending us his own divine Son, Jesus Christ. (*United States Catholic Catechism for Adults*, 526)

Ecumenical Council: From the Greek word *oikoumenē*, meaning 'the whole world', an Ecumenical Council of the Church is a gathering of all the bishops of the world, in the exercise of their authority over the universal Church. An Ecumenical Council is usually called by the Pope, or at least confirmed and accepted by him. It can be called for a variety of specific reasons, among which is to discern the direction of the life of the Church, clarifying her teachings and mission.

Eternal Life: Eternal life is living for ever with God in the happiness of heaven, entered after death by the souls of those who die in the grace and friendship of God.

Exegesis: Exegesis is the process used by Scripture scholars to determine the literal and spiritual meanings of the biblical text. (*United States Catholic Catechism for Adults*, 512)

Expiation: The act of redemption and atonement for sin which Christ won for us by the pouring out of his blood on the Cross, by his obedient love even 'to the end' (John 13:1). The expiation of sins continues in the mystical body of Christ and the communion of saints by joining our human acts of atonement to the redemptive action of Christ, both in this life and in Purgatory.

Faith: Faith is both a gift of God and a human act by which the believer gives personal adherence to God (who invites his or her response) and freely assents to the whole truth that God has revealed. (*United States Catholic Catechism for Adults*, 512)

Fruits of the Holy Spirit: The Tradition of the Church lists twelve fruits of the Holy Spirit: love, joy, peace, patience, kindness, goodness, generosity, gentleness, faithfulness, modesty, self-control and chastity. (*United States Catholic Catechism for Adults*, 513)

Gifts of the Holy Spirit: These gifts are permanent dispositions that move us to respond to the guidance of the Spirit. The traditional list of these gifts is derived from Isaiah 11:1–3: wisdom, understanding, knowledge, counsel [right judgment], fortitude [courage], reverence (piety), and wonder and awe in God's presence (fear of the Lord). (*United States Catholic Catechism for Adults*, 513)

Gospel: The term 'gospel' comes from an Old English word *godspel*, meaning 'good news'. *Godspel* was originally used to translate the Greek word *euaggelion* (Latin *evangelium*), a term the early Church used for the Good News of Jesus. The Church uses the word 'Gospel' to refer to the four New Testament books that proclaim the life, teaching, Death and Resurrection of Jesus. More generally, however, the word refers to the proclamation of the entire message of faith revealed in and through Jesus Christ, the incarnate Son of God, the Second Person of the Blessed Trinity.

Grace: The term 'grace' comes from the Latin word *gratia* which means 'free'. Grace is the free and undeserved gift of God's love to us. God shares his divine life and friendship with us. God's grace is ever at work in our lives, helping us to live as children of God and disciples of Jesus. An old proverb runs, 'There is an ebb to every tide, except the tide of God's grace.' God's grace—his effective love—is always at high tide in our lives.

Heaven: Heaven is the fullness of communion with God; it is neither an abstraction nor a physical place in the clouds, but a living, personal relationship with the Holy Trinity. (Pope John Paul II, 1920–2005)

Hell. Hell is the definitive rejection of God, a state for those who freely and definitively separate themselves from God, the source of all life and joy. (Pope John Paul II, 1920–2005)

Heresy: A religious teaching that denies or contradicts truths revealed by God. (*United States Catholic Catechism for Adults*, 514)

Holiness: Holiness is a state of goodness in which a person lives in communion with God, who is Father, Son and Holy Spirit, and, with the help of God's grace, the action of the Holy Spirit and a life of prayer, is freed from sin and evil. (Adapted from *United States Catholic Catechism for Adults*, 514)

Holy Trinity, Triune God: We believe that there is only one true God, eternal, infinite, unchangeable, incomprehensible and almighty, in three divine Persons: the Father, the Son and the Holy Spirit. (Adapted from *Catechism of the Catholic Church*, no. 202)

Hope: 'Hope' is the desire and expectation of the Salvation God promised. It is based on God's unwavering fidelity to keeping and fulfilling his promises.

Hypostatic Union: The fact that the Son of God became man in the Incarnation does not mean that Jesus Christ is part God and part man. The Son of God, the Second Person of the Trinity, became truly man while remaining truly God. Jesus Christ is true God and true man. Jesus possesses two natures, one divine nature and one human nature, united in one divine Person, the Son of God. The term 'Hypostatic Union' refers to this unity of God and man in one divine Person, Jesus Christ.

Imago Dei means 'Image of God'. We are all made in the image and likeness of God.

Immaculate Conception: 'The Immaculate Conception is the dogma proclaimed in Christian Tradition, that from the first moment of her conception, Mary—by the singular grace of God and by virtue of the merits of Jesus Christ—was preserved immune from Original Sin' and 'she

FAITH GLOSSARY | 313

remained pure from all personal sin throughout her life'. (*Catechism of the Catholic Church*, Glossary and no. 508)

Incarnation: By the Incarnation, the Second Person of the Holy Trinity assumed our human nature, taking flesh in the womb of the Virgin Mary. There is one Person in Jesus and that is the divine Person of the Son of God. Jesus has two natures, a human one and a divine one. (*United States Catholic Catechism for Adults*, 515)

Inerrancy: Because the authors of Sacred Scripture were inspired by God, the saving meaning or truth found in the Scriptures cannot be wrong. (*United States Catholic Catechism for Adults*, 516)

Inspiration: 'Inspiration' is the word used to describe the gift of the Holy Spirit given to the human writers of the Bible, so that, using their talents and abilities, they wrote the truth that God wanted people to know for their salvation. (See *Catechism of the Catholic Church*, no. 137.)

Kingdom of God: The Kingdom of God is the actualization of God's will for human beings proclaimed by Jesus Christ as a community of justice, peace, mercy, and love, the seed of which is the Church on earth, and the fulfillment of which is in eternity. (*United States Catholic Catechism for Adults*, 517)

Last Judgment: The moment at the end of time when everyone will appear before Christ and receive an eternal recompense in accord with their earthly life. (*United States Catholic Catechism for Adults*, 517)

Lectio Divina: A manner of praying with Scripture; the person praying either reflectively reads a passage from Scripture or listens attentively to its being read, and then meditates on words or phrases that resonate. (*United States Catholic Catechism for Adults*, 518)

Liturgy: Liturgy refers especially to the public worship of the Church, including the Mass and the Liturgy of the Hours. (*United States Catholic Catechism for Adults*, 518)

The word 'liturgy' originally meant a 'public work' or a 'service in the name of/on behalf of the people'. In Christian tradition it means the participation of the People of God in 'the work of God'. (*Catechism of the Catholic Church*, no. 1069)

In the liturgy of the Church, God the Father is blessed and adored as the source of all the blessings of creation and salvation with which he has blessed us in his Son, in order to give us the Spirit of filial adoption. (*Catechism of the Catholic Church*, no. 1110)

Magisterium: The Magisterium is the living teaching office, or teaching authority, of the Catholic Church, made up of the Pope and bishops, guided by the Holy Spirit, whose responsibility and task is to give authentic interpretation to the Word of God contained in both Sacred Scripture and Sacred Tradition.

Martyr: From the Greek word *martyr*, which means 'witness'. In a Christian context, a martyr is 'one who witnesses to Christ and the truth of faith, even to the point of suffering' (*United States Catholic Catechism for Adults*, 519).

Mediatrix: The title 'Mediatrix' was given to Mary to express her unique relationship to Christ and to the Church. The word 'mediator' means 'one who links or reconciles separate or opposing parties'. Jesus Christ is the 'one *mediator* between God and the human race' (1 Timothy 2:5). . . . Mary too is sometimes called Mediatrix in virtue of her cooperation in the saving mission of Christ, who alone is the unique mediator between God and humanity. (*Catechism of the Catholic Church*, Glossary)

Mezuzah: In Jewish homes today, we can often find a small decorative rectangular object nailed to the doorpost. This is called a *mezuzah*, and it contains a tiny scroll. On the scroll are the words of the *Shema*, the Jewish prayer quoting Deuteronomy 6:4–9, which begins: 'Hear, O Israel: The LORD is our God, the LORD alone. You shall love the LORD your God with all your heart, and with all your soul, and with all your might.' Devout Jews observe this tradition, each time they exit and enter their homes, as a reminder to love and honor God above all.

314 | CREDO | THE PROMISED ONE: SERVANT AND SAVIOR

Miracles: Miracles are signs of the presence of God at work among us. 'The miracles and other deeds of Jesus are acts of compassion and signs of the Kingdom and salvation' (*United States Catholic Catechism for Adults*, 80).

Original Holiness: The grace of 'original holiness' was to share in divine life. (*Catechism of the Catholic Church*, no. 376)

Original Justice: The inner harmony of the human person, the harmony between man and woman, and finally the harmony between the first couple and all creation, comprised the state of 'original justice'. (*Catechism of the Catholic Church*, no. 376)

Original Sin: Original sin is the personal sin of disobedience by the first human beings, resulting in the deprivation of original holiness and justice and the experience of suffering and death. (*United States Catholic Catechism for Adults*, 522)

Parables: A characteristic feature of the teaching of Jesus. Parables are simple images or comparisons which confront the hearer or reader with a radical choice about his invitation to enter the Kingdom of God. (*Catechism of the Catholic Church*, Glossary)

Paschal Mystery: In speaking of the Paschal Mystery we present Christ's Death and Resurrection as one, inseparable event. It is *paschal* because it is Christ's passing into death and passing over it into new life. It is a *mystery* because it is a visible sign of an invisible act of God. (*United States Catholic Catechism for Adults*, 522)

Pentecost: The 'fiftieth day' at the end of the seven weeks following Passover (Easter in the Christian dispensation). At the first Pentecost after the Resurrection and Ascension of Jesus, the Holy Spirit was manifested, given and communicated as a divine Person to the Church, fulfilling the paschal mystery of Christ according to his promise. (*Catechism of the Catholic Church*, Glossary)

Perpetual Virginity of Mary: The perpetual virginity of Mary states the faith of the Church that 'Mary was a virgin in conceiving Jesus, in giving birth to him, and in remaining always a virgin ever after' (*United States Catholic Catechism for Adults*, 523).

Prayer: The raising of one's mind and heart to God in thanksgiving and in praise of his glory. It can also include the requesting of good things from God. It is an act by which one enters into awareness of a loving communion with God. (*United States Catholic Catechism for Adults*, 523)

Protoevangelium: The term *protoevangelium* literally means 'first gospel' and refers to the very first Revelation we have in the Bible that God would send a Savior. In Genesis 3:15 God promises to send an 'offspring of the woman', who will crush the head of the serpent—the symbol of temptation and sin. (See *Catechism of the Catholic Church*, nos. 410-411.)

Purgatory: Purgatory is not a place but a condition of existence where Christ removes the remnants of imperfection. (Pope John Paul II, 1920–2005)

Real Presence: When the bread is consecrated, it is changed into Christ's Body. When the wine is consecrated, it is changed into Christ's Blood. Jesus Christ is substantially present in a way that is entirely unique. This happens through the power of the Holy Spirit and the ministry of the priest or bishop acting in the person of Christ during the Eucharistic prayer. (*United States Catholic Catechism for Adults*, 525)

Redemption: Redemption is the Salvation won for us by Jesus by his paying the price of his own sacrificial death on the Cross to ransom us, to set us free from the slavery of sin. (*Catechism of the Catholic Church*, Glossary)

Resurrection: This is the triumph of Jesus over death on the third day after his crucifixion. Christ's body is real, but glorified, not restrained by space or time. (*United States Catholic Catechism for Adults*, 525)

FAITH GLOSSARY | 315

Sacrifice: 'Sacrifice' is a free offering, a gift, made by a person for the welfare of others. The word comes from two Latin words meaning 'to make sacred'. Such a gift is deemed to be sacred—a special and a sincere sign of love and life. The greatest sacrifice of all is to give one's life for another. In a religious context a sacrifice is 'a ritual offering made to God by a priest on behalf of the people as a sign of adoration, gratitude, supplication, penance, and/or communion' (*United States Catholic Catechism for Adults*, 527).

Salvation: Salvation is the forgiveness of sins and restoration of friendship with God, which can be done by God alone. (*Catechism of the Catholic Church*, Glossary)

Sanctifying Grace: Sanctifying grace is a habitual gift of God's own divine life, a stable and supernatural disposition that enables us to live with God and to act by his love. (*United States Catholic Catechism for Adults*, 514)

Sin: Sin is an offense against God as well as against reason, truth, and right conscience; it is a failure in genuine love for God and neighbor caused by a perverse attachment to certain goods. It wounds the nature of man and injures human solidarity. It has been defined as 'an utterance, a deed, or a desire contrary to the eternal law' [*Catechism of the Catholic Church*, no. 1849]. (*United States Catholic Catechism for Adults*, 528)

Social Sin: Sins that produce unjust social laws and oppressive institutions. They are social situations and institutions contrary to divine goodness. Sometimes called 'structures of sin', they are the expression and effect of personal sins. (*United States Catholic Catechism for Adults*, 528)

Social Teachings of the Church: The official social doctrine developed by the Catholic Church in response to the industrial and technological revolutions. This social doctrine is built on the Church's reaching out and responding to orphans, widows, aliens and others from the days of the early Church. (Based on *United States Catholic Catechism for Adults*, 528)

Son of Man: Jesus used the title 'Son of Man' to identify himself and his mission in the four accounts of the Gospel (thirty times in St. Matthew, fourteen times in St. Mark, twenty-five times in St. Luke, and twelve times in St. John). Rooted in the Scriptures of ancient Israel, most especially the Books of Ezekiel and Daniel, the term 'son of man' refers to the 'ideal human', the one most faithful to YHWH.

Steward: A steward is someone who has the responsibility of caring for what belongs to another person or group of people. In the biblical accounts of Creation, God designates humanity the responsibility to have dominion over, or serve as the stewards of, creation. The root word for 'dominion' is *domus*, which means household. God has entrusted creation, his household, to humanity.

Temptation: Temptation is 'an attraction either from outside or inside oneself' to choose to sin, or to act in ways that are contrary to the will of God.

Theosis: Theosis means 'divinization' or 'the process of becoming like God'. From the Greek word *theos*, meaning 'God', *theosis* is a central concept for many Eastern Rite Catholics. St. Athanasius, Father of the Church, wrote (about AD 319), 'The Son of God became man so that we might become God.'

Tithe: Tithe, an ancient word for 'ten', refers to the practice of giving over one tenth of one's earnings for sacred purposes. The Bible often mentions and mandates tithing; for example, Deuteronomy 14:22–29 lists as a law of the Torah that people give over one tenth of their harvest of grain, wine, oil and first-born animals. Some of these were to be used in sacred banquets, some to support the priests, and some to go to the poor.

Tradition: The Tradition of the Catholic Church refers to the body of teaching of the Church, expressed in her beliefs, doctrines, rituals and Scripture, that has been handed down from the Apostles to their successors, the Pope and the bishops, through the ages, in an unbroken line of succession.

Transcendence: Transcendence refers to the idea that God is so 'beyond' the universe, and so different from anything else that exists, that God cannot be directly experienced by human beings. A shorthand way of saying that God is transcendent is: 'God is the absolute Other.'

Transfiguration: The word 'transfiguration' means 'change in appearance'. The Transfiguration is the mysterious event in which Jesus—in the sight of Peter, James and John—was transformed in appearance, revealing himself to be truly divine, the Son of God.

Acknowledgments

Scripture quotations taken from or adapted from the New Revised Standard Version Bible: Catholic Edition, copyright © 1989, 1993, Division of Christian Education of the National Council of Churches of Christ in the U.S.A. Used by permission. All rights reserved.

Excerpts from the English translation of the *Catechism of the Catholic Church* for use in the United States, second edition, copyright © 1997, United States Catholic Conference, Inc. Libreria Editrice Vaticana. All rights reserved.

Excerpts from the *United States Catholic Catechism for Adults*, copyright © 2006, United States Conference of Catholic Bishops, Washington D.C. All rights reserved.

Excerpts from the English translation of *The Roman Missal* © 2010, International Committee on English in the Liturgy, Inc. (ICEL). All rights reserved.

Excerpts from documents of Vatican II taken from A. Flannery (ed.), *Vatican Council II: Constitutions, Decrees, Declarations* (New York/Dublin: Costello Publishing/Dominican Publications, 1996).

Excerpts from *Rerum Novarum* (1891), *Centesimus Annus* (1991) and *Munificentissimus Deus* (1950), copyright © Libreria Editrice Vaticana.

Excerpts from *Catholic Household Blessings & Prayers*, Revised Edition, copyright © 2007, Bishops Committee on the Liturgy, United States Conference of Catholic Bishops, Washington, D.C.

'Better or Better Off?', p. 25, by Peter Maurin. Reprinted from *www.catholicworker.org/roundtable*. Used with permission.

Song 'Where Is the Love?', pp. 30 and 33, by Black Eyed Peas, words and music by Will Adams, Allan Pineda, Jaime Gomez, Justin Timberlake, Michael Fratantuno, George Pajon Jr., Printz Board and J.

Curtis. Copyright © 2003 BMG Sapphire Songs (BMI), Will.I.Am Music Inc. (BMI), Jeepney Music Publishing (BMI), Nawasha Networks Publishing (BMI), Tennman Tunes (ASCAP), Tuono Music (BMI), El Cubano Music (BMI) and Printz Polar Publishing (BMI). Worldwide rights for BMG Sapphire Songs, Will.I.Am Music Inc., Jeepney Music Publishing and Nawasha Networks Publishing administered by BMG Rights Management (US) LLC. All rights for Tennman Tunes administered by BMG Rights Management (US) LLC. All rights for El Cubano Music controlled and administered by EMI Blackwood Music Inc. International copyright secured. All rights reserved. *Reprinted by Permission of Hal Leonard Corporation.*

Reflection, p. 50–51, adapted from *A Sacramental People* by Michael Drumm and Tom Gunning (Dublin, Ireland: Columba Press, 1998), copyright © 1998, Michael Drumm and Tom Gunning. Used with permission.

Quotation from artist Know Hope, p. 54, from *www.thejc.com/arts/arts-features/21923/know-hope-meet-israels-answer-banksy*.

Description of God as 'the Promise-Keeper', p. 63, from Anglican theologian N.T. Wright.

'Did You Know?', p. 78, from *Fully Alive 3*, Susan Morgan, M.Phil and Peter O'Reilly, STL (Dublin, Ireland: Veritas, 2006), copyright © 2006, Susan Morgan and Peter O'Reilly.

Poem 'Annunication', p. 83, from *A Door in The Hive* by Denise Levertov (New York: New Directions Publishing, 1989), copyright © 1989, Denise Levertov. Reprinted by permission of New Directions Publishing Group.

'Honoring the Virgin Mother', p. 85, adapted from the *Catholic Encyclopedia* on line at *www.newadvent.org/cathen*, copyright © 2009, Kevin Knight.

Prayer Reflection, p. 98, adapted from 'Magnificat', in *Benedictine Daily Prayer: A Short Breviary* by Maxwell E. Johnson (Minnesota:

Liturgical Press, 2005), copyright © 2005 by Order of St. Benedict. Published by Liturgical Press, Collegeville, Minnesota. Reprinted with permission.

The dictionary definition of the word 'parable', p. 115, is from *Interpreters Dictionary of the Bible* (Nashville TN: Abingdon Press, 1980), copyright © 1980, Abingdon Press.

The description of a parable that begins 'Parables are tiny lumps of coal. . . .', p. 115, is from the contemporary biblical scholar Walter Wink.

The definition of 'parable' under 'Let's Probe Deeper', p. 116, is from 'Listening to Your Life', from *Wishful Thinking: A Seeker's ABC* by Frederich Buechner (New York: Harper Collins, 1993), copyright © 1973, 1993, Frederich Buechner.

Excerpt from poem 'Resurrection: an Easter Sequence', p. 159, by W.R. Rodgers (Meath, Ireland: Gallery Press, 1993), copyright © 1993, W.R. Rodgers, reprinted by kind permission of the Estate of W.R. Rodgers and The Gallery Press, Loughcrew, Oldcastle, County Meath, Ireland from *Poems* (1993).

Extract from 'Aslan the Great and the White Witch', p. 174, from *The Lion, the Witch and the Wardrobe* by C.S. Lewis (London, United Kingdom: Geoffrey Bles, 1950), copyright © 1950, C.S. Lewis.

Poem, 'Easter', p. 178, by Joyce Rupp, from *www.joycerupp.com/easter2001.html,* copyright © 2001, Joyce Rupp.

Quotation p. 187, St Irenaeus, from Pentecost, Office of Readings, copyright © 1970, 1973, 1975, International Committee on English in the Liturgy, Inc. (New York: Catholic Book Publishing Company, 1976), copyright © 1976, ICEL.

Mother Teresa quotation, p. 188, from *Mother Teresa in My Own Words* by José Luis González-Balado (Missouri: Ligouri Publications, 1997), copyright © 1997, José Luis González-Balado.

'Pentecost-Poem', p. 205, by Sr. Patricia Schnapp Ph.D., published in the *National Catholic Reporter*, September 14, 2001, copyright © 2001, Patricia Schnapp. Used with kind permission.

Quotation, p. 211, by St. John Damascene, from 'Sermon on the Dormition of the Mother of God, the Blessed Virgin Mary'.

Song 'Pray', p. 231, words and music by Justin Bieber, Nasri Atweh, Adam Messenger and Omar Martinez. Copyright © 2010 Universal Music Corp., Bieber Time Publishing, Sony/ATV Music Publishing LLC, Tre Ball Music, Messy Music and Omar Martinez. All rights for Bieber Time Publishing controlled and administered by Universal Music Corp. All rights for Tre Ball Music controlled and administered by Sony/ATV Music Publishing LLC, 8 Music Square West, Nashville, TN 37203. All rights reserved. Used by Permission. *Reprinted by Permission of Hal Leonard Corporation.*

The dictionary definition of 'holy', p. 242, is from *www.merriam-webster.com/dictionary/holy.*

Excerpt from ''The Inner History of a Day'', p. 248, copyright © 2008 by John O'Donohue, from *To Bless the Space Between Us: A Book of Blessings* by John O'Donohue. Used by permission of Doubleday, a division of Random House, Inc.

Poem 'The Difference', p. 260, by Grace L. Naessens, copyright © 1960, Grace L. Naessens.

St. John Chrysostom quotation, p. 272, from *The Purpose in Prayer* by Edward M. Bounds (Pennsylvania: Whitaker House, 1997), copyright © 1997, Edward M. Bounds.

Material on Frère Roger and the Taizé community, p. 274, adapted from Taizé website *www.taize.fr*, copyright © Ateliers et Presses de Taizé. Used with permission.

Image credits

Main cover image: Detail from *Jesus of the People* by Janet McKenzie. Copyright © 1999 Janet McKenzie, *www.janetmckenzie.com*

p. 12: Photo by POM²

p. 14: Photo: Marie-Lan Nguyen. Purchased with the help of ARMMA (Friends of the Museum).

p. 16: Photo: Gunnar Bach Pedersen

p. 23: Photo: Rašo

p. 24: Photo courtesy of Department of Special Collections and University Archives, Marquette University Libraries.

p. 36: Photo: Gunnar Bach Pedersen

p. 45: Photo: Mattana

p. 48: Sr. Thea Bowman during a September 1989 talk at Walsh University, Ohio. (Courtesy of Walsh University.)

p. 54: Know Hope, *How We Got There/Like Pigeons in the Rain*, 2009, installation at *No Soul for Sale* at X-Initiative, New York, commissioned by Artis. (Photo by Erin Leigh Pierson.)

p. 64: Photo: Andreas Praefcke

p. 65: Photo: MPorciusCato

p. 68: Photo: Rüdiger Wölk

p. 69: Photo: Csanády

p. 71: Photo: Ophelia2

p. 79: Painting courtesy of Donato Giancola

p. 82: Photo: Andreas Franz Borchert

p. 83: Photo: Marie-Lan Nguyen

p. 86: *Saint Joseph in the Rocking Chair* by Michael O'Neill McGrath, OSFS. Copyright © Bee Still Studio, www.beestill.com, 410.398.3057. All rights reserved. Used with permission.

p. 89: *The Holy Family at Nativity*, 2007, by Laura James (Private Collection/The Bridgeman Art Library).

p. 93: Photo: Kandi

p. 97: Members of Pax Christi protesting against the Iraq war in London, England, 2005. (MAX NASH/AFP/Getty Images.)

p. 102: Reverend Martin Luther King Jr. at Lincoln Memorial. (Photo by Paul Schutzer/Time Life Pictures/Getty Images.)

p. 129: Photo: Toby Hudson

p. 130: 'The Marriage at Cana', 1819 (oil on canvas) by Julius Schnorr von Carolsfeld. Kunsthalle, Hamburg, Germany. (Bridgeman Art Library.)

p. 143: Reproduced by permission of Alexander Gassel.

p. 158: Pope John Paul II at the Wailing Wall in Jerusalem. (SVEN NACKSTRAND/AFP/Getty Images.)

p. 161: Photo: GFreihalter

p. 164: Photo © Roman Eisele / Wikimedia Commons / CC-BY-SA-3.0 & GFDL 1.2 or any later.

p. 169: Photo: PA

p. 183: *The Risen Lord* by He Qi. Courtesy of He Qi (*www.heqiarts.com*).

p. 186: Photo: Hiart

p. 188: Nuns of Missionaries of Charity pray at Mother House, Calcutta, India, during Good Friday. (© Piyal Adhikary/epa/Corbis.)

p. 189: Jazz Funeral Through the Streets of the French Quarter, New Orleans, Louisiana. (© Philip Gould/CORBIS.)

p. 191: Photo: Miaow Miaow

p. 199: Photo: Anthony Majanlahti

p. 202: Photo: Jose Goncalves

p. 203: Photo: FA2010

p. 208: *Pentecost*, 1909, by Emil Nolde. (Private Collection/Bridgeman Art Library.)

p. 214: Pilgrims at the Sanctuary of Our Lady in Lourdes. (PASCAL PAVANI/AFP/Getty Images.)

p. 216: Photo: Andreas Franz Borchert

p. 221: Ash Wednesday services at St. Patrick's Cathedral, New York City. (Photo by Mario Tama/Getty Images.)

p. 225: Photo: Cadetgray

p. 227: Photo: Reinhardhauke

p. 235: Catholic Relief Services provide food for Migrants in Calais, France. (Photo by Franck CRUSIAUX/Gamma-Rapho via Getty Images.)

p. 242: Photo: Lforzini

p. 254: Brother Lawrence of the Resurrection by Rebecca LaChance (*www.divinelycommonicons.com*).

p. 264: Michael Conner Humphreys as young Forrest Gump and Hanna R. Hall as young Jenny in *Forrest Gump* (1994). (Copyright © Mary Evans Picture Library 2010.)

p. 274: Photo: akg-images/Michael Zapf

p. 284: Plaque commemorating the Catholic martyrs of Tyburn, London, England. (Photo courtesy of *linenonthhedgerow.blogspot.com*.)

p. 285: Photo: akg-images/Interfoto

p. 286: Photo: Josep Renalias

p. 290: William Blake, Illustration from *Jerusalem*. (Photo: akg-images).

Every effort has been made to contact the copyright holders of the material reproduced in *The Promised One: Servant and Savior*. If any infringement has occurred, the owners of such copyright are requested to contact the publishers.

Index

Abel, 59
Abraham, 57, 63–65, 71
Acts of the Apostles
    the Ascension, 201–02, 207
    the early Church, 297
Adam and Eve, 22–23, 39, 40
agape, 165, 311
Ahaz, king, 109
Andrew, St., 129
angels, 43–44, 89
    fallen angels, 45
Annunciation, 14, 81–82
'Annunciation' (Levertov), 83
Anointed One, 93
Anselm, St., 90, 92
anti-Semitism, 158
apartheid, 68
Apostles' Creed, 280, 302
Ascension of Jesus, 199, 201–04
Assumption of Mary, 199, 211–14
Athanasius, St., 92
atonement, 91
Augustine, St., 142

Babylonian exile, 69, 111
Baptism, 40, 251
    of Jesus, 104–05
basileia, 118, 119
Beatific Vision, 290
Benedict XVI, Pope, 73, 274
'Better or Better Off?' (Maurin), 25
Bible, 'active reading' of, 8
Bieber, Justin, 231
Black Eyed Peas, 30, 32, 33
Bowman, Sr. Thea, 48–49
brokenness, of the world, 31, 33

Caiaphas, 155
Cain, 59
Catherine of Siena, St., 243
Catholic prayers, 302–07
Catholic Worker, 24, 25
charity, 234
Chartres cathedral, 281–82
chesed, 55–57, 71

'Childhood Prayer', 260
Christian identity, 220–21, 235
Church
    early days, 297
    precepts of, 309
    social doctrine, 310
Clarke, Sr. Maura, 169–70
Commandments, see Great
    Commandment; Ten
    Commandments
commitment, 55–57
community, of the Church,
    252–53
contemplation, 276
Council of Trent, 39
covenants, 14
    God and Abraham, 57, 63–65,
    71
    God and Moses, 71
    God and Noah, 59
    the new covenant, 68
Creation, 16–17, 20–21
Crucifixion
    historical context, 154
    of Jesus, 152–53
'Crucifixion, The', 159
Cur Deus Homo? (St. Anselm),
    90

Damien of Molokai, St., 73
David, king, 12, 62, 67
Day, Dorothy, 24
death
    of Jesus, 165–66
    life after, 177, 189, 280
Decalogue, 66, 309
Devil, 45–46, 106, 107
Dickinson, Emily, 74
discipleship, 225–26, 228–30,
    231–34
    of Mary, 213
    of St. Paul, 236–37
Dismas, St. (Good Thief), 191,
    293
divinization, 23
dogmas of faith, 199, 211
Donovan, Jean, 169, 170

Easter' (Rupp), 178
Egypt
    exile in, 65, 87–88
    the Holy Family in, 86, 87
El Salvador, 143–44, 169–70
Elijah, 133
Elizabeth, St., 84
Emmaus, 154, 160, 183, 185, 203
Epiphany, 89
Eucharist, 138–42, 230, 269
Eve, 59
evil, 41, 43, 45–47, 249
exile, of the Israelites, 65, 69, 111
expiation, 90–91

faith, 180–81
Feast of Tabernacles, 133
Feeding of the Multitude, 114
Felicity, St., 96
Final (Last) Judgment, 282–83
Forde, Sr. Ita, 169–70
foreshadowing
    the Messiah, 88–89
    the Paschal Mystery, 131
    the Resurrection, 134
Forrest Gump, 264
Francis of Assisi, St., 220
friendship, 62, 210, 262

Gabriel, angel, 44, 81–82
generosity, of God, 15–19
Gifts of the Holy Spirit, 250, 308
glossary, of faith words, 311–17
God
    the Good Shepherd, 224
    as Judge, 286–87
Good Samaritan, parable of, 9,
    232–33
grace, 246
Great Commandment, 111,
    229–30, 231–34, 297
Great Depression, 24
Great Flood, 59

habits, 294–95
Hail Mary, 85
He, Qi, 183
healing, 155–56, 222
Hell, 292–93

Herod Antipas, 108
Herod, king, 87
Hezekiah, king, 109
holiness, 242–44, 247, 251
Holocaust, 158
holy, 242–44
Holy Family, 86–88
Holy Spirit, 244, 251
	Fruits of, 308
	Gifts of, 308
	guidance of, 247, 249–50
	and Pentecost, 206
Holy Trinity, 20
hope, 54–55
Hosea, 67
'How Can I Keep from Singing?'
	(Lowry), 42
hypostatic union, 80, 313

icons, 275
identity, 124–25
	of Jesus, 125–26
Ignatius of Loyola, St., 255
image of God, 20–22, 248–49
Incarnation, 80
influences, negative, 32
'Inner History of a Day', 248
Institute for Black Catholic
	Studies, 48
Irenaeus, St., 187
Isaac, 65
Isaiah, 89, 109, 161, 162, 185

Jesus
	the Agony in the Garden,
		162–63
	the Ascension, 199, 201–04
	the Crucifixion, 152–53
	the Death of, 165–66
	and expiation, 90–91
	and Jewish Law 155–56
	the Messiah, 93, 161
	the Redeemer, 91
	the role model, 103
	the Savior, 91–92, 161
	the Son of God, 94
	the Son of Man, 135
	the Suffering Servant, 70–71,
		161

the temptation of, 45,
	106–07, 249
the unique identity of, 125–26
the Way of, 235
the wisdom of, 10–11
Jesus Prayer, 95, 97
Job, 249
John the Baptist, St., 84, 104,
	108, 271
John Damascene, St., 211, 261
John the Evangelist, St.
	and love, 165, 230
	and Nicodemus, 156
	and the Resurrection, 180–81
	the Trial Council, 222, 223
	the miracle at Cana, 128–29
John Paul II, Blessed Pope,
	118–19, 120, 158, 214, 220,
	274
Joseph of Arimathea, 156, 179
Joseph, St., 86–88
Jubilee Year, 111
judgment, 286–88, 298
Judgment of Nations, parable
	of, 286

Kazel, Sr. Dorothy, 169–70
kenosis, 165
King, Martin Luther, Jr., 43
Kingdom of God, 108–09, 113
Know Hope (artist), 54

Laborers in the Vineyard,
	parable of, 15
Last Things, 282–83
Lateran Council, 45
Lawrence of the Resurrection,
	Br., 254, 262
Lazarus, 155
Leo XIII, Pope, 119–20
leprosy, 73
Levertov, Denise, 83
Lewis, C.S., 174–75
Lion, the Witch and the Wardrobe,
	The (Lewis), 174–75
Liturgy
	of the Eucharist, 269
	of the Hours, 145, 270
	of the Word, 13, 268

Lord's Prayer, 229, 273, 302
love, 165–66, 223, 296
	and holiness, 247
	see also Great
		Commandment
Lowry, Joseph, 42
Lucy, St., 215
Luke, St., 162–63

Magisterium, 211, 314
Magnificat, 84, 304
Malvin and Bandit, 210
Mandela, Nelson, 68
Mark, St., 156, 204
Martha and Mary, 155
Martín-Baró, Fr. Ignacio, 143–44
martyrs, 96, 112, 143–44, 284–85
Mary, Blessed Virgin, 36
	the Annunciation, 80–81
	as disciple, 213
	the Incarnation, 80
	Marian titles, 213
	the miracle at Cana, 130, 131
	perpetual virginity, 82–83
	prayers to, 305–07
	the Visitation, 84
Mary Magdalene, 179, 180
Mass, structure of, 269
Matthew, St., 87, 111, 156–57, 245
Maurin, Peter, 24–25
Maximilian Kolbe, St., 165, 285
	(illus.)
Maximus the Confessor, St., 38
meditation, 275
mercy, works of, 309
metanoia, 118
mezuzah, 229
miracles, 113–14, 129–31, 155
Molokai, 73
Moses, 94
	the Covenant with God, 65–67
	the law of, 11, 133
	the Ten Commandments, 67,
		285
Munificentissimus Deus, 211–12
Mustard Seed, parable of, 116–17

Naomi, 60–61
Nathaniel, 129

Nero, 236
Nicene Creed, 165, 189, 302–03
Nicodemus, 156, 179
Noah, 59

original holiness, 35
original justice, 35, 118
Original Sin, 35, 40

Palm Sunday, 137
parables, 115
    the Good Samaritan, 9,
        232–33
    the Judgment of Nations, 286
    the Laborers in the Vineyard, 15
    the Mustard Seed, 116–17
    the Prodigal Son, 37
    the Rich Man and Lazarus,
        289–90
    the Wedding Feast, 117
Passion, the events of, 162–63
Passover, 139, 141
Paul, St.
    and baptism, 167
    conversion of, 236
    and the Eucharist, 140, 141,
        142
    and hope, 55
    and love, 223, 253, 296
    the 'New Adam', 36
    and prayer, 263, 274
    and the Resurrection, 176, 177,
        184
    and the Savior, 92, 105, 161
Pax Christi, 97
Pentateuch, 11
Pentecost, 199, 205–09
'Pentecost-Poem' (Schnapp), 205
perfection, 245–46
Perpetua, St., 96
Peter, St., 129, 153, 168
    Quo Vadis Domine?, 227
    and the Resurrection, 179
    the Trial Council, 222, 223
Pharisees, 154–56, 222
Philip, 129
Pilate, 154, 157, 159
Pius XII, Pope, 211–12
Plinius Caecilius, 41

Practice of the Presence of God,
    254
'Pray' (Bieber), 231
prayer, 228–29, 260–63
    of the Church, 267–70
    and contemplation, 276
    forms of, 264–66
    how to pray, 271–73
    and meditation, 275
    the power of, 272–73
Precepts of the Church, 309
Pressure Cooker, 198
Prodigal Son, parable of, 37
promises, 210
Prophets, writings of, 12
Protoevangelium, 37
Psalm 104 (Praise of God), 17–18
Purgatory, 291–92

Real Presence, 138, 140
Rebekah, 65
Resurrection, 175–76
Rich Man and Lazarus, parable
    of, 289–90
Risen Lord (He Qi), 183
Robben Island, 68
Roger, Frère, 274
role models, 102–03
Roman law, 157
Romero, Archbishop Oscar, 169,
    220
Rosary, 306–07
    the Glorious Mysteries, 217
Rupp, Joyce, 178
Ruth, 60–61

Sacraments, 307–08
Salvation, 32–33
Samson, 66, 67
Samuel, 12, 109
Sarah, 65
Schnapp, Sr. Patricia, 205–06
Second Vatican Council, see
    Vatican II
Septimus Severus, 96
shekinah, 133
sin, 38–39, 58–59, 166
    Original Sin, 35, 39
suffering, 150–52

Suffering Servant Songs, 69–70
symbolism
    in Sacred Scripture, 34, 37
    the Transfiguration, 132–33
    the Wedding at Cana, 129–31
Synoptic Gospels, 130, 132, 140

Taizé Community, 274, 275
Tanakh, 109
temptation, 107, 226, 249
    of Jesus, 45, 106–07, 249
Ten Commandments, 66, 309
Teresa of Ávila, St., 142, 220, 261,
    276
Teresa of Calcutta, Blessed
    Mother, 188, 220
theophany, 132
theosis, 23
Thérèse of Lisieux, St., 261
Thomas the Apostle, St., 180, 181
Thomas Aquinas, St., 273
tomb, of Jesus, 179
Torah, 11, 111
Transfiguration, 132–34
Trial Council, 222, 223
trust, 10, 13
typology, in Old Testament, 69

University of Central America
    (UCA), 143–44

Vatican II, 21, 40, 158
virtues, 294–96, 308
Visitation, 84

Wailing Wall, 158
war, 30
Way, of Jesus, 235
Wedding at Cana, 129–31
Wedding Feast, parable of, 117
Westminster Abbey, 112
'Where is the Love?' (Black Eyed
    Peas), 30–31
Wisdom, books of, 12
wisdom, of Jesus, 10–11
world, Christian view, 6–7

YHWH, 94, 109

STUDENT NOTES

STUDENT NOTES

STUDENT NOTES

STUDENT NOTES